Lecture Notes in Computer Science 4417

Commenced Publication in 1973
Founding and Former Series Editors:
Gerhard Goos, Juris Hartmanis, and Jan van Leeuwen

Andreas Kerren   Achim Ebert
Jörg Meyer (Eds.)

Human-Centered Visualization Environments

GI-Dagstuhl Research Seminar
Dagstuhl Castle, Germany, March 5-8, 2006
Revised Lectures

 Springer

Volume Editors

Andreas Kerren
Växjö University
School of Mathematics and Systems Engineering
Computer Science Department
Vejdes Plats 7, 351 95 Växjö, Sweden
E-mail: kerren@acm.org

Achim Ebert
University of Kaiserslautern
Computer Science Department
P.O. Box 3049, 67653 Kaiserslautern, Germany
E-mail: ebert@informatik.uni-kl.de

Jörg Meyer
University of California Irvine
Department of Electrical Engineering and Computer Science
Department of Biomediacal Engineering
The Henry Samueli School of Engineering
644 E Engineering Tower, Irvine, CA 92697-2625, USA
E-mail: jmeyer@uci.edu

Library of Congress Control Number: 2007931237

CR Subject Classification (1998): I.4, I.2.10, I.5, I.3, H.5, J.3

LNCS Sublibrary: SL 6 – Image Processing, Computer Vision, Pattern Recognition, and Graphics

ISSN   0302-9743
ISBN-10   3-540-71948-2 Springer Berlin Heidelberg New York
ISBN-13   978-3-540-71948-9 Springer Berlin Heidelberg New York

Springer is a part of Springer Science+Business Media

springer.com

© Springer-Verlag Berlin Heidelberg 2007
Printed in Germany

Typesetting: Camera-ready by author, data conversion by Markus Richter, Heidelberg
Printed on acid-free paper   SPIN: 12048748   06/3180   5 4 3 2 1 0

Preface

Human-Centered Visualization Environments combine traditional Visualization techniques with the ability of the human visual-brain system and the haptic-motoric system to explore and analyze complex data comprehensively. This kind of visualization merges several aspects of different research areas, such as Information Visualization, Scientific Visualization, Human–Computer Interaction, Data Mining, Information Design, Graph Drawing, and Computer Graphics. From all subfields in Visualization, this textbook focuses mainly on Information Visualization, which centers on the visualization of abstract data, e.g., hierarchical, networked, or symbolic information sources, in order to help users understand and analyze such data.

For most practical applications, researchers try to find the best visual representation of the given information. That is the core problem of each visualization; but sometimes the seemingly best representation does not suffice if the human information processing and the human capability of information reception are not adequately taken into account. Additionally, these aspects depend on the data to be visualized and on the user's background. While developing Human-Centered Visualization Environments, user abilities and requirements, visualization tasks, tool functions, and visual representations should be equally taken into account. The design of Human-Centered Visualization Environments is one of the big challenges of Information Visualization, Software Visualization, and of many application areas, such as the visualization of biological/biochemical or geographical information.

This textbook is the outcome of a GI-Dagstuhl Research Seminar organized by the editors, which was supported by the Gesellschaft für Informatik e.V. (GI) and took place at the International Conference and Research Center for Computer Science (IBFI) at Schloss Dagstuhl, March 5-8, 2006.

GI-Dagstuhl Research Seminars are targeted at doctoral students and recent post-doctoral graduates who are interested in learning actively about new developments not well covered in textbooks. They were selected mainly according to their scientific qualification.

Subtopics from the area of this seminar were assigned to the participants, who prepared comprehensive overview papers. During the seminar, their summaries and findings were presented and discussed. After the seminar, close to 9 months was spent on writing the chapters of this book, which were cross-reviewed internally. The editors intend the textbook to be used as an introduction to the field and as a basis for graduate-level courses in Human-Centered Visualization, Information Visualization, etc.

We would like to thank all participants of the seminar for the lively discussions during and after the seminar as well as for writing the chapters of this textbook. Special thanks go to Wim Fikkert, Carsten Görg, Olga Kulyk, Robert S. Laramee, and Martin Nöllenburg for serving as chapter coordinators. We are also grateful to the GI and Schloss Dagstuhl, Germany, for their support and the privilege to hold the seminar at such a great venue.

December 2006   Andreas Kerren
                                                              Achim Ebert
                                                              Jörg Meyer

List of Contributors

 **Marco D'Ambros** is a Ph.D. student at the Faculty of Informatics of the University of Lugano, Switzerland, where he is working together with Prof. Michele Lanza. His current interests lie in the domain of software engineering with a special focus on software visualization, software evolution and software defect analysis. In 2005, he received his master degree "cum laude" from the Politecnico di Milano and from the University of Illinois at Chicago. In his graduation thesis, he introduced a new approach, called software archeology, to study the evolution of software systems in case of incomplete information. He was the co-organizer of MSR2006 Challenge and co-reviewer for various conferences and journals. He is also a member of the COSE project, a research venture which aims to analyze and control the evolution of complex software systems.

 **Torsten Bierz** is a Ph.D. student in the International Research Training Group (IRTG) for the visualization of large unstructured datasets of the University of Kaiserslautern, Germany. After obtaining his Master degree in Computer Science in 2004, he was working on the HapTEK project in the Computer Graphics and Visualization Group at the University of Kaiserslautern, which focused on the design and development of a human machine interface for advanced simulation in developing and production processes. In January 2005, Torsten joined the International Research and Training Group as a Ph.D. student dealing with the topic of immersive visualization systems. His research interests within this topic are haptic interaction, visual representation on large displays and interaction with optical tracking systems, which include the usage of GPU accelerated methods and techniques.

 **Achim Ebert** is an Assistant Professor with the University of Kaiserslautern, Germany, since 2005. Dr. Ebert is also affiliated with the German Research Center for Artificial Intelligence (DFKI GmbH) in Kaiserslautern, Germany. He received his Ph.D. from the University of Kaiserslautern, Germany, in 2004. Dr. Ebert's research interest include virtual and mixed reality, human computer interaction, information visualization, mobile visualization, and artificial intelligence in the visualization context. The application scenarios are manifold: document management, visualization of search

engine results, waste water treatment, virtual clothing, process visualization, etc. Dr. Ebert has lead and has served on multiple conference and program committees. Since 2005, he is the co-chair of the IASTED Visualization and Image Processing (VIIP) conference.

Wim Fikkert is active as a Ph.D. student at the Human Media Interaction (HMI) group of the University of Twente, The Netherlands. Wim obtained his Bachelor degree in Computer Science in 2003 at the Saxion Universities in The Netherlands by creating a simulator able to control a team in real and simulated robot soccer matches. He obtained his Master of Science in Computer Science in December 2005 at the University of Twente by researching how to unobtrusively estimate the gaze direction of a student in a commercial driving simulator. Wim started his academic career as a Ph.D. student at the HMI group in January 2006. Presently he is active in the Dutch nation-wide BioRange project in which the research group he works in aims to develop a multidisciplinary scientific collaborative environment. Wim's personal research interests therein lie with natural, human-like gestural input and visualizing the requested output. These interactions are influenced by contextual information that describe (current) user(s') tasks.

Carsten Görg is currently working as a postdoctoral research fellow, funded by the German Academic Exchange Service (DAAD), at the College of Computing at the Georgia Institute of Technology in Atlanta. He studied computer science and mathematics as a double major at Saarland University in Germany where he also received his Ph.D. in computer science. His research interests include graph drawing, in particular dynamic graph drawing, information and software visualization, and also software engineering and software evolution.

T.J. Jankun-Kelly is an assistant professor of computer science and engineering within the James Worth Bagley College of Engineering, Mississippi State University. His research areas are at the intersection of scientific and information visualization. His goal is to make visualization techniques and systems more effective by improving interaction methods and visualization utilization. Towards this end, he focuses on visualization interfaces, visualization modeling, and applications such as volume, graph, and security visualization; recent efforts include extending these to large-scale displays. T.J. has a Master's and Ph.D. from the University of California, Davis and a B.S. from Harvey Mudd College. He is a member of the ACM, SIGGRAPH, IEEE, and the IEEE Computer Society and was a founding Contest Co-Chair for IEEE Visualization during 2004-2006.

 **Andreas Kerren** is currently a Senior Researcher at the Computer Science Department of the University of Kaiserslautern, Germany. He will move to Växjö University, Sweden, in Spring 2007, where he has been appointed for a position as Associate Professor in Computer Science. Until the end of his Ph.D. studies in 2002, he was Research Assistant at the Computer Science Department of the Saarland University in Germany. From 2002 to 2004, he worked as Assistant Professor at the Institute of Computer Graphics and Algorithms at the Computer Science Department of the Vienna University of Technology, Austria. Andreas Kerren was involved in various successful research projects, e.g., in the DFG project "Generation of Interactive Multimedia Visualizations and Animations for Learning Software in Compiler Design" or in the FWF project "Hierarchies of Plane Graphs for the Acquisition, Analysis and Visualization of Geographic Information". Dr. Kerren was and is a member of several program and organizing committees, for example, the ACM Symposia on Software Visualization 2005 and 2006 or the IASTED International Conferences on Graphics and Visualization in Engineering as well as on Visualization, Imaging, and Image Processing in 2007. He has served as reviewer for several international journals. His main research interests lie in the areas of Software Visualization, Information Visualization, Software Engineering, Computer Science Education, Human-Computer Interaction, and Programming Languages.

 **Robert Kosara** is currently an Assistant Professor at the Department of Computer Science, College of Information Technology, at the University of North Carolina at Charlotte (UNCC), where he is also a member of the Charlotte Visualization Center. He received both his Ph.D. (2001) and M.S. (1999) degrees from Vienna University of Technology, Vienna, Austria. Before coming to Charlotte, he worked at the VRVis Research Center, and the "in-silico" pharmaceutical research company Inte:Ligand. His main research focus is Information Visualization (InfoVis), which is the search for methods to depict abstract data in ways that allow one to find patterns, correlations, clusters, etc., by simply looking at and interacting with the resulting images. His goal is to bring together computer science, statistics, perceptual psychology, and the arts. His main interests are developing effective means of visualization and interaction with large and complex data, and finding the link between InfoVis and the visual arts.

 **Olga Kulyk** is a Ph.D. student at the Human Media Interaction Group, University of Twente, The Netherlands, since October 2005. Her research interests include human-computer interaction, collaborative visualization environments, computer-supported cooperative work, analysis and design of complex interactive systems, and situational awareness. Her current research within Bsik project BioRange is on the user-centered de-

sign and evaluation to enhance scientific collaboration and creative problem solving of multidisciplinary research teams in bioinformatics domain. During 2003-2005 Olga was a research trainee at User-System Interaction Design postmasters program, Department of Technology Management, Technical University of Eindhoven, the Netherlands. There she received a degree of 'Professional Doctorate in Engineering' in 2005. During her final project at User Centered Engineering Group, Industrial Design, Technical University of Eindhoven, Olga worked on the design and evaluation of a service providing real-time feedback on visual attention during meetings, as a part of the EU-funded CHIL project. In 2003, she received masters and in 2001 bachelors in computer science from the National University of 'Kyiv-Mohyla Academy', Ukraine.

Robert S. Laramee received a bachelors degree in physics, cum laude, from the University of Massachusetts, Amherst in 1997. In 2000, he received a masters degree in computer science from the University of New Hampshire, Durham. He was awarded a Ph.D. from the Vienna University of Technology, Austria at the Institute of Computer Graphics in 2005. His research interests are in the areas of scientific visualization, computer graphics, and human-computer interaction. He has contributed research papers to IEEE Visualization, the Joint EUROGRAPHICS-IEEE TVCG Symposium on Visualization, EUROGRAPHICS, and the CHI conference on Human-Computer Interaction as well as their respective journals. From 2001 to 2006 he was a Researcher at the VRVis Research Center (www.vrvis.at) and a software engineer at AVL (www.avl.com) in the department of Advanced Simulation Technologies. Currently, he is a Lecturer (Assistant Professor) at the University of Wales, Swansea, in the Department of Computer Science.

Mircea Lungu is a Ph.D. student at the University of Lugano, Switzerland, where he is working together with Prof. Dr. Michele Lanza. Before joining the University of Lugano, he received his Diploma-Engineer title from the Computer Science Faculty of the Polytechnic University in Timisoara, Romania. His diploma thesis, developed in collaboration with the Software Composition Group in Bern, proposed a novel way of aggregating metrics into higher level abstractions that can be used for software quality analysis. His current research interests are related to software engineering and reverse engineering with a special emphasis on program understanding and software visualization. He maintains a live interest in generic information visualization and programming languages.

Andrés Moreno is a Ph.D. student at the University of Joensuu, Finland, since May 2005. He received his Master's degree from the Polytechnic University of Madrid, Spain. His Master's thesis developed an intermediate code for Program Animation, and was jointly supervised by professors Erkki Sutinen and Mordechai Ben-Ari. He is currently researching on program visualization and animation for novices, focusing on how to make current visualization tools aware of the personal differences of the users. Having published in conferences such as ACM ITiCSE and IEEE ICALT, he is an active member of the Algorithm Animation community. He has also taken part in several working groups at ITiCSE.

Jörg Meyer is an Assistant Professor with a shared appointment in the Department of Electrical Engineering & Computer Science and the Department of Biomedical Engineering in the Henry Samueli School of Engineering at the University of California, Irvine. He joined UC Irvine in 2002. Dr. Meyer is also affiliated with the Center of GRAVITY (Graphics, Visualization and Imaging Technology) in the California Institute for Telecommunications and Information Technology (Calit2). He received his Ph.D. from the University of Kaiserslautern, Germany, in 1999. He held an appointment as a post-doctoral researcher and lecturer in the Computer Science Department at the University of California, Davis, from 1999 to 2000, and maintains an Adjunct Assistant Professorship at the Computer Science and Engineering Department at Mississippi State University, where he was also affiliated with an NSF-sponsored Engineering Research Center (2000-2002). Dr. Meyer's research interests include large-scale scientific visualization, biomedical imaging, digital image processing, interactive rendering and virtual reality. His research efforts are aimed at developing interactive rendering methods for large scientific data sets. Medical data sets range from Magnetic Resonance Imaging (MRI), Computed Tomography (CT) and Confocal Laser-scanning Microscopy to Opical Coherence Tomography and other modalities. Other applications are in the field of Civil Engineering and include ground motion and structural response simulations. The common theme in these interdisciplinary domains is the occurrence of giga- to tera-byte volumetric data sets that need to be rendered interactively. Dr. Meyer has developed multi-level-of-detail data representation techniques based on hierarchical space-subdivision algorithms and wavelet-based compression schemes, enabling interactive data storage, transmission and rendering of large volumetric data sets. Dr. Meyer has lead and has served on multiple conference and program committees for various professional organizations, including IEEE, ACM SIGGRAPH and IASTED. He has published over 112 journal articles, book chapters, conference papers, abstracts and posters in his field.

Martin Nöllenburg is a Ph.D. student at Karlsruhe University, Germany since October 2005. He is working as a Research Assistant in the group GeoNet of Dr. Alexander Wolff. He received his Diploma with Distinction in Computer Science from Karlsruhe University in August 2005. In 2002/03 he was a visiting student at McGill University, Montreal in the computational biology group of Dr. Mike Hallett. In his Diploma thesis he studied the problem of automatically drawing schematic metro maps and implemented an algorithm based on mixed-integer programming. For this work he received the NRW Undergraduate Science Award 2005. His current research interests are in the field of graph drawing and computational geometry, specifically algorithms for the visualization of geometric graphs and networks, e.g. metro maps.

Mathias Pohl is a scientific assistant at the chair for software engineering at the University of Trier, Germany, since March 2006. He graduated in January 2005 at the University of Saarbrücken. From April 2005 to February 2006, he was a member of the Ph.D. program at the University of Kaiserslautern, Germany. His research interests cover the visualization of time-varying data and graph drawing.

Ermir Qeli is a research assistant at the department of mathematics and computer science at the University of Marburg. He is working at the "Distributed Systems" research group of Bernd Freisleben on visualization techniques for systems biology. He received his diploma in Computer Science from the University of Tirana, Albania, in 2000. His research interests include: Information Visualization and its application in Systems Biology, Data Mining and Machine Learning, especially unsupervised learning techniques (clustering), as well as Comparison of structured data, such as XML files etc.

Jaime Urquiza is a lecturer of Computer Science and a Ph.D. student at the Rey Juan Carlos University, Spain. He received his Advanced Studies degree in 2003 from the Rey Juan Carlos University and his Bachelor degree in Computer Science in 1999 from the Polytechnic University of Madrid, Spain. His research areas are information visualization and, program and algorithm visualization applied to computer science education. His research goal is the development of usable program and algorithm animations in computer science education, taking into account both students and teachers.

 **Ingo H.C. Wassink** is Ph.D. student at the University of Twente, the Netherlands, of the sub department of Human Media Interaction of the department of Computer Science. He did his master thesis in dynamic scenario generation for driving simulators. The system is based on the movie world, where a multi agent system is developed for orchestrating the driving scenarios. His main interests are in visualization, computer vision, artificial intelligence and multi agent systems. Currently, he is doing research in computer visualization techniques for physical scientific collaborative environments. In such an environment, visualization and interaction with different kinds of display devices play an important role. These displays can differ in size and the way things are visualized (e.g. 2D or stereoscopic) and therefore require different kinds of visualization techniques. On these displays devices, information should be presented in an efficient way that helps researchers discussing their experiments. Important research topics are visualization of experiments, visualization and control of the flow of the experiment and visualization for comparing (intermediate) results of the experiment.

 **Kai Xu** is currently a researcher at National ICT Australia. He is also an Honorary Associate of School of Information Technologies at University of Sydney. He received his Ph.D. in Computer Science in 2004 from the University of Queensland, Australia. Before that, he received his bachelor degrees in Computer Science and Business from Shanghai Jiao Tong University, China in 1999. His main research interest is applying graph visualization in bioinformatics, which involves modeling, visualizing, and analyzing various biological networks such as metabolic pathways and protein-protein interactome.

Table of Contents

Part II. Domain-Specific Visualization

1 Introduction to Human-Centered Visualization Environments

Andreas Kerren, Achim Ebert, and Jörg Meyer

The title of this book—Human-Centered Visualization Environments (HCVE)—is composed of two key components: "human-centered" and "visualization environments". While the first part refers to the research area of *Human-Computer Interaction* (HCI), the second one refers to the design of *Visualization* systems. Thus, the focus of this textbook is on the intersection of both fields. These two terms can be defined as follows:

Visualization can be defined as: "The use of computer-supported, interactive, visual representation of abstract data to amplify cognition." [145]. The aim of visualization is to aid people in understanding and analyzing data. While other subfields, such as Scientific Visualization (SciVis), involve the presentation of data that has some physical or geometric correspondence, Information Visualization (InfoVis) centers on abstract information without such correspondences, i.e., usually it is not possible to map this information into the physical world. In this textbook, the focus is mainly on InfoVis.

Human-Computer Interaction is "the study of interaction between people (users) and computers. It is an interdisciplinary subject, relating computer science with many other fields of study and research. Interaction between users and computers occurs at the user interface (or simply interface), which includes both software and hardware, for example, general purpose computer peripherals and large-scale mechanical systems such as aircraft and power plants." [895]. The aim of HCI research is to improve the interaction between users and computers in the sense that this interaction should become more user-friendly and better adapted to the needs of the users.

The combination of these two areas is a prerequisite for the development of really "effective" visualizations that benefit from the capabilities and functionalities of the human visual system, e.g., visual perception and other cognitive abilities. Furthermore, this approach merges several additional aspects of different research areas, such as Scientific Visualization, Data Mining, Information Design, Graph Drawing, or Computer Graphics on the one hand as well as Cognition Sciences, Perception Theory, or Psychology on the other hand. All of these issues also depend on the data to be visualized and on the user's background, see Figure 1.1.

The creation of this textbook was motivated by the following reasons: The authors would like to increase the reader's awareness that when designing a new

A. Kerren et al. (Eds.): Human-Centered Visualization Environments 2006, LNCS 4417, pp. 1–9, 2007.
© Springer-Verlag Berlin Heidelberg 2007

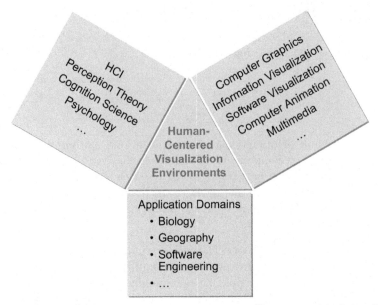

Fig. 1.1. Overview of the most important components of human-centered visualization.

visualization system, research results from the fields of HCI, Cognitive Sciences, Psychology, and others, should be taken into account. Intuitive interaction with a system and human-centered software usability design can increase productivity and efficiency in a work flow. It is the authors' goal that this textbook provides a good overview of popular visualization techniques with respect to both hardware and software. A human-centered point of view is the premier principle for selecting the described techniques. At the beginning of the book, an overview of the most significant human-centered design aspects is given, such as users' aims, users' requirements, and usability, followed by design evaluation methods, such as user studies and performance tests.

The authors' wish is that the reader—and thus a potential user or developer of visualization systems and environments—is capable of choosing an appropriate visualization technique that fits a given requirement *and* evaluating the quality and efficiency of the design by means of user studies or performance tests. A comprehensive bibliography at the end of the textbook provides additional reading material for those readers interested in further study of the subject areas.

This textbook was written as a self-contained study book that can be used for self-study or for a graduate-level semester course on human-centered visualization environments.

Structure

The content of this textbook is divided into two parts: The first part covers fundamentals of human-centered design, hardware- and software-related technologies for interaction, and base methods for visual representation. It then leads to a classification of future challenges and unsolved problems in human-centered visualization. The second part addresses the most important methods and common solutions for domain-specific visualizations, especially in geosciences, software design (algorithmic structures), and biomedical information.

Part I: Fundamental Principles and Methods

What makes visualization a human-centered approach? In Chapter 2, possible definitions of the therm "human-centered" are given. One out of the definitions and maybe the most important one—the ISO standard [394]—refers to human-centered design as "an approach to interactive system development that focuses specifically on making systems usable". Without doubt, the most prominent term in this definition is *usable*. The meaning of the term *usability* contains a number of aspects: effectiveness, efficiency, satisfaction, learnability, flexibility, memorability, ease of use, and error tolerance. Some of them can be easily measured in an objective way, others are users' subjective opinions about a tool or functionality.

How can all those usability factors be formalized? A key instrument is user studies which describe how critical information about the user can be obtained, so that the designed system is usable. Therefore, the central questions in interaction and visualization designs are: Who are the users of the systems? What kind of data are they working with? What are the general tasks of the users? These questions form a set of arguments for a good user study before one can start with designing visualization techniques.

What is a good visualization? A user study is helpful in addressing this question, even if the answer is sometimes ambiguous. A good visualization for one user could at the same time proof insufficient or inappropriate for a different user due to the variations in user and task characteristics. Several elements can be defined that help in the development of a suitable visualization system. In some cases, however, compromises are necessary, and it will not be possible to score equally high on all factors.

Visualization design and user interface design are closely related. Therefore, some of the same strategies can be applied to both areas. One such strategy is an iterative process which consists of a four-step analysis of user requirements and tasks, visualization design, implementation, and validation. This iterative approach is known as the *design cycle.*

Interacting with Visualizations (Chapter 3) describes the different aspects of interaction when dealing with virtual environments. Every time when communicating with other humans, speech, multiple gestures, or other ordinary signals are used in order to express ourselves. Multiple forms or modalities of interaction are present in such a conversion which can be summarized in the term

Fig. 1.2. Human-computer interaction in an immersive visualization environment. *Image courtesy of Fakespace Systems.*

multimodal interaction. This consideration is not only limited to inter-human communication, it can easily be transferred to the interaction and visualization paradigms used in a human-centered visualization environment (cp. Figure 1.2).

In such an environment, the display type has the largest effect on the design of the system, because most information in a virtual environment is communicated to the brain using the visual sense. All other interactions must be placed in its context. The display size greatly affects the way humans interact with a system. For example, the interaction potential of a PDA certainly differ from the interaction capabilities and possibilities of a large display system. Small displays are typically embedded in hand-held devices; this leaves only one hand free for interaction. Larger displays, in contrast, leave both hands free but cannot be easily accessed in a single physical movement. This leads to the conclusion that human-centered interaction and human-centered visualization are closely interconnected. Consequently, the interaction is dependent on the visualization and vice versa.

Which interaction modalities are considered feasible and which ones are not? Considering the term *interaction*, the terms *modality* and furthermore *multi-modality* must be explored first, before focusing on the huge spectrum of current interaction devices. These devices are trying to rise to the challenge of natural human interaction, based on the current technologies and developments.

Normally, a visualization researcher works in a team and collaborates with experts of other domains. Consider a team member who is not able to participate in a current meeting or presentation, and an important feature has to be examined or presented, or furthermore his advice or help is needed. The team member must also be able to interact with the visualization in order to provide the necessary expertise. This implies the necessity to use a collaborative workspace or collaborative environment. Current applications trying to handle this issue are facing many problems, e.g., user authentication (access management), creation of multiple, personalized views (personalization), and others. Efficient models for multi-user interactions are the key factor to a successful collaboration. The efficiency of these models must be proven by different criteria. Finally, an overview of current collaborative visualization environments is given to provide insight into features of current systems and into their benefits and shortcomings.

Visual Representations (Chapter 4) explains how data models can be expressed using visual metaphors and converted into representations suitable for interaction, as described in Chapter 3. Edward Tufte, one of the leaders in the field of visual data exploration, describes in his illustrated textbooks [835–837] how information can be prepared so that the visual representation depicts both the data and the data context. His suggestions reach far beyond coordinate axes, labels and legends. The human brain collects data and attempts to correlate the information with previously acquired knowledge. The brain is an associative memory that gathers and sorts information based on contextual information. The task of memorizing information can be supported by providing the brain with additional context information. The use of visual metaphors assists the brain in its endeavor to connect new information received through the visual input channels to existing information stored in short- or long-term memory.

For instance, in a weather analysis chart seasonal temperature changes could be presented as a bar graph showing absolute temperature values over time. Such a diagram would provide the necessary information, but it would not be obvious what the bar graph represents if the axes were not labeled. Such an abstract representation contains no context information.

The first, more intuitive alternative would be a time axis depicted as a calendar. The calendar serves as an icon for the abstract concept of time. A clock icon to represent the time would be misleading, because the time frame comprises of not of minutes or hours, but of months or several years.

In addition, the temperature axis could be shown as a thermometer, which by most people will be recognized immediately as an indicator of temperature. However, the temperature scale and the units (Kelvin, Fahrenheit, or Celsius) are not immediately obvious, especially when viewed from a distance. Colors chosen by universal, culturally accepted or experience-based methods can help to identify hot (red) and cold (blue) temperatures, but the assignment of particular hues within a given range to certain temperatures is about as random as the assignment of unitless numbers to those temperatures. The depiction of physics-based phenomena, for example, frozen or evaporating water, next to the temperature scale would make the visual representation universally understandable and recognizable, even without any knowledge of the language of the annotation or national unit systems.

There are many ways to extend the example given above. For instance, if the temperature changes are too small to be seen in a given graph, the visual metaphor could be extended by superimposing a magnifying lens on the thermometer, maximizing the space for the illustration of temperatures and using only a small add-on for the context. Why not use trees and the color and number of their leaves to illustrate seasonal temperature changes? How about a stream of water that is either liquid, steaming or solid? Be creative and think outside the box!

The authors would like to stimulate a new way of thinking regarding visual representations. Rather than just plotting multi-dimensional coordinate systems, the scientist should keep the message in mind that is to be communicated in the visualization. A convincing diagram is one that people immediately recognize and memorize. It should convey sufficient information for someone to make a decision, and it should resonate in the viewers' (associative) minds.

The chapter on Visual Representations will make the reader familiar with basic visual representations for various types of one- and multi-dimensional data, and it will give some inspiration for the use of visual metaphors. A special section is dedicated to graphs and trees, as these represent a well researched range of visual metaphors.

All technologies and human-centered design methods discussed so far have certain benefits and shortcomings. Most approaches are an intermediate step on the way to solving concrete visualization problems and to building "effective" visualization tools, which aim to incorporate useful knowledge of visual perception into the system. Chapter 5 presents a comprehensive list of top unsolved problems and future challenges in visualization with a main focus on human-centered visualization. This list surveys related literature and classifies future challenges into three different categories: human-centered, technical, and financial.

Each discussed challenge is exemplified with the help of concrete examples and problems. The chapter ends with a careful outlook into the future. Here, the authors try to foresee—with caution and some margin of error—what problems could be solved in 20 years. They recognize that the list of solved problems is shorter than the list of unsolved problems. Thus, the reader of this textbook will realize that research on human-centered visualization environments is a hot and agile one.

Part II: Domain-Specific Visualizations

Geography is one of the best studied and most ancient domains in which visualization can help to understand, explore, and communicate spatial phenomena. Most people are familiar with cartography or so-called thematic maps that display the spatial patterns of climate characteristics, population density, etc. in intuitive and comprehensive ways. There are several definitions of *Geographic Visualization* (abbr. *Geovisualization*): The International Cartographic Association (ICA) Commission on Visualization and Virtual Environments defines: "Geovisualization integrates approaches from visualization in scientific computing (ViSC), cartography, image analysis, information visualization, exploratory data analysis (EDA), and geographic information systems (GISystems) to provide theory, methods and tools for visual exploration, analysis, synthesis, and presentation of geospatial data" [528]. Other authors prefer a more human-centered point of view and describe geovisualization as "the creation and use of

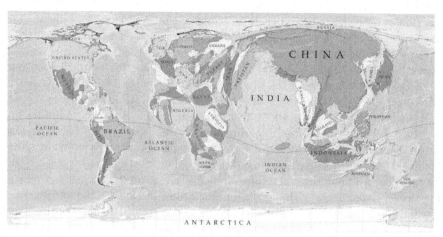

Fig. 1.3. Visualization of world map areas scaled proportional to size of population by country. *Image courtesy of M. Newman.*

visual representations to facilitate thinking, understanding, and knowledge construction about geospatial data" [513] or as "the use of visual geospatial displays to explore data and through that exploration to generate hypotheses, develop problem solutions and construct knowledge" [473]. Chapter 6 surveys the most important geovisualization techniques and methods, shows frequent problems, and in this context also discusses human-centered issues, such as usability and quality assurance by means of user studies.

The first two sections of this chapter discuss aims and driving forces of geovisualization. Because of the historic relevance of cartography, there are several approaches to evaluating the concrete perception of maps and images. The main part of the chapter covers visualization techniques and methods, especially 2D and 3D map-based visualization techniques (see Figure 1.3, for example), animation, interaction, and the integration of multivariate or time-varying data. The challenge for designers of geovisualization tools is to put these methods and techniques together effectively in order to help users solve their respective tasks. To exemplify these processes, five geovisualization systems are briefly described which show how the discussed techniques can be combined and used either individually or jointly.

Cartography has a long-standing history of applying perceptual and cognitive principles to map design. However, the cognitive theory for static maps cannot easily be generalized to apply to modern and interactive geovisualization tools. The last two sections of the chapter present usability issues and evaluation with respect to geovisualization, as well as future trends in the development of geovisualization tools, the impact of new hardware technologies (e.g., large displays or portable devices), and—of course—human-centered aspects.

The next domain discussed in the second part of this textbook (Chapter 7) is *Algorithm Animation* which is a subfield of Software Visualization (SoftVis). Algorithm animation visualizes the behavior of an algorithm by producing an abstraction of both the data and the operations of the algorithm. Initially, it maps the current state of the algorithm into an image which then is animated based on the operations between two succeeding states in the algorithm execution. Animating a visual representation of an algorithm allows for better understanding of the inner workings of the algorithm. Furthermore, it makes apparent its deficiencies and advantages thus allowing for further optimization.

Knowlton's movie [453] about list processing using the programming language L6 was one of the first experiments to visualize program behavior with the help of animation techniques. Other early efforts often focused on aiding teaching [37,365] including the classic "Sorting Out Sorting" video [38,39] that described nine different sorting algorithms and illustrated their respective running times. Experiences with algorithm animations made by hand and the wide distribution of personal computers with advanced graphical displays in the 1980's led to the development of complex algorithm animation systems.

After a brief overview of the field, Chapter 7 defines several groups of potential users of algorithm animations. This is important because a later review depends on the aims the users want to follow. Additionally, there are many taxonomies in this field that are presented from a human-centered point of view. The main part of this chapter covers a review of a selection of current algorithm animation tools summarizing the different ways users can interact with them, the methods that have been used to evaluate them, and the results that have been reported.

Biomedical Information Visualization (Chapter 8) addresses the needs of the emerging fields of quantitative biology and medicine on a molecular or genetic level. Large collections of information, such as the Protein Data Bank (PDB) or the Human Genome Project, typically sponsored by large, national and international funding agencies and maintained on supercomputers, have changed the way we look at life.

The tree of life, also known as a phylogenetic tree, represents the evolution of life according to the state of the art in genetic research. Subtrees contain various species, and special phylogenetic trees can be generated for species with related DNA sequences. Due to the complexity of the sequenced material, such trees can become quite complex. They are also subject to change when new research provides evidence for the existence of a new species. Once a new "missing link" is found, an entire tree may have to be restructured. Both their complexity and their subjectivity to change make phylogenetic trees difficult to interpret when plotted on paper. Two- and three-dimensional, interactive visualization software can help to display trees and to interact with their data.

Automated alignment of DNA sequences has enabled great advances in deciphering the human genome. Now we know that the human genome consists of approximately three billion DNA base pairs containing an estimated 20,000–25,000 genes. After collecting all the data, the problem of interpreting these genes and the functions they code for remains. Observation of genetic disorders caused by defects in the DNA is only one way to decode the functions of the proteins transcribed by a particular sequence of DNA. Another method is the observation of the effects of changes in the DNA in other species, such as mice, rats, or fruit flies. These species share an estimated 50% of their genes with humans. Visualization algorithms for sequence alignment aid scientists in the discovery of patterns hidden in the vast amount of data collected in the sequencing.

Understanding the complex biochemical processes within a cell or an organism is another emerging branch in the field of quantitative biology. Rather than looking at a single process, circuit, feedback or control mechanism, a complex system of interdependent, simultaneous processes can be simulated using computational models. Visualization currently helps to organize and understand these complex simulation models. Some illustrative examples are given in this textbook to inspire the reader to drill down deeply into the complex processes that keep an organism alive.

The next part of this chapter deals with a new technology called microarrays. This technique allows scientists to test thousands of gene variations simultaneously in the same experiment, thus speeding up large screening experiments significantly. Visualization of data obtained from such microarrays aids in an analysis of the level of gene expression in each variant. Typical visualization tools include clustering and tree view algorithms.

Medical records can be a useful scientific tool. In 1850, a typhoid epidemic was traced back by Sir John Snow to a sewage contamination of a particular public well. This incident became known as the Broad Street Pump Affair. Since this time it became evident that a systematic analysis of statistical data can reveal patterns in the outbreak, course and spread of a disease. A useful method for obtaining statistical data on pathological conditions is the analysis of patient records. Medical Record Visualization reveals patterns in particular pathological observations and allows clinicians to draw conclusions from comparing an individual patient's record to other patients' data stored in a database. This textbook provides some examples how patient data can be organized and visually presented efficiently.

Summary

The close interconnection between *visualization* and *human-computer interaction* suggests that visualization software design should incorporate human-centered principles of interaction and usability. The assessment of these priciples is primarily done by means of user studies and performance tests. The purpose of this textbook is to provide some inspiration and an overview of existing methods. The authors would like to encourage the reader to experiment with novel interaction techniques to find out which tools are useful and suitable to humans, and what type of interactive visualization helps to gain new insights in information contained in the data. Human-centered visualization environments can be the key to enlightenment!

Part I:

Fundamental Principles and Methods

2 Human-Centered Aspects

Olga Kulyk, Robert Kosara, Jaime Urquiza, and Ingo Wassink

Humans have remarkable perceptual capabilities. These capabilities are heavily underestimated in current visualizations [759]. Often, this is due to the lack of an in-depth user study to set the requirements for optimal visualizations. The designer does not understand what kind of information should be visualized, how it should be presented or what kind of interactions should be supported. The key elements of successful information visualization are the correct data using the best visualization technique and the best interaction techniques with respect to users. If one of these elements is ignored, people might interpret the data in the wrong way and thus might not understand the underlying information or a pattern.

In order to design effective interactive visualizations, it is important to take into account the limitations of human perception, context of use, and the goals and activities that are to be performed to reach these goals. In order to obtain a *usable* application, developers have to pay attention to the user's working environment and tasks; this *focus-on-user* idea is comprised in the human-centered concept.

The next section discusses usability (the property of being usable) from the human-centered point of view. Usability has application in many areas, but our focus is on the *human-centered* approach to design of interactive systems, also called *user-centered*, in order to inform the reader on how to design visualizations according to human cognitive and perceptual abilities, specific to the context of use and goals of potential users. Then, the usability concept is explained in the "Usability in Human-Centered Design" section. The next Section "User Aims and Requirements" discusses how to define a user group, establish user goals and requirements. Finally, an overview of the different evaluation methods and current evaluation practices, including the practical issues of experiment design that can help to improve the effectiveness of visualizations is presented in the "Evaluation of Visualizations Environments" and "User Studies and a Science of Visualization" sections.

2.1 Human-Centered Approach

Stone et al. [798] describe a human-centered design giving the following definition:

A. Kerren et al. (Eds.): Human-Centered Visualization Environments 2006, LNCS 4417, pp. 13–75, 2007.
© Springer-Verlag Berlin Heidelberg 2007

>"An approach to user interface design and development that views the
>knowledge about intended users of a system as a central concern, in-
>cluding, for example, knowledge about user's abilities and needs, their
>task(s), and the environment(s) within which they work. These users
>would also be actively involved in the design process." [798, Page 628]

Focusing on the field of human-computer interaction (HCI), the International Organization for Standardization (ISO) produced the standard *ISO 13407 Human-
Centered Design Processes for Interactive Systems* [394], also described in Stone
et al. [798]. The general idea is that a human-centered system has to: adapt
to the user's needs, skills and limitations; engage users; adapt to the context;
and work in real life. This standard presents a set of human-centered processes.
The main aim of the principles described in this standard is to build interactive
systems that are more effective, efficient and satisfying for its users. Also, ISO
describes four essential elements of the human-centered design:

– The active involvement of users in the design process and a clear understanding
  of them, their tasks, and their requirements.
– An appropriate allocation of functions between users and technology, specifying which functions can be carried out by users.
– An iteration of design solutions in which feedback from users becomes a critical
  source of information.
– A multidisciplinary design perspective that requires a variety of skills. Multidisciplinary design teams should be involved in the human-centered design
  process. The teams should consist of end users, purchasers, business analysts,
  application domain specialists, systems analysts, programmers, as well as marketing and sales personnel.

Finally, the ISO standard includes the list of benefits when adopting the human-
centered approach:

– Systems are easy to understand and use, thus reducing training and support
  costs.
– Discomfort and stress are reduced, therefore the user's satisfaction is improved.
– The productivity of users and the operational efficiency of organizations is
  improved.
– Product quality, aesthetics, and impact are improved, therefore a competitive
  advantage can be achieved.

The first phrase of the introduction in the ISO's standard states that *"Human-
centered design is an approach to interactive system development that focuses
specifically on making systems usable"*. As usability characterizes how usable is
a system, following we will focus our attention on the usability concept.

2.2 Usability in Human-Centered Design

Before giving a more formal description, consider the following situation: Weather
forecasters have to predict the maximum and minimum temperatures of a geo-

graphic area in a country. The Weather State Department of this country has a historical archive with all information available about rain, wind, pressures, temperatures, etc. Although all information needed by the forecasters is in the archive, the computing of maximum and minimum temperatures will take them a lot of time. They will have to extract information about a concrete geographical area, ignore obsolete and useless information, e.g. rain or wind data, and finally organize data and apply the meteorological prediction models needed to obtain the information about minimum and maximum temperatures of that geographic area. This is an example of *information overload*, where the user has more information available than needed, and more than he can readily assimilate.

Now, consider a second situation: The Weather State Department conducted a number of interviews of the weather forecasters all around the country. They concluded that information technologies could help forecasters in their prediction tasks, so they provided them with an application to manage the weather information. To develop the application, the development team analyzed how the forecasters used the weather data in their job, thus they developed information visualization systems which helped forecasters filter out the useless information and work with the useful data to apply the meteorological prediction models. The previously mentioned analysis is intended as a *usability* analysis, leading to a set of design decisions. The result should be that the forecasters can work with valid data to apply prediction models, and that they do their job using a reasonable amount of time. It could be said that the application is *usable*, and here, a human-centered approach has helped to deal with problems generated by information overload.

Finally, if the weather prediction models are changed, they need more information. The application could get obsolete (and non-usable) because it cannot handle the amount of information that the new models need to function. Then, the users will have to mix pencil and paper with computers, and information overload will reappear.

How does the design team ensure that the developed information management system is *usable*? What does the *usability* mean? To answer these questions, a formal definition of the term usability is introduced next.

2.2.1 Defining Usability

What is *usability*? What do we evaluate when we test the *human-centered* approach of a visualization system? When can we affirm that a visualization system is *usable*? The term usability is a property, rather than an independent entity of a system. Moreover, it is related with the successful utilization of a system.

From a formal point of view, Larking & Simon [497] give a rationale about advantages of using diagrammatic representations instead of textual ones. It can be applied to the successful use of a visualization system to the effect that the three reasoning processes—searching, recognition and inference—are also present in the use of visualization systems. Thus, to be successfully used, a visualization system should provide facilities to search for information, recognition of interesting information, and making inferences from it.

From a more practical point of view, consider the following question: What does it mean for a system to have low usability? It is sure that such a system will be rarely used, if it is not compulsory to do. Imagine a situation where the users of a visualization system are asked about their opinion about it. What can be concluded, if they answer: *well, it is a good system*. It can be concluded that the system has provided to the users all that they expected to receive from it. Thus, the users will not say that they could not complete the task, the users will not think that they have used more resources than was really needed to complete the task, and the users will feel comfortable while using the system.

Obviously, it is important to check if the users are able to complete their tasks, and the amount of resources expended in doing it. Still, why is it important that users feel comfortable with a system? We discuss it next.

User's Satisfaction. Traditionally, software systems have been evaluated in terms of its performance. The human-centered approach pays attention to the user interaction features rather than just software performance. One of these features is the user's satisfaction. Talbert [813] gives some ideas about what features should be supported by a human-centered system:

- Take into account human perceptual skills and limitations.
- Work in real life.
- Be flexible and not restrict the user.
- Be context sensitive, adapt to changes in user needs.
- Engage user and be enjoyable.

Four of the five points mentioned before, deal with user's satisfaction, while only one, *work in real life*, deals with other aspects as effectiveness or efficiency. In real life, problems must be solved (effectiveness) using a reasonable amount of resources (efficiency).

User's satisfaction is a quite general term. It can not be simplified to the question: *Do you like the system?* As it is the user's subjective opinion, it is broad enough to accommodate most of the reasons that can cause the rejection of a system by the user. Some examples are: systems difficult to learn to use, systems without short-cuts that can be used by experienced users, e.g. keyboard short-cuts to menu options, or systems with unpleasant graphical designs (colors, fonts). User's satisfaction highly depends on the application domain, but it is clearly related to usability [176]. In fact, to be usable, an interface should be perceived as being usable by the specified users [798].

Definition of Usability. Three important concepts have appeared associated with usability: the completion of a task, the resources used to complete a task, and the user's comfort level while using the system.

Furthermore, from its beginning, "human-centered" has been understood as a general concept that is related to a number of specific aspects. Gould & Lewis [301] write:

> "... any application designed for people to use, should be easy to learn (and remember), useful, that is contain functions people really need in their work, and be easy and pleasant to use." [301, Page 300]

Bennet [77] identified four particular aspects: learnability (ease of learn), throughput, flexibility, and attitude. Nielsen [606] defined five usability parameters: learnability, efficiency, memorability (ease of remember), errors, and satisfaction. In this chapter, ISO's usability definition will be used as the working definition:

> *"The extent to which a product can be used by specified users to achieve specified goals with effectiveness, efficiency and satisfaction in a specified context of use."* [395, Def. 3.1]

Therefore, usability is broadly defined as consisting of three distinct aspects:

Effectiveness represents the accuracy and completeness with which users achieve certain goals.

Efficiency is the relation between (1) the accuracy and completeness with which users achieve certain goals and (2) the resources expended in achieving them.

Satisfaction is the user's comfort with and positive attitudes towards the use of the system.

Similar definitions of these three aspects can be found elsewhere [606, 683, 798]. It is clear that the lack of any of these aspects could determine the user not to use the system. But importance of each aspect depends on the domain where usability is analyzed. Thus, usability could be modeled as a three dimensional space with the effectiveness, efficiency and user's satisfaction as its axis (see Figure 2.1).

Fig. 2.1. The three orthogonal aspects of usability.

Correlations among these three aspects have been studied [40, 273, 607]. One could expect some kind of correlation following simple ideas as: a satisfied user would be both a user that has been able to complete the tasks, and a user that has not expended more resources than expected in completing those tasks. A clear correlation is that there is no efficiency to evaluate without effectiveness.

But conclusions in these studies varied. While Bailey [40] questioned the existence of correlations between efficiency and satisfaction, Nielsen & Levy [607] found evidence of the opposite. They analyzed the relationship between efficiency and user preference from 113 experiments extracted from 57 HCI studies. The result of this study was that user's satisfaction predicts efficiency quite well.

However, in 25% of the 28 cases, the users did not prefer the more efficient system. This situation can also be seen in Hornbaek et al. [367], where they analyzed usability of zoomable and overview+detail interfaces (cp. Page 27). In this study, users clearly preferred overview+detail interfaces, but they completed task faster with zoomable interfaces.

Studies about the relationship between satisfaction and effectiveness have not been found. Finally, Frokjaer, Hertzum & Hornbaek [273] found no correlation between efficiency, measured as task completion time, and effectiveness, measured as quality of solution. They conclude that the correlations among the usability aspects depend in a complex way on the application domain, the user's experience and the use context.

Therefore, if this general correlation can not be found, the application domain must be carefully analyzed to assign the correct degree of importance to each aspect of usability. Different domains can be represented in the usability 3D space, depending on how important each aspect is considered. *ES*, *EY*, and *US* are the abbreviated names of effectiveness, efficiency and user's satisfaction (see Figure 2.2).

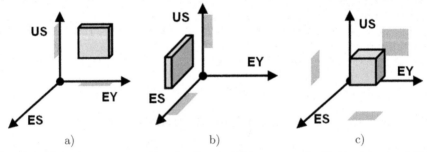

a)   b)   c)

Fig. 2.2. Domains representation in the usability space: a) effectiveness is of little importance (probably because it is supposed), b) efficiency is of little importance, c) the three aspects are important.

Figure 2.2a represents domains with simple tasks, where the efficiency aspect will be more important, because effectiveness is supposed (values of *ES* near 0)

Figure 2.2b represents domains with complex tasks, where the effectiveness aspect will be more important. Probably, users of this domain need more resources to complete tasks correctly, and efficiency is not considered important (values of *EY* near 0)

Finally, domains where users are not obliged to use a system, although it has good effectiveness and efficiency rates, should pay attention to user's satisfaction. Figure 2.2c represents real life domains, where all three aspects are important. An example could be a decision making tool, which has to help in decision making (*ES*), has to do it before a deadline (*EY*), and has to get the user to trust the results (*US*).

In summary, we can define usability as a complex property that is composed of three aspects: effectiveness, efficiency, and user's satisfaction. While effectiveness and efficiency are specific components with a clear definition, user's satisfaction is a broader term, where a number of different aspects are grouped. These aspects have some impact on a user's attitude toward the use of an application, and are not measurable in terms of accuracy, completeness, or resources usage.

Although this chapter will work with the ISO's description of usability, recent research efforts have provided new definitions and concepts related to usability. Quesenberry [683] gives a new definition, also called *the five Es*. She has maintained the effectiveness and efficiency aspects. She has renamed *user's satisfaction* to *engaging*. And she has added two components:

Error Tolerant: That is how well the design prevents errors or helps with recovery from those that occurs.

Easy to Learn: That is how well the product supports both initial orientation and deep understanding of its capabilities.

Table 2.1 summarizes different aspects taken into account through all definitions of usability cited in this section. There exist seven aspects, the most important one is the *user's satisfaction*, taken into account in all definitions of usability. In addition, the *effectiveness*, *efficiency* and *learnability* aspects are also considered in four out of the five definitions cited.

Table 2.1. Different aspects of usability.

Aspects/Definitions	Bennet [77]	Gould & Lewis [301]	Nielsen [606]	ISO [395]	Quesenberry [683]
Effectiveness		•	•	•	•
Efficiency	•		•	•	•
User's satisfaction	•	•	•	•	•
Ease of learn	•	•	•		•
Flexibility	•				
Ease of remember		•	•		
Easy of use		•			
Error tolerance					•

A new term related with the human-centered approach is the *Universal Usability*. It was initially addressed by Shneiderman [651]. It deals with making visualizations usable from a general point of view. Visualization is recognized as a powerful aid for decision making processes, but it is becoming important for services related to every citizen. Thus, many aspects need to be addressed: user diversity, variety of existing technology, and users' knowledge. New technological advances are needed to deal with different users (age, language, disabilities, etc.), the different used technologies (screen size, network speed, etc.) and the gaps in user's knowledge (general knowledge, knowledge of the application domain, and knowledge of the interface syntax or semantic).

2.2.2 Evaluating Usability

Usability has been defined as a general term composed of a number of aspects. Therefore its evaluation should be component driven. Measurements for each component should be defined. A number of components can be measured in an objective way: effectiveness with error rate, efficiency with resources used to complete tasks, learnability with the time used to reach a specific level of effectiveness/efficiency, and memorability with the level of effectiveness/efficiency after a period of time without using the system. Other components are more subjective from the point of view of the evaluator: flexibility and error tolerance. Finally, user's satisfaction is the user's subjective opinion about the tool. The evaluation methods and protocols that could be applied to these components will be covered in depth in Section 2.4 "Evaluation of Visualization Environments".

2.2.3 Improving Usability

Improvements in usability can be reached by improving each of its components. First, improvements of three interfaces are described here, specifying which aspect is related to which improvement. Finally, new areas of improvement are described.

Three Examples of Usability Improvement. The first example is the transformation from the FilmFinder (see Figure 2.3) to Spotfire (see Figure 2.4) [650]. Basic features of the original visualization technique were maintained, but a number of modifications and additions have been done to increase its utility, therefore improving *effectiveness*: ease of data importation, ease of results publication and sharing, combination of other visualizations with the former one, and integration of analytical tools to facilitate quantitative analysis. In summary, the success of the improved tool seems to be based on its ease of adaptation to specific applications.

The second example [650] involves Treemaps (see Figure 2.5) and the Smartmoney's Map of the Market [774] (the transformed interface). Many factors could be responsible for the popularity of Smartmoney's Map of the Market. With respect to the *effectiveness*: the data is important, the color mapping is familiar to most users (using green for gains or increased values of the stocks, red for losses), with alternative colors for those with color impairment, and finally, it was developed trying to maximize platform independence using lightweight Java. With respect just to the *efficiency*, the hierarchy is simple, being shallow and of fixed depth. With respect to both the *effectiveness* and the *efficiency*, the names and groupings of elements are familiar to users. And finally, with respect to the *user's satisfaction*: in conjunction with *effectiveness*, the data are familiar to the users; and in conjunction with *efficiency*, a new algorithm was developed, and a better aspect ratio for all the rectangles was obtained, making the display more readable and pleasing.

R-Zoom [841] is the third example on usability improvements. This interface is designed for dealing with large number of images, helping the users in choosing those that they are interested in. In this case, the images were graphical

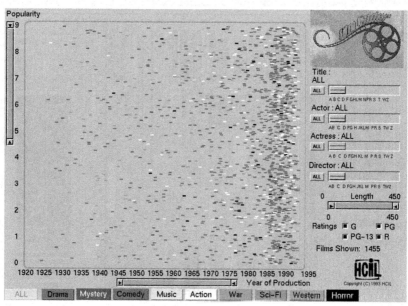

Fig. 2.3. The FilmFinder interface [7]. *Image courtesy of Catherine Plaisant.*

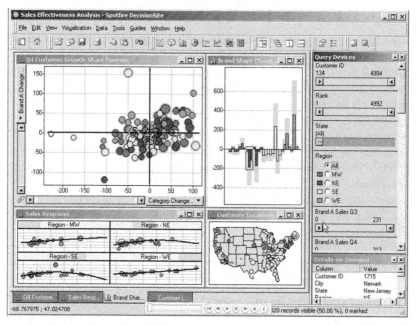

Fig. 2.4. The Spotfire interface. © 2005-2006 Spotfire, Inc. All Rights Reserved.
http://www.spotfire.com

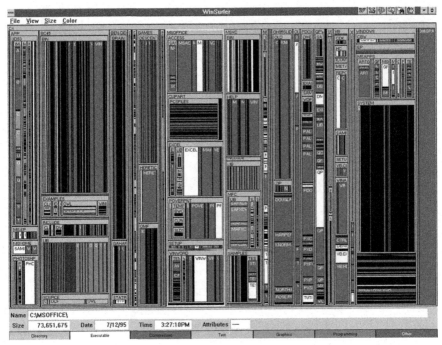

Fig. 2.5. The Treemaps interface [408]. *Image courtesy of Catherine Plaisant.*

representations of execution stages of a particular algorithm. The size of images could vary from small to complex ones. The first version of the interface just use the scroll bar on a one-column list of images. The main aim of the second version is to improve *efficiency* by using an overview+detail solution (see Figure 2.6), where all images are reduced using semantic fisheye views and a simple scaling algorithm. They are distributed with a typical grid layout, and each selected image is shown in original size in another window. But, in spite of this additions the use of the interface has not been successful. The third version of the interface tries to improve *effectiveness* by modifying the scale algorithm, so reduced versions seem to be better understandable. Improvements in *efficiency* are achieved by changing the visualization technique to a focus+context style called R-Zoom (see Figure 2.7). This technique also improves *user's satisfaction* by being tailored for an algorithm animation environment. After a usability test comparing both overview+detail and focus+context, results showed that effectiveness was very similar. But efficiency and user's satisfaction were significantly improved with the focus+context approach.

New Areas of Usability Improvement. From a different point of view, Amar & Stasko [16] identify new areas for improvement in usability. Regarding to the *visual analytics* field [906], they identify two areas that lack of development, they call them *analytic gaps*, in information visualization for high level analysis. The main problem in this field is the *representational primacy*, that is *the pursuit*

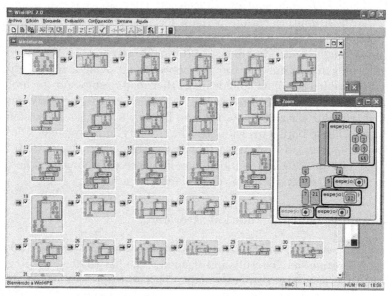

Fig. 2.6. A typical overview | detail interface, implemented in the WinHIPE environment [841]. The detail window (on the right) has the detailed view of the 13th image in the overview window.

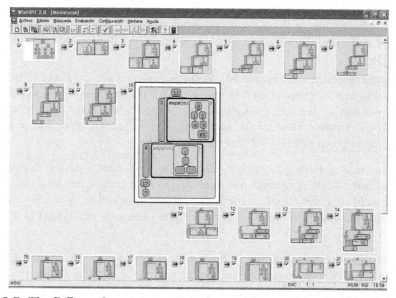

Fig. 2.7. The R-Zoom focus+context interface, implemented in the WinHIPE environment [841]. The focus of attention is on the 10th image (detailed view), while the rest of images are seen as context images (reduced versions).

of faithful data replication and comprehension. They say that representational primacy can be a limiting notion, perhaps focusing on low-level tasks that do not map well to the true needs and goals of users. Then, two gaps between representation and analysis are identified: the Rationale gap and the Worldview gap. The Rationale gap is defined as the gap between perceiving a relationship and actually being able to explain confidence in that relationship and the usefulness of that relationship. The Worldview gap is defined as the gap between what is being shown and what actually needs to be shown to make a decision. It is expected that filling both gaps will result in usability improvements [16].

Information overload is an important factor that effects usability. It is discussed next how information overload may influence environments where visualization systems are used and its connections with usability.

2.2.4 Usability and Information Overload

The term *overload* refers to the state of having *too much* of something. Applied to the term *information*, it results in somebody who has to do something using information, but has too much of it available. This term appears in many different fields, leading to various constructs, synonyms and related terms, e.g., cognitive overload, communication overload, knowledge overload, or sensory overload.

As it was stated in the introduction, information overload can affect human-centered aspects, but also usable systems should deal with information overload. In this subsection, information overload and its influence on usability are discussed. First, the term information overload will be defined, then the effects of information overload will be described from a general and from the usability points of view, and finally some ways of dealing with information overload are presented.

Defining Information Overload. What is Information Overload? The term information overload was coined by Toffler [828]. Information overload refers to the state of having too much information to complete a certain task. It appears to be an effect rather than a fact, property, or an independent entity. A similar description is given in the Usability glossary [194]:

> *"... a state of having too much information, such that a person is overwhelmed. When information is available in enormous quantities (as on the web) and not clearly structured, people have difficulty finding relevant information and grasping important principles embedded in the information."*

From a subjective point of view, information overload comes from having more information available than one can readily assimilate. As the ability to collect information has grown, the ability to process that information has not kept up. Information overload can be caused by many situations:

- Large amounts of currently available information.
- A high rate of new information.
- Contradictions in available information.
- Low signal-to-noise ratio (proportion of useful information found to all information found).
- Inefficient methods for comparing and processing different kinds of information.

General Effects of Information Overload. Information overload thus impacts the information visualization reasoning process: searching, recognition, and inference [497].

The search process can be affected by large amounts of information. This increases the size of the set where the search will be performed. From this point of view, computational efficiency will be affected because the search process will be slower. The search process may also be affected by a high rate of new information because the search should be performed each time that the information is updated, possibly interrupting other processes (e.g. recognition, inference). And low signal-to-noise ratio has adverse effects because a large part of the information set is not useful but still has to be processed.

The recognition process can be affected by large amounts of information. Selected information can contain a large number of attributes, where only target attributes should be searched. The recognition process may also be affected by a low signal-to-noise ratio if useful attributes make up a small percentage of the whole attribute set.

The inference process could be affected by a high rate of new information. Any change in the information could affect to currently working inferences based upon it. The inference process may also be affected by contradictions in available information because it could create inconsistent knowledge.

Hetzler & Turner [347] give a real-life example of the effects of information overload. They study how professional analysts' work is influenced by information overload. Professional analysts must constantly work to separate out the valuable data within a high volume of information [517]. But the problem is that they have to do it without reading all returned documents from a search. Thus, many efforts are dedicated to query refinement, where excluding valuable documents along with the useless ones is a risk. This has also been studied by Paterson et al. [642]. Hetzler & Turner show how the In-Spire visualization tool [903] can help in this environment.

Effects of Information Overload on Usability. These effects can be analyzed in a component driven way, focusing on how effectiveness, efficiency and user's satisfaction can be affected:

Effectiveness can be affected by a fast rate of new information and contradictions in available information.

Efficiency can be affected by large amounts of information. The more information to be processed, the more resources are needed. Of course, effects on effectiveness will impact efficiency.

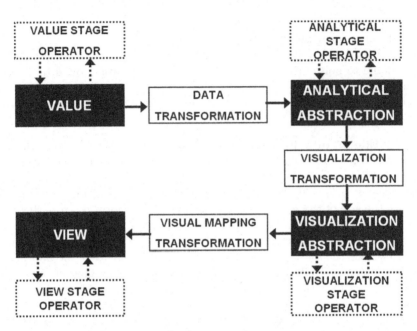

Fig. 2.8. Chi's Data Stage Model [158].

User's satisfaction can be also affected by large amounts of information. The user could be overwhelmed by a fast rate of new information and thus might not be able to assimilate new information. Contradictions may occur in available information. The user may not trust in the information. Low signal-to-noise ratio may cause user's feeling that there is no, or little, useful information available.

Dealing with Information Overload. Ways of dealing with information overload can be described from a theoretical or a more practical point of view. Larking & Simon [497] pointed out a way to deal with information overload from a *theoretical point of view*, decreasing sets where a search of relevant information is performed. Shneiderman's guideline for design of information visualization [759], *"overview first, zoom and filter, then details on demand"*, is another way to prevent information overload. Chi developed the Data State Reference Model [158] where processes performed by the information visualization techniques on the data are represented divided in stages, transformations and operators (see Figure 2.8). With regard to the information overload, information visualization techniques deal with it during the *visualization transformation*, where information, that is relevant to the user, is selected and, if relevant information is still a large set, during the *visual mapping transformation* and with *view stage operators*.

Navigation through large data sets is addressed by Furnas [280]. He pays attention to issues that arise when information structures (represented as graphs with nodes and links) become very large and where interaction is seriously limited by the available resources of space and time. To this end, Furnas defines two concepts:

Efficient View Traversability (EVT): This means how well the structure can be traversed. It consists of a pair of requirements: the number of links from one node to other nodes in the structure, and the distance (in number of links) between a pair of nodes in the structure must be "small" compared to the size of the structure.

View Navigability (VN): This means if efficient paths (good EVT) can be really found in the structure. Good VN can be reached by storing navigation information in the nodes.

From *a more practical point of view*, three families of information visualization techniques [145] deal with information overload, in the perspective of large amounts of information. These families are zoomable, overview+detail, and focus+context interfaces.

Zoomable interfaces allow users access information by panning and zooming [646]. Space and scale are the fundamental means of organizing the information [282,646]. The most common appearance of elements is geometric zoom, but there exist more complex ones as semantic zooming [72,267,646], constant density zooming [911], or non-linear panning and zooming [283,383]. Also, smoothness in zooming transitions have been studied: smooth zooms [72,316,853] and non-smooth zooms [646,734].

Overview+Detail interfaces show an overview of the entire information space together with a detailed view of part of the contents [652]. These interfaces deal with information overload by allowing the user to see a global view of the information space with the overview window, and allowing a detailed view with the detail window, see Figure 2.6. These interfaces are used in a variety of situations, e.g., editors for program code [233] or interfaces for image collections [619].

Overview+detail interfaces improve efficiency of user's navigation. Users navigate using the overview window rather than using the detail window [66]. Orientation is also improved: the overview window aids users in keeping track of their current position in the information space [652]. Finally, overview+detail interfaces give users a feeling of control [762]. The most visible drawback of these interfaces is that they require more screen space than interfaces without overviews; also, the spatially indirect relation between overview and detail windows increase the time used for visual search [145]. Blending of zoomable and overview+detail interfaces is being studied [658]. More information about overview+detail interfaces can be found in [145,366].

Focus+Context interfaces join the current focus of attention and its context (in overview+detail they were separated), see Figure 2.7. The origin of focus+context visualization is a non-interactive distortion-based technique for visualization of map data [421]. But the first interactive technique was introduced with the Fisheye Views [279,281]. Fisheye Views are a general interaction framework for information filtering according to the user's current point of interest in the material. Other focus+context interfaces are: Bi-Focal Display, Perspective Wall, Document Lens, Graphical Fisheye View, Rubbersheet View (all in [145]), R-Zoom [841], or Flip zooming [92]. Also, graph visualization is a field where focus+context techniques has been extensively used, further information can be found in [346,403] and in Section 4.4 of this book.

Other Approaches to Deal with Information Overload. Nesbitt & Barras [602] found promising results in using sounds and images to deal with information overload in stock market information, but further work is needed.

Trafton et al. [832] studied how expert meteorological forecasters deal with large amounts of data. They found that three heuristics are used: (1) attending to information in a goal-driven manner, (2) integrating information across visualizations, and (3) building a qualitative mental model from which they can abstract quantitative information.

Interactive systems have to be designed focusing on the *user working with the system* (e.g. information overload situations), rather than focusing on the system performance. This comprises the *usability* concept, which is a result of the *human-centered* approach. The next section will explain in detail *user studies*, describing how to obtain the critical information about the user, so that the designed system is usable.

2.3 User Aims and Requirements

Normally, visualization is used for two main purposes. The first one is using visualization for communication purposes which is also known as presentation [144]. The visualization of the data is the message between the communicators. In this case, it is important that each of the communicators understands the graphical representation. Otherwise, misunderstanding can arise.

The second goal of visualization is analysis. In that case, the user manipulates and perceives the data to gain more insight into the data and to solve a research problem [144,784]. Insight is defined as how users recognize and categorize information [731]. This goal can be achieved by three steps, namely: data exploration, interacting with the visualization, and drawing conclusions [436].

In this section, the focus will not be on visualization design itself, but on the important steps that are needed to construct successful visualization designs. This essential step is called *user study*. Espinosa et al. [241] argue that a good user study should yield usable information for visualization design. User studies are not atomic tasks, but a non-hierarchical activity. It is neither bottom-up nor top-down. It is an interchanging activity between them [149]. The process of visualization design consists of interim solutions that may play no role in the final design of the product. These intermediary results are used to discover new goals or to get more insight in the desired product.

We discuss the whole process from user analysis to the steps of creating visualization design. The steps have much in common with Human Computer Interaction (HCI) design, because user visualization design is a special kind of HCI design. The central questions in interaction design and so in visualization design are [499, 762]:

- Who are the users of the systems?
- What kind of data are they working with?
- What are the general tasks of the users?

These questions form a set of arguments for a good user study before one can start with designing visualization techniques.

At the University of Twente, research is done on a collaborative environment for life scientists like biologists, bioinformaticians, and medical researchers. The goal of this collaborative environment is knowledge sharing in a multidisciplinary research environment. This means that users with different background knowledge are working together in the same (possibly virtual) environment. The problem with such an environment is that each of the researchers has their own visualization techniques for representing the data. So how can these different visualization techniques be combined to generate a successful collaboration environment? This project will be used throughout this section as an example to show why a user study is so important in the field of visualization design.

Further, this section is organized as follows: Characteristics of good visualization designs are presented in the next subsection. Then, the first step of the user study, user profiling will be explained. Central questions are: Who is the user of our system, in what kind of environment is he/she working, and with what kind of data is he/she working with. The next step is task analysis. Task analysis is the process of defining which tasks are done and how these task are executed. After task analysis is finished, task modeling can be done. This shows the interactions of the user with the system. When task modeling is done, the design phase can start. During task modeling, the set of user requirements of the visualization is established from the data collected during the task analysis. It is important that the final product meets the user requirements for acceptance of the product among the target users or user groups. This means that the product needs to be tested during the design process. Prototypes play an important role during the design and test phase, because they support problem detection in the early stage of the development. We describe how to use prototyping in the design of visualization and how the users are involved in this process.

2.3.1 Characteristics of Good Visualizations and User Interfaces

Humans can interpret visualized data a thousand times faster than they can interpret text [689]. Of course, this depends on the manner the data is visualized. For example, in chemistry, there exists a molecular family called hydrocarbons. These are characterized by a chain of carbon. Consider three carbon chains: hexane, cyclohexane, and benzene. Each of these has a chain of six carbon atoms. When one sees the chemical formula, one expects that these three molecules will

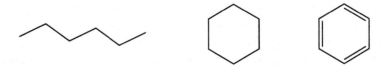

Fig. 2.9. Examples of visualization of hydrocarbons. A chemist can see in one glimpse which of these hydrocarbons is hexane, cyclohexane and benzene.

have almost the same structure. But if one sees the 2D structure, even a non-chemist can see that there are large differences. So, a successful visualization can say more than a thousand words (see for example Figure 2.9).

The next question is: What is a good visualization? There is no clear answer to this question, since a good visualization for one user may be a poor visualization for a different user due to the variations in user characteristics [927]. HCI design and visualization design can be understood as a design-oriented research field [247]. Often, visualization is a component of multimodal HCI, see Section 3.3. To simplify the problem of creating a visualization, it is split up into several dimensions. The usability factors for good user interfaces are listed in Shneiderman & Plaisant [762] and Lauesen [499]. Many of these factors are also applicable to visualization and therefore are discussed below.

2.3.2 Essential Elements of Successful Visualization

There are several elements of a successful visualization system. First, the system should *support the tasks* the user wants to perform. This means that the visualization should be functional with respect to the tasks a user wants to perform. Therefore, it is important to know what kind of information the users want to extract from the data. Often, data can be represented in several ways. This is related to the users' goal in viewing the representation [720].

Second, for acceptance of the application among the whole target group, it is important that the application is *easy to use* and *easy to learn*. The less experienced user should be able to learn the application without spending to much time in how to explore the visualization, because the visualization is just a tool for supporting the researcher. The learnability of the visualization depends on both the representation of the data, and the interaction with the data [499, 762].

Third, data should be *easy to explore* [499]. The frequent user should be able to explore the data, make certain details visible or hide some information. Some visualizations contain too little detail, some others contain too much detail. Figure 2.10 contains visualizations at three levels of the molecule benzene. The left side of the figure shows a chemical formula of benzene. Of course, the life scientist will recognize the figure, but it is not so easy to interpret the formulas. On the right side, the graphical representation of benzene is shown with maximum detail. Because there is so much detail, it is difficult to interpret the data. The representation in the middle of the figure is the best compromise between abstraction and detail, possibly.

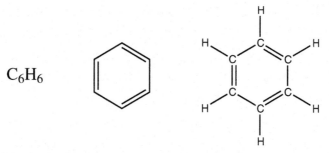

C_6H_6

Fig. 2.10. Benzene can be shown in different levels of detail.

The fourth element is *effectiveness*, as defined in Section 2.2 above. In visualization this can be translated as: Did the user extract the information he was searching for? For most types of applications it is possible to visualize the data in several ways. For example, a molecule can be represented in three different ways: like a formula, a 2D representation, or a 3D representation; each with its own purposes. The 2D structure is easy for flat non-interacting interfaces, like documents. The 3D structure is useful for exploring structural information [731, 886].

The fifth element is *expressiveness*. Expressiveness criterion defines the consistency of the representation which is required for doing measurements using the visualization [731, 886].

The last element is *subjective satisfaction*, also defined in Subsection 2.2.1. This means that a user likes to use the application to solve his/her research problem and thinks that this application is helpful to him/her [499].

It is often not possible to design a single visualization that scores high on all factors [499]. Therefore, there is a trade-off between these factors. Another solution is the use of different visualization techniques simultaneously. Each of the visualizations will emphasize a specific aspect of the data.

2.3.3 Dimensions in Visualization

To deal with the complexity of choosing good visualization techniques, many researchers have defined orthogonal dimensions to split up the problem. Shneiderman distinguishes two kinds of visualization [759]: scientific visualization and abstract information visualization. Scientific visualization typically involves spatial data, like 3D models of molecules, protein structures, or medical images. Abstract information visualization typically involves abstract non-spatial data, document clustering, or financial data.

The *data model* is the important element, not the data itself [831]. The data model can be split up into two categories: continuous versus discrete. This property is almost always fixed for a specific type of data. For each of these two categories, a separate set of visualization techniques may be used. Besides the inherent nature of the data, the data contains a set of attributes which can be mapped to color, transparency, or time. These attributes influence the interactions that can be done with the visualization.

A distinction is made between *presentation* and *representation* [146]. Representation is the model used to create an image of the information. Presentation is the method of displaying this image with respect to the complete overview and emphasizing the areas of interest. Dividing visualization into several dimensions makes visualization easier to understand, but it does not provide a direct solution for creating a good visualization.

2.3.4 Steps in Visualization Design

Visualization design itself is a process that consists of four steps from the object or phenomenon to be visualized to the visualization itself [831]. The first step is determining the *object* of study. This is the idea or the physical object itself. The object itself cannot usually be studied directly. For example, it is not possible to study a molecule directly. In the second step, the researcher studies the *representation models* of the objects. The data that stem from these models are often stored in databases. The third step is creating a *design model*. The design model consists of a set of assumptions about the data, e.g., whether or not these can be interpolated, what the type of data is, such as spatial or abstract. The fourth step is specifying the *mental model* of the user. The mental model is the internal model in the mind of the user. This model contains information about how the data is interpreted by the users. This is translated into the *user model*. The user model is the designer's model of the user's mind. There is always a gap between the user model created by the designer and the mental model of the user [845], because mental models

- are constrained by the user's background, expertise and structure of the human mind;
- have vague boundaries, i.e., things within the same context may overlap;
- are unstable over time, because people may forget and the mind is evolving;
- are unscientific and are highly influenced by superstitions;
- are incomplete, because people prefer only a limited part of the reality of what they model.

Based on the user model and the underlying data, the designer has to choose a visualization technique that closely matches the user model. Therefore, it is important that the user model matches the mental model. A perfect match is impossible, but doing a good user study can limit the gap between those two.

   This gap is a problem in visualization. The user model is based on the designer's point of view on how the data will be interpreted by the user. These assumptions are translated into a set of algorithms. This means that it can be different for different users. The problem is that users can not explain this model and there is no single user model that matches the mental models of the whole target group. To get acceptance of a tool, visualization designs should fit the users' approach for interpreting and manipulating the data and it should support the analytic flow better than currently used tools do [347]. So, the user model should fit the mental models as closely as possible. Mental models and user models are discussed further in Subsection 2.3.6.

2.3.5 The Design Cycle

In order to realize useful visualization designs, a good user study is necessary, see Subsection 2.3.2 above. In a user study, the following questions need to be answered [83, 665]:

- Who will be the users of the visualization?
- What is the data that will be viewed?
- What tasks can be performed with the data?
- What are some of the insights that the visualization will allow?

Task analysis and modeling can help to determine the tasks the users perform and therefore it should be the first step for creating successful visualization techniques [665].

Considerable research has been done on creating strategies for good user interface design. This research has resulted in much literature containing information ranging from do's and don'ts, such as the work of Johnson [416], until to complete user interface design strategies, such as the work of Mayhew [548], Shneiderman and Plaisant [762], or Lauesen [499].

User interface design and visualization design are closely related [518]. So, it is not very surprising that strategies used in user-interface design can also applied to information visualization design [665]. One such strategy is an iterative process which consists of the following steps:

1. Study users and their tasks
2. Design a visualization method
3. Implement the visualization method
4. Review and test the visualization method. If the result is not satisfactory, then go to step 1 and repeat the cycle.

This iterative approach is also known as the design cycle, which is shown in Figure 2.11. The focus of this section will be on the top right quarter of the circle "User Analysis, Requirements Analysis and Task Analysis". The "Visualization Design" and "Implementation" are steps of generating the visualization based on the first step. The last quarter of the circle contains tasks for "Evaluating the Visualization". This part is discussed in Section 2.4.

The disadvantage of this model is its simplicity. First of all, it contains no information about how to create the visualizations. Of course, there are a lot of usability guidelines, such as Johnson's work [416], but there is no general guideline for creating successful visualization designs.

Furthermore, there is no systematic way to correct usability problems once they are detected. When usability problems are encountered, a study needs to be carried why these problems arise. It can be due to using wrong visualization techniques for the kind of data or the visualization may be too abstract or contain too much detail. Maybe, the visualization techniques do not fit to the tasks of the users, the designers focused on the wrong target group, or the test group does not represent the target group [499]. When usability problems are

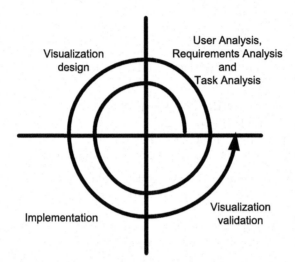

Fig. 2.11. The visualization design cycle [762].

encountered, analyzing the cause of these problems also requires user analysis and task analysis.

Fallman divides the design cycle into analysis, synthesis and evaluation steps [247] which is almost the same as the design circle in Figure 2.11, if the design and the implementation steps are taken together. But Fallman also noticed that all these steps are not clearly separated. The steps can overlap and the process is not always a clear iterative process. It is just a guideline. Before this cycle can be useful, it has to be more concrete about how to apply these steps.

The design cycle that is used here is not the only existing model. Other models are the spiral lifecycle [97] and the waterfall model [664]. There are also special HCI software design cycles like the star lifecycle [336] or the usability lifecycle [548].

2.3.6 User Analysis

Users of different research fields often use different kinds of visualization techniques, even if they are working with the same kind of data. A single user can also use several visualization techniques for the same kind of data. The visualization technique that is used depends on the kind of information one wants to extract. For example, if one wants to know the active sites of a protein, one can look at the 3D structure of the protein. Active sites are the part of the molecule where chemical reactions occur. If one wants to find out whether or not two proteins have similar function, one can look to the sequence of the amino acids the proteins consist of. In both cases, the user looks at the structure of a protein, but he uses two different visualization techniques. Also the level of detail can be different for different research questions. One can look to a protein at the level of amino acids, but it is also possible to look at the level of single atoms. Again, for each level, different representations will be used.

A common strategy used by many visualization tools is: "Overview, Zoom, Filter, and Details on Demand" [83, 436, 759] (Figure 2.12). Shneiderman calls this the Information Seeking Mantra [759]. *Overview* means getting insight into the entire collection which is presented with a low detail level. Once the user has established the items of interest, he/she will *zoom* to this area or these areas to gain more insight. The next step is filter out uninteresting items. *Filtering* can be done by using queries or by turning some details off. The last step is getting *more details* about the items of interest. Every visualization design should at least support these actions.

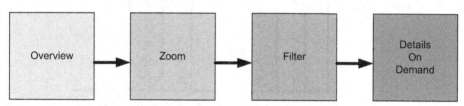

Fig. 2.12. The general strategy of working with visualization [759].

Besides these four basic steps, there are other important reoccurring steps. The first is searching for related information. This can be done using cross references. For example, a biologist has discovered that some structural modification exists in an enzyme. He can use cross references to a disease database for getting more information about the effects of the mutation.

Secondly, the interaction and distortion techniques to be used is a very important aspect of visualization design [436]. Users need to interact and to modify the data to gain more insight into the data. So, interaction helps users to explore the data [505].

History functions can also play a role. For example, the user is exploring the data set using the visualization. If the user wants to explore other parts of the data after zooming and filtering, a history functions can help with actions like undo, replay, and progressive refinement.

Another characteristic is extracting the gathered information so that the results can be saved for using these results in papers or in other tools.

Now, the characteristics of good visualization are defined, the next step is to determine how to reach the goal of a successful visualization. The first step is understanding the potential users or user groups of the system, as Shneiderman & Plaisant describe [762]. Amar and Stasko wrote that understanding the users and their cognitive styles is an important aspect for creating interfaces for a specific group of users [16].

Vertical vs. Horizontal User Analysis. It could be the case that one type of visualization will not satisfy everyone in the user group. It may be necessary to create multiple versions of the visualization [762]. It can also be the case that a fraction of the user group uses a different kind of representation of the data. Zhang et al. distinguish two dimensions in user analysis: horizontal and

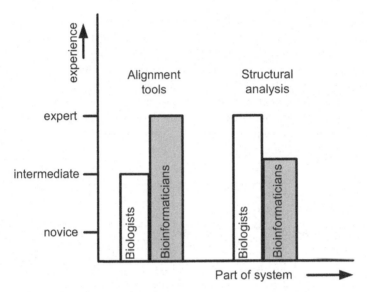

Fig. 2.13. Vertical and horizontal analysis.

vertical [927]. Horizontal user analysis means analysis of different users who use different parts of the system. Vertical analysis focuses on different users who have a different experience level using a certain component. Both analyses can be plotted in a diagram like Figure 2.13. This diagram shows the differences of experience level of two different groups (biologists and bioinformaticians) for two different components of the system. For each part of the system, it is important who uses that part and how experienced they are in using the part of the system.

Different Levels of Experience. Designing visualization techniques is a user-centered approach. The user is the one who has to work with the visualizations and to draw conclusions about the data that is visualized. Therefore, it is important to know who the target user group is or maybe who the target groups are. There are three different kind of interesting target groups. The three groups in the list below are based on the work of Shneiderman and Plaisant [762]:

1. *The early adopters*: the people in this group are well motivated users. They want to try out new technologies.
2. *The late adopters*: the people that will use the product through a technology push.
3. *The resistant users*: the group that will not use the product as long as it is not necessary.

They argued that late adopters are reluctant users and that the resistant users are non-users. However, it could be the case that these late adopters are willing to use the technology when it is mature. Even the non-users could change their opinion, if they see the advantages of the new techniques, because the environment forces them to use the technology. The difference between these three groups is the motivation for using a new application.

The first group, the early adopters, are the most motivated users. They are willing to use new technologies and are not afraid to do so. They are eager in using the application and are willing to explore the application. This is the easiest group to create applications for. This group type is often used for testing techniques, because they are very technology-driven.

The third group is on the other side of the coin. They will only use the application if it is absolutely mandatory. These users need an easy to use application which contains no unnecessary features.

The second group is somewhere in the middle of these two extremes. They will not use new technologies, but only when the technology has shown to be suitable for their activities. The group is also influenced by a technology push. They accept new technology with little resistance when it seems to be useful.

It is important to distinguish these three groups, because it can help to define the target group of the product. One can imagine that creating applications for the first group is much easier than creating applications for the second group. The first group can be used as a test group. But of course this group is not representative for the second group, since this first group is technology-driven. In most cases, the second group will be the target group, because this group contains the large audience that should use the product. The third group is not willing to use the product, maybe because the product does not fit in their daily work or due to resistance of using new technologies. Therefore, this group is not the target group for creating new products.

User Profiling. To make visualization successful, it is important to identify the target group. This step is called *user profiling*. User profiling consists of several categories [762, 927]:

Physical abilities and physical workplaces. Physical abilities focuses on the human perceptual, cognitive, and motor abilities. These contain information about basic user characteristics such as age and gender. Related to visualization design, there has been much research performed on differences in human perceptual ability [873]. Physical abilities can result in special peripherals in the physical workplace. Different people may use different kinds of input devices. But the physical workplace can also be related to the tasks that the users are performing. For example, biologists can use special 3D screens for visualizing 3D models of proteins. Such kind of virtual reality can help in perceiving structure [235, 338, 360, 505].

Diverse cognitive abilities. This topic relates to the interpretation of the information, remembering information and making decisions [689]. Related to visualization design, this refers to the abilities of the user to interpret the visualization in the right way. For example, in Figure 2.14, two 3D pictures of a cube are shown. People not familiar with 3D pictures on a flat surface often have problems interpreting them. The cognitive abilities are not always fixed for a person. For example, fatigue, influence of medicine, etc. may heavily influence the cognitive abilities of the user.

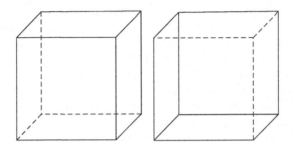

Fig. 2.14. Some people have problems distinguishing these two figures of cubes.

Personality differences. Differences in personality play an important role in visualization design. It influences the manner in which people think. These personality differences can be described using four dimensions [762]:
- Extroversion versus introversion
- Sensing versus intuition
- Perceptive versus judging
- Feeling versus thinking

Shneiderman and Plaisant give only a vague relationship between personality differences and user interface design [762]. But in visualization design, such differences can play an important role. Especially the dimensions sensing versus intuition and perceptive versus judging are important. For example, a tailored visualization may help people that follow their intuition to review their decisions. People who are perceptive have problems with making decisions. Specialized visualization can help them moving towards a conclusion.

Cultural and international diversity. This does not mean only cultural diversity at international or regional level. There are cultural differences at any level, for example, computer scientists have different ways of thinking than biologists or even bioinformaticians. Cultural differences can also be related to the users' experience with software, computer tools and peripherals, or graphical representations. If users see a 3D projection on a wall for the first time, it can be difficult for them to interpret such a projection. They expect it to behave just like normal 3D objects in the real world. But they can not walk around it and its projection is independent of the users' orientation and position.

Other cultural aspects are related to nationality. For example, in most western countries, people are reading from left to right, from top to bottom. However, in China, people are reading from right to left, from bottom to top. Therefore, it is very important to know for what kind of people the target group consists of. However, cultural aspects are not only related to reading style. Also a large difference can exists in the way symbols are used.

Users with disabilities. People can have physical limitations, such as color-blindness. These people sometimes need special kinds of user interfaces or special kinds of visualization and interaction designs, like enlarged fonts and icons or magnification tools for enlarging parts of the screen. Also other techniques can be used, for example, voice output and haptics for blind or weak-sighted people.

User Models. When the user is studied, one wants to establish a user model. The *user model* is a model which approximates the mental model of the user. The mental models contain information about how the user sees the world (or application) [845]. The user model can be divided into four dimensions [499]: the user model for data, functions, domain, and mapping. These single models will be discussed below.

The *user model for data* contains information about how the user perceives the data. For example, the user's mental model of an enzyme can be a chain of amino acids or it could be that his mental model is a 3D presentation of the enzyme. The mental model may also contain information about the data that is not visible. For example, it is not possible to see the back of the 3D structure of an enzyme, but the user knows, due to his/her mental model, that there is a backside, even when he can not see it. When data is visualized, it is important that the representation closely matches the mental model of the user in such a way that it is easy to him/her to interpret the visualization.

The *user models for functions* consist of the supposed functions of the system interface. This is more like the mental model about the cause and effect relation of triggering some event. For example, when the user moves a mouse cursor over the 3D model of an enzyme, the enzyme will rotate like in some chemical software such as Chime, JMol, or Yasara. A good match between the user's mental function model and the system functions is necessary for an easy to use application, for navigating, and for displaying the interesting information.

User models for the domain contain information about how objects in the domain are related to each other. For example, a biologist knows that gene expressions are closely related to enzymes and he/she knows that enzymes consist of a chain of amino acids and he knows the chemical properties of amino acids. This kind of information forms the background knowledge a biologist will use in doing his research.

Finally, the *user model for mapping* contains information about how things work in the domain and how these things are related in the computer. If two enzymes look similar, then they will probably have the same function. To check whether they are almost the same, the researchers can use sequence alignment tools. So, the sequence alignment is a measure for the equality of the two enzymes, see Section 8.2.

The total sets of user models is called the cognitive collage [499] (see Figure 2.15). The cognitive collage plays an important role in HCI-design and so in visualization. Studying the cognitive collage of the user will give an overview of the user's expectation about the visualization [831]. It is not easy to be determined. In fact, describing a perfect cognitive collage is impossible [831], because

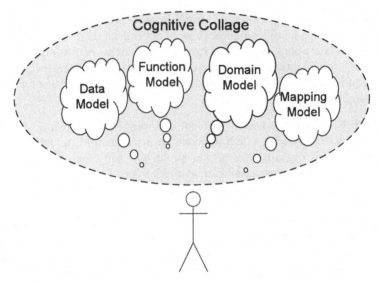

Fig. 2.15. The cognitive collage of the user.

one cannot fully specify user's mental understanding. Besides that, mental models are hard to discover for the designer. Thus, there will always be a gap between the user's models and the mental models.

The solution is to create user models that closely match the mental models of the whole group. If the whole group consists of users with several completely different mental models, maybe due to different research areas, then it may be necessary to generate distinct user models for each kind of user group.

User profiling will give the right data about the information structure that matches the users needs [927]. However, user profiling is not only important for getting insight into who are the users of the visualization, but also for determining the target group. The test group that will be used needs to represent the whole target group as much as possible.

Working Environment of Users. The second key element of user profiling is knowledge about the environment of the users. This means, before one can visualize things, one has to learn the structure of the domain, the group of user tasks and the list of visualizations needed [241]. This can be done by following training courses of the target environment, reading books of the domain, etc. In the case of visualization for biologists, one can follow introductory courses in biology or in bioinformatics, or one can read textbooks in these areas. The designer will get insight into the data the users are working with and will learn about the research questions that interest them. During such studies, the designer gets a first impression about:

The domain. The domain undoubtedly plays an important role in the mental model of the user. Therefore, the domain provides information that helps to create a user model. The user models are directly related to visualization techniques they are familiar with.

The environment. What kind of environment are we trying to mimic? Is the user working in groups? Does he/she work sitting or standing in front of the peripheral? What kind of interaction is suitable for the user? What kind of interaction is the user experienced with? Further in Chapter 3, it is discussed how to deal with the problem of finding successful interaction techniques.

The vocabulary. It is important to speak the users' language. This concern is twofold. The designer should be familiar with the terms that are used in the domain of the user. In the molecular biology case, he should know about terminology like amino acids, sequence alignment, etc.

On the other hand, he/she should prevent the use of terms that are unknown or not well understood by the user. In particular, a product may not refer to computer science related terms, because the users do not understand them.

If the users work in groups, it may be promising to investigate how they work together. In the case of a collaboration environment, it could be the case that all users are working on their own computer. It is also possible that they are discussing in front of a large screen that displays data [218]. And if they do, who is the one that has control of the visualization, i.e., is interacting with the application? Another important aspect is how they are looking at the screen. Do the users have the same orientation to the screen? Do they use special devices for showing the data? For example, in 3D visualizations, one can use special 3D screens for showing the data such as the work of Einsfeld et al. [235] and Hascoët et al. [338].

In the case of a multidisciplinary environment, it could also be the case that each user will have a different kind of visualization of the same data. Gaver et al. call this ambiguity of the representation of the data [291]. Ambiguity in data representation allows users with different cultural backgrounds to find their own representation of the data [218].

Data Users Are Working with. The central element of visualization design is the data set. Data contain information about what general disciplines or phenomena are, but it also can give an idea about the research questions that play a role in the domain [16]. For example, bioinformaticians work with databases that contain 3D structure information about proteins. This data may be related to research questions about the functionality of a protein or equality of two proteins.

Because people tend to be very perceptual, large data sets are often meaningless to human beings. It is the combination of data and its visualization model that are useful to humans, rather than the data itself [831]. So, the focus should not only be on which data they are working with, but the kind of visualization techniques they currently use. These visualization techniques are not limited to on-screen visualizations. Other techniques such as paper based sketches can be very valuable. Besides that, one can look at textbooks to discover which visualization techniques are used. Currently used visualization techniques give an idea of the research strategies of the users and their mental models of the data and can result in new visualization and interaction designs. These new kind of visualization interaction designs can be close to existing designs. Moreover, existing HCI styles can be combined with new HCI styles, such as in the work of Holman et al. [360].

2.3.7 User Requirements

In order to create a successful interaction and visualization design, it is necessary to establish the user requirements or user goals, and to satisfy them [548]. The aim of requirement analysis is to find out what the users' needs and expectations are.

User requirements identify the users' needs of the design. The new design should make users doing their job more efficient and enjoyable [78]. To do this, it is important to know who the users are, what their capabilities are, what kind of activities they do and the context in which they work. So, the user requirements contain information about [78]

- what kind of activities do people do;
- what kind of activities do people want to do;
- what kind of problems do people currently have;
- how can it be done better;
- how do practitioners do what they want to do.

This information can be translated into a set of requirements that form a stable basis towards a design [78].

Defining User Requirements. The requirements can also be split up into several categories [78, 664]:

- *Functional requirements* tell what kind of functionality the system should have or what the application should be able to do.
- *Data requirements* tell something about the type, the amount, persistence and accuracy of the data the system is working with.
- *Physical environment* defines the environment in which the users are working with the system.
- *Social environment* in which the users are working with the system explains, for example, how much pressure users work under or whether they collaborate with other users.
- *Required technologies* that should be supported by the environment. For example, some types of visualizations require special types of display devices or interaction devices.
- *Required user skill*, which defines the abilities, capabilities and the skills of the user groups.
- *Usability requirements* are subjective quality measures like efficiency, effectiveness, safety, utility, learnability and memorability.

The *usability requirements* mentioned above are only functional usability requirements. Besides these, experience usability requirements or *satisfaction goals* [548] are also important, such as enjoyability, pleasurable, aesthetically pleasing, and motivation.

How requirements are modeled is important, because different models emphasize different aspects of the requirements which can be expressed using functional models, like class diagrams or data flow diagrams [665]. More user centered approaches are use case designs and scenario descriptions. To deal with this challenge, it is important that complementary information gathering methods and complementary methods for modeling the requirements are used [664].

Finding User Requirements. Finding user requirements is the fourth stage of the design process [78]. The first step is gathering information. Direct contact with the users is very important during this stage. Information can be collected by performing interviews, observation, questionnaires, or workshops.

In the second step, the collected data need to be interpreted and structured. Interpreting and structuring the data will show what information is missing. This step needs to be done carefully.

The structured data forms the base for the third step, in which the requirements are derived from the structured data. The derived requirements define a list of needs, expectations and wishes about the design. These requirements needs to be sorted based on their relevance. Benyon et al. recommended the MoSCoW rules [78][1] which is part of the Dynamic Systems Development Method (DSDM) [212]:

Must have—*fundamental to the projects success*
o
Should have—*important but the projects success does not rely on these*
Could have—*can easily be left out without having impact on the project*
o
Won't have *(this time round)—can be left out in the current state, but can be added in later project increments*

Preece et al. [664] define a fourth step, validating the requirements. The designer and the users discuss the requirements. During the discussion, it can become clear that some requirements are missing or some information is interpreted in the wrong way. Then, the requirements need to be adjusted, which makes establishing the user requirements an iterative activity [664].

2.3.8 Task Analysis

Task analysis is the research process of identifying which activities are performed by the user groups. It is done using various exploration methods like interviews and observations [499]. The goal of task analysis is discovering necessary and sufficient features that need to be delivered in the resulting product. This means that the product needs to contain not more, but also not fewer features [927]. Too many features will result in unnecessary complexity while missing features will restrict users in performing their job.

Stammers and Shepherd [787] summarized a task as a set of actions that are performed by an individual to reach a specific goal. Vincente argues that the analysis of tasks can be divided into two ways [860]:

---

[1] The *o*'s state nothing, but they could represent "on time" and "on budget".

Work domain analysis: This approach is used when the task requires instructions which leaves little freedom to the user.

Analysis of activities: This is a constraint-based approach which needs to enable multiple ways of accomplishing the task.

Bartlett [55] proposed a combination of task analysis and information behavior to reach a deeper level of analysis. Information behavior is defined as "those activities a person may engage in when identifying his or her own needs for information in any way, and using or transferring that information" [901].

Task analysis is hierarchical. Tasks can be expanded to several levels. At the highest level, the task is described in a very abstract manner, such as "find the function of a protein". This task can be described in more concrete subtasks, like: Take a sample of the protein, search information about the protein in the database and extract the required information. Subtasks are identified during the task analysis.

Task analysis is not only used for discovering present tasks, but it is also used for discovering future tasks. If one is creating a virtual collaboration environment for biologists, then there is no real-life example of the desired system for the biologists. One can look at the current working environment to find out which tasks should be supported by the collaboration environment in the future. Another method is doing task analysis in other fields where a similar system is running. Combining those two sources of information can give a good idea what tasks will be supported by the desired system.

The end product of task analysis is a taxonomy of tasks. This taxonomy is based on the types of information processing needs [927]. The collected information will be used in the task modeling.

Methods for Doing Task Analysis. There are several methods for doing task analysis. Each of these methods has its own goal and has its pros and cons. The most popular techniques are discussed below.

Interviewing is often seen as the main activity for gaining insight into the user group. Because interviewing is a time-consuming task, only a small selection of the user group is used for an interview. Therefore, it is important that a high diversity of users is chosen, so that the interviews are taken from a representative proportion of the target group [762].

Lauesen [499] distinguishes two kinds of users that should be interviewed: the *average users* and the *expert users*. The average users can be used to establish a user profile. The expert users can give information about exceptional cases. The first goal of an interview is to gain insight about the daily tasks and the daily problems in the work area. After that, more detailed questions can be used to get more detailed task descriptions. Bartlett et al. notice that interviews relies on recall rather than direct capturing tasks. This results in an analysis missing some details which seem to be irrelevant to the users or are forgotten by them [55].

Questionnaire are used to get statistical information or to get a public opinion [499]. They can consist of open or closed questions. The disadvantages of open questions are that they are difficult to compare and responses may be misunderstood.

In comparison to interviews, questionnaires have two main disadvantages. Firstly, one cannot ask explanations during the taking of a questionnaire. Secondly, questions may be misunderstood by the respondent. To prevent these problems, a careful design is necessary and the questionnaire needs to be tested on a small pilot group. Discussing these tests with this group and revising the questionnaire can help solve the problems mentioned above.

Ethnographic observation is a method where the designer observes the users' working environment in practice. During the observation he/she gains not only insight into the individual behavior of the user, but also into the observational context. The goals of the observation are to understand the users' subject, the visualization and interaction styles they are currently using, and how to improve the working environment by creating new user interfaces [762]. A good example is the work of Latour & Woolgar [498], where they perform an ethnographic observation in a live science laboratory. This method is based on ethnographers that are observing people of other cultures without interacting with them.

One problem with questionnaires and interviews is that people often find it hard to explain what their activities are using words. Another problem is that people often explain how activities need to be done theoretically instead of how it is done in practice. Ethnographic observation deals with these problems since the target person does not have to explain anything [78]. Ethnographic observations can be very useful, but there are several problems. First, it is easy to misinterpret the observations, because it is possible that the observer does not know the context of the actions the target group is performing. The observer is not allowed to ask the target group to explain something since this will disrupt the practice.

Second, an observation can disturb the actions that the target group is performing because they know that they are being observed. Then, they can make mistakes or change their normal practice.

Third, the observer can overlook important information, because he/she does not know what information is important and what is not. To deal with these problems, it is important to verify the observations with the participants.

Participatory workshops are useful for gathering information about the product requirements [78, 664]. These workshops are organized for a specific focus group. Clients, users, and designers meet each other and discuss issues and requirements of the system. A participatory workshop can be structured or unstructured. If it is structured, it has a set of topics to be discussed. Then, its contents and participants are carefully selected and described. If the workshop is unstructured, a facilitator is required who assists the workshop, and directs and stimulates the discussion.

The advantage of a participatory workshop is its multiple viewpoints. To get valuable information, a careful selection of the participants is essential [664]. If this is neglected, it is possible that one participant or a small group of participants dominates the discussion. This is especially the case when a participant has higher status or has influence over other participants.

Task demonstration implies the users demonstrating the task to the observer. In contrast to observation, task demonstration allows the observer to explain some actions in order to gain more insight. However, the task is described from the perspective of the observed users, so the feedback may be very limited. Another disadvantage is that existing problems may not become visible during the observation, since most experienced users are not aware of these problems (anymore) [762]. A partial solution is giving the user a set of predefined tasks. A third disadvantage of task demonstration is that it could be the case that the tool to be demonstrated is discussed rather than demonstrated [55].

Task Analysis Completeness. Task analysis is useful for discovering the tasks the system needs to provide [439]. But how does one know whether all tasks are covered? There is no guarantee for completeness. Some guidelines to solve this problem are given below [499]:

Are all domain events covered? Task descriptions often start with abstract event-based task descriptions. The first question will be: Have all tasks been taken into account?

Are there difficult tasks covered? Difficult tasks often take a lot of time. They are frequently done under difficult circumstances with time constraints. These kinds of tasks require extra investigation.

At least as good as before? Will the system be at least as good as the current system? When some tasks are more difficult to do or take more time than in the current system, people will not use the new system.

Fulfills the CREDO check? The CREDO check stands for Create-Read-Edit-Delete-Overview [499]. For every kind of data, it should be checked that there are tasks for creating, reading, editing, and deleting the data. Besides that, it should be possible to generate an overview of the piece of data.

Another basic checklist for evaluating visualization is given by Amar and Stasko [16]. The checklist consists of a set of primitive tasks that are used to investigate the basic components of users' interactions with visualization when he/she is working with a data set:

- *Retrieve values:* Find the attributes of a given set of cases.
- *Filter:* Find the sub set of the data that satisfies a set of conditions.
- *Compute derived value:* Given a data set, compute some aggregate numeric representation of the set (like average, standard deviation).
- *Find extremum:* Find the data that is over a specific range for some attributes.
- *Sort:* Sort the data with respect to one or more attributes.
- *Determine range:* Find the span of values of one or more attributes of the data.

- *Characterize distribution:* Characterize the distribution of values with respect to an attribute in the data set.
- *Find anomalies:* Look for inconsistencies within the data set with respect to some expected relationship (function, heuristic).
- *Cluster:* Find related subsets within the data sets.
- *Correlate:* Find useful relationships among attributes of the data.

These ten primitive tasks are always reoccurring in the analysis of non-spatial data. They can be used as a vocabulary when discussing the capabilities and the weaknesses of different visualization techniques. The limitations of this checklist are that it is specialized for statistical information visualization.

Use Cases. Use cases are abstract representations of the users' tasks from the system's point of view. The design of use cases is a vital process for designing a visualization system. Good use case studies can help the design process. However, bad use case studies can hinder the process, since the designer can take the wrong direction. Often, use cases tend to be too abstract or too concrete [83]. Use cases that are too abstract give too little information about the users and too much detail in use cases can limit the new application.

Use cases are used to describe a users' task. The distinction between use cases and task description is, that in use cases, it is made explicit what is done by users and what is done by the system. Use cases are not suitable for visualization design in the early stage, because use cases contain too much detail with respect to task description and therefore can limit the usability of the system. It is better using use cases only for the final dialogues and for evaluating the usability.

Use cases are described by use case diagrams [665]. Use case diagrams describe the lower level actions done in a task. They represent dialogues between the user and the system and describes the interaction between them.

Scenarios. An instance of a use case is called a *scenario* which is a "informal narrative description" [149] of a real life situation or a future situation. Unlike a use case, a scenario is described from the user's point of view. A scenario contains a well specified and sufficiently detailed description of individual instances of events, artifacts, and procedures. It is described in full context of use from the point of view of the practitioners.

A scenario can be formatted in several ways, such as a written story, a video or a script to be acted using a mock-up. The main actors in the scenarios are the users. Scenarios are useful for usability testing [499]. A scenario should be executed by different users in order to see alternative approaches. In order to find alternative approaches or to find problem areas, it is essential to design more than one scenario from the same use cases. However, designers of scenarios have to keep in their mind that scenarios need to be described at an abstract level, because things may be done differently in the future.

Guidelines for Doing Task Analysis. Doing task analysis in the right way is not a straightforward activity. The goal of task analysis is to learn how users' tasks are executed. The scenario should be a real world case. Its description needs to be done in an abstract manner. The name of the task is an abstract action, like "searching for proteins with equal structure" instead of "the biologist searches proteins with equal structure", because the tasks form the base of the research. Lauesen [499] defines a set of guidelines for defining good scenarios:

Closure rule: Every task has one fixed goal. The path to reach this task may contain several subtasks. The task should be executed from trigger to closure without breaks.

Session rule: Small, related tasks performed in the same work session without breaks should be grouped together under a single task description.

Domain level: Hide the performers in the task description. Describe only what should be done. Things will be done differently by different users. Too much detail about the future is premature.

Don't program: A task description should not be a step-by-step description. It is not the goal of the task analysis to discover these steps in detail, because it may be done differently in the future. During task analysis, one can get information about alternative paths.

These guidelines show that it is important that the user should know what to do, but it should not limit the user on how to do it. The goal of task analysis is learning how things are done. The result of the task analysis should be an overview of which steps are performed when doing the task.

2.3.9   Task Modeling

During task analysis, high volumes of task data and user data is collected. The next step of structuring the collected data and visualizing ideas into structured pieces of knowledge is called *task modeling*. There are several methods used for structuring these types of data, where each method emphasizes its own specific aspect of the data.

Just like visualization, each representation type of the data needs to be effective, efficient, and unambiguous. It should not contain too little information, but also no irrelevant information. Each representation is for a specific kind of audience with a specific purpose. This means that task modeling can be a visualization problem on its own.

Visualization of tasks has several purposes. First, it can act as a mean of communication between designers, customers, and users. Second, it can be easier to find bottlenecks and opportunities. Third, different presentation techniques may fit to different designers that are looking at the same data model using their own mental model of the structure of the tasks. Fourth, the task models can be used as discussion elements for designers about changes, additions, or alternatives in the design.

To make a selection of suitable visualization models for visualizing task models, there are several questions that should be answered [850]:

– *Intended purpose:* What kind of information should be emphasized?
– *Coverage:* Does the representation used show the information that needs to be shown?

- *Complexity:* Complexity should be not too high. Select the representation that shows the necessary concepts and number of relations, not more.
- *Intended audience:* Who is working with the task visualization? Some representations are more familiar to designers than to customers or designers from other disciplines.
- *Understandability:* The representation should be easy to understand by the intended audience. This means the intended audience should be familiar with the presentation or should be able to learn the principles quickly.

In Welie et al. [850], four view points are used to represent the data that is gathered from task analysis. Each of the following four views has a specific purpose based on the ideas mentioned above.

Representing Work Structure. The work structure model is used to visualize the tasks people do and how they divide them into smaller sub-tasks and actions in order to reach certain goals [850]. The work structure model is a tree structure diagram with on the upper-left-corner the goal to be reached and on the bottom-right side the task and sub tasks to be executed. The horizontal axis is used for defining tasks to sub-tasks. The vertical axis denotes the tasks at the same level. The vertices between the tasks can also contain extra information about the relationships like Choice, Concurrent, AnyOrder, Successive, or Any [850].

Representing Work Dynamics. Work Dynamics models are used for showing the order of tasks, the time aspects of tasks and which people are involved in them. These models can also be used to show how people work together and what kind of information or objects they exchange.

In Welie et al. [850], a modification of the UML Activity Graph is used to represent such Work Dynamics Models. These models are similar to the workflow diagram. They describe the tasks to be done by who performs these and the order of the tasks.

Representing Tools and Artifacts. To give an overview of tools and artifacts that are relevant to the system, all the objects being used working with the system are modeled [850]. All of these objects are assigned to their corresponding users of the systems.

The models themselves are visualized as a set of ovals representing the user types. These ovals contain the objects that are used by the user. Since different user types can use the same object, ovals may overlap.

Representing the Work Environment. The representation of the work environment consists of two models. The first one is a physical map of the work environment. If looking at the working environment for bioinformaticians, this will be a map of a laboratory or a map of a collaboration room, where researchers can discuss a research item. The map can contain information about the position of objects that are in the room, such as a video wall or whiteboard. In addition, it contains information about the position and orientation of the researchers in the room. Are all researchers looking in the same direction (for example to the video wall), or are they sitting in a circle?

The second model contains information about the culture, i.e., the roles the users play. For example, bioinformaticians play other roles than biologists. Bioinformaticians can be seen as the domain experts in the use of microarray analysis [692] or extracting knowledge from the databases and filling the databases with new data. Biologists are novice users in using these databases for doing their research. The cultural model contains a set of ovals representing the users, and arrows between these ovals representing the relationship between these users.

2.3.10 Designing for and with Users

Based on the task analysis and task modeling, a representational analysis needs to be done [926] which is the process of identifying the best visualization technique for a given task performed by a specific user (group) and the interaction modes required for them. The three important aspects are again: users, data, and tasks, since a specific user group needs a specific kind of visualization of the data for a certain task, based on their mental model [762].

Prototyping. Prototypes are intermediate products, not necessary resulting in (parts of) end products. A prototype is used for two main purposes. First, it can be used as a proof of concept to test whether the design works or not. This is usability testing. Testing is not only focused on functionality testing, but also on usability. Usability testing is a user centered approach that focuses on whether or not the application fits the users needs. An important requirement of this test group is that it should represent the whole target group [480]. Second, it can be used as a means of communication with the users for evaluation.

Prototypes are useful when there are changes in the design. They can give feedback whether the design ideas correspond the end users' ideas about the product. Besides that, they can give information about whether or not the user is willing to use the new product [762]. It is very important to start very early with prototyping to prevent major problems as soon as possible.

Prototyping can be performed in several ways. The types Lauesen distinguished are [499]:

Sketches: Sketches range from hand-drawn paintings to electronic drawings using painting/vector graphics tools, from cardboard modeling to 3D computer graphics [247]. The advantage of sketches are that they give the designer complete control about the visualization. They require very little technical support. The designer is not limited by technical tools. The designer does not have to focus on the tools for creating visualizations, but can put his focus completely on his inspiration.

Screen prototypes: These prototypes are usually created with tools. The prototypes consist of real software components, but it is not possible to interact with the prototype. These prototypes are more like screenshots of the products.

Functional prototypes: These kinds of prototypes look like real products. The user can interact with the product. There are two types of directions in creating functional prototypes. In the first one, the designer puts as much functionality as possible in the prototypes, with a limited set of options. This one is useful to test the functionality of the whole prototype. In the second type, the designer puts little functionality in, but the functionality is highly configurable. This kind of prototype is useful for testing some functionality (like some visualization techniques).

Each type of prototyping has its own advantages and disadvantages. Sketches are very suitable during discussions, brain storm sessions, while functional prototypes are very useful for testing the system in an operating environment.

Participatory Design. The design of the visualization and interaction can also been done interactively with the end users. The advantage of participatory design is that users can give feedback and that they can give more accurate information about tasks. Having direct influence on the design can increase the acceptance of the final product [762].

There are also disadvantages of participatory design. For a start, it is very time consuming. Besides that, it can be possible that some people get irritated, because their ideas are rejected or in order to prevent this, the resulting design can be a compromise of the ideas of the participants to satisfy them [762].

To solve these problems, a careful selection of participants is necessary for successful design. To have useful influence, the participants need to learn the goals of the design and the technologies that are available. Last but not least, they should know that they are not representing only their own ideas, but the ideas of the whole user group they are a member of.

Participatory design in combination with prototyping can be very useful in visualization design for discussing visualization techniques that are currently used and for evaluating new visualization techniques. But the key element in participatory design is the careful selection of the selected user group.

Personas. Personas is a technique of describing fictional people for production design [177,667]. These fictional people are used for clarifying the vague definition of the typical users. Personas are created based on studying the user group using, for example, the previous mentioned techniques. In contrast to the classical user profile, personas are put down as real people. The advantage of this approach is, that designers could talk like "what if (fictional) person 'A' does this or how does (fictional) person 'B' like this feature?". It is easier for designers to talk about concrete users. Besides that, designers do not base scenarios on people similar to themselves [667].

Pruitt stated that personas are powerful in combination with other modeling techniques [667]. Personas are very useful as communication means among designers and clients, because it is easy to explain and justify design decisions. But Pruitt mentioned that personas do not explicitly cover every conceivable user.

By building on results from psychology and other fields, and adding new aspects to them, visualization will be able to become a proper science, and produce relevant solutions for many types of problems. The next section discusses evaluations of visualizations environments by giving an overview of the different evaluation methods and current evaluation practices of visualizations, including designing experiments.

2.4 Evaluation of Visualization Environments

Advanced visualization interfaces are developing rapidly. Modern technologies open the door for advanced visualizations. New generations of interactive interfaces not only have to meet the usability requirements, but also have to enhance exploration of large heterogeneous data and knowledge construction [470]. This raises challenges in evaluations that play a crucial role in human-centered design of visualizations. Innovative and complex designs need to be tested in order to check whether they meet user requirements. The challenge for designers and developers of applications is to reach not only early adopters but the early majority of the target users as well. Existing evaluation methods are not fully applicable for new interactive applications that involve new visualization spaces and advanced user interfaces [470]. Usability evaluation of any visualization technique has to include both evaluations of visual representation and interaction styles [902]. Experienced researchers in visualization recently underlined the low quality of published evaluations, as most of the findings do not lead to design principles to guide future research and are not appealing for potential collaborators [370]. Therefore, there is a constant need in reliable and practical evaluation methods to test the designs and optimize the applications and interaction styles that satisfy the needs and meet the expectations of the intended user group.

The scope of this section is an overview of the different evaluation methods and current evaluation practices by means of the ongoing BioRange project[2], including the practical issues of experiment design that can help to improve the effectiveness of visualizations. We also discuss additional aspects of evaluation in the context of the evaluation of visualizations in collaborative environments.

2.4.1 Human-Centered Evaluation in Visualization Practice

Research at University of Twente within the BioRange project is devoted to the *user-centered design*, also defined as *human-centered design* in Section 2.1, and evaluation of visualizations and enriched interactions for biologists and life scientists in order to enhance their exploration of different bioinformatics resources. Current application interfaces are designed for bioinformaticians, cheminformaticians and, computational biologists. They are too complex for pure biologists [785]. User studies should help to overcome the barrier between biology experts and the available bioinformatics resources, so as to promote discovery of new knowledge.

Currently, user analysis studies in bioinformatics domain are carried out, including contextual field observations, interviews, and questionnaires (see Section 2.3), in order to get insight into the needs and working practices of researchers from different domains. Unobtrusive observations of students from different backgrounds have been collected during the practical assignments of a

---

[2] The project BioRange is a research activity of the Netherlands Bioinformatics Centre (NBIC). BioRange aims to enhance collaboration between bioinformatics and genomics research and to stimulate bioinformatics development in the Netherlands.

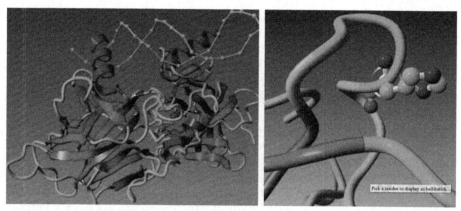

Fig. 2.16. Alternative protein views in Yasara: Ribbon (left), Sticks (right), a tool for 3D visualizations of proteins, CMBI, Radboud University of Nijmegen. *http://www.yasara.org/*

bioinformatics introductory course. The collected observations were translated into simple questions about the way students approach practical bioinformatics problems using different information resources and tools. Using these questions, a questionnaire was designed based on self-reflections from the latest practical assignment. Students had to apply knowledge from the whole course and use different bioinformatics databases and tools for this assignment. Visualizations of familiar proteins from a 3D visualization tool were used to correlate the questions with recent practice, see Figure 2.16. Students were asked to fill out the questionnaire at the end of the course in order to gain insight into their experience and interaction preferences while working with bioinformatics interfaces.

Next, the interviews were conducted with researchers from different institutes in the field of bioinformatics, biology, and biomedical technology, employing a contextual inquiry technique [86, 482]. It is expected that different research institutes have different working cultures within the same domain. The *contextual inquiry* technique, developed by Karen Holtzblatt and Hugh Beyer of InContext Enterprises, is a specific type of interview for gathering field data from users [86]. It is a hybrid methodology combining face-to-face interviews and observations, where users are interviewed in their context when doing their tasks, with as little interference from the interviewer as possible [361]. Collected observations, questionnaire and interview results were analyzed and translated into the user requirements and user profile description which will serve as the input for design of future user interfaces, visualizations, and more intuitive interactions [482].

The rest of the subsection is organized as follows. The next part provides the reader with insight on the question: "Why Evaluate?" by explaining the role of evaluation in the user-centered design cycle. Next, the approaches in evaluation of visualizations are presented. Then, an overview of the existing methods used in evaluation of different visualizations is given.

Reasons for Performing Evaluations. The goal of usability evaluation is to discover the needs and expectations of users. Every design needs to be tested to determine how well the visualization fits its intended purpose and meets user requirements. It can also help to diagnose the usability problems and errors that can be an input for optimization of visualization. Performance evaluation is valuable for testing the efficiency of interactions with visualization. This is often done by comparing alternative visualizations.

Users can give valuable input for improvement of the data representation. By observing people in their natural environment, a designer can learn about their way of exploration and style of interaction.

Another reason to perform evaluation is to check whether a future visualization product will be adopted by the target audience. There are known examples showing that involvement of the users during the design process has paid off by turning a visualization tool into a successful commercial product [785].

Evaluation in Human-Centered Design. The central drive of human-centered design is to serve the needs of users. It is important to involve users as early as possible in the interaction design cycle to ensure the relevance of the visualization [302]. The main motivation to do evaluation before actual implementation is: the earlier the evaluation takes place, the more successful is the design. This increases the chances of the visualization to be adopted by the target users. Usability evaluation should be carried out throughout the whole process of an interactive application design. Therefore, the design and development of any system should be done ideally in an iterative way. This means that the design process should include several iterations of analysis, design, and evaluation, see Figure 2.17.

However, practice shows that even though evaluation methods are promoted in visualization research [650], controlled experiments are the most common practices that take place only after the design is finished. One of the reasons is the aim to build the prototypes and software that are clear demonstrations of the performed work. Researchers in the information visualization field have become more aware of the importance of involving users in early stages of design. Therefore it is believed that the research through design approach is a way to increase the effectiveness of visualizations [33]. The *Research through Design* is a form of *Action Research*, defined by Archer [33] as:

> "Systematic enquiry conducted through the medium of practical action, calculated to devise or test new, or newly imported information, ideas, forms or procedures and to generate communicable knowledge."

Here, the designs are put in the real world in order to generate new knowledge. The findings are extremely valuable as they can advance practice, by providing material for more generalizable studies. This approach helps the designer and researcher to balance between users needs, skills and the design problem, and to prevent the design from becoming irrelevant [290]. In addition to the usual research output as such publications, research through design also generates designs and prototypes. These designs should provide vision into the future,

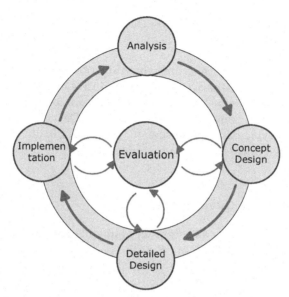

Fig. 2.17. Iterative Evaluation in Human-Centered Design Cycle.

demonstrate what is possible and stimulate the imagination. This might help the information-evaluation research balance between the urge toward innovation and design of visualizations for real problems of users. Overviews of the studies reporting different evaluation frameworks for visualizations are presented in the following section.

Evaluation Approaches of Visualization. According to Kobsa [454], success of visualization systems depends on the following factors: flexibility of visualization properties, freedom of operating the visualization, visualization paradigm (vertical versus horizontal), and visualization-independent usability problems. This study concludes that users achieved only 68-75 percent accuracy on simple tasks involving different commercial visualization systems. It indicates that there is room for improvement in effectiveness of visualizations.

Several studies report a framework for design and evaluation of information visualization techniques [16, 470, 902]. Such models can help to perform evaluations in a structured way. For example, Figueroa et al. introduce a methodology for the design and exploration of virtual reality visualizations [255]. They evaluated performance and user preference with several versions of a prototype during the early stage of design. Several alternatives of interaction techniques were presented by means of different prototypes in order to choose a design that users prefer the most [255].

Koua and Kraak developed a framework for the design and evaluation of exploratory visualizations for knowledge discovery [470]. This study points out the lack of evaluation methodologies and task specifications for user evaluations of exploratory geovisualizations. In contrast, a knowledge task-based framework aims to support decision making and learning in design and evaluation of visualizations [16]. A task-based model to construct abstract visual tasks and generate test scenarios for more effective and structured evaluations was proposed by Winckler and Freitas [902].

The next subsection describes different evaluation methods, namely summative versus formative, qualitative versus quantitative and their employment in different stages of the design cycle, including the examples of the practical use of different methods in evaluation of visualizations. Then, the practical steps for designing and carrying out experiments are provided. Finally, the challenges in evaluation of collaborative visualization environments are discussed in the last Subsection 2.4.4.

2.4.2 Evaluation Methods

There are several general classifications of evaluation methods in User-Centered Design. The evaluation methods are classified as *formative* and *summative* evaluation, depending whether the evaluation takes place during or after the design phase. Usually, there is also a distinction made between *analytical methods* and *empirical methods* [664]. Formative and analytical evaluations are usually qualitative methods, whereas summative and empirical evaluations are quantitative. These methods and their application in the evaluation of visualizations are described below. Later in this section, we will compare controlled experiments versus field studies.

Analytical Methods. Analytical methods involve the analysis of user interface features to discover potential usability problems. These methods are often done by usability experts evaluating the preliminary design and may not involve users. Some of the well-known techniques are described below:

Heuristic evaluation is a method in which several interaction design experts examine the system to evaluate it according to a set of usability criteria, known as heuristics. Experts try to provide feedback about the quality of the interface and to come up with suggestions for improvements. The outcome of heuristic evaluation is a report on the usability problems found, referring to the criteria which were not satisfied. An overview of ten basic heuristics can be found in Nielsen [606]. This evaluation method is a fast technique that does not involve actual users.

With respect to evaluations of visualizations, Tory and Moeller recently used the heuristics evaluation for two visualization applications [829]. Their study reports that expert reviews provided valuable feedback on visualization tools. They recommend to include experts as well as users in the evaluation process. This study stresses the need for development of visualization heuristics based on visualization design guidelines.

Cognitive walkthrough is aimed at identifying potential usability problems, often focused on specific aspects like learnability and perception. It is also done by experts, but this time experts in cognitive psychology or perceptual theory. They work on the basis of the interface, task description, and a list of actions required to finish the task. The user profile information, including users' background and experiences, has to be provided to the experts as well.

Allendoerfer and colleagues have recently adopted the cognitive walkthrough method to assess the usability of a particular type of visualization [13]. They focused on the usability of CiteSpace social network visualizations to envisage the cognitive tasks that need to be supported by knowledge domain visualizations tools. It was difficult for the researchers to create action sequences for experts, since the accurately completed task had to be a representation of designer's intentions of how to complete the task. This study confirms that each method has to be adjusted for the specific domain, users and the evaluation purpose.

Early concept evaluations are a way to ask users whether a future design is what they need, whether they like it and would use it. Focus groups and interviews combined with questionnaires are the most common techniques used for this method [570].

The *Focus group* method is a form of group interviewing but it is important to distinguish between the two. *Group interviewing* involves interviewing a number of people at the same time, the emphasis being on questions and responses between the researcher and participants [570]. Focus groups however rely on interaction within the group based on topics that are supplied by the researcher. Compared to *observations*, a focus group enables a researcher to gain a larger amount of information in a shorter period of time. Observational methods tend to depend on waiting for things to happen, whereas the researcher follows an interview guide in a focus group. In this sense, focus groups are not natural but organized events. The main purpose of focus group research is to draw upon users' attitudes, feelings, beliefs, experiences, and reactions in a way in which would not be feasible using other methods, for example the interviews or questionnaire surveys. For more information about the interviews and questionnaires see Subsection 2.4.3.

A simple mock-up or a sketch design together with a context scenario can be used to demonstrate the design idea in a focus group. The number of users is not crucial in this case, as the main purpose is to get feedback on ideas about a new design. However, an optimal focus group should include eight to ten participants [570]. The recent usability study of Figueroa and colleagues shows the use of this method in evaluation of interactive visualizations [255]. Several preliminary prototypes were presented to choose a design that users prefer the most.

Empirical Methods. Empirical methods collect usability data by observing or measuring activities of end users interacting with a prototype or an actual implementation of a system. In general, usability measurements may include different factors, such as effectiveness, efficiency, satisfaction, learnability, etc. [664]. These factors vary in importance in the evaluation of every specific system, depending on the application domain, task types and the target group. Often, the main purpose of empirical evaluations is an assessment of the system's effectiveness. The task design and usability measures will be discussed later in Subsection 2.4.3.

The most widely used empirical methods to assess usability are observational evaluations [664], controlled experiments, field studies, and query techniques (interviews, questionnaires). The comparison of controlled experiments versus field studies is given in the next paragraph, as empirical methods are often used in combination during user evaluations.

Empirical evaluation is the most widely used method in the context of visualization interfaces. Most published studies focus on the evaluation of one or several visualizations [618,708,802]. The weaknesses of these evaluations are the artificial settings and simple tasks, focusing mostly on visual representation and much less on user experience. Another drawback of such experiments is that they are usually carried out when the visualization tool is already implemented and are not combined with user analysis studies. As a result, the changes are difficult to make and visualizations may have little relevance to the users.

Controlled Experiments vs. Field Studies. In addition to the controlled experiments done in the lab, it is necessary to study the use of visualizations in the field [217]. Unfortunately, there are very few studies in which the evaluation of visualizations is done in the users' natural environment. One of the examples is an exploratory investigation of Trafton et al. of how complex visualizations are comprehended and used by weather forecasting domain experts [832].

Three longitudinal case studies, including participatory observations and interviews were done by Seo and Shneiderman to evaluate an interactive knowledge discovery tool for multiple high-dimensional data [749]. This contextual evaluation aimed to understand the exploratory strategies of users and to encourage knowledge discovery designers to adopt similar evaluation approaches. Biology users were enthusiastic while exploring the interactive visualization to discover the genes with the same functions. However, evaluators confirm that users are not aware of the metrics to identify meaningful clusters of genes. Seo and Shneiderman conclude that further research in Bioinformatics Visualization is needed in order to meet future challenges of bioinformatics.

Another work of Graham, Kennedy and Benyon [302] presents a case study of visualizing and exploring multiple hierarchical structures in botanical taxonomies. This is a great example of the iterative human-centered approach in design of a visualization interface. They involved users from the very first paper-based prototype. Thus, it allowed them to encourage participants to come up with the new ways of interacting with information. This study discovered that user preference for visual representation strongly reflects their mental model and not the structure of the information. It was also found that traditional metrics are not suited for the multi-dimensional interactive visualizations. Therefore, they focused on initial testing by observing representative users trying out the prototypes using representative tasks. The authors state that the performance measure is not always useful in the context of visualizations that are not aimed to improve the performance. Instead, ease-of-use, enjoyability, and frequency of use might be more important for evaluation of novel interactive visualizations. They used a combination of techniques for data capturing, namely logging software, video recordings, note taking, and verbal protocol, which helped to disambiguate detailed interactions [302].

Formative and Summative Evaluation. *Formative evaluation* is done in the design phase to get the first feedback from users about the visualization concept and to check whether the design meets their expectations and needs. Formative evaluation methods provide qualitative results and correspond to analytical methods described above. *Summative evaluation* is a quantitative evaluation method performed to test a finished design or an application [664]. The main purpose is to evaluate the usability aspects and usefulness of the system by comparing it to one or more alternative systems or the previous version. Alternatively, the finished interface can be compared to the condition in which there is no such interface present, for example, when the design is completely new and there are no similar ones available. Examples of empirical evaluations of visualizations presented above are summative evaluations.

To conclude, several practical issues play a role in selection of the evaluation technique. Some of them are stage in the design, particular questions to be answered, user profiles, etc. Some techniques are better than others for getting around practical problems. It is important to select a method that matches the evaluators' expertise, as training evaluators costs a lot of time and money. Table 2.2 contains a summary of the discussed evaluation methods. A number of important issues concerning the setup of the experiments are discussed next.

2.4.3 Designing Experiments

It is important to think about the questions that have to be answered before starting with experiment design, in order to discuss the feasibility and estimate the budget and time needed to carry out the evaluation with the whole design team. There are many decisions to be made during a user evaluation planning. The most important issues are described below.

What to Start with. It is recommended to start with defining the goals for the experiment and important issues to be addressed in the evaluation. Then, it is time to decide which visualization design, preliminary prototype, finished design, or existing system, or a number of them, to evaluate. Depending on what aspects are going to be tested there may be a need to adjust the prototype in order to engage users in evaluation scenarios.

With Whom. It is useful to prepare a *user profile* description in order to make a proper selection of the representative users from the target group. For example, controlled usability studies often need to involve participants with a particular level of experience, namely novice or expert users, or users with specific expertise. The following aspects have to be taken into account: balance in genders, age range, level of experience with particular technology, cultural diversity, personality differences, etc. Therefore, it is important to prepare a user profile before starting to look for participants. To learn more about user profiling and user requirements see Subsection 2.3. After defining the target group, possibilities of

Table 2.2. Comparison of evaluation methods.

Method	Design Stage	Advantages	Disadvantages
Heuristic Evaluation	Concept design	Investigates individual usability problems; can address expert user issues; fast	Does not involve real users; can not reveal "surprises" relating to their needs
Cognitive Walkthrough	Concept design	Puts the focus on the user; recognition of user goals	Bias because of task selection; tries to make the designer the user
Focus Groups	Analysis, Concept design	Takes a short period of time; produces variety of design choices and new features; spontaneous reaction and group dynamics	Records what users think they want; doesn't test actual interaction
Interviews	Analysis, Concept design	Flexible; in-depth attitude and experience probing	Time consuming; hard to analyze and compare
Observations	Analysis, Detailed design, Implementation	Made in real-use environment	Very costly; difficult to analyze and reason the behavior
Empirical Experiments	Detailed design, Implementation	Allows to design hypotheses or alternatives; close approximation to actual usage	Experts knowledge required; limited generalization of results due to controlled settings
Field Studies	Implementation	Made in real use environment; reveals real-life problems	Costs a lot of time; impossible to control the settings

reaching users should be discussed with the design team to make appointments with the users in advance.

Another method that can be used to create a description of the user is the popular *'personas'* method [667], already presented in Subsection 2.3.10 above. Personas represent real users and help to discuss design decisions. They are archetypal users that represent the needs of a whole target group, in terms of their goals and personal characteristics. Personas identify the user's motivations, expectations, and goals. Designers bring users to life by giving those names, personalities, and often photos [667].

How?-Tasks and Metrics for Evaluation of Visualizations. The design of tasks for user studies requires additional expertise from one or more domains. Brainstorming with the design team and consulting the evaluation and domain experts is a common approach. In the evaluation of new exploratory visualizations, the tasks have to be realistic, motivating, and engaging for the domain experts [650]. Currently, used tasks in empirical evaluations of visualizations are often only simple ones. Therefore it is recommended to let users to explore the visualization interface freely using their own data and ask them to explain what they were able to see and understand [650]. Another possibility is to analyze the related work for relevant tasks or adopt a task from the Information Visualization Benchmark Repository [251] based on the collection of the results from InfoVis context [250]. The repository contains low-level tasks for software visualizing multiple datasets. Amar and Stasko [16] proposed a taxonomy of higher-level analytic tasks that can provide a better support for designers and evaluators of information visualization systems.

The common usability measurements in empirical evaluations of visualizations are user performance, behavior, and attitude [802]. As already described in Subsection 2.2.1, *usability*, according to ISO 9241 Usability Standard [395], can be defined in terms of three factors:

- *Effectiveness*
- *Efficiency*
- *Satisfaction*

Effectiveness and efficiency are quantitative descriptions which can be measured objectively by user performance. The common *objective measures* of performance are accuracy and time for task completion. Testing the performance of a specific task using specific visualizations can yield reliable information about which visualization provides better performance of the task. However, such results are not generalizable across populations, tasks, visualization methods, and data sets. People are good in finding visual patterns, but have different perceptual abilities. Thus, it is important to ensure comparability of performance at the sensory, perceptual and cognitive level. To large extend, the effectiveness of the perceptual process will depend on the perceptual learning skills, e.g., in fields of medical image analysis. Therefore, when different visualizations are compared, evaluators must ensure that the observers in each test have adequate perceptual training and experience [306].

User satisfaction may play an important correlation of motivation to use an interface or a system and may affect performance in some cases. User satisfaction is a qualitative description that cannot be directly captured by data or observations. Commonly used measures of satisfaction are user attitudes collected by means of interviews and questionnaires. Most of widely used questionnaires include several *subjective measures* of usability, such as *satisfaction, usefulness*, and *ease of use*. During interviews, users are asked about their experiences and perception of interacting with visualization systems. Interviews can be semi-structured or free-form and can be very flexible. Still, results may be hard to analyze and interpret. In contrast, questionnaire can be structurally analyzed.

Questionnaires used to measure satisfaction and associated attitudes are commonly built using Likert [506] and semantic differential scales [664]. Likert-scale questionnaires consist of a set of statements; users are asked to indicate their level of agreement with each of the statements (for example *"The system was easy to use"*). In a semantic differential scale, evaluators use two opposite adjectives of the same dimension (for example *difficult* versus *easy*) [664]. Evaluators may choose to use validated published satisfaction measures or may submit satisfaction metrics they have developed themselves. In the latter case, questionnaires should be thoroughly analyzed for *reliability* and *validity*. The reliability is the ability of the questionnaire to evoke the same user responses when filled out by similar users in similar circumstances and thus concerns its internal consistency and reproducibility. The validity of a questionnaire can be based on its consistency with other questionnaires. Since developing a questionnaire and testing requires a lot of time and expertise, it is recommended to adapt the standardized questionnaires to a specific experiment. However, adding, changing or removing items from the questionnaire may affect its reliability and validity [216, 722].

Furthermore, novel visualization applications pose additional questions for evaluation. Probably, usability measures are not enough for specific aspects, for example new ways of interaction and perception of visualizations. Therefore, there may be a need for adjusted or completely different metrics in every particular case [302]. We will discuss this issue in more detail in the next section on evaluation of Collaborative Visualization Environments and Awareness Displays.

When and Where. Planning the experiment also includes estimating the time for preparation, finding participants, performing a pilot test to measure how much time each part and the whole experiment will take. Choosing an optimal location, i.e., lab, natural environment, or simulated environment close to real conditions, is very important for the success of the experiment.

How to Avoid Being Biased. Some experts suggest that it is better to invite an outside experiment facilitator [570]. However, in some cases it is hard to explain the whole idea of the design and not to forget important details that have to be observed during the experiment. Another effective solution is to split up the roles (experiment facilitator, technical support with prototype, observer, video/audio, and measurements monitoring person) and use a separate experiment protocol for each person. It helps to organize the evaluation team and divide tasks effectively [216].

The design of the experiment in terms of optimal tasks and metrics can be improved by consulting domain experts, psychologists, and colleagues. Performing pilot tests is essential to discover the pitfalls that could happen during the real test.

To conclude, designing and conducting controlled experiments requires a substantial amount of time and resources. The clear objectives and tasks are hard to formulate during the exploratory phase of the research. Therefore, it is important to be aware of the alternative evaluation methods that can be applied in different stages of the design in order to insure the effectiveness and relevance of the visualization. For further information on the practical steps in evaluation see the *"Practical Guide to Usability Testing"* [216].

Ethical Issues. It is important to ensure privacy of users which means that their names and other personal information can not be associated with data or be revealed in public reports. Video and audio recordings should always remain confidential as they contain very personal data about behavior of users. People give their trust when they agree to participate in the evaluation study and this should be respected. Therefore, it is sensible to use a special *consent form* which explains the aim of the user study, asks permission for audio/video recordings, and ensures participants that their personal details and performance will not be made public and will be used only for the purpose stated. It is a common practice as well to give the users a money reward for their participation as this creates a formal relationship in which mutual agreement and responsibilities are respected by both parties, namely users and evaluators [530].

Data Analysis. Collected objective and subjective data can be first analyzed by inspecting the graphs and plots, e.g. histograms, to check the distribution of the variable in the population. Next, the statistical analysis of the data should be performed, for example to find out whether any of the observed differences between two conditions are statistically significant. The type of statistical analysis (parametric, non-parametric test) depends on the type of data and questions to be answered [722]. The commonly used types of parametrical tests are t-test and ANOVA (Analysis of Variance). A t-test is used to test the significance of the difference between or within subjects. A t-test between subjects assumes that both groups are sampled from a homogenous population. ANOVA is similar to the t-test in cases with two samples and is also used to compare more then two samples. ANOVA employs the difference between the variance[3] within and between groups to draw interferences regarding mean. When reporting the results, a method by which the data were analyzed should be described in sufficient detail to allow replication of the data analysis methods by another organization. Particular items that should be addressed include statistical procedures (e.g., transformation of the data) and tests (e.g., t-tests and statistical significance of differences between groups). Scores that are reported as means must include the standard deviation and optionally the standard error of the mean [722].

Interpretation of the results has to be done very carefully for several reasons. One of the considerations is is that subjective ratings of users can be biased towards the peak difficulty and most pleasant experience rather then average difficulty and pleasure. It is also important to establish the relation between objective performance data and subjective user satisfaction and preferences. For more information about statistics and data analysis see [216, 606, 722].

When to Stop Evaluating. Every evaluation test will reveal some area in which improvements can be made. Therefore, there is never a time when visualization is perfect. Budget and time constraints usually determine when to stop [664]. Dumas and Redish [216] pointed out that for the iterative design approach each test should take as little time as possible while still providing useful information. So called 'quick and dirty' techniques [664] are sometimes a reasonable alternative in view of the time. For example, expert analysis is a reasonable first step, yet it will not discover all problems. Therefore it is very important to let potential users explore the interactive design [78].

---

[3] The variance is the square of the standard deviation.

From Evaluation to Design Guidelines. A common problem in evaluation of visualizations is that a generalized framework is lacking and there are only few attempts to transform the results from different evaluation experiments into the general guidelines or heuristics [370,829]. The general guidelines are useful for the visualization society including designers, developers and marketing specialists of interactive visualizations design. In order to provide design guidelines, another evaluation approach is needed, namely comparison of many visualizations in the similar area in order to make generalized conclusions.

2.4.4   Challenges in Evaluation of Collaborative Visualization Environments

Most of the currently known evaluation studies focus mainly on integrated software visualization tools, with interaction like "single user - single integrated visualization". However, novel visualizations can be much more complex in situations where a group of users will be interacting with multiple visualizations and communicating with each other at the same time. Enhancing collaboration and exploration of information is a new challenge for the interaction designers of a new wave of advanced visualizations environments. Multiple methods of evaluation are needed in order to adequately address all the aspects of collaborative work [688].

Figure 2.18 illustrates Collaboration in a Geovisualization Environment (left) for Knowledge Construction and Decision Support [526]. I-Space (right) is a demonstration of a Multidisciplinary Visualization Environment for discovering human genome, developed by Barco Visualization Solutions and Bioinformatics department of Erasmus University, Rotterdam [797]. One more example of such advanced visualizations is the Persuasive Displays Environment designed in Mitsubishi Research Lab [200]. Such environments can also include *Peripheral Awareness Displays*-systems that reside in user's environment within the periphery of user's attention [655]. These ubiquitous computing services provide feedback on the periphery of user's attention. The feedback is generated on the basis of multimodal cues sensed by the perceptive services embedded in the environment [390]. The evaluation of awareness displays focuses on effectiveness and unobtrusiveness and the ability of visual representation to communicate information at a glance without overloading the user [481,655].

The possibilities of the multidisciplinary group collaboration in visualization environments are to be explored within BioRange project. User studies are aimed to find out whether such collaboration takes place in daily work practices between biologists, bioinformaticians, and biomedical researchers. Use case scenarios for empirical studies in micro-array experiments are provided by the project partners [692]. Refined methodologies and reliable measures are needed for evaluations to asses aspects like knowledge discovery and decision making quality. Similar aspects, for example in design and evaluation of a groupware and decision making and satisfaction with group processes, have to be integrated into the evaluation framework. Such a framework can be constructed using the evalua-

Fig. 2.18. Collaboration in a Geovisualization Environment (left), Pennsylvania State University [526], © *2004 IEEE. Reprinted with permission*; I-Space (right), Multidisciplinary Visualization Environment for discovering human genome [797]. *Image courtesy of the authors.*

tion practices of fields like computer supported cooperative work and ubiquitous services [390, 601].

As an example of alternative measurements, eye gaze direction is used as an indicator of users' attention and preference in visual information representation [481, 783]. North and Shneiderman evaluated the users' capability to coordinate and operate multiple visualizations in spatial information representations [618]. House et al. point out that evaluation of perception should be included in the evaluation framework of visualizations [370]. Another study reports the evaluation of spatial and associative memory ability posing additional cognitive demands [890]. Some of the other important evaluation aspects are: influence of visualization environment on multidisciplinary collaboration, cognitive load, peripheral attention, awareness, engagement, and more. In every case, particular aspects will have a priority depending on the goal of the evaluation.

In any evaluation it is important to answer questions like: what do we want to find out, what makes this particular visualization useful for the users, and what does it aim to enhance: visual representation, information exploration, interaction, collaboration, creativity, knowledge discovery, etc. Furthermore, fundamental comparative research is needed to assess the reliability and validity of different techniques for human-centered design of collaborative visualizations environments. The development of a generalized framework for evaluation of such environments requires connections between the areas of design, evaluation, and perception. Essential insights in a wider range of disciplines such as human visual perception, cognitive science, and social psychology in combination with traditional HCI evaluation methods can guide us towards the most potentially promising venues of investigation. Future challenges in human-centered visualization are discussed in Chapter 5.

2.5 User Studies and a Science of Visualization

More than most other areas of computer science, visualization is communication with the user. Any method developed for this purpose, regardless of its theoretical merits, is only of relevance if it shows a particular pattern, draws the user's attention to previously unknown structures, or helps answer a particular question. Unlike most other areas in computer science, visualization methods cannot be proven mathematically and can only be verified using models at a very crude level. Evaluation requires the use of empirical studies involving real humans as test subjects. This should be seen as an opportunity rather than a challenge, because much useful information can be gathered from user studies besides answering the question which method is better suited for a particular task.

Many researchers still shy away from performing studies, either because they feel they do not need them, or because they fear the amount of work that is involved. Studies also require a lot of work in planning, execution, and assessment, and all that work can lead to inconclusive results. Kosara et al. [464] discuss possible problems and ways around them, and Ware's book [873] gives some guidelines for successful user study design.

In addition to the points above, a recent NIH/NSF report on Visualization Research Challenges [411] considers evaluation a vital part of visualization research. Johnson's list of top scientific research problems [409] also includes research into perception and evaluation as two important points. These examples, together with the rising number of publications that either include user studies as part of a new design, or whose main topic is a study, show the growing awareness of the importance of this type of evaluation.

Finally, user studies provide an avenue for a more scientific way of conducting visualization research. The quantifiable nature of studies, together with the necessity to formulate explicit hypotheses, helps our young field grow. In the development of a foundational theory of visualization, the results of user studies and the lessons learned about perception will play a key role.

2.5.1 Survey of Information Visualization Studies

The following survey presents a sampling of studies that were published in the InfoVis literature, with a special focus on study design and outcome. It largely follows the structure of Chen's discussion of the matter [152].

There are two large groups of user studies in InfoVis: basic perception studies, and application-oriented ones. Both types serve different purposes, and it is unfortunately not easy to transfer knowledge gained in a basic perception study to an application area (or vice versa).

Basic Perception. Basic perception studies are the simplest in terms of their design, and the ones that are the most likely to yield statistically significant results. By performing a simple task or answering a simple question many times, sufficient data can be gathered relatively easily. At the same time, however, the

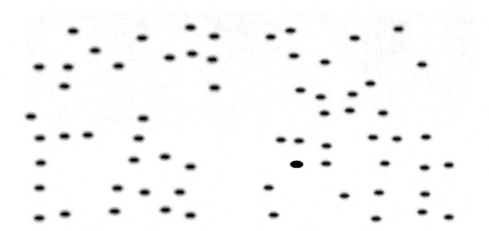

Fig. 2.19. Images used in the SDOF study [467]. The left image contains only blurred *distractors*, while the right image also contains one sharp *target*. Different numbers of targets and distractors, and different blur levels were tested.

applicability of these results for real-world tasks is not always clear, and needs to be tested separately.

As Chen points out, even basic perception studies can not easily be compared. Different thresholds, numbers of objects, repetitions, and other differences in study design can make it impossible to draw further conclusions from combining several studies. In the interest of proper embedding of one's work, it is therefore advisable to base a new study on an existing design, or to provide another avenue for comparability.

Preattentive processing (see Section 4.1.3) has received some attention from the visualization community, and there have been several studies trying to establish the usefulness of preattentive properties in visualization, and also whether particular visual cues are in fact preattentive or not.

Healey et al. investigated the use of bars of different height, color, and density [344], which represent different data channels in a salmon tracking system (e.g., plankton density, ocean current strength, surface temperature). These are called *pexels*, for "perceptual element". In their study, they found that users could interpret the separate dimensions of information presented easily, and were also able to answer questions combining two or more visual cues. The latter was of course not preattentive (the combination of preattentive cues is not preattentive), but still proved feasible in a visualization setting.

Semantic depth of field (SDOF, [466]), which uses blurring to direct the users' attention to relevant objects (which are crisp), was also tested (Figure 2.19, [467]) and found to be a preattentive feature. This is an interesting result not only for the use of SDOF for visualization, but also because blur and sharpness had not been tested for their preattentive nature before. Work in visualization was able to contribute to psychology this way.

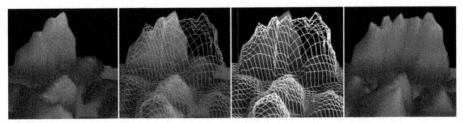

Fig. 2.20. Conquering change blindness [621]. This transition from one state to another makes changes obvious, and also creates static displays that clearly show which is the old state, and which the new one.

Another well-known effect in psychology is change blindness. After an interaction, users may not be able to tell what has changed on screen, so the interaction has to be repeated, several times perhaps. A way to conquer change blindness is by using a transition between the old and new display (Figure 2.20, [621]). In addition, a temporal "asymmetry" is created, by using a different method when fading out the old image than when fading in the new one (transparency and drawing a wireframe). This way, even for a static frame (e.g., a screenshot) one can tell which objects are disappearing, and which are new.

An interesting aspect of InfoVis, that is very likely to become much more important in the future, are secondary tasks. When visualization is used in cars, appliances, etc., the user will concentrate on a task, and only use the visualization occasionally, when the need arises. In such a case, it is necessary to convey the information without distracting the user too much from the primary task. Visual attributes, such as color, size, closure, etc., that can be used for such a purpose were tested in user studies [157,779].

Automated Mini-Studies. An interesting variation on the user study are simple, automated tasks, that do not yield new insights, but that help adapt a program to the user's environment. One application area for this is the calibration of displays, so that color scales work in the way the designer expected them to.

Colormaps that are monotonically uniform in luminance are widely recommended for use as a visualization dimension. A simple method for generating such colormaps without the need to calibrate the display, but with user participation, was developed, the "Which Blair Project" [715]. A black and white photograph of a face is colored with the colormap to be tested, and presented to the user. Because humans are very sensitive to faces, they can easily tell if such a colormap is increasing in luminance or not, by judging how natural the image looks.

Based on this idea, a system for face-based colormap generation [448] was developed, which uses two binary images of a face (one the inversion of the other, Figure 2.21) to generate perceptually uniform colormaps on any display. The comparison of the two faces is intuitive and quick, making this mini-study an effective way of calibrating a display.

Fig. 2.21. Face-based generation of colormaps [448]. Each pair of images compares a color to a shade of gray. The user moves a slider towards the face (changing the color's brightness) until it flips to the other side. When the user can't decide any more which image shows a face and which doesn't, the color is perceptually as bright as the grey tone.

Application-Level Studies. Different from low-level perception studies, application-level studies are aimed at more complex visualizations and interactions with a system. Such studies are much more difficult to do than low-level studies, but have the advantage of being directly applicable to the complete application, without the danger of other effects interfering with the desired ones. Studies can be done to compare a method to another one, or to find out how users work with a method and what could be improved.

A large user study (with 83 participants) of different visualization applications (Eureka (formerly TableLens) [690], InfoZoom [691], Spotfire [8]) was performed [454] to compare how fast users could solve different tasks with them. Not surprisingly, different tools were better for different types of tasks. For example, for tasks where it was necessary to ascertain the existence of a correlation between two variables, users found Spotfire's default visualization of a scatter-plot very useful, while InfoZoom users had difficulty seeing correlations due to misunderstandings of how to manage the interface. On the other hand, a task that involved finding the answer to a question about the proportion of cases with a particular attribute found that InfoZoom users obtained the result much faster than either Eureka or Spotfire users, because a simple combination of interactions leads directly to the answer, while Spotfire users first had to determine the appropriate visual representation. Eureka users had other, different issues involving being able to backtrack easily from mistakes. The point seems to be that the more "natural" a particular task is for a particular interface, the more easily a user will perform it. Thus, the issue is not that a visualization system *can* do any particular task, but whether a user will be able to quickly find and apply the appropriate tool.

An evaluation of cone trees [168] showed that while users liked cone trees (because of their appearance and interaction), they were significantly slower when navigating through cone trees than when using a more traditional 2D visualization.

Another study of different tree visualization methods [54] showed that different visualizations scored very differently for certain tasks—a result similar to the study done for SpaceTree [653].

A study of an implementation of the reorderable matrix [764] was done to discover usage patterns and possible improvements of the method. The results include some interesting ideas for new interactions (such as moving groups of rows and columns, not just single ones), as well as different strategies when comparing data rows and columns.

The effect of animation on building a mental map was investigated in another study [70], which used family trees that the users had to memorize from only seeing a zoomed-in version that they could pan. Interestingly, only the reconstruction of the whole tree was aided significantly by animation, not the answers to specific questions. The high level of dissatisfaction of users with the task also showed that not providing an overview of the whole data makes the user extremely uncomfortable.

2D vs. 3D. The question as to whether 2D or 3D visualizations are more useful was investigated in a number of studies. While 3D theoretically provides more space and enables the user to make use of his or her spatial memory, it brings with it problems such as depth perception and occlusion.

One study [507] tested participants' capability to perceive the space around them as "Euclidian", i.e., to estimate sizes equally well in all directions, even that pointing away from them. They were shown (physical) objects at a relatively flat angle, and had to point to the 2D shape that matched them. The result was a high error in the perceived shape. Even when a comparison object (which was the same in all cases) was presented, accuracy did not improve significantly. The results of this study very clearly show the possible problems with 3D visualization methods, which restrict what can be done in practice. This does not mean that 3D could not be used in InfoVis at all, however.

The Data Mountain [710] is a user interface for storing and retrieving documents on a tilted 2D plane. Documents can be moved in two dimensions on the plane, and thus be arranged from back to front and in groups. An initial study showed that this method was clearly superior to simple lists (like bookmarks or favorites). Another study [169] later compared this method to a version that had fewer depth cues (no tilted plane, no perspective projection). Interestingly, no significant differences were found in retrieval time between the interfaces, not even when the display got cluttered by many objects (where the authors had expected the 3D version to be clearly superior).

Similar techniques were implemented and tested against real-world interfaces made from steel frames and fishing lines, where little printouts of web pages could be placed [170]. To interact with pages in the real world, study participants pointed at them with a laser pointer, and told the experimenter where to put them. The results of this study showed a decrease in performance and subjective assessment of effectiveness from 2D to 3D. It also turned out that occlusion in 3D was less a problem than the subjects forgetting page locations in 3D; and also the gained flexibility, which led to less efficiency.

A different study [820] came to the conclusion that 3D can indeed increase performance for special tasks, in this case memorizing the structure and contents of a small tree. The 2D display was a display similar to the Windows Explorer, while the 3D version showed the depth structure of the tree as the distance of the objects from the screen, and presented the information on vertical "cards" which did not overlap. The choice of visualization (no overlapping objects) and task make it questionable, however, if the results can be generalized.

The question of whether to use 2D or 3D is quite a crucial one, that will need more studies to gain more insight and concrete recommendations what to use for which application.

2.5.2   The Future of User Studies

While user studies undoubtedly serve an important purpose today, they are still largely unconnected and do not provide us with a complete image of what direction visualization should be taking. There are clearly a number of shortcomings, which are described in the following.

User Expertise. The most available subjects for user studies are college students, who usually have no in-depth knowledge of particular domains or data sets. Studies can be adapted to this audience to use data that almost everybody is an expert in, like Kobsa's experiment [454] using data from dating web sites (Kobsa calls this data "ecologically relevant").

People working with data in the real world, however, will approach a visualization in a different way, and will ask different questions. These differences need to be addressed and accounted for when reporting results. The real difference between expert and lay users also needs to be assessed, to be able to judge the true impact of this requirement.

Two-way Validation. The usual test of a visualization method consists of looking at a particular data set and trying to find those patterns or structures that one expects from knowing the data. Another approach is to look at a data set that one does not know, and trying to find any kind of structure.

This does not give a complete picture of how good the method is, however. A visualization might produce false positives as well as false negatives—a fact that is readily recognized in most engineering fields, but hardly considered in visualization (with the exception of a panel discussion at the Visualization conference in 2003 [529]). Currently, there is no discussion of the relative merits of visualization techniques with regard to this problem, nor is there an understanding of which is preferable (false positives or negatives). Clearly, some high-level research is needed to inform future developments and experiments.

Double-blind Tests. The standard approach to tests in most of empirical sciences is the double-blind test: neither the experimenter nor the subject knows whether the tested substance is effective or a placebo. In visualization, the usual approach is what could be called the double-seeing test: both the experimenter and the subject know what is being tested, and what results

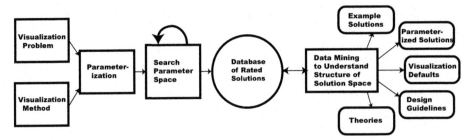

Fig. 2.22. Phases of human-in-the-loop exploration [369]. *Image courtesy of D. House, A. Bair, and C. Ware.*

the experimenter is interested in. There is a high danger of skewed results because of the subject wanting to please the experimenter, and the experimenter explaining his or her new method in more detail or in a more positive light than the one being tested.

Double-blind tests are certainly much more difficult to design in visualization, especially for application scenarios. But there are ways to improve the situation, e.g., by using synthetic data sets (see below) or designing appropriate study protocols.

Thorough Understanding and Experience. For most visualization methods, there is only a very small number of real experts: their developers. Even those often do not know what exactly to look for when trying to find clusters or correlations. A trained and experienced user would be able to spot more complex and subtle patterns than an untrained one, similar to a physician developing an eye for certain types of symptoms that a layperson would ignore.

As visualization is maturing, the number of expert users for particular methods will increase, and these users will require different types of tools that will need to be evaluated differently than those developed for naive users.

Exploring the Search Space. With any new parameter tested in a user study, the number of possible combinations quickly reaches a point where an exhaustive test becomes unfeasible. Recent work by House et al. [369] (Figure 2.22) addresses this problem by storing the possible parameter combinations as well as those tested in experiments in a data base that can be mined for both knowledge about the tested methods and holes in the knowledge. While covering the whole search space may still be impossible, covering the meaningful parameter combinations is greatly facilitated.

In order to increase the importance and usefulness of user studies, we propose a number of steps that we regard necessary for the further development of the field. These go beyond simple improvements in study design, and into the quest for a science of visualization.

A Guidebook. There is a vast body of knowledge of and experience with empirical studies in psychology. And despite the fact that some excellent guides exist [873], there is still little information available for visualization researchers that can be used directly. Guides are needed for different kinds of studies, including not only designs, but also answers to some difficult questions. One foray in this direction is currently being undertaken by Russell Taylor in the IEEE Visualization 2006 Visualization Design Contest.

Data Generator. The biggest obstacle in performing an effective user study is data. We often have only limited access to real-world data (if at all), and manually manufacturing data is likely to skew test results. Therefore, a data generator is needed that will generate data with given characteristics (dimensions, types of data, clusters, correlations, noise), as well as data that is structurally and statistically equivalent to a real data set. Analyzing a data set that has an unknown number of structures of unknown type (or perhaps none at all) will sharpen the senses of visualization researchers, and evoke a more critical response to their own work and that of others.

Synthetic data sets are also the only way to achieve true double-blind tests. If the parameters are chosen correctly, the user will be presented with a data set that he or she knows nothing about and has to explore without any preconceptions. The experimenter cannot influence the result so easily, because he or she will not know what to look for, either. This is certainly not sufficient for double-blind tests, but it is undoubtedly necessary.

Experience. Even though we would like visualization to be directly accessible and intuitive to use, the visual representation of abstract data and relationships in high-dimensional data requires a certain amount of experience and training to understand. We also tend to concentrate too much on specific types of data or structures that we are looking for, and ignore others—and thus missing these other gems that are hidden in the data. Elaborate case studies are therefore needed that demonstrate the use of different kinds of visualization for different kinds of data, showing not only the principal way of working with a technique, but also what different kinds of structures look like, and how to recognize them.

Real Users. We need access to real users who know their data, and who have real questions they want to have answered, or real tasks they need to fulfill. Experience shows that techniques that look good and useful in the lab often prove to be of little use in practice. Getting access to users can be extremely difficult, but researchers have done successful work with people in practical settings, and can share their experiences and ideas how to approach users. There also needs to be a reward system for companies and individuals to take part in experiments.

Reproducibility. Studies must not only be documented at a level of detail that will allow others to confirm them, the software used should also be made available. It must be possible to build on existing study data to add new questions to a study and get a more complete picture. A complete archive of user study software and data is therefore needed that will allow researchers not only to reproduce results, but also learn from examples. Expanding existing study designs will allow much quicker results, and thus reduce the threshold for performing experiments.

Value of Studies. User studies are still undervalued in visualization. There needs to be an incentive not only to perform user studies for own work, but also to confirm and extend the work of others. At the very least, publication of studies that expand the knowledge about existing visualization techniques must be publishable, just as original studies about the same technique are. Studies that lead to inconclusive results or failed to prove their hypotheses must be publishable, to show which approaches failed or did not lead to significant improvements. This is important not only to learn from the mistakes of others, but also to get a more complete picture of which changes produced significant advantages, and which did not. Other researchers might build on failed designs and existing data to produce conclusive results that can improve the work.

2.6 Chapter Notes

Application of a human-centered approach in design practice of visualizations will result in usable visualization systems. In this way, users can complete tasks in a comfortable way using a reasonable amount of resources. This means that designing visualizations is based on the user needs, wishes, and knowledge. A good visualization should be both understandable and easy to interact with. It should represent the desired information, no more, no less.

To create such visualizations, good user studies are essential. During a user analysis study, several types of information are extracted. Firstly, information will be collected about who the users are. Secondly, information about the working environment will be gathered. Lastly, it is important to know what data they are working with. User analysis can give the designer a good insight into the mental model of the users. After having a clear overview of these elements, the design phase can start. The design phase is an iterative process of task analysis, task modeling, design, implementation, and evaluation.

Most of the current usability evaluations in visualization take place when the design is already finished. In order to improve the effectiveness of visualizations it is important to get users' feedback in the early stages of design. Applying an iterative approach will help to create system designs that closely match users' needs and improve the visualizations continuously throughout the whole design process [302]. As the field of visualizations evolves, the evaluation methods cannot remain limited to only empirical usability studies [370]. Experts in the field of evaluations are making an effort to make the collection of material for evaluations accessible to the researchers and designers.

Another crucial aspect is to make sure that visual representation matches the user's mental representation of the information to be navigated [890]. Operation of multiple visualization environments and interactive visualization spaces requires additional cognitive demands. Cognitive aspects of the visualized information processing have to be taken into consideration in design and evaluation.

There is a need in the evaluation framework for collaborative visualization environments. Such frameworks for design and evaluation of visualizations for multidisciplinary group collaboration can be developed by applying the iterative approach in user-centered design. During user studies and task analysis the following aspects will be addressed: what are the daily working practices of users, what resources, visualizations and artifacts do they use and which of them are preferred, what interaction styles are the most suitable for them, and do these user groups need visualization support in experiments and collaboration.

The advantage of a human-centered approach in visualization is that it results in a system with fewer problems during the development stage and has lower cost over time. In addition, it reduces the gap between the technical functionality and the users' need.

3 Interacting with Visualizations

Wim Fikkert, Marco D'Ambros, Torsten Bierz, and T.J. Jankun-Kelly

In human-media interactions, visualizations occur in a large variety of forms. However, they remain but a single form of possible feedback towards a user. In this chapter it is argued that human-centered visualization is a fundamental part of human-media interaction and vice versa. To that end, the focus in this chapter lies first on the more general topic of interaction research, thus providing a solid literary ground for the rest of this chapter (Section 3.1). In Section 3.2 the focus shifts towards the question how a display technology influences the way(s) in which interaction with visualization takes place. This path is then broadened in Section 3.3 by focusing on approaches towards interacting multimodally with visualizations. To that end a chronological overview of developments in that field is given, thus providing an insight of trends and required steps in realizing multimodal interactions. Also, future work in this field is deducted from literature and those development trends. Fourthly, Section 3.4 describes the issues at hand for effectively applying visualizations in group-based collaborative and distributed environments. The aim in this chapter is to provide an overview of developments and the current state-of-the-art of approaches in which visualization supports the human-machine interaction process and vice versa. For that, this chapter is finalized with a short summary of issues to deal with while designing interaction for visualization. In addition current and future challenges in interacting with visualizations will be discussed.

3.1 Interaction

Typically, "we"—humans—interact extensively with one another on a daily basis. "We" are hardly aware of the enormous complexity of these human-human interactions. When reviewing the research field of interaction studies this complexity becomes painfully clear by the sheer number of research efforts on a seemingly even larger number of research topics, all concerning themselves with various aspects of interaction. When humans communicate with one another, each participant in the conversation uses a combination of various modalities to express himself. Apart from a speaker being able to send multimodal signals, the listener is able to receive and interpret those multiple input signals. Mehrabian [556] found that only 7 percent of human interaction in a dialogue setting is provided by verbal cues in contrast to 38 percent vocal cues and 55 percent facial expressions. In addition, Qvarfordt and Zhai [686] found that eye gaze

A. Kerren et al. (Eds.): Human-Centered Visualization Environments 2006, LNCS 4417, pp. 77–162, 2007.

patterns provide a more rich and complex information source with respect to a person's intentions and interests. If anything, these exemplary studies should indicate the relevance of looking into this interaction complexity in depth.

Illustrating the complexity of a human dialogue, think of a dialogue between two persons in which person A describes to person B the size of the fish he caught. Apart from speech, the fish's size is described using a (often extravagantly large) gesture with both hands. This is a simple example to indicate the importance to look further than just one form of interaction, especially toward nonverbal forms. Although humans are not always aware of its complexity this type of (natural) interaction is preferred when interacting with another human being [127, 631, 685, 870]. Comparing this to the topic of man-machine interaction, e.g., a human interacting with a computer, typically limited natural interaction is found there. As an example, consider the Windows-Icons-Menu-Pointer (WIMP) paradigm that is well known from, amongst others, the Windows operating systems. In the WIMP paradigm, a keyboard and mouse typically make up the interactive devices while feedback to the user is provided via display and possibly audio. The Human-Computer Interaction (HCI) research field is one of the main fields in which these and, more importantly, new kinds of interaction are studied, aiming to improve these interactions, often based on these complex inter-human interactions.

This section describes how interactions are considered amongst humans and between humans and machines. Therefore, various settings in which interaction can take place are introduced in addition to interaction metaphors that describe forms of interaction.

3.1.1 Describing Interaction

This book deals with the ins and outs of human-centered visualization environments. In such an environment, interaction is bound to take on an important role, i.e., the human/group of humans interacts with the visualization. However, visualization is but a part of the whole interaction process; it provides feedback toward a user (group) in the form of a visual representation of the data that is dealt with. The opted visualization is most often tuned to the person using it, as was described in Chapter 2. Visualizations support the whole interaction process while being a fundamental part of it. However, in numerous visualization research areas, e.g., in information visualization (InfoVis) and visualization (Vis), the user is typically left out of the picture whereas in this book it is argued that he should be the main focus to tune visualizations to. The previous chapter provided footholds regarding how to design a visualization that is suited for its audience. Here, settings in which interaction can take place in a Human-Centered Visualization Environment (HCVE) are discussed in addition to interaction metaphors.

Interaction settings vary between parties in a visualization environment. They range from a single user with a single machine, to multiple users with multiple machines. In addition, interaction between these parties can be distributed spatially, teleconferencing is a simple example, or situated at the same physical location. Section 3.4 goes into more detail on this topic. For now it is important to realize that interaction does not only take place between a single user and a machine but more typically between multiple users in a computer supported visualization environment. The QuickSet system [172], the virtual meeting room that is being developed in the Augmented Multi-party Interaction (AMI) project [696], and the famous CAVE [182, 183] are only some examples of these kinds of visualization environments.

Interaction Metaphors. Apart from the interaction setting, e.g., multiple users with a visualization, the interaction itself is important. Interaction is the way in which communication between the user(s) and the machine(s) takes place. The focus now shifts on how (parts of) interactions in general can be classified in order to better understand the interaction possibilities. Amongst communicating partners, three basic human-computer interaction metaphors can be distinguished [257, 327]:

- *Navigation* enables users to browse through (a set of) data, similarly to navigating (three dimensional) space;
- *Direct Manipulation* in which the machine is viewed as a mere tool, as a passive collection of objects waiting to be manipulated;
- *Human Interaction* in which the communicating partner is perceived *through* the interface having human characteristics, or being human-like.

Navigation. In a virtual environment, it is one of the basic and most common interaction techniques. Examples such as walking and flying are well known to everybody. Every navigation technique consists of two basics: *traveling*, which is the control or motion of the user's viewpoint in the environment, and *wayfinding*, where the user determines the path by the knowledge of the environment, extended visual information, e.g., signs, and supporting aids like maps or top-views. These issues are combined to the navigation and require a good understanding when designing an effective virtual environment navigation interface. However, traveling typically is a basic task that enables one to perform a more more extensive interaction with the virtual environment, e.g., grabbing or moving of an object.

There are various proposed metaphors for the viewpoint control in virtual environments [103, 136, 443, 818, 876, 880]. It is beyond this piece to extensively discuss these metaphors. One well known approach is the World in Miniature (WIM) metaphor for navigation proposed by Pausch et al. [643, 796]. A miniature representation of the current visual representation is added to the virtual scene in order to simplify the navigation. Objects may be directly manipulated either in the miniature representation or in the 3D environment.

Navigation alternatives to reaching an object exist, such as altering acceleration and velocity. One possibility is steering to a target object or the target selection after which the user chooses the target object [534]. Considering acceleration and velocity, the simplest approach is using a constant rate. However, when interacting in a huge virtual environment, it is quite inefficient to move at a constant rate, because the navigation from a place A to a distant place B will take a long time. Concerning this issue, more efficient adaptive approaches have been proposed and implemented, see e.g. [102, 103, 534].

Manipulation. After the user has efficiently navigated to the desired object or target, the manipulation of the object is usually the next step. Selecting objects can be performed by different means, for example, by a command. Then, manipulation, e.g., translation or rotation of the object, can be performed. Based on trying to focus on interacting with the virtual environment in a natural way, which might not always be the ultimate solution, natural mapping simply maps the location and the scale of the user's physical hand directly to the virtual hand. So, when the user tries to grab an object in the virtual world, it is automatically selected and manipulated [447].

Although this interaction is very intuitive and is easily adapted to most users, a big disadvantage of the basic approach is the difficulty of interaction in large environments. For instance, if the user is interacting with an object, he has a limited physical arm reach for performing the action. For placing the object to a place out of reach, the user needs to travel to the correct coordinates.

To avoid this issue, the Arm-Extension Technique focuses on the limited reach of the user. This approach allows the extension of the virtual hand and interaction with distant objects. Within the threshold distance, the user interacts in a normal way. Outside the threshold, the virtual arm follows a nonlinear function relative to the distance of the physical arm from the user's body. The mapping function is the important contribution of this approach. However, precision over distances still lacks accuracy as will be discussed in more detail in Section 3.2.2.

In order to select objects, ray-casting techniques are commonly used. This technique is based on the two dimensional Desktop Metaphor [775] in which the mouse—visualized by a pointer—is used to interact with, amongst others, icons and menus. The three dimensional approach is comparable to the well known computer graphics ray casting technique. So, the object is selected pointing a virtual ray into the scene. When the interaction is performed with a users hand and not a pointing device, the orientation of the hand is mostly used for specifying the direction of the virtual ray. When an object intersects the ray, it is selected and ready for further manipulations [558]. Based on this technique is also the image plane technique, where the user performs the selection by covering the desired object with the virtual hand [648].

The previously mentioned World in Miniature technique is also one of the powerful interaction techniques for selection and manipulation. This technique has been extended by the *voodoo dolls* technique by Pierce et al. [649], where the user creates his own miniature version of the environment. This miniature can then be manipulated with both hands.

The Human Interaction Metaphor. It attributes a form of agency to the computer: it can act on its own—at least so far as the user's mental image of the computer is concerned. This is not the case for the other two metaphors as Fineman [257] argues; direct manipulation results in the computer doing exactly what the user requests. In Section 3.1.1, this human-like interaction with the computer is discussed in more detail.

Most interactive interfaces implement instances or combinations of these three basic metaphors. Especially, the distinction between the direct manipulation metaphor and the human interaction or intelligent agent approach has been the subject of considerable debate in the literature [761]. Supporters of the direct manipulation metaphor praise the fact that such interfaces are typically made very transparent by displaying the options available to the user on a screen. Moreover, because the effects of the undertaken user actions are known *a priori*, direct manipulation interfaces are predictable. This predictability makes them easy to learn and remember. Finally, direct manipulation systems make the user feel in control of the interaction. Researchers advocating the use of communication agents believe that agent-based systems are much more versatile and offer users the opportunity to delegate some of their tasks. In their opinion, systems that act as intelligent agents can alleviate problems that are due to the increasing complexity of systems, which makes them more suitable for untrained users [761, 801].

Computers Are Social Actors. While interacting with a machine, some scientists [190, 257, 597, 611, 826, 922] believe that humans would like to experience the same kind of interaction like communicating with other humans, the kind of interaction we are most familiar with.

In these research efforts, amongst others, it has been suggested that when given certain social cues humans will interact in social ways with computing technology. These feelings are compounded when the technology is providing cues that encourage an individual to perceive its actions as they would another social actor's, leaving the impression that the users are dealing with an autonomous rational social actor who in some way exerts control over their environment. However, other researchers argue that machines are just tools to control in order to reach a certain goal [699, 745, 761, 762]. Either way, the importance and complexity of interaction studies for human-machine interaction is paramount.

In inter-human communication, modalities that are being used to express meaningful conversational contributions include speech, gestures, touch, facial expressions, possibly smell, etc. Bunt and Beun [166] expect that including the possibility to use various modalities in interfaces may contribute to a more efficient and satisfactory human-computer interaction. They base this hypothesis on the fact that in everyday conversation, people effortlessly combine multiple modalities; human perceptual, cognitive and motor abilities are well adapted to the real-time processing of these various modalities. Reeves and Nass [693] argue—on the topic of interacting with a social actor—that *"all people automatically and unconsciously respond socially even though they believe that it is not reasonable to do so."*

This indicates that machines are typically not considered a mere tool "to get the job done" but more so an assistant, communicating partner, a social actor, helping or collaborating with the user to reach his goal. In their famous work *"The Media Equation"*, Reeves and Nass [693] report on their experiments regarding humans assigning human characteristics to computers. The authors suggest that people tend to respond to computers and other media as they do to other people. They state that

> "[Individuals'] interactions with computers, television, and new media are fundamentally social and natural, just like interactions in real life."

The Media Equation became known as the "social reactions to communication technology" perspective in which "computers are social actors". In addition, the experiments by Reeves and Nass made clear that it is not only a matter of contributing personality characteristics to computers; it is also a matter of being influenced by these properties while communicating. Users exhibit behavior toward a computer or form of media as if it was a social actor. Other research on this topic further supports this view as is argued by Van Welbergen of [849]:

- In the work by Wang et al. [868], it is shown that a teacher-agent[1] exhibiting politeness in his interaction with a student, not only lets this student score on average 10% better on a difficult learning test's outcome, but is also liked more by this student, when compared with a teacher-agent that does not make use of politeness strategies.
- Lester et al. [503] observe the so-called *persona X*: the presence of a lifelike character in an interactive learning environment can have a strong positive influence on a student's perception of his learning experience.
- Van Es et al. [846] suggest that subjects perform their tasks faster when they are supported by an avatar[2] that exhibits realistic gaze as opposed to an avatar that uses a random gaze or no gaze strategy at all. The subjects also liked interacting with the realistic gazing avatar better than interacting with randomly or non-gazing avatars. This showed that feedback via a method exhibiting more human-like characteristics, possibly but not necessarily in the form of an avatar, is preferred.

As the above indicates, researchers have reached consensus on the hypothesis that human-like interaction with a computer/machine will increase user efficiency, effectiveness, and satisfaction, defined in Chapter 2 on user-centered aspects. Whether it is the most preferred approach remains a point of vivid discussion (as was described earlier). The focus now shifts toward interacting with and in a Virtual Environment (VE). In any VE, interaction plays a major role, enabling users to interact in an large number of ways with the visualization. It enables the user of such a VE to navigate and manipulate—the most abstract tasks in an interaction—the objects in that virtual world. This is true more so for a HCVE, a more specific type of VE[3]. Providing appropriate, simplistic, and

---

[1] "An Agent can be a physical or virtual entity that can act, perceive its environment (in a partial way) and communicate with others, is autonomous and has skills to achieve its goals and tendencies." [253]

[2] When speaking of an avatar, one refers to an Embodied Conversational Agent that typically exhibits human-based behavior in communication.

[3] See Chapter 1 for the definition of a Human-Centered Visualization Environment

above all human-centered interaction techniques and devices supporting those techniques is one of the currently most challenging research issues in the field of human computer interaction studies.

3.1.2 Defining Interaction

In literature on interaction and multimedia systems, researchers have been defining and using the terms media, modality, and mode in different and mostly confusing ways. This confusion originates from the fact that different properties and functionalities are assigned to each of these terms. As an example, André [18] defines the term modality as being both the input and output of multimodal systems whereas Maybury and Lee [547] define it in relation to the human senses that process, e.g., visual or auditory information. This section enumerates definitions of terms important in (parts of) interaction. Concluding this section, the definitions that will be used throughout this chapter are listed.

Numerous definitions for modality and media have been proposed and are being used. Most researches seem to agree on the idea that the term *modality* is associated with the human senses and that the senses are used to process information. The term *media* however, is related to the device or medium used to convey the information. Bunt and Beun [166] define numerous often occurring terms in multimodal research in an effort to clarify their use. Bunt and Beun will be followed in their definitions of modality and media here [36, 844].

The term modality typically refers to an attribute or circumstance that denotes the mode, manner, or form of something [166]. Moving from this general case to that of human-computer interaction, the modality of a message usually relates to particular aspects of the surface structure or form in which information is conveyed. Modality is thus used to denote the form in which the information is presented, e.g., spoken or written language and gestures.

In addition to Bunt and Beun's definition of the term modality, it is associated with the human channels of perception as defined in the domain of cognitive psychology. In this, modality is associated with the human channels of perception; channels that are deployed in storing, decoding, delivering, and processing information [36]. In its definition, modality encompasses the human senses like the linguistic, visual, and haptic systems. Although the modality is defined based mainly on the human cognitive system, Bachvarova [36] does not exclude it entailing the interaction with the computer/machine—also referred to as artificial multimodal systems—and as such allowing the modality term to acquire characteristics that are usually associated only with artificial systems. The definition of modality thus draws on the form and function of the cognitive processes associated with each channel of perception and which channel can ensure a relevant and optimal interaction between the human and the computer [36].

The term medium, although often used in literature in a similar if not identical manner, is distinctly different compared to modality. Although both notions are related to the form of a communicative message, a medium refers to the various physical channels and carriers that are used to transfer information, ranging from the human perceptual channels, e.g., sight, to carriers, e.g., radio waves or paper [166]. On the other hand, as the previous paragraph explains, a modality often refers to a particular communicative system, i.e., conventions of symbols and rules on how to use these symbols and to express messages. A *multimodal system* is multimodal when it combines two or more different modalities in the communication process. Note that several media are typically required in a multimodal system. However, a medium need not be a determining factor of the modality information it conveys; multimodal information can be passed along using a single medium. The term *multiplexing* is used to denote multimodal communication using a single medium whereas its counterpart-term *diviplexing* is used when speaking of a system in which different messages are transferred through different media [166, 821]. Bolt's [99] system, often referred to as "*Put that there*", is an example of a diviplexed system that uses deictic messages, i.e., pointing gestures in combination with speech that can only be understood unambiguously while using information from both sources (the uttered 'that' and a pointing gesture).

A fine-grained distinction is introduced via the term "*representational modality*". Representational modality is defined as the "*mode or way of exchanging information between humans or between humans and machines in some medium*". In Bernsen's [82] Modality Theory (see Section 3.3.1) the term medium entails:

"*[Medium] is the physical realization of some presentation of information at the interface between human and system.*"

In this respect, media are closely related to the classical psychological notion of the human *sensory modalities*. Bachvarova [36] follows Maybury and Lee [547] and makes the following distinction between medium and mode. The term *mode* or *modality* refers to the human sense employed to process information, while the term *medium* refers to the material object or carrier of information, different kinds of physical devices and information types. The information that is transferred can be coded in the form of, e.g., sign languages or pictorial languages.

In multimodal systems, two or more input modes, e.g., facial expressions, gaze behavior, bodily gestures, touch, pen, speech, etc., are being processed in a coordinated manner with multimedia system output. Comparing these types of systems with the conventional WIMP interface, a new direction for computing is represented. Oviatt [631] describes this new class of interfaces to aim at recognizing and subsequently interpreting—based on the recognized interaction context—naturally occurring forms of human language and behavior in which at least one recognition-based technology, e.g., speech, pen, or vision, is incorporated. Multimodal systems are discussed in detail in Section 3.3.

The claim that people will not leave useful and available modalities unused in a given situation is known as the "Multimax Principle" [130]. This is a fundamental topic in diviplexed and multiplexed use of different modalities and media in natural communication. The integration of multimodality in the human information process is such a prominent characteristic that the inclusion of integrated multimodal communication in human-computer interfaces will open the way for more effective and efficient forms of communication, as is described by Oviatt [631], Oviatt and Cohen [632], and Bunt and Beun [166]. Taking this chain of thoughts, a step further the hypothesis of Bunt and Beun is reached stating that:

> "Taking care of the appropriate combination of modalities can be considered a feature of cooperativeness."

Cooperation, a topic that is discussed in Section 3.4 further, involves mutual consideration of each other's goals and the activity to achieve those goals, helping each other where possible. In a collaborative workspace, users can work together, using multimodal communication between themselves and their surroundings. The scientists in such an environment can be said to be cooperating amongst themselves *and* with the collaborative workspace in which they find themselves. This entails that such an environment should be able to ascertain user desires, goals, mode, and possibly even the form of interaction.

Summarizing the main terms used in this work:

Agent A physical or virtual participant in a communication process that can act on and perceive its environment, communicate, is autonomous, and has skills to achieve its goals and tendencies [253], e.g., human or computer.

Media Physical devices to capture input from or present feedback to a human communication partner, e.g., microphone, keyboard, mouse, or camera.

Modality The way a communicating agent conveys information to, or receives information from a communication partner (human or machine), e.g., speech, gaze, hand gestures, or facial expressions.

Multimodal system A system that represents and manipulates information from different human communication channels at different levels of abstraction.

Display devices are used to show any visualization to the user and thus greatly influence the way an interaction takes place. In the following section, this topic is looked into in detail, analyzing the variety of display technologies and the even larger variety of interaction possibilities with those displays.

3.2 Influences of Display Technologies

Of the machine components that are part of human-computer interaction for visualization, the display has the largest effect. The display device determines the physical size of the viewport, the range of effective field-of-view and resolution possible, and the types of feasible interaction modalities. All other interactions must be placed in context of the display.

This section discusses the human-related factors that affect visualization design stemming from the display device; devices from cellular phones to multi-projector display walls are considered. The technical challenges required to create such systems are not significantly discussed—that is beyond the purview of this piece. Only aspects which affect the usability of the display system are considered. This section starts with an overview of display technologies; this leads into the effect of scale on interaction. Scale affects both the physical interaction modalities and possible interactions; both of these elements will be discussed. Finally, the consequences for human-centered visualization will be summarized.

3.2.1 Survey of Display Technologies

Displays serve several purposes; this purpose affects the technologies used in their manufacture. This section discusses three primary purposes of displays—*general purpose displays, electronic paper displays,* and *volumetric displays.* The technologies used for each, and the consequences upon physical size and interaction based upon those technologies, are outlined.

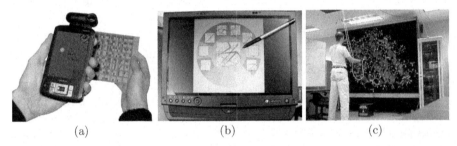

(a)   (b)   (c)

Fig. 3.1. General purpose displays: (a) Small-scale, *image courtesy of M. Hatchet,* Iparla project (LaBRI—INRIA), (b) medium-scale, (c) large-scale, *image courtesy of O. Kreylos.*

General Purpose Displays. General purpose displays must fulfill a range of needs including document presentation, image viewing, and entertainment purposes. Thus, the display technology used must have reasonably high resolution with fast response times and vivid colors. The primary technology used for these devices are cathode ray tubes (CRTs), liquid crystal displays (LCDs), digital light processing (DLP) monitors/projectors, liquid crystal on silicon (LCoS) monitors/projectors, and plasma display panels (PDPs). Due to the variety of technologies, general purpose displays can be found in many different shapes and configurations. This is categorized into three size scales, depicted in Figure 3.1: *Small-scale* (mobile phones, personal digital assistances (PDAs), in-vehicle displays), *medium-scale* (tablets, laptops, single monitor configurations), and *large-scale* (multi-monitor configurations, projection-based display walls, immersive virtual environments). Visualization research has traditionally been focused on medium-scale displays; however, the growing ubiquitousness of smaller and larger displays is driving visualization to novel uses.

Small-scale displays are those smaller than 0.1 m (measured diagonally). These "little screens" are often considered ideal for checking email, personal navigation, and digital picture previewing [405]. They are designed primarily for portability, and thus are limited in their computational and display power. At the small scale, LCDs predominate, and can be found in devices from cellular phones to PDAs. In visualization, the primary use of such small displays is *in situ* visualization—visualization which occurs at the physical location of the item being visualized. Visualizing telecommunication traffic on site is one example of such visualization [561].

Medium-scale displays have dominated visualization, many due to the proliferation of computer monitors. Such displays—between 0.1 and 1 m in size—were primarily CRTs. However, the commoditization of LCD and other similar technologies have lessened the use of CRTs. Medium displays may be portable (such as LCD tablet displays) or immobile (such as DLP back-projected interactive tables). Medium-scale displays are the largest devices where LCD technologies are feasible; larger single LCD screens are generally less cost-effective than DLP, PDP, or similar technologies. For larger LCD screens, multi-monitor configurations are popular.

Large-scale displays are either a single display device (e.g., a front-projected LCoS system) or collection of display devices (e.g., a tiled collection of back-projected DLP displays). Displays larger than 1 m are considered to be a large display; they are common in entertainment and large-scale visualization. A single display can be driven by a single computer; such displays are limited by the maximum resolution of the technology. PDPs made for entertainment are limited to HDTV resolution, for example. Projection can make a single display physically larger, but does not increase the pixel density. To increase pixel density, arrays of smaller display devices must be used. However, this introduces issues with bezels, as discussed in Section 3.2.4.

Electronic Paper. Electronic paper distinguishes itself from general purpose displays due to the relaxation of the need for fast updates and the significantly higher resolution requirements—ideal acuity to recognize a written character is five arc minutes per character [873], or about 229 pixels per centimeter at reading distance (57 cm). Color is not as important, as many print products do not require it. Organic electronics are currently the preferred technology for such devices; such electronics allow a pixel value to be set once without flicker—an important consideration for long term use. Electronic paper is used largely for electronic books and other print media; in this respect, they compete with the more interactive but lower resolution/higher flicker "virtual books" that appear on general purpose displays (e.g., Card et al.'s 3Book: A Scalable 3D Virtual Book [143]). Since electronic paper devices are primarily used for reading and not visual communication, they have been little used for visualization.

Volumetric Displays. The displays discussed so far produce two dimensional images; however, humans perceive in three dimensions. Volumetric displays attempt to depict 3D volumes with true stereo cues (Figure 3.2). Traditional stereoscopic displays involve a single or collection of 2D displays; the stereo cues are created using special glasses—colored glasses for anaglyphs, polarized glasses for multi-screen displays, and shutter glasses for multi-view rendering [202]. Polarized and shutter glasses, when head-mounted, are often tracked; this enables the volumetric view to appropriately update as the user's gaze changes. These

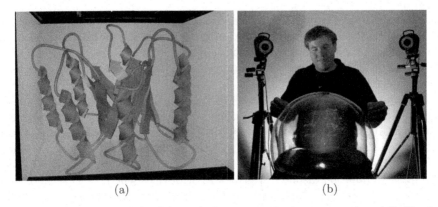

(a)   (b)

Fig. 3.2. Volumetric displays: (a) Tracked-stereoscopic, *image courtesy of O. Kreylos*, and (b) autostereoscopic, *image courtesy of T. Grossman.*

tracked-stereoscopic displays have found significant use in scientific visualization; the CAVE, a four rear-projection display configuration, is the most famous example (Figure 3.2(a)).

In contrast to anaglyph and tracked-stereoscopic displays, autostereoscopic displays project true volume images; no extra glasses are required. Autostereoscopic displays support multiple users, but tracking may be required in this case [202]. One example autostereoscopic display is the Perspecta Spatial 3D display (Figure 3.2(b)); it projects an updated image on a swept screen over 6,000 times per second [248]. Autostereoscopic technology is still in its early stages, and limitations on the complexity of surfaces, number of users, and voxel density prevent its wide scale adoption. However, as the technology matures, such displays hold the promise of high fidelity 3D realism for visualization applications.

Consequences for Visualization. The size and the type of display limits the feasible interactions. The time between subsequent renderings of the screen limits the display fidelity of pointer movement, for example—an input medium with a low update rate will appear choppy. Synchronization of displays is also important in multiple display configurations; this is also true of stereo displays. Limits in pixel/voxel density (such as in autostereoscopic devices) affect the needed precision of pointing devices. However, the largest effect on iteration is the size of the display. Small devices are typically carried; this leaves only one hand free for an interaction medium. Larger displays, in contrast, leave both hands free but cannot be easily accessed in a single physical movement. The effect on display scale upon interaction is explored next.

3.2.2   Scales of Interaction

As the size of a display increases, certain kinds of interactions are enabled; similarly, other interactions become impractical. Analogous to the three display scales discussed previously, there are three major interaction distance scales of interest—*hand-held* (distances up to 0.5 m), *arms-length* (distances between 0.5 m to 1.5 m), and *distal* (distances greater than 1.5 m). According to common psychological categorizations, the first two interaction scales fall within *personal space* (with hand-held interaction within *intimate space*), while distal interactions occur within a person's perceived *social* or *action space* [184, 325, 780]. Generally, hand-held or arms-length interactions with a device are preferred, while interactions on scales larger than the device are not favored, especially in collaborative contexts [343]. Table 3.1 summarizes different physical interactions at different scales.

Table 3.1. Interaction scenarios at different display and interaction distance scale.

	Distance		
Display Scale	Hand-held	Arms-length	Distal
Small-scale	Manipulate	Passive Viewing	N/A
Medium-scale	Manipulate	Active Viewing	Passive Viewing
Large-scale	Manipulate	Device-based Input	Active/Passive Viewing

Hand-Held Scale Distance. At hand-held distances, users can physically manipulate the display. For small-scale devices, this corresponds to actually holding the device in the hand and using finger or tool-based (e.g., stylus) input. Larger devices cannot be physically held, so touch-based input predominates at the hand-held scale. For medium-scale devices, interactions can be stylus-based or facilitated via touch-screens (e.g., interactive white-boards). For large-scale devices, touch-sensitive screens are impractical; however, computer vision-based approaches have been used to allow gesture and touch movements on this scale [577]. Section 3.2.3 discusses these input modalities in more detail. Hand-held scale is also the domain of reading; average reading distance is 30 cm [873].

Arms-Length Scale Distance. Arms-length distances are still considered personal space, and there is a direct sense of control within this distance [343]. However, this sense of control is relative to the size of the display. At arms reach, small-scale devices are impractical to control via device-based input (e.g., mouse) due to their size with respect to the device and other discomfort issues [452]. Passive viewing interaction, where the user does not interact with the display, is common for small-scale devices at this distance. Examples include in-car movies and in-car navigation systems, which are infrequently manipulated during use.

For medium and larger-scale displays, arms-length interactions utilize direct manipulation—a control device is used to directly maneuver a cursor or another object on the screen. Viewing distances for monitors fall within 50–70 cm, with an acceptable average of 57 cm [873]. At arms-length distances, typical monitors fill 20°–30° of visual angle, or the useful field of view—areas outside this region are not optimized for visual search as they have significantly fewer receptors [211,873, 891]. Thus, a user can directly manipulate objects on medium screens without turning their head. In addition, such direct manipulation is within a reasonable physical range: For a 30 cm × 30 cm square mouse pad, a user needs only to pick up and reposition a mouse once when moving a cursor from one side of a display to another on a 22" monitor (assuming a one-to-one correspondence and no mouse acceleration). As the display gets larger, however, mouse-based interaction becomes infeasible—for a 2.5 m wide screen, the same mouse would have to picked up eight times to scroll across the screen (again, assuming constant velocity motion and a one-to-one correspondence). Non-linear mouse-to-screen space mappings are considered inappropriate for most large-scale interaction tasks [809], though success for specific tasks has been demonstrated [94,136,167, 441,662]. Many interaction methods have been designed to address this *reaching problem* for large displays; these will be further discussed in Section 3.2.4.

Distal Scale Distance. Direct interaction at distal distances is active viewing—the users interact with what they can see. These are viewing interactions since the display is contained within the user's field of view. Interaction with large-scale displays at arms-length distances is not active viewing since the display extends past the user's field of view. At distal distances, direct interaction with large-scale displays can be considered active viewing—there is still a strong sense of presence for large displays at these distances [138,819][4]. However, at this distance, a user becomes psychologically disconnected from medium displays, and thus passive viewing applications are appropriate. Passive viewing applications are common for large, public displays, such as digital theaters.

Consequences for Visualization. From this discussion, a few visualization design precepts can be enumerated:

- Small and medium-scale displays favor one human to one machine interactions for active visualization. Small devices are too limiting for collaborative use, and medium displays have one effective control (a single mouse/keyboard or stylus).
- In contrast to the above statement, large-scale displays are appropriate for collaborative use. Several researchers report increased collaboration on large-scale displays [260,343,809].
- For small-scale displays, interaction devices other than finger, stylus, or keyboard are not appropriate.
- For large-scale displays, arms-length interactions are appropriate for an area close to the user. Specially designed interface metaphors must be used for distant objects.

These factors are independent of the interaction device used with the display. An input device for small screens is probably not suited for larger displays, for example. Such interaction media are discussed next.

---

[4] Presence is a sense of the display being an extension of one's environment: *"A state of consciousness, the (psychological) sense of being in the virtual environment."* [771]

3.2.3 Display Interaction Modalities and Media

Mice and keyboards were designed for desktop interaction; these devices do not scale well to smaller and larger sizes. For small-scale devices, one cannot manipulate both the display and the input devices simultaneously; for large-scale displays, indirect keyboard/mouse interaction is generally unsatisfactory [343,809]. In this section, a summary of research into alternate interaction modalities at the three major interaction scales—hand-held, arms-length, and distal is provided. Media are listed based upon the most extreme appropriate range; thus, speech interaction, which could be used at any interaction scale, is listed with distal interactions. This section discusses possible interaction modalities and a few specific input media; for in-depth discussion of interaction devices, see Section 3.3.4.

Hand-Held Scale Interaction Modalities. Hand-held interaction devices work best when they do not interfere with the operation of the display device. For small-scale displays such as PDAs, this requires that the input device be integrated into the display, be usable with one hand, or operated hands-free. For medium or larger displays, this restriction is not as stringent; both hands become free for control devices. At this distance, the primary display interaction is selection and pointing. Therefore, input modalities for this scale should be designed for this task—speech input, for example, is inappropriate. Modalities only appropriate to hand-held scale tend to be incorporated into the display device or require direct contact. Three such modalities are presented.

Touch. Touch-based systems use a variety of methods to accept input. Traditional touch screens work by detecting changes in electrical field, surface charge, or surface-layer acoustic signal [647]; recent advances have utilized vision-based or infra-red optical signals [181, 269, 326, 404, 577, 701, 788, 899, 900]. Whatever the technology, touchscreens provide a two-dimensional location on the display surface whenever the surface is touched. Traditional touch-based devices have high spatial resolution; the SMART Technologies SMART Board has 4000×4000 spatial resolution over a 1.5 m × 1.2 m region. Resolution for optical methods depends on the camera's sample resolution, the number of cameras involved, and the vision algorithm utilized. Both methods require a fast sampling rate—70 to 100 samples per second are recommended for writing tasks [577]—and thus require visualization algorithms to possess similar response times to support full touch-based input.

Touch-based input is ideal for small-scale devices, and is often pre-installed. Finger or stylus-based inputs are common. There is also a long history of human-factors studies utilizing small display touchscreens [745]. However, traditional touchscreen technologies do not scale effectively to large displays; vision-based approaches are preferred [578]. There are two main challenges with vision-based methods for touch input. First, the resolution of the touch input will degrade as the size of the display increases unless more cameras are installed; however, more cameras increase the computational load. Some efforts have begun to address this limitation [12]. The second challenge, common for all vision-based methods, is the discriminability of targets (fingers, styli) vs. background objects (especially objects displayed by the display itself). Common solutions utilize specialized color segmentation for the hands [181, 269, 404] or infra-red optics which do not register visible light [326, 577, 701, 899, 900]. Vision-based input modalities are a large, current area of interest and the fidelity of these methods improves steadily every year.

Writing and Pointing. Styli are often bundled with small-scale devices such as PDAs. They provide a higher-resolution pointing surface than finger-based input. One benefit of combining stylus and finger-tracked input using vision-based tracking is that input devices can be distinguished, allowing the stylus and finger to control different aspects of the visualization. When not combined with touchscreens, pen-based input uses powered devices such as light pens. These devices require optical detection by the display system; the Liveboard and Interactive Mural are representative displays which utilize light pens [237, 314]. Styli and pen-based devices are supplemental to touchscreens, and thus possess all their benefits and limitations. In addition, care must be taken when designing a visualization interface that requires any input device so as to avoid fatigue [351].

Text. Integrated keyboards or smaller keypads are common on small-scale devices; the numeric pad on cellular phones is a prevalent example. Keypads are similar to traditional keyboard based input, though they may support chorded (multi-key) input for increased efficiency. Due to their small size, keypads are appropriate for text-input on small-scale devices; on a large-scale device, a keypad would be often out of reach if embedded within the display. If keyboard input is required on a large display, indirect input (via a proxy device) or a simulated, tracked keyboard on the display itself would be suitable. Again, for ergonomic issues, input typed directly onto the keyboard should be limited.

Arms-Length Scale Interaction Modalities. At arm's length, the user can still touch the device if desired, and has a feeling of direct control over the display. As mentioned previously, the devices in this section are more appropriate to medium and large-scale devices, though a few (such as gesture tracking) have been used on small-scale displays.

Gaze Tracking. Gaze tracking uses a variety of eye-tracking technology to capture the eye's motion. Eye motion is significantly faster than other methods for pointing [879]; however, its primary use as the means of perceiving a visualization conflicts with usage as an input method [924]. In addition, eye tracking technology is not suited to selecting targets smaller than one degree of visual angle [879], though recent efforts have begun to address this limitation [781]. Gaze tracking has been used successfully in conjunction with other input devices (such as a keyboard) to augment pointing tasks. For example, eye tracking can be used to set the initial selection point, with manual adjustment via an external device [925]; this tracking can be extended to collaborative environments [924]. Gaze detection can also be used as means of detecting a user's focus; this information could be used as a basis for gaze-contingent rendering [64, 191]. Such rendering is important as displays get larger; the massive communication bandwidth needed to deliver gigapixel or higher graphics at sufficient refresh rates will be a significant challenge in visualization [884].

Isotonic Input. Isotonic input devices provide input by their position; six-degree-of-freedom (6DOF) mice, wands, laser pointers, and similar are isotonic. These devices work by being tracked in two or three dimensions. The tracking technology is either tethered to a tracking processor or untethered; untethered tracking is preferred for display device input to allow multiple users freedom of movement. The tracking itself can be performed via a range of technologies including magnetic, inertial, ultrasonic, and optical [717, 889]; see Section 3.3.4 for more detail on traditional tracking. When using a tracking-based system, care must be taken to ensure that the entire range of expected user motion is covered; if a user is free to move within a 30 m wide strip in front of a display, the trackers must have sufficient resolution to track this motion. One solution to this problem is to use vision-based tracking.

Computer vision-based tracking has received considerable attention in the past few years, especially for performing input for large displays. The advantage of vision-based methods is that they are untethered and scale with the number of cameras involved—more cameras increase either the spatial resolution of a fixed area or increase the total area covered. In addition, optimized algorithms and processor speed have combined to the point where such approaches are practical [181, 269, 270, 746]. Vision-based methods exist for most of the input modalities discussed below. For isotonic devices, the VisionWand [142] is an exemplar vision-based approach. The VisionWand is a specially colored wand that provides three-dimensional input (a 3D ray). The vision-based tracker uses color segmentation to determine the orientation of the wand, allowing a variety of input gestures; example gestures are *"tapping"* and *"dragging"*. Wands of different color can be tracked in parallel to allow multi-user interaction. One can imagine combining VisionWand-based input with one of the vision-based input methods mentioned later to build a comprehensive input system.

Of special consideration for large scale and table-based displays is the use of laser pointers for input [188, 449, 623, 624, 641]. Laser pointers are ubiquitous and low cost, and thus have high appeal as an input device. In addition, laser pointers can be used both at arms length and touching a screen in a manner similar to a light pen. However, laser pointers are limited to only two degrees of freedom and have accuracy problems due to hand jitter [588, 623]. Though there are approaches to limit the effect of jitter [9, 624, 641], laser-based methods are not recommended as a primary/sole input modality.

Isometric Input. Isometric devices use pressure or motion to provide input, such as joysticks or trackballs (Section 3.3.4). The physical location of the isometric device does not matter, and thus a user is free to move about with the device. Isometric inputs are well suited to small-scale displays [767]; for example, a joystick with a clickable mode for selection has been used to augment personal navigation devices [433]. However, for medium-scale and larger displays, they are not ideally suited, at least for remote pointing tasks [532, 588]; these devices suffer from poor throughput (a combined measure of accuracy and movement time based upon Fitt's Law [259, 531]) (For further discussion on Fitt's Law, see Section 3.2.4). New devices which combine isometric and isotonic input, such as the CAT [318], have demonstrated improvements over the stand-alone isometric design, and deserve further investigation. In addition, for object manipulation tasks, isometric input can be effective. For example, dual isometric wands have been used for 3D object construction on large displays [310].

Embedded joysticks in small devices are not the only option for isometric input. With the addition of tilt or inertial sensors, the small-scale display itself is the isometric device [41,240,261,262,353,698]. Such couplings have been used to virtually rotate around an image of real-world objects, control menu items, or to navigate a 2D space. It is discussed later how the use of a smart phone for isometric input can benefit large-scale display interaction.

Finger, Gesture, Head, and Body Tracking. Excluding gaze tracking, the previous interaction devices in this section use an intermediary such as a wand, mouse, or pointer. However, utilizing the body directly has benefits such as integrating proprioception (a person's perception of body alignment and position) with navigation [559], providing a kinesthetic frame of reference [43], and increased task performance with two-handed input [502]. Body tracking can be decomposed into finger, gesture/hand, head, and full body tracking. The vast majority of recent applications of these tracking methods use vision-based tracking.

Finger tracking can be achieved with touch-based input; gestures constrained to the plane can also be detected this way. At arms length, however, additional technology is needed. Glove-based non-optical trackers have been used extensively in virtual reality applications to track fingers and gestures [661], though tracking resolutions have limited their applicability for fine-detail tracking until recently [864]. Vision-based methods can segment the fingers and hand and thus detect gestures either on a surface [311,329,355,540,682,751,899,900] or in the air [99,179,864]. Finger and gesture tracking is ideal for selection, though the wrist is not well suited to six degree-of-freedom tasks [923].

Head tracking is often used to identify a user's location or the direction of their gaze; head tracking can be combined with eye tracking for this latter application. Head tracking can be done in a tethered (magnetic/inertial-based) or untethered (vision-based) fashion. One example of head tracking is its use to augment the accuracy of finger/gesture tracking [605]. A novel application is using gaze and facial expression (such as frowning) as input [806]; for example, one could consider using frowning as negative feedback to a semi-automatic visualization technique. However, except for its use in collaboration (indicating gaze), head tracking is not an ideal input for visualization applications which require fine motor control.

Full body tracking determines the body's location and pose. Untethered body pose/position tracking has been used with some success for 3D navigation tasks [419]. However, body pose tracking is less fine-grained than even head tracking [863]. Thus, while it may be useful for macro-scale or rough initial interaction, it is not suitable for fine-grain manipulations common in visualization selection tasks.

Indirect Input. Indirect input includes any external device input that is not included in the above list. Here, the focus lies on alternate, secondary displays which are used to control a primary display. A popular example is the use of a PDA or tablet PC to show a scaled down or cropped version of the large display; this "semantic snarfing" approach has some demonstrated success as a remote pointing mechanism for large displays [588,589]. This form of input has potential for utilizing some of the novel interaction methods discussed in Section 3.2.4; a scaled-down "dollhouse" version of the large display on a PDA could be used to remotely manipulate the real version [809]. In collaborative visualizations, a remote proxy should be provided for each user; users dislike indirect interaction with displays when only one remote interaction device is provided [343].

Distal Scale Interaction Modalities. At long range distances, smaller displays are more akin to ambient pictures than a dynamically controlled device. Depending on the size of the display, some sense of presence may linger. However, most of the previously mentioned input devices are not usable at distal scales—tracked sensors may not extend to significant range and the accuracy of pointing-based devices falls off. At long distances, some interactions are still possible using speech or photographic input; even-so, these interactions are predominantly used at arms reach or closer distances.

Speech Input. Speech recognition, as a mode of input, has been widely used for accessibility in desktop environments. The recognition software comprehends a fixed vocabulary that requires no training or allows flexible vocabularies which require both voice training (for recognition) and macro development (for determining what the voice command does). For typical tasks in visualization (selection, navigation, etc.), voice input alone is not as useful as direct manipulation [174]. The benefits of speech technology is when it is combined with direct input or gestures to form a multimodal input device for 2D and 3D selection and manipulation tasks [99,172,173,179,422,477]; see Section 3.3.5 for more details. Combined with some sort of object recognition by the visualization system, a small vocabulary may be utilized at long ranges to interact with a large display. When used by itself, speech is ideal for querying tasks, since voice is significantly faster than typing [174]. In this setting, the visualization system would require a natural language processor to translate spoken queries to visualization queries.

Photographic/Video Input. Photograph or video based input has been used for displays of all scales. A distinction is made between cameras used for computer vision-based input (such as gesture tracking), and cameras which process the image in some other manner. Vision methods have already been discussed; image-based methods are discussed here.

By either photographing real-world objects or specialized coded-glyphs, different tasks can be accomplished. For small displays such as camera phones or PDAs, built in cameras have been used to interact with their environment; examples include identifying special tags for information retrieval, identification, and visualization [47,536,561,716,777], using visual codes for 2D and 3D display navigation [319,320], and using images or real-world objects as feedback into querying and navigation systems [41,135,778]. The key to each of these methods is the ability of the camera to discriminate the visual glyph or real-world object from the background. For digital codes, they can be designed to be unique visual keys used in information lookup; in this case, all that is required is that the codes be distinct from each other. Visual codes can also be used to encode commands to the visualization system; TangiMap, for example, uses 6-bit colored codes to communicate navigation commands—different color combinations over the six locations correspond to different directions to scroll the display [320]. Orientation of the glyph can also be taken into account. Wilson [900] and Owen et al. [634] have an in-depth discussion of the design of visual codes. The most difficult scenario is real-world object recognition, where variance in lighting conditions and camera orientation complicates matching with exemplar images. However, if the camera or PDA is also spatially–aware, such as through the use of the global-positioning system (GPS) or other sensors, this information can augment the visual-only information when identifying targets [135, 261, 478, 918].

Large-format displays can also utilize photographic and video input. Visual codes have been used to provide virtual target recognition and to discriminate between users and input devices for table-top, wall-mounted, and augmented reality displays [430, 540, 634, 700, 900]. A more novel application is to integrate detection and communication between a camera phone/PDA and the larger display. Examples include using a blink on a camera phone to perform state changes on a large display [562], detecting the change in a camera phone's relative position on the screen to control a pointer [48], manipulation of visual code tagged user interface elements [537], and using a phone's camera to select a visual glyph via a *"point-and-shoot"* protocol [48]. Ballagas et al. [49] provide a survey of such interaction methods. This fusion of small and large displays reaps the benefits of semantic snarfing-type interactions with the more open potential of camera-based input.

Consequences for Visualization. A large collection of alternate input modalities are available for interaction with small and large-scale displays. Many of these modalities have capabilities which complement each other or that are appropriate for different interaction distances. In summary:

- Due to the versatility of vision-based algorithms, camera systems should be considered a vital part of any large display system.
- At hand-held distances, touch-based modalities should be the primary form of input. Stylus or keypad inputs are useful as secondary tools.
- At arms-length distances, vision-based tracking, be it wand-like, gesture-based, or similar should be primary. Proxy displays or "semantic snarfing" are beneficial as secondary devices. Gaze tracking and laser pointers are too error-prone to be used as primary input sources.
- Voice recognition and photographic input can be used to augment the previous interaction devices discussed above. Secondary displays, such as camera phones and PDAs, are especially useful in this respect due to being voice- and image-capable devices.

For visualization software, there are multiple advantages to these sorts of input modalities. Secondary displays can be used both to manipulate a visualization (e.g., to rotate a volume visualization on the large display, to change the values of a dynamic query) and to show ancillary visualizations (e.g., a histogram of depicted volume data, previous dynamic query values). Small-scale devices can visualize details of real-world objects if they are tagged with codes. However, these "beyond-the-desktop" applications pose another challenge—what user interfaces are needed for these systems? These usability aspects are discussed next.

3.2.4   Interfaces and Usability for Novel Displays

There are five common perceived issues in large display interaction: Reaching distant objects (selection tasks), tracking the cursor (navigation tasks), bezels (viewing and navigation tasks), managing space, and transitioning between interactions/tasks (managing control) [604, 709]. In small-scale devices, the lack of suitable input modes (keyboards) and a dearth of pixel real-estate are paramount. Each of these has consequences for visualization user interface design. These issues are broken into four categories: selection issues, navigation issues, viewing issues, and management issues. Each issue is outlined and current solutions are discussed.

Selection. Interactive visualization requires the ability to select and interact with data objects. Selection tasks are a well understood problem, and have received significant attention in human-computer interaction research. The complexity of selection tasks is determined by three factors: The size of the target, the distance to the target, and an associated lag between the human's physical movement and the corresponding screen pointer movement. This relationship is formalized by Fitt's Law [259, 531], with the inclusion of lag by MacKenzie and Ware [533]. Here, the formulation from Ware is used [873]:

$$t_s = a + b\left(t_r + t_l\right)\log_2\left(d/w + 1\right) \qquad (3.1)$$

where t_s is the mean selection time, a and b are measured constants dependent on the device and user, t_r the mean response time of the human to the visual stimulus that causes the selection, t_l the mean lag time of machine response, d is the distance to the target's center, and w the width of the target; height or depth may be used as appropriate. The value $1/b$ is the *index of performance*; it is measured in bits/second. The index of performance is based upon the user. The term $\log_2\left(d/w + 1\right)$ is the *index of difficulty*. It depends entirely on the targets. Larger indices of difficulty correspond to more difficult selection tasks— either the relative distance to the target is very large or the relative width of the target is very small.

For small-scale displays, though the distance between any two selection targets will be small, the corresponding width of these targets will also be small. Thus, the index of difficulty is comparable to desktop displays. Using a 10 pt font character (an observed legibility limit for small screens [427]) as a target on a cell phone with a height of 3.7 cm, the maximum index of difficulty would be about 4 bits. For comparison, a target that is 40 cm away with a width of 2.5 cm would have a similar index of difficulty. Since the size of the device is fixed (and thus the maximum distance), a solution to reduce the difficulty is to increase the size of the targets. However, uniformly increasing the size decreases the amount of information that can be communicated. A common solution in both desktop and smaller devices is to use *focus+context* techniques—enlarge the data of interest while leaving the other objects untouched. Conversely, one can leave the focused objects alone and shrink the context objects. Regardless, the effect is the same—targets of interest have an increased width, and thus a lower target difficulty.

Several focus+context techniques have been explored for small devices [71,93, 916]. Both the PowerBrowser [93] and DateLens [71] display calendar information on PDAs. The PowerBrowser displays different date scales (month, week, day) at once; only one focus scale is displayed at full resolution while the others are minimized. Thus, to select an event at a different time scale, multiple selections are required. The DateLens uses a Furnas fish-eye lens approach [279]; events near the time of interest are given the most screen real estate while those farther away are given corresponding less. To lessen the multiple selection required by the PowerBrowser to jump time scales, the DateLens will "lock" the current focus level between selections. This decreases the "virtual distance" between neighbors. Yang and Wang use a similar fish-eye technique for displaying hypertext on PDAs, though their method is based upon a fractal weighting function [916].

Focus+context is not the only solution to improving the usability of selection tasks on small displays. Liquid scatter space [867] uses a lens to separate items near a focal region—this removes occlusion which interferes with selection. Due to small screen size, occlusion is much more likely in comparison with larger screens. Liquid scatter space also draws attention to targets perceptually using motion. A complementary selection process is used by the bubble cursor [309]; it expands the size of the selection area to cover the nearest available target while not covering any other targets. Thus, a target is always under the cursor—the effective distance to the nearest object is always effectively zero. Improved small target selection was demonstrated for similar bubble techniques where the target was grown instead of the selector/cursor [167]. Either approach would be beneficial on small and large displays.

For larger displays, the index of difficulty is governed predominantly by distance—objects of interest can be much farther away than their relative size. This *reaching problem* has been addressed in several ways. Focus+context methods are popular [314, 709, 711, 744]; others use interactions with proxies [62, 88, 175, 337, 442, 709, 809] or a combination of the two [89].

The focus+context methods used to assist selection on large displays leave the majority of the display alone while moving the compressed context to the periphery of the display. ZoomScapes [314] uses a three layer approach: The center region of the display is at full resolution while the upper and lower horizontal bands have smaller magnification levels. Moving beyond the focus/context boundary changes the scale of the manipulated object. Scalable Fabric [711] uses a similar approach, but allows user-control regions of the screen to be scaled-down context areas and can group selected objects (usually full windows). The context region can also be limited to a small area; this compressed, localized region can then be used to store objects for later interaction [744]. The Tablecloth metaphor [709], designed primarily for multi-monitor displays, uses a slightly different approach. Instead of dragging a particular object from a context area into a focus, the user "pulls" the entire context region containing the target into the focus area. The previous focus area is then compressed and merged with the non-selected context area—this effect mimics how a tablecloth is compressed when one drags it. Thus, the user's pointer never leaves the center focus area (usually the center monitor); the virtual space is scrolled beneath it.

Instead of changing the scale of large portions of the display, proxy interaction methods create copies of other objects which can be manipulated. There are a suite of such methods which involve dragging or throwing a cursor. Drag-and-pop [62] brings icons of relevant objects (such as applications) towards the cursor; other variations launch selected objects towards relevant targets [337] or merge the two approaches [175]. The Vacuum metaphor [88] and the Target Chooser [709] are similar to the cursor-based methods in that they shoot rays from the currently selected point to targets; targets are then either brought to the center for proxy interaction (the Vacuum) or one of the distal objects is selected and becomes the focus (Target Chooser). Like the vacuum, the Frisbee metaphor [442] allows selection and manipulation of distant targets; a remote region of interaction is positioned using the frisbee. By manipulating the locally controlled frisbee widget, distant regions can be highlighted, targets selected, and moved between the local and remote areas. Finally, the Dollhouse metaphor [809] uses a miniaturized version of the entire display for remote selection and interaction. Thus, the effective distance to a distal target is the distance to its dollhouse representation.

All proxy methods reduce the index of difficulty by decreasing the effective distance; this contrasts with the virtual target magnification caused by focus+context methods. These benefits have been combined into a common framework by Bezerianos and Balakrishnan [89]. Their *"canvas framework"* can express most of the previous metaphors using some combination of scale factors and linked portal windows. All of these methods reduce the need to reach for distance targets, increasing the usability of the interface.

Navigation. Selection is the process of choosing objects on the screen; navigation is the process of moving between selectable and viewable objects. Thus, the various techniques which distort space mentioned previously have applications for navigation. By using a spatial compression or eliding scheme, navigation tasks can be made significantly faster [280]. However, care must be taken when designing how the view transitions between different positions; van Wijk and Nuij provide guidance on spatially and cognitively efficient transforms between views at different scales [854].

For small screen devices, many specialized input devices have been designed to assist navigation in the absence of keyboards and mice [41, 240, 319, 324, 353, 433]; these are discussed in more detail in Section 3.2.3. As for user interfaces, most mobile devices have limited themselves to traditional 2D text and graphics; the extra pixel overhead to represent 3D objects consumes too much of the limited screen resource [79]. Icons have been shown to assist mobile device navigation [427, 704]; well designed icons can save significantly on screen real estate. Some initial work has explored design principles for 3D mobile device interfaces [324]. In this experiment, navigation was performed over a tree-like, 3D file browser using constrained motion—users were only allowed to descend deeper into the hierarchy, move to neighboring siblings, or open up the contents of a folder. Various visual cues (a spotlight-like effect [444]) were used to assist navigation through focusing attention. This design space needs further investigation.

Navigation on small devices can also be facilitated by novel interaction methods. Contextual pop-up menus and marking menus (radial context menus [485]) have been used for navigation and control purposes [427]; two-handed marking menus have performance comparable to hot-keys [622]. In a similar vein, a radial scrolling tool has been used to quickly navigate document spaces [776]. This radial tool is an example of gestural techniques for input; similar gesture-based input, such as the Graffiti system for Palm Pilots, have been very successful on small devices [427]. A system of gestures has also been developed for navigating between multiple small devices in a collaborative setting [354]; this type of system would be beneficial in visualizations using multiple, smaller devices to control a larger display.

On large scale devices, two main issues affect navigation beyond the reaching problem: *cursor tracking* and *bezel interference*. The cursor indicates a user's current selection focus; navigation tasks often involve moving this cursor to the new physical and virtual location. On multi-monitor configurations or large projection screens, it is easy to lose track of this cursor's location due to the large number of potential distractors; the cursor can also be lost during its movement. One solution is to utilize a high-density cursor that uses temporal sampling to ensure a perceivable path [63]; for lost cursors, various visual signals can be used to call attention to its new location [444, 709]. Alternatively, a "bubble cursor" that grows in relation to the density of targets could assist cursor tracking [309].

Bezel interference occurs on multi-monitor configurations predominantly, though some DLP display systems have significant bezels. The bezel introduces a physical barrier between areas of the screen that is not present in the virtual (screen) space. Thus, motion from one side of a bezel to another does not follow the proper path; it seems to be deflected by the space caused by the bezel. Mouse Ether [61] accounts for the bezel separation; after calibration, cross-bezel motion is appropriately linear. This bezel-free movement can be combined with methods to properly communicate pointer position; this delegation of control is especially important in collaborative environments [407]. However, even with the presence of bezels, navigation on a multi-monitor configuration has been shown to be more efficient than a pan-and-zoom navigation on a single monitor [46].

Viewing. The human visual channel dominates sensory input; significant cognitive resources are devoted to sight. Visualization utilizes this perceptual focus by depicting information. Thus, considerable effort must be spent on how the information is presented. Small and large displays add new challenges to effective visual communication: Small screens have significantly fewer pixels and field of view, while large screens saturate the field of view with potentially distracting information. Additional care must be taken to present and highlight information on these devices.

As previously mentioned, icons are effective for quickly communicating information on small displays [427, 704]. In addition, layering of information and user interface elements are common, with interface transparency depending upon active control [427]. Liquid browsing uses an inverted opacity scheme; objects in the lowest layer have the highest opacity in order to maintain context at the different levels [867]. Transparency, however, can cause significant visual interference, and should be used only in regions of low-density backgrounds for maximum effectiveness [873].

The main issue with viewing on large displays is drawing a user's attention where it is needed. Motion can be used for this purpose; movement in the peripheral vision is a strong, pre-attentive cue [873]. For example, motion has been used to inform a user when the state of peripheral motion has changed [56]. Another approach is to "spotlight" the important information: The brightness of data of interest is fixed while the brightness of unimportant data is diminished [444]. The brighter areas become pre-attentive beacons to the data.

Bezels also cause interference with viewing on large displays. A bezel visually breaks a display. Again, since this physical distance is usually unaccounted for, a continuous image displayed across the bezel will have a false "gap." Methods similar to those used for Mouse Ether can be used to account for the missing physical space; this correction has the effect of removing the part of the visualization that "falls underneath" the bezel [709]. However, like all calibration methods, it must be repeated for each different bezel configuration.

When discussing viewing, special mention must be made of stereoscopic visualizations using large displays. While large displays are ideal for collaborative visualization, stereo applications limit full collaboration. This limitation stems from tracked nature of stereo-rendering—only one viewer's position is tracked and thus used for rendering. While passive collaborators can interact with the display, there will be visible distortions caused by this tracking mismatch. Some techniques using multiple viewpoint projections have been explored to enable multiple user stereoscopic interaction [768, 769]. In the future, autostereoscopic, non-head tracked displays will allow stereoscopic viewing for multiple viewers without special tracking [202].

Management. Users must manage their information—either they must manage its compartmentalization (e.g., positioning windows from different applications on a screen) or manage their time related to each task (e.g., switching between current tasks). Management of tasks and windows has been significantly studied for large displays; smaller displays do not have enough screen real estate to display multiple tasks at once.

The chief concern with window and task management on large display is the tendency for the amount of information to grow to fill the visual space. With so many windows and related applications, transferring between them and locating related windows can be difficult. As many visualization systems utilize multiple windows (querying control palettes, linked visualizations, etc.), multiple window management is important to visualization. Any of the selection mechanisms discussed previously can be used to select a single window; however, they do not deal with sets of windows. Apple Exposé [31] facilitates window switching by providing a dollhouse-like overview of all open applications or application windows on demand; again, this method is limited to single window operations. Microsoft has developed a suite of grouped window interactions such as grouping items in the taskbar based upon user set categories [709] to allowing portions of different, active windows to be manipulated as one window [817]. Scalable Fabric takes this grouping one step further, by allowing users to arbitrarily group windows/applications into a single collection in the compressed periphery; any single window in this collection can be brought to the focus, manipulated, and then returned to its same group [711].

Though bezels interfere with navigation and viewing on large displays, they assist task management [312]. Studies have shown that long time users of multi-monitor configurations naturally partition their work by the bezels—email in one partition, web browsing in another, and work related applications in a third [45]. Such partitions are a human-based application of locality of reference—objects most related to a task are nearest to that task. This partitioning has been used for large flow visualization parameters studies [728]; users of the Hyperwall, a 7 × 7 collection of LCD monitors, visualized a collection of linked parameter spaces (pressure, velocity, etc.) across the display. A similar grouping strategy has been used for managing web exploration histories [709]. Thus, tiled displays are a natural setting for spreadsheet-like visualization environments [65, 159, 339, 402, 504].

Consequences for Visualization. Small and large devices pose new challenges to visualization user interface designers. The following list should be considered when addressing those challenges:

- Focus+context solutions are suitable to small and large scale displays; their use should be considered for any peripheral information management.
- For small devices, careful partitioning and layering of information can be used to expand the amount of information displayed.
- For large devices, proxy interaction widgets (Frisbee, Vacuum, etc.) can be combined with interaction devices (secondary displays, tracked wands, etc.) to address the reaching problem.
- Bezel distortion can be corrected to reduce pointer misdirection and continuous image breaking; in addition, they facilitate compartmentalization of information.

3.2.5 Display Device Challenges in Visualization

Novel display technologies present new opportunities for visualization. Small devices allow visualization to be mobile, forcing the visualization to come to the user instead of the usual way around. Large displays encourage collaboration, macro- and micro-scale visualizations, and "hands-on" interaction. To realize these opportunities, the challenges visualization faces on these devices must be understood. Towards that end, the effects of display scale on interaction have been discussed, a variety of input modalities to communicate with the display have been presented, and interaction methods to enable this communication have been outlined. The guidelines presented here should assist in creating appropriate visualizations given the interaction scale, device, and interface used.

Visualization research on small- and large-scale devices is a fruitful area. Besides addressing issues of scalability, fundamental, human-centric challenges remain:

- How does the size of a visualization affect its perception and cognition? How does the resolution affect it?
- Is there a prescriptive theory of interaction that can encapsulate findings at different interaction distances and display scales?
- What is the most effective way to display millions of items on a small-scale display? How best to interact with these items?
- How do we satisfy the demand for interactivity and high pixel density on large displays when graphics bandwidth is growing very slowly?
- What alternate interaction metaphors can be explored?
- What is the best way to utilize bezels for large, multi-monitor displays?

Answers to these questions will not only benefit visualization, but other users of these displays.

3.3   Multimodal Interaction

The previous section argued that display technologies greatly influence the inter-action that takes place with a visualization on that display. In this section, this topic is broadened towards multimodal interaction, introduced in Section 3.1. Interfaces that allow for multimodal interaction are expected to increase the level of computing accessibility for users of varying ages, skill levels, cognitive styles, sensory and motor impairments, native languages, and even temporary illnesses as Oviatt and Cohen argue in [632]. Firstly, multimodal interaction will be described in more detail. For that, the interaction definitions from Section 3.1 are built upon further. Secondly, the differences between unimodal and multimodal interaction are compared in Section 3.3.1; what kind of interaction differences can be found there? Thirdly, in Section 3.3.4, the technologies that can enable these kinds of interactions are focused upon. To that end, not only the technologies are described but also (research) applications thereof in the field. Note that Section 3.2 already described the display technologies that fall in this category; for that reason, this topic is only briefly touched upon here. Section 3.3.5 aims to provide a chronological overview of research efforts and appliances of multimodal interaction. In addition, future work in this field is identified. This part is concluded in Section 3.3.6 with a description of necessities when aiming to create a multimodal enabled interface for human-centered visualizations.

Based on the impressions received in films (e.g., The Matrix, Minority Report), computer games (e.g., first person shooters and real-time strategy), science fiction books (e.g., Isaac Asimov's Foundation series), the public already has a state of mind when it comes to new forms of human-media interaction. Based on these suggested science fiction factors, there are high user demands on visual representation and also on interaction technologies. However, only few technologies presented in these futuristic scenarios are feasible with the current state-of-the-art devices and systems. However, many research groups are rising to the challenge to improve and enhance human interaction with new technological developments, often based upon natural human behavior.

Interacting with virtual environments is quite challenging. Although numerous research initiatives are found concerning themselves with the topic of human computer interaction (HCI), the interaction in three dimensional space is not simple at all. It is dependent on different issues, e.g., the input and output devices, user ability differences, the objectives of the applications, and so on. Norman [616] described guidelines for interaction, characterized by four usable artifacts: affordances, constraints, good mappings, and feedback. Affordance is a property of an object that links to the usage of the object, e.g., a filled glass with soda affords the possibility of drinking [101]. The constraints limit the actions or interaction possibilities of the user. A good mapping tries to focus on the object based concept or metaphor, which should be as easy as possible for a defined task. In order to provide the user with the information whether he is interacting correctly, feedback should be presented in a comprehensible way.

In Section 3.1, a comprehensive definition of multimodal interaction based on usage of this term in literature was provided [166, 609, 693, 801]. Communication between two social actors/agents using more than one modality to convey useful contributions to the communication process is known as *multimodal interaction*. Such an agent need not be human but can be a computer or other type of (part of a) machine as well, as is argued by (amongst others) Reeves and Nass in their Media Equation [693], see Section 3.1. Human-Computer Interaction (HCI) is the research field in which the interaction between human and computer agents is studied extensively. Application of multimodal interaction in HCI systems is thought to provide a large step forward in the perceived naturalness of the interaction. Taking this towards the human-centered view on multimodal interaction, Reeves et al. [694] argue that

> "Multimodal interfaces should adapt to the needs and abilities of different users, as well as different contexts of use."

This argument couples nicely with the user-centered design approach that has been described extensively in Chapter 2. The user is central in the design of a MI system. This section focuses on multimodal interaction in human-centered visualization environments. A recurring example in this section is the collaborative workspace [692]. Rauwerda et al. [692] define their virtual laboratory *"e-biolab"*, a collaborative scientific workspace, as

> *"[...] an electronic workspace for distance collaboration and experimenta-*
> *tion in research or other creative activity, to generate and deliver results*
> *using distributed information and communication technologies."*

In a collaborative workspace such as the e-biolab, users collaborate to solve a common problem, e.g., medicine discovery. For example, visualizations of discussion points, workflows, results of experiments are required for each user. Using new technologies, the research is moving towards computer supported collaborative work (CSCW). Rauwerda et al. expect to have various visualizations tuned to specific users of their multidisciplinary team. Multimodal interaction may contribute to such an environment by supporting user-specific interaction forms matching the user-specific visualization. The following sections discuss issues that have to be dealt with in order to adequately apply multimodal interaction in visualization environments.

3.3.1 Unimodality Versus Multimodality

This section looks into the differences between unimodal and multimodal interaction. In an effort to classify modalities, Bernsen [82] has developed the Modality Theory. He observed a lack of theoretical understanding how to get from the requirements specification[5] of some application of innovative interactive technology to a selection of the input/output modalities for the application which will optimize the usability and naturalness of interaction. Bernsen's Modality Theory was developed to address this issue, providing better theoretical understanding regarding the principles that should be observed in mapping information from some task domain into presentations at the human-computer interface. To be able to promote this understanding, Bernsen uses his own definitions for medium and modality, albeit virtually identical to the ones proposed in Section 3.1.2.

Modality Theory concerns itself with (representational) modalities and is not about the devices that machines and humans use when they exchange information, such as hands, joysticks, or sensors. This implies that there exists a stable set of modalities that is suited for theoretical treatment. The negative implication of this is that Modality Theory in itself does not address the—often tricky—issues of device selection that might arise at the point where a particular set of input/output modalities for a specific application to be built needs to be chosen [82]. In literature, this topic is not studied very closely. Most often some modalities are selected seemingly out of the blue. The most natural and complementary forms of interaction, speech, and gestures are chosen in many research efforts [122, 131, 172, 257, 399, 629, 761]. Modality Theory further claims to address the general information-mapping problem:

> *"Given any particular set of information which needs to be exchanged*
> *between the user and system during task performance in context, iden-*
> *tify the input/output modalities which constitute an optimal solution*
> *to the representation and exchange of the information."*

---

[5] Again, see Chapter 2 for more information.

Multimodality. Multimodality is referred to as being the combination of two or more modalities. Typically, when speaking of an actual system, speech with vision-based technologies or pen-input are the most mature forms of multimodal interactions, represented in the field in the form of multimodal speech/pen systems and speech/lip movement systems. However, other combinations of modalities may prove even more useful, efficient, and intuitive. Thus, the explicit goal for any multimodal system is, or should be, to integrate complementary modalities in order to combine the strengths of various modalities and overcome their individual weaknesses. In addition, user-specific interaction desires should be included, i.e., allowing a user to find his own best form of multimodal interaction. When selecting modalities for a multimodal-based system, media interference will also need to be taken into consideration—arising whenever two of more media sources provide or obtain mismatching information. This issue is even more substantial when differences between input and output modalities are considered.

Input Versus Output Modalities. The Modality Theory by Bernsen [82] provides a taxonomy of modalities. His starting point is the assumption that modalities can be either unimodal or multimodal and that multimodal modalities are combinations of unimodalities. This means that multimodality can be completely and uniquely defined in terms of unimodalities. Bernsen adopts a generative approach for building the taxonomy, the core of which centers on how to generate the unimodalities. Then, through intuition, analysis, and experiment, the unimodalities generated from basic properties are tested whether they satisfy the following requirements:

- *Completeness.* Any piece of—possibly multimodal—output information in various media, such as graphics, acoustics, and haptics, can be exhaustively described as consisting of one or more unimodalities.
- *Uniqueness.* Any piece of output information in those media can be characterized in only one way in terms of unimodalities.
- *Relevance.* The set captures the important differences between different modalities.
- *Intuitiveness.* The interaction developers recognize the set as corresponding to their intuitive notion of the modalities they need or might need.

The difference between multimodal input and output is still unclear. Thus, Bernsen [82] describes multimodal *input* as the interactive information going from a source A to a receiver B, where B has to decode the information sent by A. Notice that A and B may be either humans or systems. Typically, A will be a human and B will be a system. Bernsen takes for granted that humans know a lot about what can take place in an interaction in which both A and B are humans, or in which several humans interact together, possibly in a cooperative setting, as well as interacting with a system. However, this assumption by Bernsen is not necessarily true, think simply of miscommunication in a dialogue between humans: ambiguous information is not decoded correctly in all cases. Multimodal *output* is directly opposed to the definition of *input* and is thus defined as the interactive information going from B (typically the machine) to A (typically a human). Note that visualization is thus a single type of multimodal output. In Table 3.2 an overview of input and output modalities is given. This table describes the important contributing research areas in the field of multimodal interaction systems. Note that some research areas overlap between research topics, i.e. those found in the bottom row. As should become clear by observing Table 3.2, the number of research areas brushing against the topic of multimodal interaction is vast. Topics like user modeling (Chapter 2) and cognitive science (Chapter 4) have already been or will be described in this book. In Section 3.3.4, more details on sensor technologies enabling multimodal input and output are found. Other research areas have been described extensively, for example by Russel and Norvig [724] (machine learning) and Varci and Vieu [857] (formal ontologies).

Table 3.2. An overview of enabling technologies and important contributing research areas regarding multimodality [609].

Multimodal input	Multimodal interaction	Multimodal output
Sensor technologies	User modeling	Smart graphics
Vision	Cognitive science	Design theory
Speech and audio technology	Discourse theory	Embodied conversational agents
Biometrics	Ergonomics	Speech synthesis
Machine learning, Formal ontologies, Pattern recognition, Planning		

Jaimes and Sebe [399] describe a multimodal human-computer interaction system simply as one that responds to inputs in more than one modality or communication channel. They advocate a human-centered approach to multimodal HCI systems in that he distinguishes between the mode of communication according to human senses or type of computer input devices. When speaking in terms of the former, the categories of sight, touch, hearing, smell, and taste can be identified, i.e., the human senses themselves. Speaking in terms of the latter, computer input devices—referred to as modality output in the user-centered definition— are equivalent but not identical to the human senses: cameras (sight), haptic sensors (touch), microphones (hearing), olfactory (smell), and even taste. Most of the more familiar input devices do not map directly to a human sense, or set of senses. Think of the keyboard, pen, or mouse. In research on multimodality, speech and language take primacy [609]; other modalities are often considered mere add-ons.

Perceptive interfaces are highly interactive, multimodal interfaces that enable rich, natural, and efficient interaction with computers. They seek to leverage sensing and rendering, input and output respectively, in order to provide interactions that are infeasible using only current standard interfaces. Gestures are assigned a crucial role in human-human and human-computer interaction schemes.

In literature, scientists seem to agree on the thesis that multimodal communication is a form of interaction that holds the promise of solving the problems associated with traditional unimodal interaction by combining multiple modalities such as pen and speech interaction, thus taking the best of both worlds [632,801]. However, several points of attention can be discerned when choosing and, equally if not more important, combining modalities.

3.3.2   Issues to Deal with in Multimodal Interaction

When choosing a multimodal interaction scheme for a system, various issues arise. These issues include but are not limited to selecting the ideal combination of input and output modalities, devices that provide the opted interaction possibilities, ambiguity of individual modalities, and designing the underlying hardware/software of the system. This section describes the most important and well known issues that one comes across when creating a multimodal interaction scheme.

The Wait Problem. The best known problem when combining modalities is the *wait problem*, occurring in cases in which a system should wait for a speech utterance to modify the intention of an observed gesture [800]. Waiting in such a case is necessary, because the modification may express an intention that is not compatible with the action that would be triggered without the modification. Long delays are not acceptable as normal behavior of any system; thus a (wait) problem has arisen. In principle, it is not restricted to the case of determining the intention of a deictic gesture. Streit [800] exemplifies this statement by describing a system enhanced with features of natural communication. In natural communication, one can also think of modifying a manipulation instead of completely skipping the manipulative meaning. One could specify an action by gesture and in parallel specify by speech that the action should be performed in a certain mode (e.g., fast or as usual), thereby unfolding the hidden communicative nature of direct manipulation. Streit proposes several ways with which the wait problem may be resolved:

- Promoting synchronization of multimodal user utterances and thus keeping gaps between multimodal input as short as possible.
- Identifying the cases in which gaps are harmless.
- Providing certain features to reduce the critical cases.

Oviatt [630] describes the discovery that when users speak and gesture in a sequential manner, they firstly gesture and then speak within a relatively short time slot; speech rarely precedes gesture. This silent assumption is found at the basis of the wait problem; a gesture should always precede or occur simultaneously with speech, otherwise the possibility arises that modifying speech by gesture will not result in a complete change of meaning of the spoken utterance.

Efficiency Gains. It has been assumed in the field of multimodal systems that efficiency gains would be the main advantage of designing a multimodal interface and that this advantage would derive directly from the ability to process input modes in parallel. Although it is true that multimodal interfaces sometimes support improved efficiency—especially when manipulating graphical information, e.g., recall the "Multimax Principle" from Section 3.1.2—this is not necessarily the case. In research on simulation, comparing speech-only with multimodal pen/voice interaction, empirical work demonstrated that multimodal interaction yielded a 10% faster task completion time during visual spatial tasks. However, no significant efficiency advantage in verbal or quantitative task domains was observed [172]. Notice that the amount of obtained system efficiency need not necessarily increase when selecting multimodal interaction for that system. This should be studied and, equally if not more important, evaluated with care in order to yield the meant efficiency gain(s).

Combining Modalities. A typical issue of multimodal data processing is that multisensory data is typically processed separately and is only combined at the end. Yet, people convey multimodal, audio and visual, communicative signals in a complementary but also redundant manner [131,399,484,633,641,859]. Jaimes and Sebe [399] conclude, based on this observation, that in order to accomplish a human-like multimodal analysis of various different input signals, those signals cannot be considered mutually independent and cannot be combined in a context-free manner at the end of the intended analysis. The input data should be processed in a joint feature space and according to a context dependent model. A potential way to achieve multisensory data fusion is to develop context-dependent versions of a suitable method.

Mutual Disambiguation. An advantage of a multimodal system is that it provides the possibility of mutual disambiguation [629,631]. Mutual disambiguation involves the disambiguation of signal or semantic-level information in one error-prone input mode by making use of partial information supplied by another. Mutual disambiguation can occur in a multimodal architecture in which two or more semantically recognition-based input modes are found. It leads to recovery from unimodal recognition errors within the multimodal architecture, the net effect of which is suppressing the errors experienced by the user. Bourget recently addressed this topic and proposes a taxonomy to guide choice and design of error-handling in multimodal interaction systems [100]. One main conclusion of Bourget's work is that context-awareness is of paramount importance for error-handling in multimodal interaction systems.

System Architecture. The advance of multimodal systems is not just a matter of adding modalities although, from a technological point of view, systems that combine several modalities are believed to be more suitable for relatively demanding applications, e.g., a computer-supported discovery environment [190]. Multimodality should be adjusted to human cognitive and perceptual processing.

Currently, multimodal systems are being developed rapidly, with an increased interest in multimodal dialogue systems as a subgroup. The goal of such a dialogue system is to listen and understand a typed or spoken user request and to subsequently generate a suitable response. By nature, multimodal dialogue systems process information from different types of input and output modalities in parallel. Multi-Agent System (MAS) architectures are typically used in multimodal dialogue systems because of the need for parallel processing of different modalities. The Open Agent Architecture [171] and Adaptive Agent Architecture [483] are examples of Multi-Agent Systems that provide a flexible infrastructure for the different information flows employed by multimodal dialogue systems. In these MAS architectures, different tasks for processing multimodal input and output are often coordinated by a central agent; in the Quickset system [172] this agent is named the *Facilitator*. Collaborating agents include those that facilitate speech and gesture recognition, database access, multimodal integration, and so on.

Van der Sluis [844] describes how a multimodal dialogue system can be, and typically is, roughly split up into three parts:

- *The input side* which focuses on understanding and interpretation of the user input. This information is then typified by hypothesis management, i.e., by selecting the most suitable interpretation for a given combination of user inputs[6].
- *The output side* which addresses language generation and which can be characterized as a process of choice, i.e., deciding what to respond and how the response is formulated, given the means available.
- *The dialogue management* which takes the care of the coordination between the input and output of the system.

In a multimodal dialogue system architecture, there are two ways for integrating different modalities: early fusion and late fusion as is extensively discussed by several authors [74, 131, 484, 631, 633, 641, 859]. With early fusion [484, 641], the modalities are integrated at the feature level which is suitable for modalities that display a strong temporal connection, such as speech and facial expressions or gestures. Bellik [74] noted that in general technologies do not provide a means to fuse modalities at a low level. She addresses this issue and proposes to design new technologies to support successful integration. In contrast, late fusion integrates the modalities at the semantic level. Late fusion is therefore applicable to modalities that contain complementary information that is not strictly temporally bound, like speech and pen input.

3.3.3 Myths of Multimodality

There are some misconceptions on the principles of multimodal interaction which this section will clarify. Oviatt [630] described ten myths of multimodal interaction—empirically proven false—which can guide us in the application of multimodal interaction. First of all, when users are confronted with a multimodal system, there is no guarantee that they will interact with it in a multimodal fashion. Note that this contradicts with the Multimax principle that was introduced

---

[6] Note that a multitude of input modalities is not required.

in Section 3.1.2. Most of the time, unimodal interaction is likely to be observed. As described before, in speech and gesture multimodal systems, signals are not simultaneous. This is not only true for an example system combining speech and pointing modalities but also for other combinations of modalities. In addition, speech and pointing are falsely thought to be the dominant multimodal interaction pattern. Speech is not even the primary input mode in a multimodal interaction system [630, 822].

Multimodal language is different from unimodal language. Deictic gestures can be made that are accompanied by greatly simplified spoken utterances, e.g., *"Put that there"* [99] whilst subsequently pointing towards an object and a location. Modalities cannot be uniformly integrated, each user can have his own interaction preference. It was shown though that a user's preference was established early and remains consistent during a session. In addition, redundancy of content between modes is opposite reality. Modalities complement one another to yield even more semantic information when compared with those modalities separately. As described above, enhanced efficiency is not *the* advantage of multimodal systems. Other more noteworthy advantages include a drop in task-critical errors and satisfying the user's strong preference to interact multimodally.

3.3.4 Survey of Enabling Technologies

As from now, the focus turns from multimodal interaction theory towards practice. It is clear by now that technological developments enable new forms of interaction. Here, a state-of-the-art overview of enabling technologies available today is provided. Display technologies have already been introduced in Section 3.2.1 and are excluded from this survey. In this piece, commercial and research concepts are described. Note that a lack of public availability is typically caused by development time and costs. When a product matures, these hold-backs diminish making innovative technologies available to the main public. This then increases the possibilities for more extensive research with those technologies.

Communicative messages observed in humans is most often thought of in the combination of speech and gestures. Gestures can be defined to include gaze direction etc. Cohen et al. [172] showed that multimodal pen/voice interaction is advantageous for small devices, for mobile users who may encounter different circumstances, for error avoidance and correction, and for robustness. The QuickSet system provides military commanders to observe and interact with a map of the battlefield using one of many interface devices, e.g., a workbench and tablet PC. A multimodal voice/gesture interface complements, but also promises to address the limitations of current GUI technologies for controlling simulators. In addition, it has been shown to have numerous advantages over voice-only interaction for such map-based tasks.

There are huge amounts of interaction devices with different functionalities and purposes. Some of them are prototypes built by research groups in order to fit their specific needs. Others are commercially available devices. They vary from a simple computer mouse or keyboard to high complex interaction systems, e.g., a virtual reality suit which is used for a full body tracking of the interacting

Fig. 3.3. Emerging and more established technologies that contribute to enabling multimodal interaction. (a) The CyberGrasp exoskeleton glove [178]. © *2006 Immersion Corp. Reprinted with permission.* (b) A pen device. *Image courtesy of Wacom Europe®.* (c) And a selection of SensAble's PHANTOM haptic devices [748]. © *2006 SensAble Technologies, Inc. Reprinted with permission.*

human or haptic devices which will be discussed later. Some of possibilities are illustrated in Figure 3.3.

The reader must also distinguish between pure input devices like a mouse keyboard and devices providing output opportunities, e.g., force feedback devices [134]. This is one of the most challenging topics nowadays. In order being able to interact properly with a virtual environment, the user should "feel" the interaction, e.g., the grabbing of an object. With the common state-of-the-art devices, it is not yet possible to do this unobtrusively because they are too big or too uncomfortable. However, the design and development has improved over the last years and will definitely evolve in the next years. So, this is one of the most challenging topics nowadays.

Every device has a different set of degrees of freedom (DOF) for movement and orientation. As an example, the PHANTOM haptic device (see Fig-

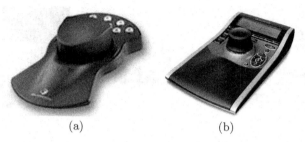

(a)   (b)

Fig. 3.4. 3D desktop devices [1]. (a) 3Dconnexion® Spacemouse® Plus. (b) 3Dconnexion® SpacePilot^{TM}. *Image courtesy of T. Kenthen, 3Dconnexion Inc.*

ure 3.3(c) [748]) has six degrees of freedom: heave, sway, surge, pitch, yaw, and roll. Note that this is only a single definition for DOF, e.g., in robotics an (human) arm is said to have seven DOF, adding up the possible pivots or movements of each joint. A difficult task is to select a suited device for a specific problem, especially given the device-specific DOF. Note that a distinction can be made between input and output devices and devices that can do both, e.g., the PHANTOM. The interaction is not only limited to one hand of the user. There are several approaches using both hands for interacting with the virtual environment. Therefore, the non-dominant hand is used as a frame of reference, where the dominant hand is used for fine or precise assignment [231, 297, 352].

Some existing, matured through practice, technologies include pen, speech, and computer vision technologies. Note that these technologies vary in the required processing steps for their user's input to be understood by the system, e.g., applying computer vision typically requires extensive image processing [256]. Less mature technologies are mostly based on haptic devices, the kind described in the survey by Khoudja et al. [445]. Note that haptic devices can provide feedback to the user in addition to the user providing input to the system, this is known as force feedback. Some examples of these technologies are depicted in Figure 3.3.

Basic Interaction Devices. Most users are accustomed to some level of interaction with a computer, typically using the combination of keyboard and mouse or joystick. These and similar devices are typically considered "basic" or relatively unsophisticated interaction devices. In case of most consumer products, e.g., computer games, these "basic" interaction devices are considered superior in user's efficiency, effectiveness, and satisfaction, when compared with more elaborate devices, e.g., data gloves. For scientific interaction, research has been performed on the question what more elaborate interaction devices, e.g., the PHANTOM, contribute to an interaction, and how and consequently for what purpose they should be used.

In order to provide suitable 3D interaction the idea of the desktop mouse has been extended to six degrees of freedom, e.g., the Spacemouse or Spacepilot [1] (see Figures 3.4). These desktop devices can be easily used in order to navigate in a three dimensional virtual environment. One disadvantage of these naviga-

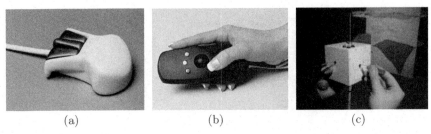

(a)   (b)   (c)

Fig. 3.5. Extended tracked interaction devices. (a) The Ascension 6D Mouse [34]. *http://www.ascension-tech.com.* (b) The Ascension Wanda device [34]. *http://www.ascension-tech.com.* And (c), the Cubic Mouse™ [272]. *Image courtesy of Fraunhofer IAO, CCVE, Germany.*

tion devices is their stationary usage, limiting the user's freedom of movement. In order to avoid this fact, hand-held devices, e.g., the bat [878], the Wanda device [34], the dragon fly and bug devices [791], or the cubic mouse [272] (see Figures 3.5), have been developed, which can be used in front of large visualization displays, e.g., a CAVE [182,183] or PowerWall [244], recall Section 3.2.1. Most of these devices are using a tracking mechanism in order to get the correct position in the real world. The tracking itself and the underlying tracking techniques will be discussed in the follow up section.

Tracking Devices. Taking into regard large display systems like CAVEs [182, 183], Powerwalls, or tiled displays, the usage of basic devices or even haptic devices for interaction is very uncomfortable, unnatural, and often downright impossible, as also described in Section 3.2. In order to control the virtual environment, several alternative approaches exist, e.g., the tracking of alternative interaction devices or even the tracking of the position and gestures of the user. In such cases, tracking a device's position and often its orientation is needed in order to make meaningful measurements on the user's intentions.

Various tracking technologies exist, each with their distinct advantages and disadvantages. A short overview about the available tracking technologies is provided, including some examples thereof. First of all, tracking devices can be evaluated based on their values of jitter, update rates, latency, drift, and accuracy (see Table 3.3). This offers the ability of evaluating the devices and their different tracking technologies.

Mechanical Tracking. The first used devices have been mechanical tracking devices introduced by Sutherland [807]. He build up a CRT-based Head-Mounted Display (HMD) which was attached to the ceiling. The position and the orientation of the user is calculated relative to a reference point using the kinematic properties of the devices. The tracking can be handled in real-time, is extremely accurate and is immune to metallic interference.

Nowadays, only few commercial mechanical systems exist, e.g., the Gypsy motion tracking suites [28] that use gyro sensors. These systems are nevertheless no *pure* mechanical tracking systems. It is not attached to the ceiling or any

Table 3.3. Tracking device parameters.

Problems	Description	Notes
Accuracy	Difference between the object's actual 3D position and that reported by tracker measurements	Measurement in translation and rotation
Jitter	Change in tracker output when tracking a stationary object	Needs to be minimized
Drift	Increase of the tracking error in time	Tracker reset needed
Latency	Time delay between action and result	Should be kept small
Update rate	Number of datasets per second recorded by the tracker	Real-time issue

desktop. A magnetic tracker, discussed later on, is used for the tracking of the user's position. Only the relative position and orientation of the joints and bones is mechanically measured. It is a so called hybrid tracking system, also discussed later on. Pure mechanical systems also have some serious drawbacks, e.g., the limitation of the workspace, the weight, and the users' freedom of motion.

Magnetic Tracking. Keeping in mind those disadvantages of mechanical trackers, many have been replaced by other tracking techniques. One of the most common is the magnetic tracking. By using a magnetic field, the position of the receiver element can be calculated without being dependent on a direct line of sight. There are two different types of magnetic trackers: AC and DC trackers. AC trackers, e.g., the Polhemus Fastrak® [656], use an alternating field of 7-14 kHz. The DC tracker, e.g., the Ascension Flock of Birds™ or MotionStar™ [34] use pulsed fields.

In addition to the more "conventional" tracking approaches using magnetic sensors, alternative applications for magnetic tracking have been studied. As an example in his Ph.D. thesis, Hansen described the application of magnetic sensors for eye tracking [328]. A metallic ring was placed on the eye, much like a contact-lens. A magnetic field and sensors where than used to detect the user's eye locations. A conclusion of this work was that although the accuracy was high, the human implications, e.g., influence of the magnetic field, is currently too badly understood for long term application.

Nixon et al. [612] showed that the trackers can be influenced or distorted by ferromagnetic metals or copper. The metallic distortion for DC fields is significantly less sensitive than for AC fields. However, the DC tracking systems interfere with magnetic fields generated by ferromagentic objects, e.g., loudspeakers or monitors. Another fact is that the error rate is increasing dependent on the distance between transmitter and receiver. This influence was also noted by Fikkert [256] whom tried to obtain ground-truth for passively obtained user head orientation estimations. The driving simulator in which these measure-

(a)   (b)

Fig. 3.6. Optical Tracking Devices. (a) NaturalPoint® OptiTrack™ [599]. *Image courtesy of K. Fox, NaturalPoint Inc.* (b) Qualisys® ProReflex® [681]. *Image courtesy of A. Lundqvist, Qualisys AB.*

ments should be obtained contained great pieces of metal, influencing measured orientations greatly.

Ultrasonic/Ultrasound Tracking. Ultrasonic trackers track an object's position using ultrasound. The speed of sound through air is used to calculate the distance between the transmitter of an ultrasonic pulse and the receiver of that pulse. This speed is depending on the density of the air which depends on temperature. The sound pulse is also reduced by the humidity of air. Another drawback is the possible interference with other present sound devices and the necessity of a direct line of sight. One big advantage of these ultrasonic devices is affordability.

Optical Tracking.. Optical trackers go beyond magnetic trackers; the most often used tracking systems. Optical sensors (cameras) are used in order to determine the position and the orientation of an object which then can be calculated using trigonometrical mathematical equations. Cameras exist that detect various parts in the electromagnetic spectrum. Camera examples include:

– Black and white
– Infrared
– Natural light[7]
– Laser

Depending on the used camera (e.g., the NDigital® Polaris® [620] or the NaturalPoint® OptiTrack™ [599] (see Figure 3.6)), very high update rates are possible. Many commercially available cameras or tracking systems are still marker-based tracking systems, (e.g., Brunnett and Rusdorf [723]) which guarantee a high accuracy. The trackable objects can be balls in every size or pattern, where pattern recognition techniques are used in order to transmit more information. However, being dependent on a marker and the position of the marker on the interacting person is not really intuitive and cumbersome.

---

[7] Typically, "natural light" is defined as the part of the electromagnetic spectrum visible to humans.

Nowadays, researchers are focusing on markerless tracking [140,277,278]. In markerless tracking the position of the users hand and head is detected and used for interaction purposes [564]. Carranza et al. [147] build up a markerless tracking system which uses common computer vision techniques in order to estimate the user's position and gestures in the real world. The data are then mapped to a virtual model. This interaction is more intuitive. As already mentioned in Chapter 3.2.3, research is also done on real time tracking of human eyes [215, 328,368,398,929] or faces without any markers [917,928]. Not being dependent on any further devices, markerless tracking and its corresponding interaction have become one of the most challenging topics in computer vision research. Moeslund and Granum [563] provide an overview of computer vision based human motion capturing which currently is the main focus of the computer vision research area.

One big advantage of optical tracking is the immunity to ferromagnetic materials and the low latency time which make them very attractive for researchers. However, optical tracking systems are also dependent on the line of sight. In order to solve this issue, different filter techniques, e.g., Kalman filters [425, 581, 887, 888] or Wiener filters [892], are used that try to estimate the position or orientation of the target depending on the previously measured position or orientation.

Inertial and Hybrid Tracking. Inertial trackers use gyroscopes and accelerometers in order to track the rate of change of the orientation and the velocity change. Inertial sensors are only influenced by gravitation. So, direct information about the current position is not provided. Advantages include the lack for a direct line of sight and the low jitter noise. A main disadvantage is the drift error that accumulates over time. This can only be solved by resetting the sensor.

These systems are typically combined with an acoustical, optical, or magnetic tracker in order to receive the correct position of the person or object. This leads to the so called *hybrid tracking systems* that combine two or more tracking technologies, e.g., the Gypsy® tracking suit (see Figure 3.7 (white)) by Animazoo [28].

Concluding, every piece of tracking technology has its advantages and also disadvantages. Researchers have to take care for what purpose or application they want to use the tracking. They should also keep in mind what update rates and what accuracy they really need. Furthermore, they should consider the visual representation they want to use in reality and where they want to setup the tracking environment. Table 3.4 can be used as a summarization and evaluation of the different technologies.

Gesture Interfaces. Finding a natural way of interaction is a huge effort, as was described in Section 3.3.2. One possibility is the usage of gesture-recognizing interfaces that provide more accuracy than tracking devices and are very intuitive. Nowadays, most devices used for this interaction technique are gloves with embedded sensors. According to the sensor values, the position of the fingers can be calculated. For gesture recognition, these positions are compared to a stored set of defined gestures in order to interact with the virtual environment. Another possibility is the interaction with virtual objects in the virtual environment. So,

Fig. 3.7. Different tracking suits [28]: inertial (left), magnetic (center) and optical (right) tracked suits. *Image courtesy of Animazoo.*

Table 3.4. Tracking device characteristics.

Problems	Mechanic	Magnetic	Acoustic	Optical
Accuracy	++	+	−	++
Latency	++ (lowest)	++	− − (highest)	++
Update rate	+	+	0	++
Line of sight	not needed	not needed	needed	needed
Range	− −	−	−	++
Interferences	none	magnetic	sound sources	illumination
Weight	− −	+	+	++

while interacting the user has the advantage of a multi finger interaction fulfilling different tasks which provides a higher flexibility and definitely simplifies many tasks. The data gloves can be used not only for grabbing issues but also for the navigation or other tasks specified by the gesture library.

In order to get the correct position in space, the data glove has to be connected to a tracking system. Otherwise the data glove is not really efficient. The well known state-of-the-art devices are the Immersion CyberGlove [385], the Fifth Technology 5DT Data Glove [2], the EssentialReality P5 Cyberglove [242], and the Fakespace Pinch® Glove [244] (see Figure 3.8). Not every device has the same properties. The main differences amongst these state-of-the-art devices are the

− amount of sensors
− types of sensors

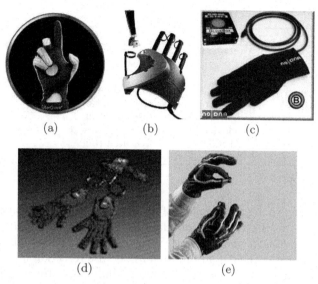

Fig. 3.8. Common commercial available data gloves. (a) CyberGlove® II [385]. © *2006 Immersion Corp. Reprinted with permission.* (b) Essential Reality P5 Glove [242]. (c) X-IST DataGlove [614]. (d) 5DT DataGlove Ultra Wireless [2]. *http://www.5dt.com.* And (e), Pinch® Glove [244]. *Image courtesy of Fakespace Labs, Mountain View, CA, USA.*

— resolution of the sensors
— sampling rates of the glove
— interface connection

A clear disadvantage of using data gloves is the varying size of the human hand between users. This results in different sensor locations for each user that needs to be accounted for. Typically, for every new user the data gloves have to be reconfigured in order to efficiently match the user specific configuration of the fingers and size of the hand. The Pinch Glove [244] need not be calibrated in this manner, it measures the contacts and the contact time of the fingertip, the finger back and palm electrodes. Consequently, there's no possibility of a specific readout of the finger configuration which are typically the angles of the fingers.

Haptics. Khoudja et al. [445] provide a state-of-the-art survey on tactile interfaces with which a user can express himself towards the system using touch but also with which the system can express itself towards the user via the same sense. The human haptic sense[8] is composed of two modalities: the kinesthetic sense (force and motion) and the tactile sense (tact and touch). It is obviously associated to the sense of touch [98,382]. Note that this distinction between modalities of the human haptic sense is not based on human physiology but is in fact based on a user's input (tactile) and output (kinesthetic) modalities. Khoudja et al.

---

[8] The term "haptic" is based on the Greek "hapthai" which means "to touch".

Table 3.5. Skin Receptors.

Receptor Types	Sensing	Comments
Thermo receptors	temperature	specialized in cold and heat receptors; sensitive between 5° C to 48° C
Nociceptors	pain	triggers the pain response
Merkel disks	pressure	slow adapting
Ruffini corpuscles	skin stretch	slow adapting
Meissner corpuscles	light touching; velocity	fast adapting
Pacinian corpuscles	vibration; deep pressure	fast adapting

show that there are a great number of devices available with which a user can interact with a system, varying from data gloves to fluid-based interfaces. Note that typically, no matter how advanced, such a device in itself allows unimodal interaction, following the definition of multimodal interaction in Section 3.1.2.

The tactile stimulus is affected by different kind of receptors under the human skin. They are located in the dermis and receive and transmit the signals to the brain. There are different kinds of receptors in the skin which are shortly summarized in Table 3.5. The density of the pressure receptors varies along the human body. On the fingertips, it is possible to distinguish distances about one millimeter and on the back about sixty millimeters. This can easily be demonstrated with the so-called two-point threshold test [201, 554, 590]. The temperature receptors (thermo receptors) are specialized receptors for the feeling of heat and cold. Humans are able to distinguish temperature changes in the range of 5° C to 48° C. The receptors for pain are called nociceptors.

The other previously mentioned kinesthetic stimuli represent the states of the joints and arms. In detail, these are the angularity and position of the bones and the tension or relaxation of the muscles. So, in a haptic sense, kinesthetic devices exert controlled forces on the human body in order to provide the interaction or feedback.

(a)   (b)   (c)

Fig. 3.9. Examples of widely available force feedback devices. (a) Logitech® Rumblepad™ [511]. *Image courtesy of G. Karbautzki, Logitech GmbH.* (b) Saitek® R440 Force Feedback Wheel [726]. And (c), Saitek Cyborg evo Force™ [725]. *Image courtesy of Saitek Inc.*

Haptic Devices. A vast amount of devices exist for the stimulation of the sense of touch. A popular example is the mobile phone with a vibrating alert function. The most popular/common devices are force feedback gaming devices, examples of which are depicted in Figure 3.9. They are enhancements of standard input devices, providing tactile feedback to the user. Nowadays, gaming force feedback devices are widely available on the consumer market. They are however, seldom used for scientific applications. Other devices with a higher accuracy of tactile feedback simulation have been developed. The amount of industries manufacturing haptic devices has been increasing in the past few years. Availability of haptic devices is not an issue (any more). There are two different kinds of haptic devices:

- (Vibro) tactile devices
- Force feedback devices

The main difference between these device types is the method in which the feedback is provided. Tactile devices, e.g., the Immersion® CyberTouch™ (see Figure 3.10(b) [385]), braille display systems [862], or the off-the-shelf mobile phones with a vibrating alert function, offer the possibility of stimulating the user into performing a specific task. This action refers to the touching of objects. In addition, touch is the most important sense for visually impaired people. Many applications are trying to help or support these users by displaying information using braille displays [5] or tactile stimuli. The stimulation of the fingertip is provided by using a pin-matrix which represents information, e.g., shapes or braille. Based on these displays, there have been approaches of simulating larger shapes, e.g., maps or images, using tactile displays [865]. Other touch-based devices include PDA's, tablet PC's, or public information terminals. These devices do not provide tactile feedback but are mentioned for completion. Most of these devices are capable of detecting a single touch location at any given time, due to technological constraints. Research is underway however to overcome this problem. Han [326] described an approach to enable detecting multiple touch locations and concluded that some of the main current drawbacks is the inability to detect touch locations of distinct sources, i.e. of two hands as opposed to one. Other researchers [199, 539] have also described a similar approach to the multi-user, multi-touch problem addressed by Han's multi-touch approach. Most often a vision-based approach is used to detect users touching a canvas. However, difficulties still remain in determining the origin of a touch location. Extending on these touch-based devices, the first thermal tactile displays have been build [387, 565] in 1993 which also give a thermal feedback. These devices are nowadays mostly controlled by heating and cooling elements, e.g., peltier cells [141, 446, 475].

The previously mentioned joysticks, depicted in Figure 3.9, belong to the group of kinestethic/force-feedback devices. These devices focus on the force output in order to represent the mass or the stiffness of objects and collisions with those objects. Example devices include the Immersion® CyberGrasp™ (see Figure 3.10(c)), the SensAble® PHANTOM™ device (see Figure 3.10(a)), the FCS HapticMASTER (see Figure 3.10(e)), and magnetic levitation haptic device

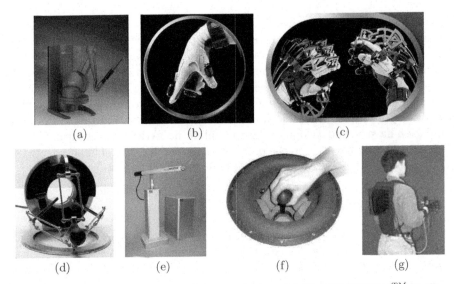

Fig. 3.10. Examples of (well known) haptic devices. (a) The PHANTOM^{TM} Desktop Device [546, 748]. (b) The CyberTouch^{TM} and (c) the CyberGrasp^{TM} Device [385]. © *2006 Immersion Corp. Reprinted with permission.* (d) The Force Dimension Omega [263]. *Image courtesy of Force Dimension, Switzerland.* (e) The FCS Haptic-MASTER [249]. (f) The magnetic levitation haptic device by Berkelman and Hollis [80,81]. *Image courtesy of Carnegie Mellon University.* And (g), the GraspPack^{TM} [385]. © *2006 Immersion Corp. Reprinted with permission.*

(developed at the Carnegie Mellon University [80,81], see Figure 3.10(f)). Most of the devices are static grounded devices, so they are not portable. This lack of portability and the freedom of movement is one of the biggest problems when using haptic devices in combination with large screen displays like PowerWalls or CAVE's® [484]. As a result, haptic devices are mostly used for single user workstations or workbenches. There are some approaches for portable haptic force feedback devices as the Immersion® GraspPack^{TM} (see Figure 3.10(g)). Nevertheless, the portability results in the weights of the devices the user has to carry while interacting with the virtual environment [133].

Haptics devices can be and are used in many different application areas. One example is the medical interaction in which applications include training of medicine students and doctors performing surgery, e.g., endoscopic surgery [460, 509]. They have a haptical force feedback of what they are really doing, training their ability to perform surgery on real humans. Haptics provide an opportunity for the visually impaired to interact with or to explore written text in addition to images and other virtual objects.

Modeling objects in virtual reality is another application domain for which haptic devices are quite suited. This area is not limited to members of the computer graphics and geometric modeling society or engineers (CAD). Many art schools or artists have begun to use haptic devices for modeling, painting, or sculpturing [155, 551].

For tele-operating systems, haptic devices can provide force feedback and improve the interaction. One useful application in this area is the disposal of explosive ordnances [476]. Tele-operating systems supported with haptic devices can be used in dangerous real environments in order to prevent injuries and save human lives.

Audio Interfaces. Other devices that can be used in order to improve the interacting of users also exist. One of them is the 3D sound output, allowing the user to co-locate the sound source of virtual objects [266]. Commonly used devices vary from simple stereo speakers to high end surround sound systems, which are based on different Dolby systems, e.g., Dolby Surround or Dolby Digital or DTS[9].

Considering the sound output, there is also the sound input or speech recognition. When talking of speech recognition, many users think about writing a text using a microphone. But, speech interaction is more powerfull than that. It can be used for different interaction purposes [192, 431, 477, 733]. One of the first interaction systems was mentioned in Section 3.1.2: the *"Put that there"* system by Bolt in 1980 [99]. This idea was extended by Krum et al., who presented an application for multimodal interaction and control using speech and gestures of a whole Earth 3D visualization environment [477]. Speech therefore is very commonly used for cursor control or object manipulation, e.g., translations or rotations [625]. The input is not only limited to a single recording device. Microphone arrays allow operators to pinpoint, track and amplify individual voices in a crowd, or a multiuser environment [111, 160, 794, 917].

Olfactory Interfaces and Taste Interfaces. Another approach to sense stimulation are olfactory devices that can add the smell to the currently presented virtual environment [434, 793, 914, 915]. An olfactory device created by Yanagida et al. [915] is able to track the users nose and uses an air cannon in order to fire small packets of scented air to the user's nose. The commercially available Scent Dome[TM] [834] provides twenty different aroma cartridges. The odour can enhance the users perception and provide additional real information, e.g., when moving in a virtual rose garden, a rose odour can be sprayed into the air in order to simulate the smell. In order to complete the list of senses which can be addressed, there's also the food simulator by Iwata et al. [397] which simulates the biting force—a form of tactile feedback. The taste of food arises from a combination of chemical, auditory, olfactory, and haptic sensation.

Skipping Technological Developments. Various studies [445, 630, 632, 801] regarding the application of multimodal interaction concede that new developments in enabling technologies increases the drive of multimodal interaction developments by providing new possibilities for humans to interact with systems. By applying emerging techniques, it is possible to devise new methods and application areas in which they can be applied. As an example, Holman et

---

[9] Digital Theather Systems by DTS Inc.

al. [360] created the PaperWindows system that makes assumptions on the currently emerging technology of flexible displays. Their system enables its users to use an ordinary piece of paper as if it were a flexible display; a beamer projects contents on the paper that is detected using a computer vision approach. By doing so, an emerging technology can be used without being developed in full. In addition, new insights gathered from such a study can then be applied in the development process of these displays thus providing practical feedback.

3.3.5 Overview of Approaches to Multimodal Interaction

The previous section described technologies enabling users to interact with a HCVE. This section aims to provide an overview of multimodal interaction approaches and research efforts, biased towards the HCVE. A chronological order is used, first describing past approaches, moving onwards to current developments in the field. This approach was chosen in order to identify trends in multimodal interaction system development resulting in future directions. Note that numerous studies of approaches to multimodal interaction have already been introduced and will be left out here. For those approaches refer to Sections 3.1.1, 3.2.3, and 3.3.2.

Past Developments. In one of the earliest multimodal concept demonstrations, Bolt had users sit in front of a projection of *"Dataland"* in the *"Media Room"*. Using the famous *"put that there"* interface [99], they could use speech and pointing on an armrest-mounted touchpad to create and move objects on a 2D large-screen display. For example, the user could issue a command to "create a blue square there" with the intended location of "there" indicated by a 2D cursor mark on the screen. Semantic processing was based on the users' spoken input, and the meaning of the deictic "there" was resolved by processing the x- and y-coordinate indicated by the cursor at the time "there" was uttered. Since Bolt's early prototype, considerable strides have been made in developing a wide variety of different types of multimodal systems.

Oviatt [631] provides some insight into past developments on multimodality in general HCI. Among the earliest and most rudimentary multimodal systems were systems that supported speech input along with a standard keyboard and mouse interface. This is not that dissimilar from Bolt's system as the gestures are in essence nothing more than point-and-click events. Conceptually, these early multimodal interfaces represented the least departure from traditional graphical user interfaces (GUIs). They belong to the WIMP paradigm with which most computer users are familiar. The initial focus of GUIs was to support richer natural language processing in order to support greater expressive power for the user when manipulating complex visualizations and engaging in information extraction. During the last decades, Automated Speech Recognition (ASR) has matured. These systems add spoken user text as an alternative to text entry via the keyboard and mouse 'gestures'. The development of ASRs indicates that the early involvement of the natural language and speech communities has played an important and often leading role in developing the technologies needed to support new multimodal interfaces. This also has a downside in that research has often been biased by the assumption that speech is the modality to use, typically supported by the thought that speech is self-sufficient [630].

Cohen's QuickSet [172] system has already been introduced briefly. It consists of a set of interfaces, including a workbench and tablet PC, that allow users to interact with a battlefield map. Strategists are enabled to interact with the workbench in a multimodal fashion using mainly gestures combined with utterances, e.g., "move this battalion to here" while subsequently making a circular selection gesture followed by a movement gesture. Various interface devices were used. Note that Cohen tried to enable users to use a random interface device for a single action; the method in which the communication of that action was performed differed greatly depending on the used interface device, e.g., workbench versus tablet PC.

Brønsted et al. [122] created a similar system to Cohen's QuickSet, named the IntelliMedia WorkBench. It is a multimodal input and output system with which a user is able to perform 2D building plan-based tasks such as obtaining the location of a person's room verbally. Sensors that are used are a laser system, microphone array and speech recognizer. Output modality generation is done using a speech synthesizer. A distributed agent structure is used. Similar to this research, there are multiple ventures towards tabletop interaction systems [199, 326, 539, 573]. As was noted in Section 3.3.4, these workbench applications provide intuitive input in a rather similar fashion to the traditional GUI approach, i.e., combining pointing gestures and issued commands—using hand-gestures and speech rather than mouse and keyboard. A trend in these research ventures is a turn towards multi-user, multi-touch interaction rather than the more traditional single-user, single-touch interaction.

Perhaps one of the most famous immersive systems is the CAVE—introduced in Section 3.2.1, a projection based virtual reality system developed at the Electronic Visualization Lab [182, 183]. Its technology is currently being exploited commercially by a Fakespace Systems [244]. The CAVE is a stereoscopic, shell display device that is created by projecting a virtual environment on a combination of floor, walls, and ceiling surfaces. The original CAVE was created as early as 1991. Back then, it consisted of three wall segments and a floor on which the environment was projected. CAVE users wear stereoscopic-enabling goggles in order to get a 3D illusion. Note that the size of the CAVE walls—10 foot—fills the user's field of view, immersing them in the virtual environment. The CAVE provides excessive visualizations towards the user, with added interaction possibilities such as speech, and tactile sensory input. Various user studies (including collaboration test cases) have been completed using the environment provided by the CAVE. In addition, studies focusing on emerging technologies, e.g., gloves and wands (see also Section 3.3.4), were done. An Immersive Environment, such as the CAVE, is a very helpful tool for researching the effects of emerging or existing technologies in such a context. A still active continuation of the CAVE system are the FLEX and reFLEX systems. Figure 3.11(a) illustrates this newer version of the CAVE: the FLEX system. The FLEX system is based on the same principle as the CAVE but has added flexibility as it is modular by design. A

(a)   (b)

Fig. 3.11. Examples of current developments in multimodal interaction systems. (a) The FLEX immersive environment[TM] [244]. *Image courtesy of Fakespace Systems.* And (b), Illustration of a single user large display-based workstation [125]. *Image courtesy of the Dutch BioRange 4.2.1 Subproject.*

variety of configurations is thus possible; a "spatially immersive environment, flat wall, or immersive theater". This added flexibility provides researchers with added freedom to study phenomenon in user studies and interaction possibilities, e.g., remote communication and more large-scale collaboration cases.

It should be clear by now that in the past, multimodal systems have been designed and created in a highly context-based and task-oriented manner; explicitly for their domain. Systems such as the CAVE paved the way for more flexible systems, in the mean time allowing various multimodal approaches to be studied. The next section will expand on this notion towards current techniques in development in which modality dynamics is advocated; the user can choose from a set of (a limited number of) modalities with which to express himself.

Current Developments. GUI-based interaction is rapidly losing its benefits, especially when a large number of entities need to be created and controlled, often resulting in enormous menu trees. At the same time, for reasons of mobility and affordability, there is a strong user desire to be able to create access large data sets on small devices (e.g., PDA's). This impending collision of trends for smaller screen size and for more entities requires a different paradigm for human-computer interaction with simulators [172]. The same user input capabilities for hand-held, desktop, and wall-sized terminal hardware are required in future collaborative environments. However, the shape/form these input capabilities will take will differ to large extent depending on the actual device that is used.

The previous section described the move from a static modality selection in a system towards a more dynamic—and often considered more natural—selection and use of multimodality. In Figure 3.12, the roadmap for the near-past by Bunt et al. [131] is found. A subsequent roadmap for the continued work on this road is depicted in Figure 3.13. Nijholt [609] describes these roadmaps' description of integration and synchronization of input modes during interaction and the coordination of the multimodal output. The three lanes in both figures distinguish

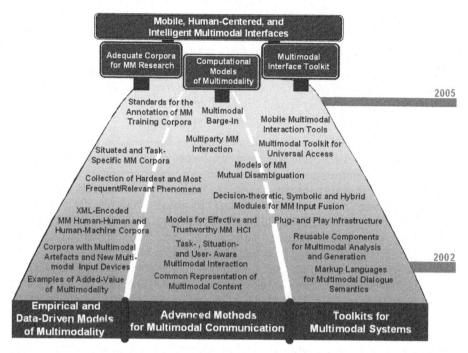

Fig. 3.12. Near-past roadmap for multimodal communication as proposed by Wahlster [866]. *Image courtesy of W. Wahlster.*

the collecting of multimodal corpora, including coding schemes and annotation tools; the computational modeling of multimodality, including modeling of multimodal syntax, semantics and pragmatics; and, as a third lane, the development of toolkits for input fusion and output coordination.

Numerous catch words are found in Figure 3.12; some of which have already been explained in the previous sections. Mutual disambiguation models have been seen as a by-product of designing a multimodal architecture [629] that was best used for superior error-handling techniques. In addition, note that in Figure 3.12 the individual user that interacts in a multimodal way is the research starting point. The choice of modalities is still denoted in a similar fashion to systems in the past. Gradually, the roadmap in this Figure converges to the point where a user can interact multimodally in a "barge-in" scenario, i.e., a setting in which the user can interact in a non-predefined manner. Also note that techniques for multi-party interaction are being researched. As an example of such a system, the COMIC system [264] allows multi-party multimodal interaction and enables users to cooperate to solve a graph-planning problem. Users can interact via speech and pen modalities with a system and perceive automated speech generation and visualized graph feedback.

Situated and task-specific multimodal corpora have also been developed, for example in the AMI project. AMI is a European project with numerous participating parties. The project concerns itself with

> "[...] the development of meeting browsers and remote meeting assistants for instrumented meeting rooms—and the required component technologies R&D themes: group dynamics, audio/visual/multimodal processing, content abstraction, human-computer interaction."

Annotation tools have been developed to support the creation of such a multimodal corpus [695, 707]. Reidsma et al. worked towards the creation of a (immersive) virtual environment used as a means for real-time remote meeting participation [696]. The authors also discuss the usage of (automatically) annotated meetings to create a 3D summary of those meetings. Reidsma, Hofs, and Jovanović describe the difficulties that arise when annotating such a corpus, e.g., think of varying interpretations of a single case [695]. The corpus that was created thus far in the AMI project is an implementation of one of the goals on the near-past roadmap in Figure 3.12. In addition, multi-party interaction is also a topic that has been researched in the context of the AMI project, as discussed by Rienks and Reidsma [707] who discuss a framework for inter-human interaction.

Another current development is the application of Embodied Conversational Agents (ECAs). An ECA is nothing more than a computer-based agent with which a human can communicate. It is however, embodied in an often visual manner. An example is Karin, an agent in the University of Twente's Virtual Music Center environment [610]. Karin performs a desk operator role and is able to communicate with the user in a multimodal fashion. The goal is to provide the user with desired information on a specific performance regarding time, date, etc. Karin aims to add a more natural communication partner to a HCI dialogue. Human-based facial expressions [610] can be generated as are gestures [849] and possibly other forms of naturally occurring human modalities of interaction. Van Welbergen [849] is one of many researchers to note that realistic human visualization can add significantly to the level of trust a user perceives when interacting with such an ECA. In addition, it has been observed that such interaction is often more believable when an agent is visualized in a more comic-based manner so that errors in the gestures, facial expressions are not perceived so much by the user. A comprehensive example hereon is the way in which a cartoon character can stretch, break, and turn in virtually any shape and still allows it to be a believable character.

Oviatt [631] describes that—while the main multimodal literature to date has focused on either speech and pen input or speech and lip movements—recognition of other modes also is maturing and beginning to be integrated into new kinds of multimodal systems. In particular, there is growing interest in designing multimodal interfaces that incorporate vision-based technologies, such as interpretation of gaze behavior [256], facial expressions, and manual gesturing [659]. These technologies unobtrusively or passively monitor user behavior and need not require explicit user commands to a "computer". This contrasts with active input modes, such as speech or pen, which the user deploys intentionally as a command issued to the system. While passive modes may be "attentive" and less obtrusive, active modes generally are more reliable indicators of user intent [631].

Poppe [659] provides a survey on vision-based human motion analysis. He describes the extensive research field of non-obtrusive vision-based estimation of human body poses. This research finds a direct application in multimodal systems in the form of, e.g., gesture recognition (HCI), automated annotation, etc. In his survey, it becomes clear that the research towards such passive non-obtrusive pose estimation systems is advanced and maturing rapidly. An application of these body pose estimation techniques can be found in [256] wherein the author describes the estimation process of a student's gaze behavior in a driving simulator. The student's head orientation is estimated in this research by detecting distinct features, i.e., eyes, ears, and mouth, and matching the feature constellation that can thus be created with a pool of predefined constellations on a similarity basis.

On the topic of multi-party multimodal interaction, an example is the work by Han [326] and Ringel et al. [573] who study multi-party interaction with a workbench application. Difficulties include identifying users interacting with the system in addition to recognizing simultaneous input from those multiple users. Mitsubishi's DiamondTouch system [199] provides a domain to study these problems. The DiamondTouch system can distinguish between individuals and their touch locations on the tabletop on which the workspace is projected. However, it does constrain the interaction due to its design, i.e. it is based on electrical currents that can be detected when the user touches the 'display'. It cannot detect a user's finger hovering slightly above the tabletop.

When studying Figure 3.12, it is clear that not all set targets have been reached. But why is this the case? One of the most important issues in this is that the development of new enabling technologies (see Section 3.3.4) has not been as swift as was expected. It still remains a challenging task to create new devices for the user to express himself, applicable on a large scale. In addition, a direct consequence of the limited enhancements in enabling technologies are the high risks for the industries, resulting in a reluctance to commit to this task. Currently, research has progressed towards roughly three quarters of the presented near-term roadmap.

One target that has not yet been reached is the creation of standards for the annotation of multimodal training corpora. Strides towards the creation of such a standard have been taken as was described above [695, 696, 707]. Another open target is the creation of models for mutual disambiguation. Again, work is well underway but a standardized model has not yet been developed. When reviewing these targets on the near-past roadmap, their successors have also not yet been reached. It must be noted that it is unlikely that these targets will not be met in the near future as can be deduced from the amount of work that is underway regarding these topics. An additional boost in developments of novel multimodal interaction systems is found in the form of the myriad input and output technologies that are currently being developed and/or becoming available;

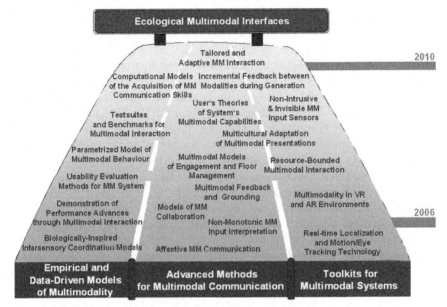

Fig. 3.13. Long-term roadmap for multimodal communication as proposed by Wahlster [866]. *Image courtesy of W. Wahlster.*

as described in detail in Section 3.3.4. These developments will contribute to the developments of multimodal interaction systems. Decrease in device prices will contribute to a more widespread availability of these technologies and vice versa.

Future Developments. Few multimodal interfaces currently include adaptive processing. When they do, the available choice is typically still limited by the system's design. Researchers in this field have begun to explore adaptive techniques for improving system robustness in noisy environmental contexts. This is an important future research direction [631]. In the long-term roadmap, depicted in Figure 3.13, the focus is more on multimodal environments, collaboration, multi-users, usability and user modeling, and affective computing. This indicates the desire and expected research into, amongst others, the collaborative (scientific) workspace. This shift of focus can also be discerned when taking the previous two sections into mind.

Like in Figure 3.12, the long-term roadmap for multimodal interaction developments that is depicted in Figure 3.13 is loaded with catch words. Here, these terms are more ambiguous, more open to a free interpretation. Like the near-past roadmap sketched, standardization of developments, e.g., models of multimodal collaboration, are likely to contribute greatly to the completion of these roadmaps. De Jong and Rip [190] envisioned this trend; they describe in great detail a futuristic scientific collaboration workspace aimed at drug discovery by a multidisciplinary team of, amongst others, biologists, and statisticians. It can be seen in this roadmap that developments of multimodal interaction converge to an adaptive multimodal interface. In this, the user interface is tailored to the user, allowing him to select interaction modalities at run-time. This development is possible only if current problems such as a lack of multimodal collaboration models, an immaturity of non-intrusive and invisible multimodal sensors, and a lacking extensive user description and cognitive model are solved. Work is underway to do exactly that but a large input from industries and multidisciplinary research groups will be required to meet the predicted roadmap's targets. This is confirmed by (amongst others) Rauwerda et al. [692] who describe their approach to design and build a virtual laboratory—the "e-biolab"—introduced in Section 3.3. They note that the reasons why it takes so long to construct an adequate virtual laboratory is due to a lacking of multidisciplinary collaboration "from applications via generic software components to networking". The envisioned goal for their "e-biolab" is to create a Problem Solving Environment (PSE) in which—amongst others—life scientists can solve complex problems in a specific domain. Note that it is a collaboration setting in which the mentioned adaptive multimodal interaction can take place between researchers and the system.

Rauwerda et al. also note that building and implementing such an environment is generally not a task for academic research groups; moreover, it will take time to bridge the multidisciplinary gap between scientists [692]. In addition to the described advances in the long-term roadmap (see Figure 3.13), the most important advancement in the construction of these human-centered collaborative workspaces can thus be said to be the added multidisciplinary commitment on the task at hand [190, 631, 692]. This should include agreement of standards and methodologies, extensive user studies, shared tools, and intuitive visualizations[10]. In addition, Bunt et al. [131] observe the need for new devices for cross modal mutual disambiguation, and new models for multimodal interaction including management of those models.

This section described approaches to multimodal interaction in the field in a chronological order, finishing with expected and—more importantly—required research improvements. The next section discusses the topic how multimodal interaction in an HCVE can be applied using the trend of advancements in the field of multimodal interaction—observed in this section.

3.3.6 Enabling Multimodal Interaction

In this piece, an overview has been provided of HCVE development. Focus point in this was the multimodal interaction that takes place in such an environment. Highlights included modality theory, empirical studies towards the use of multimodal interaction schemes and their resulting guidelines, a survey of enabling technologies with which a user can express himself using a specific modality, and a chronological overview of multimodal interaction approaches aiming to discern trends in this research domain.

---

[10] Numerous of these topics have been and will be addressed in this book.

Inter-human communication is multimodal by its nature. Modalities—denoting the form in which information is communicated—are abundant and can be defined on many different levels of detail. Combining modalities to provide multimodal interaction is an ambiguous task and is at the moment typically done by design for a specific task-domain. Various approaches to multimodal interaction have been tried and tested extensively and although those systems focus mainly on speech and gesture combinations, other forms of multimodal interaction have been devised and described. Simply providing multimodal ways of communicating with agents (either human or a computer) does not suffice; humans will often personify their combination of modalities with which to express themselves when given the chance. Current developments can not yet cope with a dynamic choice and combination of modalities as given by the user's form of interaction. It is expected that especially HCVEs will benefit from the possible forms of multimodal interaction between users and the environment in which they collaborate to solve their problems.

In order to advance towards a multimodal interaction environment in which the user takes *the* central position, added multidisciplinary collaboration, and the agreement and creation on standards are required because currently research is often performed isolated. The research on these sub-tasks requires to be combined; the framework and standards for which have yet to be developed. Regarding enabling technologies, a huge number of input and output devices have been introduced, ranging from basic interaction devices like the mouse, to tracking, haptic, acoustic and olfactory devices. These devices are the key to the interaction in HCVEs and virtual reality. However, although many different interaction devices exist, each device or technology has different advantages and disadvantages. Like choosing the modalities for a user to express himself, selecting devices to enable the use of such a modality cannot be done at random. One concern should be the desired/required dimensional range for these devices. As was argued in Chapter 2, extensive analysis of the user (group) is a main focus for these selection problems. This section also showed that choosing established devices is not always the best choice, leaping ahead—thus skipping a technological development—by using mockup versions of an emerging device can lead to exciting new insights, often applicable with matured technologies as well. In addition it pays to focus strongly on choosing a suitable metaphor for a specific interaction.

3.4 Visualizations in Multi-party Environments

Nowadays, visualizations are used in many different domains as discussed in detail in Part II of this book. Example domains include but are not limited to geography, medicine, chemistry, civil engineering, etc. In all these fields, the work is mostly carried out by teams in which each participant typically performs a specific role based on his/her specific and most often different expertise. The team's outcome results not only from how the participants work (and from their abilities) but more importantly from how they *collaborate*.

This section is structured as follows: firstly, in Subsection 3.4.1, the importance of collaboration in all types of visualization is pointed out. In the same subsection, some preliminary definitions on collaboration and cooperation are given, followed by the distinction between distributed and collaborative visualization. In Subsection 3.4.2, the models behind collaborative visualization are discussed, distinguishing between intrinsically multi-user and extensions from single-user models. Criteria for system evaluation are then described in Subsection 3.4.3, followed by an overview of the current state-of-the-art in distributed collaboration systems (Subsection 3.4.4). This section is concluded by a short summary (Subsection 3.4.5).

3.4.1 Collaborating with Visualizations

Collaboration has an important role in visualization. Wood et al. [910] argued that *"visualization must be a collaborative activity"*. Collaboration plays a key role in all the visualization categories which, according to Butler et al. [137], are:

- *Descriptive Visualization.* The visualized subject is known to a master-user a priori. The visualization is a means to present the data to the other passive users in order to make them understand the subject. In this situation, the role of collaboration is important and well defined. Descriptive visualization is widely used for educational purposes.
- *Analytical Visualization.* Defined as the process of looking for something known in the available data. Visualization is used to find out whether "it" is present in the data or not. Note that the user has an image of what "it" is.
- *Exploratory Visualization.* Defined as the process of interpreting the nature of the available data. The user does not (yet) know what he is looking for so he tries to discover recurring patterns in the visualization.

Analytical and exploratory visualizations usually involve a collaborative team work which consists in discussing and interpreting the visualization. They are used in many different fields: medicine, biology, engineering, geography, etc. Before introducing the various types of possible collaborations in visualization, it is useful to point out the difference between distributed and collaborative visualizations. The former implies a collaboration at the physical level, i.e., the computation needed to render the visualization is distributed on different machines. This is especially suitable for the so called Modular Visualization Environment (MVE) visualization tools—discussed in 3.4.2 and 3.4.4, since they are composed of several modules. Each of these modules can run on a different machine and the computationally most expensive tasks can be done on supercomputers. Note that distributed visualization are suited for single-user as well as multi-user settings.

Collaborative visualization implies a cooperation at the human level, i.e., all the participants collaborate to get an insight (exploratory, analytical) or to understand (analytical, descriptive) the visualization. This cooperation can have a different nature: it can be based on discussion only, it can involve an exchange of printed visualizations together with annotations, or it can involve several machines. The last case is called *distributed collaborative visualization* and involves a cooperation at both the physical and the human levels. Visualization tools in this category allow geographically distributed users to cooperate. They can provide modularity in order to distribute visualization tasks among different users and sharing of resources. Some tools include also audio/video conferencing facilities to improve the communication among participants.

Cooperation. Cooperation is a logical extension of collaboration. However, it is not said that collaboration entails cooperation. Allwood [14] defined an ideal cooperation framework. Two or more agents may be said to cooperate to the extent that they

- consider each other cognitively in interaction, i.e., both agents actively try to understand one another;
- have a joint purpose, i.e., both global and local purposes are jointly pursued;
- consider each other ethically in interaction, i.e., allow each other to act as freely as possible;
- trust each other to act according to the above three requirements.

When all four requirements have been met, an ideal cooperation between agents is established. In a normal communication process, only some of the requirements are or will be met. It is therefore possible to speak of degrees of cooperativeness. Cooperation between agents is not an "all or nothing" phenomenon but a matter of degree. In a dialogue, participants can be cooperative to a greater or lesser extent.

According to Reeves and Nass's "Media Equation" [693], human interaction with computers, television, and new communication technologies is fundamentally social and natural. Many supporting examples can be given: people usually are polite to computers, people treat computers with female voices differently than those with male voices, motion affects physical responses in the same way that real-life motion does, etc. Based on their studies they concluded, among other things, that the human brain has not evolved quickly enough to follow the rapid development of twentieth-century's technology. Expanding on those assumptions, it can be assumed that cooperation between a human-agent and computer-agent will take place according to Allwood's cooperation framework [14]. However, when a computer-agent tries to live up to all of the above four requirements, it is not said that its human counterpart will do the same. The way cooperation between a human- and a computer-agent is given, its content has not yet been researched extensively. This is confirmed by—amongst others—Yu who describes i^* in his PhD-thesis. The i^* approach stands for "distributed intentionality" [922]. This approach can be used to describe distributed intentions, particularly in a Multi-Agent System (MAS). Yu assumed that social settings involve social actors who depend on each other for goals to be achieved, tasks to be performed, and resources to be furnished.

Multimodal Interaction in a HCVE. The previous section described multimodal interaction in a HCVE. multimodal interaction characterizes a form of communication between user and system in which several channels of communication are used. Multimodality is often felt to be a chance given to the designer of an interface to improve the usability because it offers a larger communicative "bandwidth" to the user [663]. The true issue of multimodal user interface design is to tailor the interaction style supported by the system so as to actually define a usable and efficient interface. Randomly adding modalities for added interaction capabilities will not work on its own, as was described earlier. In addition, literature seems to agree that operation-dependent design of multimodal interaction is required for it to work effectively. In a HCVE, the user should be challenged to try new courses of action but moreover, the user should not be concerned with, or even perceive the actual form of required interaction and thus optimally manipulate the data. The system should understand the user's intent and actions. In visual analytics, information is not only presented to the analyst in the HCVE, it is a dialogue between analyst and the data, similar to the one expected to occur between two human analysts. Visual representation in such an interaction is just an interface into or view of the data. The analyst observes the current data representation, interprets it and then thinks of the next question to ask, formulating a strategy of how to continue the dialogue [826].

The Collaborative Workspace. Similarly to a single-user HCVE, a computer-supported collaborative discovery environment [190], or collaborative workspace in short, does exactly the same thing: allowing a user *team* to observe, interpret, think of a next question, follow its strategy—adjusting it when need be. De Jong and Rip [190] describe in their visionary work a highly detailed use case study of multi-user environment in which a group of molecular biologists are working in a discovery environment[11]. The scientists are able to obtain, use, and adjust all tools and data they come across—in short, they have complete freedom to discover their domain. De Jong and Rip provide guidelines for actually implementing such a system, going from the current stage of high-cost copyrighted scientific tools that are available to limited degree, towards global data manipulation results management with freely accessible data manipulation tools. Nowadays, a lot of research is being conducted in the field of molecular biology. Vast amounts of data are being obtained and manipulated. De Jong and Rip described in their work an ideal situation for these scientists to work. Currently, the first steps towards such collaborative workspaces are being made, not specifically for the described group of scientists but for a larger target group, e.g., a simple form is teleconferencing.

At the University of Twente, research is underway that also concerns itself with such collaborative workspaces. The Dutch BioRange subproject 4.2.1 is a part of the larger BSIK BioRange project [125] and has ties with the BSIK VL-E project [126]. These projects aim to develop software helping scientists

---

[11] De Jong and Rip [190] define a discovery environment as a set of tools, methods and procedures, material devices, and a shared body of knowledge in which researchers can pursue their scientific hypothesis.

to communicate with one another; be it directly in real-time collaboration or indirectly by providing better access to resources. The User Interfaces project complements these efforts by laying the interface foundations that help scientists to work with the software, maximizing efficiency and effectiveness. Their current goal is to devise the means that enable for example a biologist, life scientist, or chemist to intuitive work with the vast amount of data gathered on the human genome in the bioinformatics research field. For this reason, a broad focus has been adopted in which an extensive task analysis of the targeted user group is performed including extensive (re-)evaluations. In addition, user-centered visualization design is included to enable designers to build comprehensive, adequate, and intuitive visualizations.

Rauwerda et al. [692] describe the Virtual Laboratory (VL) as a future Human-Centered Discovery Environment. Their VL's goal is to enable life scientists to pre-process, analyze, and interpret the huge amounts of generated data on, for example, drug discovery. They stress that a VL is not meant to replace the current laboratories but to be an extension of them. The concept is meant to advance and promote opportunities for integrated teaching, research, and cross-disciplinary work [692]. Note that in such a workspace, life scientists are encouraged to move towards a virtual collaboration environment in which they can express themselves optimally and thus to come to new understandings as a team.

Collaborative Visualizations. After defining cooperation and discussing Human-Computer Interaction for collaboration in general, the next step consists in focusing on visualization. Collaborative visualization, also called Computer Supported Cooperative Visualization (CSCV) [909], requires interaction not only between people and machines, but also interaction between people and people. This type of collaboration was one of the topics of research in the CSCV community, starting from the 1980's. Applegate [32] described the collaboration using a 2×2 matrix in a time-place space. The Applegate matrix divides the space between time and place in four areas; combining different-time, same-time with different-space and same-place.

Same Time—Same Place. All participants have to be in the same place at the same time. The collaborative visualization can be performed by a group of people clustered around a workstation, with one person driving the visualization while the other people may discuss or suggest how it can be improved. This collaboration can also be done in a CAVE (see Subsections 3.3.4 and 3.3.5 for more information regarding the CAVE system). The same time—same place approach does raise some issues:

- All the participants have to be physically in the same place. This implies that either the team is a "local team", or it is necessary to spend a lot of resources for traveling. On the other hand, a possible geographical distribution would allow to share expertise without limitations on the locations.
- A single person has visualization control at any given time, possibly of only a part of the entire visualization. This does not permit a complete "sharing" of expertise.

- Only one version of the environment is available at a system. Team members without the knowledge of the environment are not able to access the visualization process.
- People usually work more efficiently in their working environments.

Non-distributed collaborative visualization belongs to this group, since the interaction between participants occurs in the same place. On the contrary, in distributed collaborative visualization the place is usually different, since the interaction takes place through geographically distributed machines.

Different Time—Different Place. The visualization is performed by different people regardless of their geographical position. These people can work on the visualization asynchronously at different time. For this reason, collaborative visualizations with different time—different place characteristics are also called *asynchronous visualizations*. As Subsection 3.4.4 will show, many tools and applications provide this feature, especially applications based on web technologies. To do this, they must keep and store the "state" of the visualization in order to restart the visualization from the point in which it was stopped.

Same Time—Different Place. This is also known as *synchronous collaboration*. All the participants are required to be connected to the collaborative application at the same time[12], without constraints on their geographical position. Typical examples of synchronous collaborations are audio/video conferencing and chatting. Distributed collaborative visualization belongs to both same and different time—different place groups.

Since the focus lies on Human-Centered Visualization, distributed visualization will be omitted. It requires a "collaboration" at the system level, i.e., the computation is distributed on several machines but there is no users interaction. Moreover, because of the limitations of the collaborative visualization (same time—same place) the focus will lie on distributed collaborative visualization, called from now on "collaborative visualization" only.

3.4.2 Models for Distributed Collaborative Visualization

Before presenting applications and tools, the main models behind them are introduced. In doing this, two main families of models for multi-user visualization applications are distinguished: extension from single-user and intrinsically multi-user. The second family includes web-based approaches whilst the first family is composed of:

- Models obtained by extending a traditional Modular Visualization Environment (MVE) data-flow paradigm. The extensions provide collaborative features which were not available in the original version.

---

[12] "At the same time" means within the same time-frame in this context. Latecomers can join and leave ongoing sessions, where the time window corresponds to the lifetime of the session.

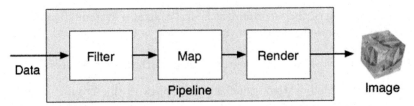

Fig. 3.14. The Haber and McNabb visualization pipeline [317].

- The Spray [637] model and its CSpray collaborative extension [638, 639], a different approach to visualization with respect to the MVE.

These models are explained later on in this section. The distinction between synchronous and asynchronous visualizations is not appropriate for models, it is more application oriented. Moreover, it is orthogonal to this distinction: most of the MVE-based applications are synchronous but some of them provide also asynchronous features, while most of the web-based are asynchronous.

MVE-Based Models. Well-known single user visualization systems, e.g., IRIS Explorer [265], AVS [514], IBM Data Explorer [4], and Khoros [921], are designed according to a common paradigm: the MVE data-flow. In this paradigm, the actual visualization is built by means of several modular components (modules) connected to form a pipeline for the data-flow. The raw data is given to the first module as input, then it is treated by each module in the pipeline, and finally, it is given to the last module which gives the rendered image as output of the pipeline. Users can choose and connect a set of modules using a visual editor. Different modules can run on different machines, allowing the computation to be distributed on a network but not allowing different participants to collaborate in the visualization process. In fact, there is a single user interface from which the whole process is controlled. In other words, this paradigm is suitable for distributed visualization but it is not for distributed collaborative visualization. That is the reason why it needs to be extended towards collaboration.

The Haber and McNabb Model. The reference model for single user MVE systems is represented by the Haber and McNabb model [317] shown in Figure 3.14. In this model, the pipeline is composed of the following modules:

- *Filter.* The role of this component is to refine the raw data it receive as input. For example, it can interpolate from an unstructured grid to a regular grid.
- *Map.* During the mapping stage the data is converted into a geometrical representation, such as an isosurface.
- *Render.* The role of the rendering module is to transform the geometrical information it receives from the mapping module in a visible image (or animation). The output of this component coincides with the output of the visualization pipeline.

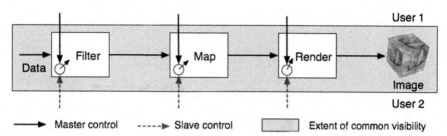

Fig. 3.15. Shared pipeline with token mechanism [909].

Extending the Haber and McNabb Model Towards Collaboration. The most simple extension to the single user visualization consists in duplicating the user interface on all the participants' machines. In this way, the application can be shared without being modified from its original version. A token mechanism is used to ensure that only one machine at a time is acting as master, while the others are slaves. The master copy of the user interface (UI) is transmitted to all the slaves whenever a change is done, making the network load very high. This approach is used by IBM Lakes [381], Intel ProShare, and COVISE [180].

As can be seen in Figure 3.15, this model is represented by a single pipeline having different sets of parameters. The token mechanism guarantees that only one of these set is active at a time.

A model which allows a more complex interaction among the collaborators is shown in Figure 3.16. Each participant can choose which parts of the pipeline he wants to share and which others he want to keep private and control by himself. In the example depicted in Figure 3.16, both collaborators 1 and 2 have control of their own rendering process, while the mapping is shared by the two in such a way that the control can be switched at any time. The filtering stage can be controlled by the master only, which is the user who launched the visualization session. Although this model is better than the previous one, it still has two main shortcomings:

- *Limited Control.* The remaining processes (the filtering in the example in Figure 3.16) can be controlled only by the participant owning the base application.
- *Shared parameters are statically defined.* The set of parameters which can be shared among the collaborators cannot change dynamically.

Examples of applications which use this model (or models which can be viewed as this one) include: two extensions of respectively IRIS Explorer and AVS implemented by Grave et al. in the context of ONERA [626] and the Tempus Fugit system developed by Gerald-Yamasaki [292].

The most complex and general model for collaborative visualization, introduced by Wood, Wright, and Brodlie [909] is shown in Figure 3.17 for N collaborators. Each participant has conceptually his own pipeline, but each stage of the pipeline can be shared with other participants. In detail, this model has the following characteristics:

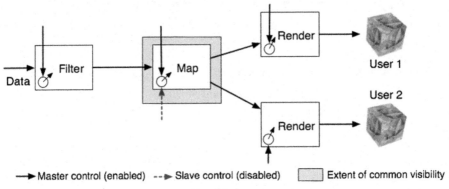

Fig. 3.16. Sharing parts of the pipeline [909].

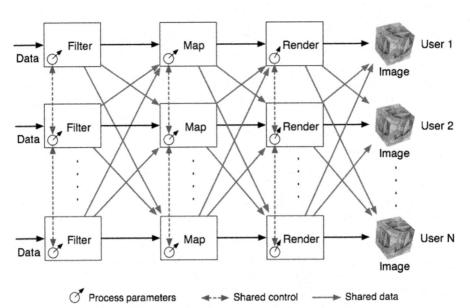

Fig. 3.17. The general model for collaborative visualization [909].

- Data can be transmitted and received at arbitrary points of the pipeline (refer to the diagonal arrows in Figure 3.17)
- At any stage, parameter settings can be controlled either locally by the user or externally by a collaborator (blue lines in Figure 3.17).
- Modules and entire pipelines can be externally launched by a participant on another collaborator's machine.

Examples. The description of the MVE models is concluded here by giving some particular examples (taken from [909]) of the general model previously described in order to see which parts of the pipeline can be shared and how. In Figure 3.18, User 1 sends geometrical data to User 2 (diagonal arrow), who renders his image independently from User 1. A similar situation is shown in Figure 3.19 in which the same data is shared (the geometrical information), but now the two views (images) are synchronized by exchanging rendering parameters (dotted arrow).

The following two examples show how the public/private data issue can be addressed. In Figure 3.20, User 2 receives filtered data from User 1 (red line). Then, they synchronize their mapping processes by exchanging control parameters. In this case, the filtered data is public. If this data needs to be private to User 1, he/she has to send the data after the mapping in a geometrical representation. However, User 2 has no control of the mapping process in this way.

The solution is depicted in Figure 3.21: User 2 sends control information to User 1 at the mapping stage, then User 1 sends the geometrical representation (obtained using the User 2 mapping parameters) to User 1. In this situation, the mapping process of User 2 is a ghost process used only to generate and send control parameters to User 1.

Spray. The model used by the Spray rendering system [637] is presented separately because this is the only one found that is not based on MVE. The system is presented in more details in Subsection 3.4.4. The model uses two main concepts: *Spraycan* and smart particles called *sparts*. A spraycan is used to transform the data by firing sparts into it. Different spraycans are provided to modify the data in different ways. Spraycans can be moved in the data-space in order to modify parts of the data only. For example, if the user wants to locate isosurfaces in

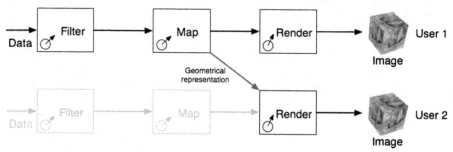

Fig. 3.18. User 1 sends geometrical information to User 2. They render the image independently [909].

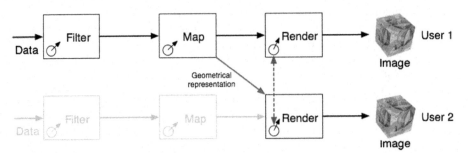

Fig. 3.19. User 1 sends geometrical information to User 2. They synchronize the rendering by sharing parameters [909].

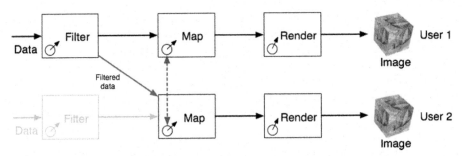

Fig. 3.20. User 2 receives filtered data from User 1. This data is public. Users 1 and 2 synchronize their mapping processes [909].

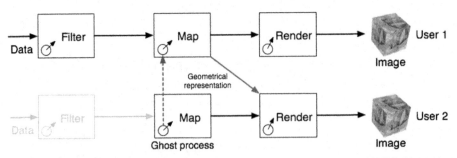

Fig. 3.21. Filtered data is private to User 1. User 2 receives geometrical information from User 1. User 2 controls the mapping stage by using a ghost mapping process to generate and send the control parameters [909].

a region of the data, he/she takes the appropriate spraycan, moves it on the region of interest and fires the sparts into it. The data is incrementally modified by means of spraycans according to the goals of the visualization task. The spraycans can be seen as modules, the reverse of MVE. Instead of having the data flowing through the modules, i.e., the data-flow model, the modules flow through the data modifying it.

The collaborative extension of Spray is called CSpray [638, 639]. There is a shared visualization space in which users and spraycans are shown. In this way, collaborators can see each other and they can also see other participants' spraycans. The results of the application of a user's spraycan are visible to the other users if they have the right permissions.

Web-Based Models. The world wide web has substantially changed over the last decade. In its beginning, it was a repository of information in which researchers could publish their results as web documents including text and images. In such an environment, descriptive visualization only was possible, where the interaction was between the publisher and the readers. With the introduction of new technologies such as VRML, Java, and CORBA, the web started to become a distributed computing environment in which reader-reader interaction is possible. This interaction among readers allows them to perform analytical and exploratory visualizations. As a consequence, new approaches were proposed and new systems were developed for web-based visualizations.

A reference model for these visualizations was introduced by Brodlie [117]. The model is based on three different players and on three different parameters:

- *Player A*: The user; is assumed that he has enough computational power to run a web browser with a VRML plug-in and a Java interpreter. In some cases, he may be capable to run a visualization system.
- *Player B*: The visualization service provider; hosts the web pages which provide the visualization facilities.
- *Player C*: The data provider. This player can be the user himself or an external data provider.
- *Parameter A*: Visualization software; can run on the visualization service provider side or on the user side.
- *Parameter B*: Computing power; may be supplied by the visualization service provider or by the user.
- *Parameter C*: Data; may be provided by an external provider or by the user.

According to this model Brodlie grouped web-based visualizations in different families [117]:

- *Full service* (server-based solution). Both the visualization software and the computational power are on the server side. The visualization is entirely created by the visualization service provider and returned to the user as an image or a 3D model.
- *Software delivery*. The computational power is on the user side, while the visualization software is on the server side. The visualization service provider sends the visualization software to the users and they execute it.

– *Data only* (client-based solution). Both the visualization software and the computational power are on the user side. The role of the visualization server provider is managerial.

Another classification of web-based visualizations was proposed by Brodlie et al. [119, 120]. This one is based on the client-server architecture of web applications. In [119, 120], visualization software is divided in two parts: the visualization design and the core software. The former, with respect to MVE, is the program connecting modules in the pipeline, while the latter is the available set of modules. Brodlie et al. distinguished two main categories of web-based visualizations, and each category is further divided into several different approaches.

1. *Client-based*. The entire visualization process, i.e., filtering, mapping, and rendering, is performed by the client. There are three different approaches for doing that:
   a) Both the visualization design and core software are on the client side and no software is downloaded from the server (it has a managerial role). This case corresponds to the "data only" group in the previous classification.
   b) The core software is on the client side while the visualization design is downloaded from the server. In other words, the structure of the pipeline is created on the server and downloaded by the client. The actual modules, which are installed on the client, are then connected according to this structure.
   c) The visualization design and the core software are downloaded from the server, usually in the form of Java applets. Both the last two cases correspond to the "software delivery" group in the previous classification.
2. *Server-based*. The visualization process up to the mapping stage is carried-out by the server. According to where the rendering stage is performed two different approaches are distinguished between:
   a) *Image display on client*. The server executes the rendering and sends the resulting image to the client.
   b) *3D model rendering on client*. The server sends the geometry (a VRML file) created in the mapping stage to the client, which renders the 3D model. The client has control of the rendering process.
   This category corresponds to the "full service" group in the previous distinction.

3.4.3 Evaluation Criteria

In Subsection 3.4.1, the importance of collaboration in visualization activities was stressed. Now, the main characteristics of a distributed collaborative visualization environment are discussed, according to Brodlie et al. [119, 120]. The main focus is on distribution and collaboration properties. These characteristics should be used for evaluating existing distributed collaborative visualization framework as well as for designing new ones.

1. *Nature of the collaboration*; should evolve over time driven by the visualization, not be predetermined.
2. *Collaboration level*; is the most characterizing factor for a collaborative environment. It allows for categorization of systems according to the level of shared control they provide over the visualization process:
   a) *Data.* Each collaborator should be able to share not only raw data but also data at any level of abstraction, i.e., at any point within the pipeline.
   b) *Parameters.* Each participant should be able to set any parameter of any module of any collaborator's pipeline. In this way, the parameters can be controlled by different experts according to their skills.
   c) *Modules.* It should be possible to launch and connect modules in a participants' environment.
3. *Participation*; Each collaborator should have his own instance of the visualization, and he can decide how much he wants to collaborate with the other participants. The environment should provide the following features to the user:
   a) *Dynamic joining/leaving.* Users should always be able to join or leave.
   b) *Floor control.* Different users having different expertise should have different privileges in accessing/controlling the data and the parameters and in launching/connecting modules in other collaborators' pipelines.
   c) *Global view.* There should be a global view of the distributed environment. This view allows a hypothetical administrator to manage the session and to help inexperienced users.
4. *Ease of learning*; The collaborative environment should be designed by extending current visualization approaches, without modifying the paradigm and the UI too much. A user should be able to switch from a single-user to a collaborative mode without having to learn a completely new environment.
5. *System*; Collaborative visualization systems are very complex applications which have to deal with many technological and implementation issues. Four criteria for evaluating these applications from the implementation point of view are:
   a) *Multiple platforms.* Since a collaborative application runs in a distributed environment which is usually composed of different workstations, the application should have support for an heterogeneous set of platforms. Moreover, taking into account the "ease of learning" criterion, it is important that a user is allowed to use his own desktop system.
   b) *Performance.* Adding a collaborator (or more generally a collaborative element) in the environment should not decrease the overall performance relevantly.
   c) *Reliability.* As in any distributed application, sharing resources implies data integrity problems.
   d) *Robustness.* As users should be able to dynamically join/leave the collaborative session, the failure of one component should not lead to a collapse of the whole session.

6. *Other features*; Besides the visualization, the environment should provide other facilities to improve the collaboration among users such as: audio/video conferences, chats, shared blackboards, etc.

According to the *Collaboration Level* criterion, collaborative visualization tools can be categorized in four main groups[13]:

1. *Local Control*. It represents the simplest form of a collaborative environment. The image is generated entirely by one user on one machine. Then, the generated image is broadcasted to all the other participants.
2. *Local Control* with Shared Data. A slightly more collaborative variation of the previous one consists in applications in which the participants can share data at any point in the pipeline, but still they cannot share neither parameters nor modules.
3. *Limited Shared Control*. The environments belonging to this group can share, in addition to data, parameters at any points in the pipeline. These parameters can affect any step of the visualization computation: filtering, mapping and rendering.
4. *Fully Shared Control*. A collaborative visualization application is considered to be "Fully Shared Control" if it allows not only to share data and parameters but also to connect/launch modules in other user environments.

3.4.4   Survey of Collaborative Visualization Systems

In this section, the tools and systems for collaborative visualizations are presented. The overview is organized as follows: in the first part, systems based on the MVE data-flow paradigm are introduced. Then, the CSpray system is described followed by a brief introduction of three systems based on slight variations of MVE. Finally, web-based approaches are discussed.

MVE Systems. In the following, collaborative visualization tools based on MVE are presented. Table 3.6 summarizes the main characteristics of the systems, while their descriptions are provided in the following paragraphs. Moreover, two MVE-based systems are evaluated after being discussed in more detail.

COVISE. The collaboration is provided by means of a shared data space to which all the collaborators' workstations have access. This data space contains the results of simulations performed by a supercomputer. Only one participant at a time can have the control of the view, but this control can be exchanged among collaborators during a session.

COVISE CE. It is a version of COVISE developed by Visenso [861]. CE stands for Collaborative Engineering. It provides collaboration by synchronizing the view points for every frame. The limited amount of data transferred (a 4×4 matrix) allows the collaborative visualization of large data sets even with an ISDN link. Audio/video conferencing facilities are not included, but they can be provided by the external ENScube package [861].

---

[13] A similar classification was proposed by Johnson and Elvins [415].

Table 3.6. MVE-based tools and systems.

Name	Applications	Collaboration level	Pros	Cons
COVISA [909, 910]	General purpose	Fully shared control	High collaboration level	No audio/video conferencing facilities provided
COVISE [180, 489, 893, 894]	General purpose	Limited shared control	It can handle huge data set	Only one user can have the control of the view at a time
COVISE CE [861]	General purpose	Limited shared control	It can be used together with other Visenso tools	Same as COVISE
MANICORAL [213, 213, 214]	Altimetry and geodesy based on GIS	Limited shared control	Easy of learning (extension of an existing visualization system)	Sharing modules should be explicitly introduced
EnSight Gold [150]	CFD, FEA, crash, hydrodynamics, SPH	Local control	Performances (it uses parallel processing and rendering)	Low collaboration level, number of participants
FASTexpeditions [596]	CFD	Local control with shared data	The audit trail allows sessions to be replayed	Low collaboration level
ONERA [304]	Aircraft simulation	Limited shared control	Easy of learning (extension of two existing visualization systems)	Few information available online
Pagendarm and Walter prototype [636]	Aerodynamics	Local control with shared data	Audio/Video conferencing facilities provided	Low collaboration level
Shastra and Poly [29, 30]	Medicine	Limited shared control	Collaborative facilities provided by the Shastra environment	Performance and robustness

EnSight Gold. A version of the EnSight software enabling real-time collaboration, based on a client/server architecture. One user, called the "pilot", starts the collaborative session by running the "hub", an external program which handles the exchange of information between participants. When a second user, called "co-pilot", joins the session, whatever the pilot does is replicated on the co-pilot's machine. The underlying hardware can be heterogeneous.

FASTexpeditions. The collaborative extension of the FAST (Flow Analysis Software Toolkit) tool, developed at NASA Ames. The collaboration is based on the concept of "pilot" and "passenger". The pilot is the user who drives the visualization. His audit trail is recorded and streamed in real-time to all the other users (the passengers). In this way, they can reproduce the visualization on their machine, using the information given by the audit-trail. The pilot role can be changed using a token mechanism: only the user who holds the token can be the pilot, where the token is passed in a round-robin fashion.

MANICORAL. Each collaborator runs his own copy of AVS/Express [35] (the approach is based on this tool). The collaboration is possible through sharing modules, which need to be launched in the environment of the user who want to share data or parameters. These modules communicate via a central distribution server. Users have to explicitly introduce the sharing modules into their environments, but once these are created, any other user can join in.

ONERA. Designed as an extension of two existing visualization systems: AVS5 [35] and IRIS Explorer [265]. A simulation result can be sent to the collaborative visualization environment which allows the parameters of the visualization pipelines to be controlled by any collaborator.

Pagendarm and Walter Prototype. Two participants work on the same data and produce the same visualization synchronously. Each image is created locally and the consistency of the data and the visualization is ensured by exchanging status and layout information. Remote cursors and audio/video conferencing are provided. The prototype is based on the HIGHEND visualization system [635].

COVISA and Shastra: Descriptions and Evaluations. Here, detailed descriptions and subsequent evaluations of COVISA [909, 910] and Shastra [29, 30] are given. COVISA was chosen because it enables fully shared control, and Shastra because it is a general collaborative environment in which several tools can run. The evaluation of these systems was done following the criteria presented in Subsection 3.4.3.

COVISA. It was created by Wood, Wright and Brodlie in the context of the CO-VISA project [909] (Co-Operative working in Visualization and Scientific Analysis). The idea behind this framework is to create an extensible base, allowing it to extend towards collaboration with existing MVE single-user visualization systems. The model of the system is the most general, shown in Figure 3.17. A particular implementation [910] was developed for IRIS Explorer. Figure 3.22 shows the general architecture of the collaborative visualization environment. The main components of such architecture are:

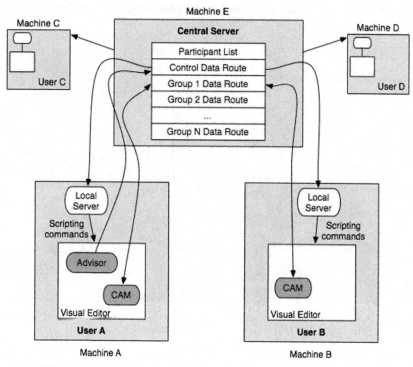

Fig. 3.22. The COVISA Architecture, adapted from [910]. *Image courtesy of J. Wood, H. Wright, and K. Brodlie.*

- *CAM* (Collaboratively Aware Module). It represents the core of the collaboration, i.e., the link among pipelines. When a CAM is launched by a participant, it causes other CAMs to be launched in the collaborators' environment. Then, each participant can connect collaborators' CAMs into his own pipeline. Each CAM module allows, at least, data and control parameters sharing.
- *Advisor Module.* It is used to duplicate pipelines or parts of pipelines. It allows the user to select a set of modules locally from his pipeline. Then, it generates the scripting code to duplicate the selected parts of the pipeline (the modules) and sends the code to the other participants through the central server.
- *Local Server*[14]. Locally manages a collaborative session, keeping the connections to the other participants via the central server.
- *Central Server.* Manages the global collaboration by: (i) storing and dynamically updating the Participant List, (ii) passing control messages about new modules (Control Data Route), and (iii) distributing data from one group member's CAM to all the other members' CAMs (Group Data Routes).

---

[14] It is assumed that the visualization system can be driven by both a scripting language and the usual visual programming system.

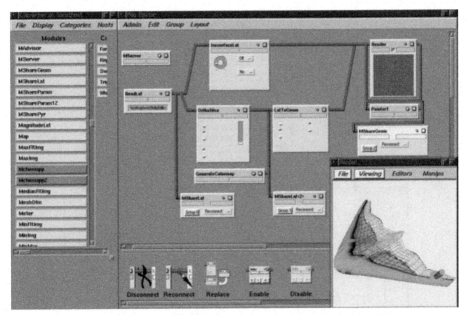

Fig. 3.23. A screenshot of IRIS Explorer running a collaborative visualization session, taken from [910]. © *1997 IEEE. Reprinted with permission.*

This architecture has been implemented as an extension for IRIS Explorer[15] (a screenshot is depicted in Figure 3.23). The local server, advisor module and CAM have been implemented as regular IRIS Explorer modules. Their names appear in the library window (in the very left of Figure 3.23) and they can be launched into the Map Editor (right part of Figure 3.23) and connected to other components in the same way as any other module. For further details refer to Wood, Wright, and Brodlie's work [910].

The main benefits and shortcomings of this approach, with respect to the evaluation criteria presented in the previous subsection, are sketched in Table 3.7. Taking into account the groups defined in Section 3.4.3, COVISA can be defined as a *Fully Shared Control* system. It is not only possible to share parameters at any point in the pipeline, but also to launch and connect to modules in other user environments.

Shastra and Poly. Shastra [29] is a collaborative multimedia scientific environment in which experts can communicate and interact across the network to solve problems. This environment provides an infrastructure for running different tools designed according to the Shastra architecture. One of these tools is Poly [30], a 3D rendering and visualization application. In the following, the general architecture of Shastra is introduced first. It is then described how to obtain collaborative visualization in Shastra using Poly. The Shastra environment is composed of the following components:

---

[15] Available for UNIX systems.

Table 3.7. Benefits and shortcomings of COVISA.

Benefits	
Collaboration Nature	It can evolve over time, it is not predetermined.
Collaboration Level	It is possible to share data and control parameters and to launch and connect modules in collaborators' environments.
Participation	It is completely dynamic.
Ease of Learning	The model is obtained by extending the Haber and McNabb pipeline. The application is obtained as an extension of IRIS Explorer with few modifications.

Shortcomings	
Performance	The tool is designed to be used by two or three people. This is not a technical constraint (scalability), but rather a human one, as it would be too hard in a cognitive sense to understand what is going on when there are many independent sessions. However, it would be interesting to do some scalability tests for applications where there is a person demonstrating to a class (descriptive visualization tasks).
Other Features	Neither audio/video conferences nor chat systems are provided within the environment, but it is possible to use external tools. Keeping these features separated from the COVISA system was a deliberate decision of the authors, since it allows separate development, and it allows COVISA to be used with whatever audio/video conference tool a user wants.

- *Kernel*: Responsible for managing the distributed environment.
- *Session Manager*: Maintains collaborative sessions among different users.
- *Services*: Provide facilities like textual, graphical, audio/video rendition and communication.
- *Toolkits*: Provide scientific and manipulation functionalities.

The environment is responsible for the distribution of the different applications (tools) running in it. It allows to create remote instances of the applications and it provides mechanisms to connect them in both client-server and peer-to-peer modes. The users can create, start, join, leave, and terminate collaborative sessions. Shastra provides many synchronous modes for the users interaction. In order to run in the Shastra environment, a tool needs to register itself with the environment providing the following information: (i) The *Directory*, i.e., the services the tool offers and (ii) the *Location*, i.e., where the tool should be contacted to provide these services.

As was described previously, Poly is a 3D visualization tool. It has capabilities for managing, manipulating and rendering graphical objects. These objects can be represented in several formats which will be converted by Poly into its own internal representation used for efficiency. A collaborative visualization session

Table 3.8. Benefits and shortcomings of Poly running in the Shastra environment.

Benefits	
Collaboration Nature	It can evolve over time, it is not predetermined.
Collaboration Level	It is possible to share data, control parameters and viewing locations, while the possibility of launching modules in collaborators' environment is not provided.
Participation	Both joining and leaving are dynamic but the former is only possible passing through the group leader.
Other Features	Audio/video conferences are provided by the Shastra environment.
Multiple Platform	The platform heterogeneity is provided by the replication of the Poly instances in the Shastra environment.

Shortcomings	
Performance	Scaling problems due to the centralized session manager. However, it performs well for typical group sizes.
Robustness	A failure of the group leader will collapse the whole session.

in Shastra consists of several instances of Poly. A user can start the collaborative session as the group leader, specifying to its local kernel the other participants he wants to invite. The kernel instantiates a session manager which starts the collaborative session with the group leader only. The users specified in the kernel are then invited to join and, if they accept, they are included in the session. At any point in time, a participant can leave the session. To participate in an ongoing session a user has to ask to the group leader to invite him, and after receiving the invitation he can join.

The activities of all the instances of Poly are regulated by the *centralized* session manager. This has performance implications discussed in the evaluation section. The control flow and access permission are managed at runtime, providing two types of interaction: (i) *regulated interaction* with a token passing mechanism or (ii) *unregulated interaction* with a free interaction mode. In both of them, one user only gets exclusive control of the shared space at a time. The centralized session manager allows users having access permission to access the view while users with modify permission can also modify visualization parameters, viewing modes and directions.

Table 3.8 presents the main benefits and shortcomings of the collaborative visualization provided by Poly running in the Shastra environment. According to the definitions given in Subsection 3.4.3, the collaboration provided by Shastra in combination with Poly is Limited Shared Control. The state is centralized and it is not possible to launch modules in other user environments. On the other hand the environment allows the users to have different parameters for the same view, e.g. different cutaway, view locations, etc.

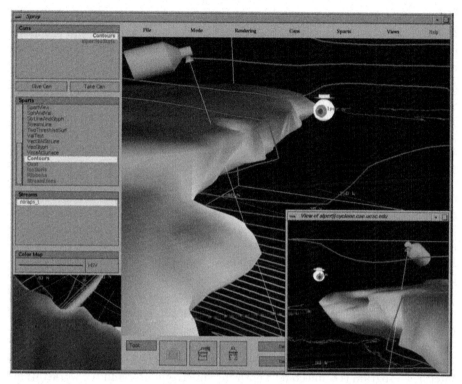

Fig. 3.24. A screenshot of a CSpray workspace, taken from [638]. © *1997 IEEE. Reprinted with permission.*

CSPRAY. CSpray [638,639] is the collaborative extension of the Spray rendering system [637] already discussed in Subsection 3.4.2. In this system, the active participants create a shared visualization space by applying one's own spraycan to the data. Each collaborator is represented in the shared view with an *eyecon* (see Figure 3.24) which shows to all the participants (included oneself) where the corresponding user is in the visualization space. He can move his *eyecon* to get a different location point on the view. A spraycan can be either private or public: in the first case the results of the application of the spraycan are visible to its owner only, while in the public case, they are visible to everybody.

Figure 3.24 shows a CSpray workspace of a two-user collaboration session. The main window is User 1's view, in which the eyecon of User 2 is visible. The window in the lower right is the view of User 2, where User 1's eyecon is visible as well. In both views, the spraycans are visible. Floor control is provided by the system. Users can get control of visualization objects isosurfaces by asking the participant who created or last modified the object. It is possible to join and leave an ongoing session, since the system records an audit trail. If a latecomer wants to join the session he has to re-run it up to that point, using the information stored in the audit trail.

Variations of MVE. The following systems are based on slight variations of the MVE data-flow model. They all have the filtering, mapping and rendering stages but the collaboration is provided in a different way with respect to the collaborative extension of MVE presented in Subsection 3.4.2.

Sieve. This is a Java-based collaborative environment [393]. The approach is similar to MVE: data-flow networks are created and maintained from an extensible set of modules. Collaboration is achieved by a replicated architecture which provides real-time information about participants' actions and locations. Users can view and modify different parts of the shared data at the same time. Sieve provides also asynchronous collaboration: the state of a session is stored in a central server in such a way that latecomers can catch-up and the visualization can be regenerated later. Collaborators can leave notes[16] on the workspace using the annotation tools provided by Sieve. These annotations are stored in the central server as well, giving another means for asynchronous collaboration. Sieve exploits JavaBeans [805] functionalities to support interaction and collaboration. As opposed to the MVE models presented in Subsection 3.4.2, collaboration was incorporated in Sieve as a design aim.

Tempus Fugit/Interview. Tempus Fugit [292] is a system for the visualization of unsteady fluid flow. It has a companion program, called *"Interview"*, which provides facilities to create a collaborative visualization environment. In the Tempus Fugit system, the filtering and the mapping are done on a supercomputer and then the created geometry is passed to a workstation for rendering. The Interview program is connected to both the supercomputer and the workstations (at most two). It receives requests from the Tempus Fugit clients and it forwards them to the supercomputer. Then, it sends the requested geometry back to the workstation for the independent rendering. It is also possible to synchronize the rendering process by exchanging the rendering control information.

Web-Based Tools. The collaborative systems overview is concluded by presenting web-based tools, summarized in Table 3.9. For each system, a brief description in the following paragraphs is provided. Three approaches (Lovegrove and Brodlie VRML Solution [516], TANGO [67,68], and WWW Visualization [907]) are discussed in more details at the end of the section.

CEV. Collaborative Environment for Visualization [700] is a client-server application implemented in Java. All the clients are connected to a central server, responsible for the computation and rendering of the visualizations. The images are sent from the server to all the clients which display them within a web-browser. The innovative aspect of CEV is the separation between 2D and 3D components. This accommodates clients with less or limited computation power. Each client maintains a local (*"private"*) view and a global (*"public"*) view on all the objects he is using. The local view can be updated at any time, while for the global one a token passing mechanism is used. The user holding the token can perform a global update. An authentication process to protect important data is not provided in the current version of CEV.

---

[16] Not only notes but also lines, arrows, text, images, and any arbitrary Java objects.

Table 3.9. Web-based tools and systems.

Name	Technologies	Applications	Type	Pros	Cons
CEV [687]	Java	General purpose	Full service	The separation between 2D and 3D components improves performances	An authentication process is not provided
DSAV Loops [42]	Java, VRML, CORBA	General purpose	Full service	High collaboration level	The Shastra collaboration substrate is needed
Engel and Ertl VRML Volume Visualization Application [238]	Java, VRML	Medicine	Full service	It is possible to synchronize the visualization with any other user	All the synchronization data passes through a single server
Habanero [151, 600]	Java	Hablet tools are provided for GIS and molecular applications	Software delivery	Easy to extend (just write a Hablet tool)	Advanced visualization is not provided
KnittingFactory [53]	Java	General purpose	Software delivery	Applets can communicate directly, without passing through the server	Only 2D visualization
Lovegrove and Brodlie VRML Solution [516]	Java, VRML	General purpose	Full service	A shared space is provided to improve users collaboration	The whole visualization is stored on a single VRML file
TANGO [67, 68]	Java	General purpose	Software delivery	Combination of Java applets and standalone applications	All the communication pass through the central server
WWW Visualization [907]	VRML	General purpose	Full service	Past visualization can be retrieved	Low collaboration level

DSAV Loops. DSAV Loops are models for collaborative work providing an intuitive understanding of the tasks which need to be done. They organize scientific visualization around a loop of project work composed of: (i) data sources, (ii) simulation servers, (iii) analysis tool, and (iv) visualization client. An implementation of this model is proposed by Bajaj and Cutchin [42]. The collaboration substrate is provided by the Shastra [29] environment, on top of which the collaborative visualization module is developed. This module is a pure Java client, available as a web-based applet. It supports VRML and collaborative navigation and interrogation of shared scene graphs.

Engel and Ertl VRML Volume Visualization Application. In the Engel and Ertl [238] approach, the collaboration is managed by a central server called "synchronization server". It maintains a list of connected users. When a participant joins a session, he/she receives the user list from the server. Then, he/she selects the users which he/she will synchronize the visualization with (registration process). When a participant changes some view parameters, like view point, transfer-function, clipping planes, etc., the changes are sent to the synchronization server which forwards them to the registered users. The system allows users to mark interesting parts of the visualization using persisting tags. These tags can be seen by other participants or by the user himself later on. A text chat is provided by the tool to improve the collaboration.

Habanero. Habanero [151] is an environment for collaborative work. The architecture is client-server, in which the server hosts and keeps track of sessions, and clients connect to and interact with those sessions. Within a session, different tools—"Hablets"—can be launched and used. They provide a variety of services, such as visualization, audio and text chats, whiteboard, physics tools, etc. The Habanero client allows the user to define, list, create and join sessions. It is possible for a single client to interact with several sessions at the same time. The client can be used in two modes: off-line, without interaction and collaboration or on-line with real-time collaboration. The whole Habanero framework (Hablet tools, client and server applications) is developed in Java.

KnittingFactory. KnittingFactory is a distributed collaborative Java application. It provides a registry service (running on a server) to which Java applets can register, publicizing their requests for partners. When a user want to start a collaboration, he/she looks for a partner-applet in the registry service. Once a suitable applet is found, it is downloaded from the server and executed within the user's browser. At this point, other participants can download the same applet and collaborate with the first user. The communication between the applet is direct, without passing through the server.

Lovegrove and Brodlie VRML Solution. Lovegrove and Brodlie [516] propose an approach to provide a shared 3D visualization environment that users inhabit and in which users can interact. The approach is built around a single VRML file including the geometry and the sensors. This file is dynamically generated using the information stored in a database. Each participant can have his own visualization by accessing the VRML file using a standard web browser with

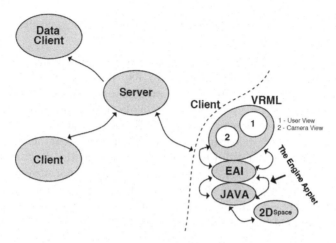

Fig. 3.25. The Architecture of the system proposed by Lovegrove and Brodlie, taken from [516]. *Image courtesy of S. Lovegrove and K. Brodlie.*

a VRML plugin and a controlling Java applet. In detail, the client, i.e., the web browser, is composed of. (i) the local visualization in which the user can navigate and manipulate the view, (ii) a second view, called *camera view*, showing an overview of the whole environment, and (iii) a 2D shared space providing facilities for user communication like whiteboard, chat, etc.

Figure 3.25 depicts the architecture of the system, showing all the system components. The most important components are:

– *The Server.* It provides message passing services to all the connected clients. The messages are passed using a broadcasting round robin policy.
– *The Engine Applet.* It is a Java applet responsible for managing the communication between the VRML world and the network socket connected to the server.
– *The VRML File.* It contains all the geometry composing the viewed world. The VRML file is composed of three elements: (i) visualization, (ii) proximity and time sensors, and (iii) external prototype widgets. The sensors are used to control user tracking: in particular the proximity sensor tracks the user position and orientation.
– *The Secondary Camera.* It is used to create the *camera view* which shows all the events happening in the virtual world. It is implemented as another VRML browser plugin running the same VRML file.
– *Shared 2D Space.* It is a whiteboard which allows users to communicate and interact by drawing shapes and text onto it. The whiteboard is placed in the Java engine applet's window.
– *The Data Client.* It represents the bridge between the database and the system. It provides the data to generate the VRML file.

The system is not scalable, since it is designed as a client-server application. A large number of clients will result in a loss of performance, due to the bottleneck represented by the server. The use of Java and VRML guarantees portability and platform independence.

TANGO. A system which integrates web-based and standalone applications written in any programming language [67, 68]. It provides a uniform interface through which different applications can exchange data and communicate. It makes it possible to run and control a collaborative application from a web-browser. The collaboration in TANGO is based on the concept of *session*. A session is a group of application instances which work together in a collaborative manner, sharing data and behavior. Every application is part of a session, even if it is not used for collaboration. Each session has a master, a particular user having special privileges. He/she is able to control the application behavior and can grant access to the other users. This provides floor control.

The communication takes place between applications belonging to the same session. In detail, they can send/receive *control* and *application* messages. The first type of messages is needed for service operations (like logging users into the system, establishing sessions, launching applications, etc.), while application messages represent the way the applications communicate. Since all the messages pass through the server, they can be recorded in a database. This is done in order to provide event logging. The recorded data can be used for asynchronous collaboration by replaying an entire system activity. Figure 3.26 shows the architecture of the system, in which the main components are:

- *The local daemon.* It manages communication between the central server and standalone applications or applets. The standalone applications can be written in any language. They communicate with the daemon using sockets. Java applets can be downloaded from an HTTP server and executed in a browser environment.
- *Central server.* It routes messages between applications participating in each session and, at the same time, it records all the messages and events in the database.
- *Control application.* It is the interface to the user for launching application locally or remotely, creating or joining collaborative sessions, etc.

WWW Visualization. The WWW Visualization project is an asynchronous collaborative visualization environment. It is asynchronous because the collaboration occurs by retrieving past visualizations through a tree structure. Information about past results is stored in the tree (together with the views) in a structured way, allowing other users to retrieve them in the future. Figure 3.27 shows the architecture of this environment. An example of the system usage is as follows:

- The user sets some pipeline parameters using the form interface.
- This information is sent to the web service which is a remote visualization engine.
- The visualization engine renders the view using the parameters received in input.
- The engine output forms a set of VRML geometry. This geometry is returned and displayed to the user in a local VRML client.

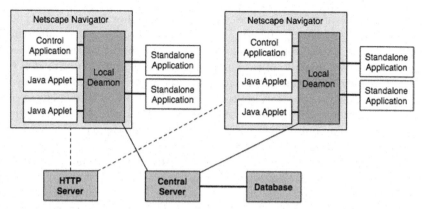

Fig. 3.26. Global Architecture of TANGO, adapted from [67]. *Image courtesy of L. Beca et al.*

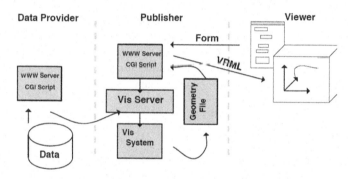

Fig. 3.27. WWW Visualization Architecture, taken from [907]. *Image courtesy of J. Wood.*

3.4.5   Challenges for Multi-party Visualizations

This section introduced three categories of visualizations: descriptive, analytical, and exploratory. It is argued that collaboration with visualizations differs per category but that the forms of cooperation at the human level are not that dissimilar. Cooperation is typically not found in its ideal form but is a matter of degree in which four characteristics define an ideal cooperation between communicative agents. Being either human or machine, the interaction between these agents has been studied extensively and, as Section 3.3 argues, more and more takes a similar form as human-human interaction. Most importantly when creating a visualization for collaboration purposes, it should be considered that the chosen cooperation model fits the user's expectations, allowing direct control via a human-like interface.

Different types of collaborative visualizations are possible, varying the time and space variables (same or different time and same or different place). Because of the limitations of the same time—same place collaboration, the section has focused on different time—different place (or asynchronous) and same time—different place (or synchronous) collaborations. Collaborative visualization can be described by two main families of models: intrinsically multi-user models (typically web-based) and extensions from single-user models. In the first family, two further classifications can be done: the first one is based on three players (user, visualization service provider and data provider) and three parameters (visualization software, computational power, and data), while the second classification reflects the client-server architecture of web applications. For the second family, two single-user visualization models can be considered and extended towards collaborations: the MVE data-flow and the Spray rendering system. In extending these models some issues arise: to which extent share the visualization process, how to ensure synchronization of user data and visualization parameters, and how to distinguish private and public parts within the same visualization.

In designing collaborative visualization systems, some criteria should be considered and evaluated. In addition to the requirements common to all distributed applications, such as reliability, robustness, performance, and compatibility, there are some criteria typical to collaborative visualization. These criteria include collaboration aspects, e.g., collaboration nature and level, participation aspects, such as floor control and global view, ease of learning and presence of facilities, like audio/video conferencing and chat.

3.5 Chapter Notes

Interaction is a crucial part of visualization and vice versa. This chapter discussed various aspects of interacting with visualizations. Starting with an extensive description of interaction studies, it was argued that although humans prefer to interact in a human-like fashion, direct control over a visualization should still be possible. Three interaction tasks can be identified and defined: navigation, selection, and manipulation, each can be performed in numerous ways. This chapter aimed to provide its reader with a detailed overview of these interaction possibilities. Display devices greatly influence the way in which a user interacts with a visualization, given its size, shape, mobility, etc. It is argued that three scale levels exist in these interaction variations, ranging from hand-held, to arms-length, to distal scale. These interaction scales also influence the suitable modalities for that specific scale. It is therefore not possible to adequately use a modality for distal-scale interaction on a hand-held device or vice versa; scaling issues arise in performing the mentioned interaction tasks.

In addition to discussing possibilities of interacting with a visualization, the way in which the interaction takes places has been discussed in detail. This, too, has a wide range of focus, starting with human-like versus direct-control interaction, ranging to the devices that are used to express oneself in an interaction. Although differences are plentiful between human-like and direct control interactions, it is argued that multimodal interaction is a paramount contribution to more "bandwidth" for a human to express himself—using for example speech and hand gestures—while interacting with a visualization. Multimodal interaction enables a user to express himself in a human-like fashion, and is arguably more intuitive, efficient, effective, and satisfying. However, it is also noted that direct control should remain a possibility. No lack of interest in interacting with visualizations was observed. However, it has become apparent that the focus has been too narrow.

Combining modalities for expressing oneself should not be done at random. Rather, this is a topic requiring careful study as it has been proven that only user-tailored modality combinations increase satisfaction, etc. In addition, users tend to select their personalized modality set when given a chance. Other topics of interest when combining modalities for multimodal interaction schemes include the approach to data-fusion (ranging from low-level, sensor based, to on the semantic level), system architecture, and mutual disambiguation.

A wide variety of technologies was introduced, enabling the described modalities. A distinction is made between input and output devices. However, some devices can perform both tasks so the difference is not too clear. Some devices are based more on the analysis of certain sensor data, e.g., automatic speech recognition. It is argued that user-worn sensors provide accurate data on the user's actions when compared to passive sensors approaches. User-worn sensors do influence the interaction itself due to their very presence. A trend toward unobtrusive interaction schemes can be identified when observing research developments in the field of multimodal interaction. In order to identify this trend, a summarily chronological research overview has been provided. It also became apparent that standards are still missing in the development of multimodal interaction schemes. In addition, it became clear that a more extensive input from industries to develop and market amongst others new devices is required to further advance developments in this field.

Multi-party/multi-disciplinary interaction with visualizations are also described in some detail. In this, collaboration can occur in various forms between users themselves but also between users and computer-based agents. Collaboration however, need not entail cooperation amongst these communicating agents. Degrees of cooperation have been introduced while noting that an ideal cooperation is unlikely to occur often—even between humans. Computer supported cooperative visualization was introduced, describing cooperation with respect to varying place and time. The topic of distributed visualizations was omitted for the reason that it is mainly a system-level affair. Instead, the focus lies on distributed collaboration tasks with visualizations. Models describing distributed collaborative visualization were introduced, distinguishing between intrinsically multi-user (typically web-based) and extensions from single-user models. The MVE data-flow model was discussed in detail, describing how to extend it for multi-users collaboration. Topics of interest here include how to synchronize user data and parameters, how to and to which extent share the visualization process, how to clarify/visualize the interactions of other users with the visualization and how to manage floor control. An extensive list of evaluation criteria were introduced with respect to both the user's and the system's point of view. The criteria for the user are mainly focused on collaboration aspects like the nature and the level of the collaboration, while the system criteria concern implementation aspects such as performances and reliability. An overview of distributed collaborative visualization tools and systems was presented, where some systems were also evaluated according to the criteria previously introduced.

4 Visual Representations

Carsten Görg, Mathias Pohl, Ermir Qeli, and Kai Xu

Visualization can help in the process of extracting insight from data during decision-making. Its advantages are based on the ability to rapidly interpret large quantities of data. The challenge in this context consists in constructing visualization systems which enable the user to understand and perceive the data effectively by providing transparent interaction methods for effective communication between the user and the data. Ware [872] states a number of advantages of visualization, namely:

- The ability to comprehend huge amounts of data.
- The perception of properties that are otherwise not anticipated.
- The extraction of problems with data itself, i.e., detecting outliers or anomalies.
- The understanding of both large-scale as well as small-scale features of data.
- The creation of various hypotheses related to the data.

Visual representations range from simple maps and schematic diagrams to computer generated 2D and 3D visualizations. They differ themselves from other kinds of representations, e.g., sentential representations, in the fact that they make use of *visual variables* to convey the information to the user. In contrast, sentential representations use the semantics of their constituent units, words, and letters, to achieve the same thing. Thus, the meaning of a word is dependent on its context and its letters but not on the spatial position of the word.

The aim of visual representations is dependent on the context of their usage. However, their advantages are usually focused on these three categories [85]:

- *Information recording*, that is related to the usage of visual presentations as a storage mechanism in order to avoid the need for memorization of data and their relationships.
- *Information communication*, where visual representations play the role of a *message* for communicating the essential features of the data visualized.
- *Information processing*, where visual representations are used as a means to derive knowledge from data.

Whereas the first two advantages are valid also for other kinds of representations, the last one is specific for visual representations.

This chapter is concerned with visual representations in the context of human-centered visualization environments. Considering the variety of issues

A. Kerren et al. (Eds.): Human-Centered Visualization Environments 2006, LNCS 4417, pp. 163–230, 2007.

that relate to visual representations, it will focus on computer-generated visual representations in different contexts. Before introducing the various techniques which are used to visualize specific data types, a short introduction to perceptual issues is given in Section 4.1. Furthermore, different issues, such as taxonomies for data, visual variables and their ability to express different data types, are discussed in Section 4.1. Section 4.2 focuses on general criteria used in information visualization and the use of metaphors. Section 4.3 presents a survey of different visualization techniques, mainly in the context of multivariate data, by discussing properties of different techniques related to their comprehensive and interaction properties, advantages, and drawbacks with illustrations given for different data sets. Section 4.4 provides an overview of existing evaluations on visualization techniques designed for graphs and trees. The survey mainly focuses on the effect of graph layout algorithms which compute the position of nodes and edges, as well as on user's understanding of graphs for different tasks. Section 4.5 covers several issues concerning multiple view visualizations. Apart from a classification of multiple view instances, design-issues are discussed. The section is concluded with a comparison based on evaluation studies between multiple views and integrated views.

4.1 Perceptual and Cognitive Issues

Knowledge about perceptual and cognitive issues is very important in order to enhance visualizations, e.g., by proper use of colors, and to avoid potentially misleading usage of metaphors in visualizations.

This section will concentrate on issues, such as preattentive processing, visual variables and their role in visualization. Before these issues are discussed, a general schema of visualization process is discussed, taxonomies for classifying data are reviewed, and the mapping between data and visual variables is illustrated.

4.1.1 The Visualization Process

The visualization process usually consists of the following steps:

1. The collection of data to be visualized.
2. The visual display of data.
3. The human perception of the visualization.

The second step can be further divided into preprocessing of data and visual rendering of the preprocessed data. Figure 4.1 adapted from Ware [873] illustrates the visualization process with the above described steps.

Depending on the context, data either possesses a clear visual representation and is visualized directly without any further preprocessing, or a proper transformation and an interactive process between the user and the visualization take place in order for the user to accomplish the tasks.

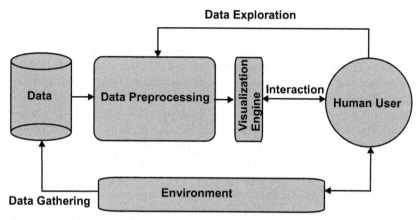

Fig. 4.1. The visualization process with its components. Image adapted from C. Ware [872].

4.1.2   Types of Data

Data is at the source of every visualization method. However, its attributes vary from one data set to the other. Below, two taxonomies related to data attributes and data types are discussed.

Attributes of Data. One of the broadly accepted taxonomies for classification of data scales is the one defined by Stevens [795]. According to this taxonomy, there are four categories for measuring data scales: nominal, ordinal, interval and ratio.

- *Nominal* scale represents a collection of identifiers, where no specific order is defined, e.g., hair color of people. Every transformation preserves the relationships between variables of this scale.
- *Ordinal* scale, in contrast to nominal scale, encompasses values that have an ordering defined in them. Examples include income of a household classified as low, medium and high; or height defined as short, medium and tall; etc.
- *Interval* scale is a further extension of the ordinal scale, where the intervals between possible values of the variables are equally spaced. Thus, continuing in the light of previous examples, consider three people with heights 160, 175, and 190 cm. In the case of ordinal variables, they would be short, medium, and tall, i.e., no presumption is possible about the differences between the three persons, whereas in the case of interval scale, we know that the difference between the third and second person is the same as the difference between the second and first person.
- *Ratio* scale is an extension of the interval scale, where an absolute zero is defined as in the case of money, size etc.

Data in Context of Information Visualization. Shneiderman [759] has defined a taxonomy of seven data types in the context of information visualization:

1. *1-dimensional* or linear/univariate data types include data which could be organized in a sequential manner, such as lists of strings, source code of programs, texts, and so on. Each item belonging to collections of this data type could possibly have attributes that characterize it.
2. *2-dimensional* or planar/map/bivariate data include geographic maps, plans and alike where each item in the collection covers some part of 2D plan. This kind of data type is extensively used in geographic information systems.
3. *3-dimensional* or trivariate data could represent real-world objects, such as molecules, the human body, and buildings. Thus, these objects have items with volume and some potentially complex relationship with other items.
4. *Temporal* data represent time lines which are widely used and crucial in the context of medical records or project management. In contrast to 1-dimensional data presented above, temporal data have a start and a finish defined and overlaps are not excluded.
5. *Multi-dimensional* or multivariate data represent relational and statistical databases. Such databases are conveniently manipulated as multidimensional data in which items with n attributes become points in a n-dimensional space.
6. *Tree* data hierarchies or tree structures are collections of items with each item having a link to one parent item (except the root). Items and links between a parent and a child can have multiple attributes.
7. *Network* or graph data represent data whose structure and relationships cannot be captured with hierarchical data types like trees. In this case, links exist arbitrarily and not only between child and parent nodes.

4.1.3 Preattentive Processing

Certain features of the visual image are identified easily after a very brief exposure to the image. This process, which logically occurs before the attention of the user is concentrated on the details of the visual image, is called *preattentive processing*. One such example, generated in analogy with an example given in [873], is presented in Figure 4.2. The same block of numbers is presented two times, in the first case (a) without any highlighting, and in the second case (b), the digits **3** are bold whereas the rest is gray. It is clear that counting 3s in the second example is much easier than the first.

In the context of visualization, preattentive processing is important because good visualizations could be enhanced to make use of factors that can be processed preattentively. Thus, if one is interested that the user identifies quickly something on a visual display, it could be made distinct from the rest by using preattentively processed features. Typically, experiments are conducted in order to find out if certain features are processed preattentively or not. If the time taken to distinguish the target is independent of the distraction level, then the subject feature is processed preattentively. Table 4.1 presents features of visual images that are processed preattentively, taken from [872].

Table 4.1 also shows that color is one of the preattentively processed features. However, in order for a color to be preattentively distinguished, it should

62469533302564284162533066088093455666026249775005
47173708707625885929151544992118585041209070762974
00814240307627367608821441631497293941734788463575
75158257142149622091596144304923114510440467803674
05161008726205613478351811614648711502830618984204

(a)

624695**333**0256428416253**33**066088093**4**55666026249775005
4717**3**708707625885929151544992118585041209070762974
008142403076273**6**76088214416**3**1497293941**7**34788463575
7515825714214962209159614**3**04**923**114510440467803674
05161008726205613**4783**51811614648711502**83**0618984204

(b)

Fig. 4.2. Preattentive processing example.

Table 4.1. Preattentively processed features grouped with respect to visual variables.

Form	Color	Motion	Spatial Position
Line Orientation	Hue	Flicker	2D Position
Line Length, Width	Intensity	Motion Direction	Stereoscopic Depth
Line Colinearity			Convexity/Concavity
Size			
Curvature			
Spatial Grouping			
Added Marks			

lie outside of the region defined by the existing colors in the CIE L*a*b* [299] color space developed for describing the colors visible to the human eye. The CIE L*a*b* color space, although not a directly displayable format, has several advantages, such as its colorimetric property where similarly perceived colors are also encoded similarly, its perceptual uniformity, i.e., color differences are perceived uniformly, and its device independency. Thus, the *convex hull* defined by certain colors in the CIE L*a*b* space defines points, i.e., colors, that have a certain similarity with all the predefined colors. Thus, colors that are preattentively distinct from the given colors lie outside this convex hull.

Figure 4.3 adapted from [872] illustrates this idea. In 4.3(a), the gray color lies within the convex hull defined by colors blue, red, yellow, and green in CIE L*a*b* color space and for this reason, the gray circle is difficult to find in 4.3(c) whereas in 4.3(b) the red color lies outside the convex hull defined by colors blue, yellow, and green in CIE L*a*b* color space, making thus the red circle in 4.3(d) easier to distinguish.

Visual Variables. In his seminal work *Semiology of Graphics*, Bertin developed a theory of what he calls *visual variables* [85]. The graphics system has according to Bertin the following seven visual variables: *position, form, orientation, color, texture, value,* and *size*. Visual variables were characterized intentionally by Bertin as retinal variables, because they can be compared effortlessly without additional cognitive processing, as if the retina were doing all the work.

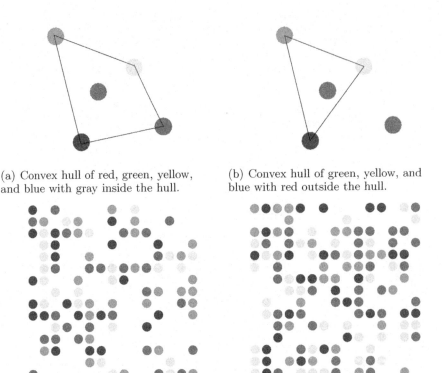

(a) Convex hull of red, green, yellow, and blue with gray inside the hull.

(b) Convex hull of green, yellow, and blue with red outside the hull.

(c) Gray is not processed preattentively.

(d) Red is processed preattentively.

Fig. 4.3. Illustration of preattentive processing of colors. Image adapted from C. Ware [872].

Figure 4.4 illustrates visually these seven visual variables. In computer-based visualization, motion is also considered as a visual variable. Furthermore, the set of visual variables is a well selected subset of preattentively processed features in Table 4.1. In the context of human processing, the differences expressed by the above mentioned visual variables are distinguished perceptually without involving cognitive steps as in the case of comparing numbers.

Two visual variables which could be confused with each other are color and value. Value represents the luminance or the grayscale value, and it is different from color, although somebody might argue that both represent subsets of RGB color space. Value is thought to be suitable for ordinal types, whereas color is thought to be suitable for nominal/categorical data types.

Thus, visual variables serve as a means of communication by encoding data in such a way as to draw distinctions between visual elements. However, depending on the attributes of data to be visualized (see Section 4.1.2), some of these visual variables have more representational power than others. Thus, when visualizing a file system, shape is not as efficient as color to make some files distinguishable from the others. For certain types of data, e.g., temperature, any one of these visual variables could be used: position on a scale, length of a bar, color of an

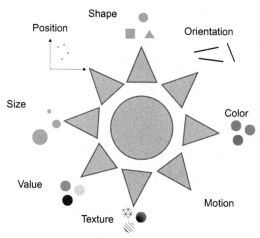

Fig. 4.4. Seven retinal variables as defined by Bertin [85] plus motion.

indicator, or shape of an icon. The choice of visual variables will strongly affect how the users will be able to perceive and use the displayed data. Visualization could be considered as a mapping between data on one side and visual variables or a combination of them on the other side.

In general, Bertin divides the characteristics of perception of visual variables into four groups:

– *Associative perception* describes how much a visual variable affects the visibility of other dimensions. The size or color of an object is unaffected by its orientation, making orientation associative whereas for very small objects we can hardly distinguish their orientation or color, making size a dissociative variable. Size and value dominate perception and are both dissociative variables.
– *Selective perception* defines how good a certain visual variable isolates particular instances from the rest. A selective visual variable is distinguished easily. This process is immediate and effortless, e.g., selection of all green objects in a visual display. All visual variables are selective with exception of shape. Thus, the process of picking out a triangle amidst a set of rectangles does not occur effortlessly.
– *Ordered perception* of a visual variable means that the objects should be able to be put into a ranked order based on its values. The perception of an ordered variable is fulfilled without consulting an index to determine the ranking of the objects. Position, size and value are ordered in human perception.
– *Quantitative perception* restricts the criteria of ordered perception further; it must be possible for a viewer to distinguish between two ordered values and to be able to determine the amount of difference. Position and size are quantitative in human perception.

Table 4.2 shows the seven visual variables and their characteristics, whereas Table 4.3 shows their appropriateness for being used to visualize different datatypes.

Table 4.2. Characteristics of visual variables with respect to their perception properties [85].

	Selective	Associative	Quantitative	Order
Position	yes	yes	yes	yes
Size	yes	no	yes	yes
Shape	no	yes	no	no
Value	yes	no	no	yes
Color	yes	yes	no	no
Orientation	yes	yes	no	no
Texture	yes	yes	no	no
Motion	yes	yes	no	no

Table 4.3. Appropriateness of visual variables for different data types with 1 lowest and 3 highest.

	Categorical/Nominal	Ordinal	Numeric
Position	3	3	3
Size	1	3	3
Shape	3	2	1
Value	1	3	3
Color	3	2	1
Orientation	3	1	1
Texture	3	1	1

4.2 Information Visualization Criteria and Metaphors

Over the last few years, the amount of digitized data has grown rapidly. Providing tools that present data in a way to help people understand and gain insight from this data is becoming more important.

Tufte [836] pointed out that *"There are right ways and wrong ways to show data; there are displays that reveal the truth and displays that do not.".* He illustrated this point via an example of miscommunication between NASA and rocket engineers caused by a bad visualization. This miscommunication was the root cause of the *Challenger* space shuttle explosion.

In January 1986, the space shuttle *Challenger* was launched on a very cold day and two rubber O-rings lost their resiliency. Consequently, the O-rings leaked and caused the explosion of the space shuttle. The day before the engineers who designed the rocket recommended to NASA not to launch the space shuttle the next day. Their decision was derived inter alia from the history of O-ring damage during previous cool-weather launches of shuttle. The Report of the Presidential Commission on the Space Shuttle Accident (Washington, DC, 1986) shows in volume V on page 896 one of the diagrams the engineers presented to NASA. Unfortunately, this diagram does not reveal obvious patterns but seems to show that the incidents of damage are few.

Tufte suggested to present the same data using a simple scatterplot[1] (see [836], page 45) that depicts the relationship between damage and temperature. The different types of damage are combined into one single value of severity. The predicted launch temperature for the following day is also marked on the graph to provide a relation to the previous launches.

This example illustrated how important human-centered visualizations are: Even though the rocket engineer's visualization contained all the data necessary to see the relationship between temperature and damage, it was not suitable to point out to a human observer the high risk of the rocket launch. If the NASA officials would have seen Tufte's scatterplot visualization instead, probably they had decided not to launch the space shuttle and the disaster might have been avoided.

4.2.1 Information Visualization Criteria

Computers, the internet and the web give people access to incredible amounts of data like news, sports, financial, purchases, and a lot more. This data explosion raises the questions how to make sense of the data, how to use it in the process of decision making, how to avoid to be overwhelmed, and finally, how to transfer the data to people.

Humans have different senses to receive data: vision, acoustic, haptic/tactile, smell, and taste. With 100 MB per second, vision has the highest bandwidth of all of these senses. Furthermore, human vision is fast, works in parallel preattentively, is very suitable for pattern recognition, and is closely connected to the humans memory and cognitive capacity. People also often tend to think visually and therefore it makes sense to use this impressive sense to convey data.

The challenge of information visualization is to transform *data* into *information*—providing understanding and insight—thus making it useful to people. Consider the following example: Given a census of the percentage of college degree recipients and the income per capita of the states in the United States (see Figure 4.5), consider the following questions:

1. Which state has the highest income?
2. Is there a relationship between income and education?
3. Are there any outliers?

Using the visualization of the data shown in Figure 4.5, it takes some time to answer the questions because one must scan over the whole table. But there are also scenarios where it is even harder to answer the questions: What if you could only see the data of one state at a time (like at the website of the Census Bureau)? Or imagine someone just reads the data to you. . . There are better ways to present this data. By using an interactive scatterplot visualization (Figure 4.6) the appearance of extrema, outliers, and such is more readily apparent.

---

[1] A scatterplot is a graph to visually display and compare two or more sets of related quantitative, or numerical, data by displaying only finitely many points, each having a coordinate on a horizontal and a vertical axis.

Table - StateData ()

Load | Snap

State	College Degree %	Per Capita Income
Alabama	20.6%	11486
Alaska	30.3%	17610
Arizona	27.1%	13461
Arkansas	17.0%	10520
California	31.3%	16409
Colorado	33.9%	14821
Connecticut	33.8%	20189
Delaware	27.9%	15054
District of Columbia	36.4%	18881
Florida	24.9%	14698
Georgia	24.3%	13631
Hawaii	31.2%	15770
Idaho	25.2%	11457
Illinois	26.8%	15201
Indiana	20.9%	13149
Iowa	24.5%	12422
Kansas	26.5%	13300
Kentucky	17.7%	11153
Louisiana	19.4%	10635
Maine	25.7%	12957
Maryland	31.7%	17730
Massachusetts	34.5%	17224
Michigan	24.1%	14154
Minnesota	30.4%	14389
Mississippi	19.9%	9648
Missouri	22.3%	12989
Montana	25.4%	11213
Nebraska	26.0%	12452
Nevada	21.5%	15214
New Hampshire	32.4%	15953
New Jersey	30.1%	16714
New Mexico	25.5%	11246
New York	29.6%	16501
North Carolina	24.2%	12885
North Dakota	29.1%	11051
Ohio	22.3%	13461
Oklahoma	22.8%	11893
Oregon	27.5%	13418
Pennsylvania	23.2%	14068
Rhode Island	27.5%	14901
South Carolina	23.0%	11897
South Dakota	24.6%	10661
Tennessee	20.1%	12255
Texas	25.5%	12904
Utah	30.0%	11029
Vermont	31.5%	13527
Virginia	30.0%	15713
Washington	30.9%	14923
West Virginia	16.1%	10520
Wisconsin	24.9%	13276
Wyoming	25.7%	12311

Fig. 4.5. Visualization using a table. *Image courtesy of C. North.*

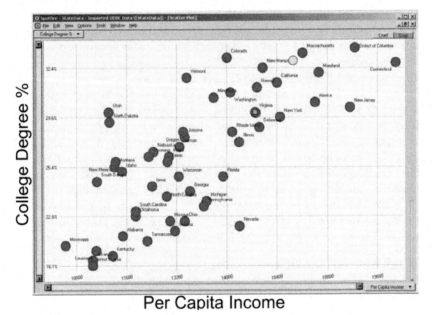

Fig. 4.6. Visualization using a scatterplot. *Image courtesy of C. North.*

The purpose of visualization is to provide insight (not pictures) to support humans in the process of discovery, decision making, and explanation. The main idea is helping people to think by providing a frame of reference and a temporary area to store cognition externally. Card et al. [145] defined information visualization as follows:

> *"Information visualization is the use of computer-supported, interactive, visual representations of abstract data in order to amplify cognition."*

In this context, information is considered as items, entities, or things which do not have a direct physical correspondence—a notion of abstractness of these entities is important too.

Information visualization differs from scientific visualization in that the latter primarily relates to and represents physical or geometric quantities like the air flow over a wing. Information visualization comprises of two components: A spatial mapping which takes items without a direct physical correspondence and maps them into a screen space, and a visual representation which provides information a depiction that supports human-centered processes, like analysis and decision-making. Information visualization takes the following tasks into account:

- *Search:* Finding a specific piece of information;
- *Browsing:* Looking over or inspecting something in a more casual manner or seeking interesting information in general; and
- *Analysis:* Comparing, differentiating, looking for outliers, extremes, and patterns.

This section provided a brief introduction to the area of information visualization. [608, 835–837] provide a much deeper insight into this topic. To produce visualizations that successfully convey information to humans it is important to understand the concept of human visual perception, as discussed in the previous section.

4.2.2   Metaphors

In this subsection, we present the application of visual metaphors in the domain of social visualization. Judith Donath defines social visualization as the *"visualization of social information for social purposes"* [207]. The PeopleGarden System [913] uses garden and flower metaphors to visualize online interaction environments (virtual communities). The system provides both individual and societal views to answer the following users' questions about a discussion group:

1. Do participants really get involved?
2. How much interaction is there?
3. Do participants welcome newcomers?
4. Who are the experts?

PeopleGarden uses data portraits (which are abstract representations of users' interaction history) to answer these questions. Physical features, such as gender, age, or race, are not incorporated into the portrait. The data portraits combine a user's history, relations between users, and represent individuals in an online environment. Over time, a user's portrait changes depending in the action of the user in the community.

Fundamental View of an Individual. Each user is represented as a flower, as shown in Figure 4.7. The user's postings are represented as petals of the flower, arranged by time in a clockwise manner. The different visual parameters of a petal are used to represent different attributes of a posting, like the time of a posting, the amount of answers, or whether a post starts a new conversation.

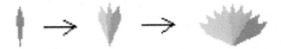

Fig. 4.7. Basic PeopleFlower. *Image courtesy of R. Xiong and J. Donath.*

Fig. 4.8. A user's PeopleFlower changes over time. *Image courtesy of R. Xiong and J. Donath.*

Fig. 4.9. Three users with same amount of postings over different durations, and with different amount of responses. *Image courtesy of R. Xiong and J. Donath.*

Fig. 4.10. The same three users from Figure 4.9, this time with magenta representing initial posts, blue replies. *Image courtesy of R. Xiong and J. Donath.*

Time Since Posting. PeopleFlower uses the ordering as well as the saturation of petals to indicate time. New posts are added to the right and older petals slide back so the flower stays symmetric. Each petal fades over time showing time since the posting. A marked difference in saturation of adjacent petals denotes a gap in posting. Figure 4.8 shows the development of a PeopleFlower over time.

Response to Posting. To illustrate the amount of interaction in the community, PeopleFlower also displays the amount of feedback from other users. Small circles drawn on top of a posting are used to represent each follow-up response, as shown

Fig. 4.11. A PeopleGarden showing messages from a message board with 1,200 postings over a two months period. *Image courtesy of R. Xiong and J. Donath.*

in Figure 4.9. The three users represented in Figure 4.9 posted the same amount of messages but at different time intervals (indicated by the saturation) and the amount of responses also varies.

Initial Post Versus Reply. Figure 4.10 shows the same PeopleFlowers, like Figure 4.9, but the color of the petals represents whether it was an original post or a reply. Here, magenta is an original post, blue is a reply. This leads to more insight into the situation: User *A* started a thread and received many responses. After that User *A* replied to other's postings. User *B* only responded to other user's postings (all posts are colored blue). User *C* made initial post as well as replies. This user received the most replies.

Visualizing Groups of People. Many portraits can be combined to make a garden. A garden with more bright flowers indicates a discussion group with more new posts. It looks healthier than one with faded flowers representing a group with old posts. Figure 4.11 shows a message board with 1,200 postings over two months. Each flower represents a different user. Height indicates length of time at the board. The metaphor shows that a flower planted earlier is taller than one planted later. This visualization can help answer the first and the last

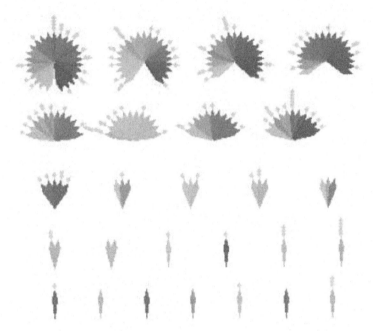

Fig. 4.12. A PeopleGarden sorted by amount of postings. Magenta denotes initial postings, and blue denotes replies. *Image courtesy of R. Xiong and J. Donath.*

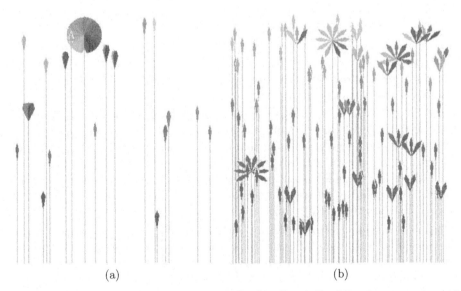

(a)   (b)

Fig. 4.13. Two different communities visualized as PeopleGardens. *Image courtesy of R. Xiong and J. Donath.*

question raised at the beginning of this section: (1) There are many users with varying level of participation, many of them posted continuously. (4) The users contributing the most have been a member of the community the longest.

To answer more detailed questions about the level of response, PeopleGarden offers an alternate garden view sorted by the number of postings (see Figure 4.12). This visualization is helpful to answer the remaining two questions: (2) People answer each other quite a lot. (3) The chances for newcomers to get a response is about 50%—their initial posts are more likely to get a response.

Figure 4.13 compares two different groups. In Figure 4.13(a), a group with one dominating voice with a large number of replies in blue is shown. Height of a flower denotes again how long a user has been at the board. A more democratic group with a large number of initial posts in magenta is shown in Figure 4.13(b).

4.3 Multivariate Visualization Techniques

The field of abstract data visualization (information visualization) deals with either high-dimensionality, like relational multidimensional datasets, or with complex structure, such as graphs, trees, etc. Although their visualization is not necessarily bound to the computer, the usage of computers has strongly affected the way it is performed. However, compared to other subfields of computer graphics, information visualization has a serious restriction: the available screen space. Whereas slow algorithms perform better on faster computers or algorithms that require too much memory become feasible by extending the memory of the computer, the screen resolution has remained nearly constant in the last years. Thus, the purpose of information visualization research is to optimally use the available screen space for conveying as much information as possible to the user. However, this task becomes challenging in the case of high-dimensional datasets which are encountered frequently in research and practical applications. Furthermore, even massive low-dimensional datasets can pose big challenges in the optimal usage of the available screen space. Issues related to visualization techniques for low- and high-dimensional datasets as well as their evaluation will be discussed in the remainder of this section.

4.3.1 Low-Dimensional Data Visualization

One of the broadly used tools in the analysis of univariate data are *dot plots* and their variants. Figure 4.14(a) presents the simplest of them, where each value along the range of values of the data set is represented as an empty circle (the data shows spirits consumption for a certain period for 50 US States [896]). This simple variant is suitable for relatively small data sets because of the *clutter effect*. Clutter is characterized by dense graphics that hinder proper perception.

For larger data sets, a variant of dot plots called *stripe plots*, where circles are replaced with lines for reducing the information overload, is shown in Figure4.14(b). Another possibility to reduce clutter is to use the second dimension to place circles either regularly like in *stacked dot plots* (see Figure 4.14(c))

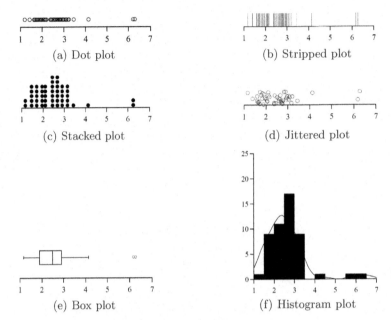

Fig. 4.14. Univariate data plots showing spirit consumption for 50 US states [896]. (a)-(d) map data directly into 2D space; (e) and (f) use statistical indicators to visualize data.

or randomly like in *jittered dot plots* in Figure 4.14(d). Figure 4.14(e) represents *box plots*, a more sophisticated technique which presents in the same view the median, quartiles, and the range of the data. Furthermore, outliers (in the right part) could be left out in order not to distort the visualization of the rest of the data. Box-plots are useful for having an overview of all the data set simultaneously with its symmetry, skewness, and possible outliers. A *histogram plot* in Figure 4.14(f) builds on a similar idea by displaying the frequencies of occurrence of values in uniformly divided ranges. However, the discretization size is crucial to the proper understanding of the histogram as different discretization values derive different histograms. The above presented techniques could possibly be combined together, e.g., the box-plot could be combined quite nicely with the histogram plot.

The common factor of the discussed univariate techniques is that they all use the visual variable position in one dimension to map data. Furthermore, some of the techniques use size as a second visual variable and some make use of another dimension, i.e., making full use of 2D position. Regarding computational issues, simple algorithms are used to generate vertical positions in stacked plots and jittered plots. For computing the discretization step in the histogram plot, different heuristics are used. Two-dimensional data is commonly depicted as the ubiquitous scatterplot which maps the two dimensions of the data to the XY dimensions of the display. In this way, a dataset is mapped to a set of points in the Euclidean space. Figure 4.15 presents a 2D scatterplot example, representing two

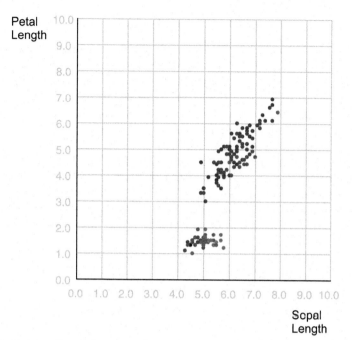

Fig. 4.15. Scatterplot of first and third dimensions of Iris dataset representing the dimensions sepal length and petal length for determining the XY position. The color of the instance is determined by the two other dimensions.

dimensions of the Iris dataset[2]. The example uses the dimensions sepal length and petal length for determining the XY position and the two other features for determining the color of the instance. One of the major usages of scatterplots is to discover possible correlations between the considered variables. The scales of scatterplot axes play a very important role in this context and should be scaled carefully.

One of the problems often considered in the context of scatterplots is the visual clutter occurring in large datasets. Different techniques ranging from simple jittering, i.e., objects that should be plotted in the same 2D position are placed randomly in a small neighborhood, to sampling, i.e., selection of fewer, more significant points.

Similar scatterplots could be created for 3D data. In this case, the three dimensions of the dataset are mapped to XYZ axes (instead of XY axes used in 2D). The whole scatterplot is then usually rotated about the vertical axis, thus revealing different structures existing in the data [208].

---

[2] The Iris dataset contains 150 random samples of flowers from the iris species setosa, versicolor, and virginica. From each species there are 50 four-dimensional observations for sepal length, sepal width, petal length, and petal width in cm [185].

4.3.2 Multidimensional Data Visualization

Multidimensional visualization is a subfield of information visualization that focuses on multidimensional datasets. Sometimes, the terms multivariate and multidimensional are used interchangeably. The distinction between the two however is often considered to be the fact that multidimensional data accounts for independent variables and multivariate data possibly accounts for dependent variables [904]. Multidimensional datasets can be thought as a set of entities (or objects), where each entity possesses a vector of attributes (or features) and these attributes may be discrete, continuous, or take on symbolic (nominal) values. Difficulties in visualizing data with more than three dimensions are mainly raised because there are no obvious ways for visualizing such data (unlike 2D plots in two dimensions), and because high-dimensional data are often massive in size. Thus, a transformation process needs to take place before rendering the data.

Depending on which visual variables they use, on how the available screen space is used, and the transformation that data undergoes, techniques for visualizing multidimensional data can be broadly categorized as:

- Dimensional subsetting, such as scatterplot matrices [165],
- Dimensional embedding techniques, such as dimensional stacking [500],
- Axis reconfiguration techniques, such as parallel coordinates [389],
- Glyph-based techniques, such as Chernoff faces [156],
- Dimensional reduction techniques, such as multidimensional scaling, principal component analysis, and self-organizing maps [544, 740, 920], and
- Tabular visualization techniques, such as the reorderable matrix and its derivatives [84].

Below, each of these categories and their most representative applications will be discussed.

Scatterplot Matrices. A simple but powerful way to extend the 2D scatterplot for visualizing high-dimensional data is by creating a grid of scatter plots for every pair of dimensions/features. Figure 4.16 presents a scatterplot matrix for the Iris dataset [258]. As in the case of a single scatterplot, two dimensions are used to define the 2D position of the object, and the two remaining features are used to enhance the scatter plots by coloring their respective objects. User interaction is commonly used to help interpret the visualizations. In this context brushing, i.e., making the selection distinguishable from the rest, and linking/coordination between different scatterplots play a very important role.

Dimensional Embedding Techniques. The methods used in this context are hierarchical in nature and require often either categorical data or a discretization of numeric data. The main idea is that a quadratic space is divided recursively into sets of embedded rectangles. The two most important dimensions are presented by the outer horizontal and vertical dimensions of the grid; each grid cell is further divided in the same way using the rest of dimensions. Color is often used to characterize the last feature represented by the finest rectangle. It is understandable that levels of hierarchy in this context cannot be endless because

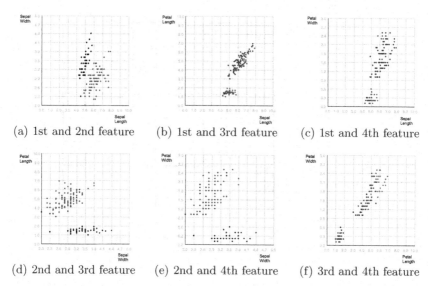

Fig. 4.16. Colored scatterplot matrix of the Iris dataset showing all possible combinations of dimensions, $\frac{4 \times 3}{2}$ for $n = 4$.

of the display resolution; indeed visualizing more than nine dimensions with this method is difficult [359]. This comes from the fact that usually 3-5 bins are used to discretize each feature and that the number of cells in horizontal or vertical direction grows exponentially. The method is effective in generating an overview of the dataset to be visualized; however, it is sensitive to the discretization step and alternate discretizations could possibly create different views that might confuse the user. Figure 4.17 shows the dimensional stack visualization of the Iris data set, taken from [359]. The color of squares presents the class each object belongs to, and as we could see also from Figure 4.16, two classes intersect each other which is reflected in the color. The dimensional stack is first discretized based on the dimensions petal width and sepal width. The inner discretization is done then based on dimensions petal length and sepal length.

Axis Reconfiguration Techniques. Parallel coordinates visualization introduced by Inselberg and Dimsdale [389] is one of the most popular methods used in multidimensional data visualization. Each feature of the data in this method corresponds to an axis; the axes by themselves are organized as uniformly spaced horizontal (sometimes vertical) lines. A point in the high-dimensional space is represented as a line connecting points on each axis. Figure 4.18(a) shows the parallel coordinates visualization of the Cars dataset[3]. This method suffers from the clutter effect. To reduce cluttering, different techniques, such as distortion or sampling, are used. However, in the case of parallel coordinates, algorithmic approaches could be used to enhance visualizations. Thus, a different order of dimensions could possibly reduce (or increase) clutter [644]. The biggest difficul-

---

[3] The Cars dataset contains information on mpg, cylinders, displacement, etc. (8 variables) for 406 different cars [209].

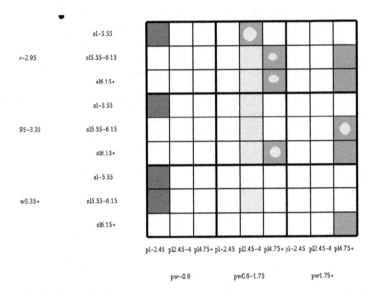

Fig. 4.17. Dimensional stacking of Iris dataset. The two outer discretized dimensions are petal width and sepal width, whereas the two inner ones are petal length and sepal length [359]. *Image courtesy of P. Hoffman.*

ties occur in the disclosing of relationships of non-adjacent dimensions. A proper order brings more clarity as Figure 4.18(b) illustrates. Efficient brushing techniques are also used to highlight or remove items from the visual display. One of this techniques, *Angular Brushing*, is presented by Hauser et al. [342]. Whereas normal brushing allows the user to mark certain subsets of interest by selecting intervals where the values of a certain feature should lie, angular brushing allows more sophisticated selection of objects which fulfill certain slope requirements for neighboring axes.

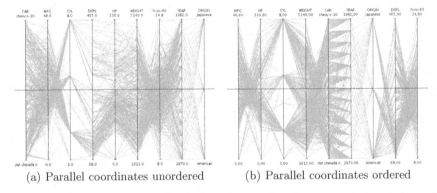

(a) Parallel coordinates unordered   (b) Parallel coordinates ordered

Fig. 4.18. Parallel coordinates [389] plot where each axis represents one feature. An object is represented by a line connecting points on each axis.

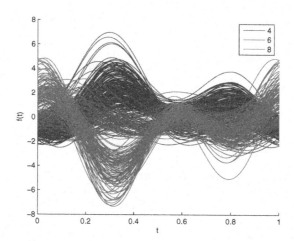

Fig. 4.19. Andrews Plot [19] of the Cars dataset.

Andrews curves [19] is a visualization method similar to parallel coordinates based on a trigonometric transformation of the object attributes. It has the property of preserving Euclidean distances between objects. Thus, close points in the dataset will result in similar plots, and plots for distant points will be distinct. These characteristics are fulfilled by parallel coordinates, too. Figure 4.19 presents the Andrews plot of the Cars dataset.

Glyph-Based Techniques. Glyphs and icons are graphical entities, which represent the attributes of data objects via visual features such as shape, orientation, color and size. In the case of Chernoff faces [156], multidimensional data is represented by means of faces with changing attributes. The changing attributes of the faces include the size, orientation, and location of facial components (mouth, eyes, eyebrows). Thus, the problem of finding similar vectors is converted into the problem of finding similar faces. The effectiveness of this method is strongly debated. Morris et al. [571] studied the effectiveness of the features used in Chernoff faces. They came to the conclusion that their perception is a serial process and is not preattentive.

Another icon-based method are the so-called *star glyphs*, where axes are arranged as radiating lines in equal angular distance, in contrast to parallel coordinates where they were arranged parallel to each other. Figure 4.20, generated with Matlab using Statistics Toolbox [824], illustrates both techniques. Multidimensional scaling is used to generate the 2D positions in the plot, and each Chernoff face or glyph plot is placed at the calculated 2D coordinates.

Dimension Reduction Methods. Dimension reduction is another alternative to visualize multidimensional data in 2D or 3D. There are two types of dimension reduction techniques: linear and nonlinear. Principal component analysis (PCA) [417] is a well known linear projection method, where the projected data is formed as a linear combination of the input data.

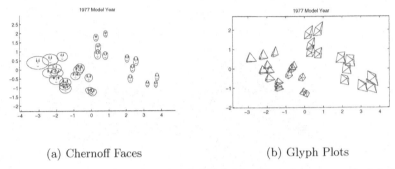

(a) Chernoff Faces   (b) Glyph Plots

Fig. 4.20. Icon-based plots combined with MDS. The 2D positions are calculated using projection. The attributes of glyphs represent features of data.

Multidimensional scaling (MDS) [544, 740, 920] represents a broad category of nonlinear projection methods such as Classical MDS [544], Sammon Mapping [727], etc. The first difference between MDS and the above presented techniques is that MDS operates on a distance matrix and not directly with raw data. MDS techniques try to construct the configuration of points in 2D or 3D which represent best the given distance matrix.

To illustrate the idea, consider Table 4.4, representing the distances between some major US cities (1=Boston, 2=New York, 3=Washington DC, 4=Miami, 5=Chicago, 6=Seattle, 7=San Francisco, 8=Los Angeles, 9=Denver) with the aim of reconstructing their map. Thus, we are looking for a two-dimensional configuration of the cities which should be "close" to the true map of these cities. Different computational approaches are used to achieve this aim, and multidimensional scaling techniques constitute one of the largest group in this context. Figure 4.21 represents one configuration of the cities generated using the classical MDS approach. As MDS solutions are insensitive to rotation, translation and reflection, the solution approximates fairly well the real map.

Table 4.4. Distance between some major US cities.

	1	2	3	4	5	6	7	8	9
1	0	206	429	1504	963	2976	3095	2979	1949.0
2	206	0	233	1308	802	2815	2934	2786	1771.0
3	429	233	0	1075	671	2684	2799	2631	1616.0
4	1504	1308	1075	0	1329	3273	3053	2687	2037.0
5	963	802	671	1329	0	2013	2142	2054	996.0
6	2976	2815	2684	3273	2013	0	808	1131	1307.0
7	3095	2934	2799	3053	2142	808	0	379	1235.0
8	2979	2786	2631	2687	2054	1131	379	0	1059.0
9	1949	1771	1616	2037	996	1307	1235	1059	0.0

It is clear that by visualizing high-dimensional data in 2D there is a loss of information most of the time. Techniques are distinguished from each other in functionality in the way that they approximate the distances between objects. Some

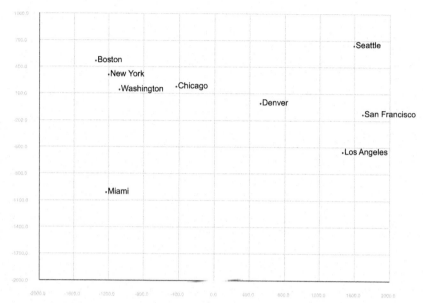

Fig. 4.21. MDS representation of US cities data from Table 4.4 generated using the classical MDS approach. MDS solutions are insensitive to rotation, translation and reflection.

methods, such as classical MDS, preserve better large distances, other methods like Sammon Mapping preserve small distances. Non-metric MDS methods consider the data not as a real distance matrix but rather as a similarity matrix.

The other difference between the visualization methods considered earlier and projection methods consist in the computational aspect of projection methods. Whereas the former concentrate on screen optimization, clutter reduction, etc., projection methods are computationally expensive, and the biggest challenge here is the computation of projections of big datasets. Current research in projection methods/MDS approaches is concentrated on the following tracks:

– Improving the computational side of MDS algorithms [575,576].
– Techniques on using MDS for discovering intrinsic structures present in datasets [721,823]. Figure 4.22 presents an example of Isomap [823]. In 4.22(a), the original dataset, which is three-dimensional but possesses an intrinsic structure, is plotted in 3D. If only Euclidean distance would be taken into consideration, then the projection of this dataset would be far from representing the right structure of the dataset. On the other side, Isomap can successfully preserve the geodesic distances by preprocessing the distances between objects. This preprocessing step takes as input the Euclidean distance matrix between points and outputs the transformed distance matrix, containing the all-pairs shortest path information.

– Inclusion of user feedback in the projection process [897].

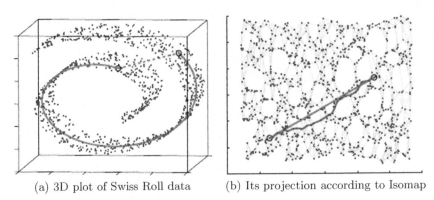

(a) 3D plot of Swiss Roll data   (b) Its projection according to Isomap

Fig. 4.22. Isomap example illustrating unfolding of intrinsic structures in multidimensional data [823]. *Image courtesy of Tenenbaum et al.*

Tabular Visualization Methods. The reorderable matrix method proposed by Bertin [84, 85] is a simple but robust approach to visualize tabular data. The main idea of the reorderable matrix method is to convert a tabular data set into an interactive 2D view. The 2D view has the same dimensions[4] as the original data, and according to Bertin, the data size should not exceed dimensions of $X \times Y = 10000$, where X and Y represent the dimensions of the rows and columns of data. Data values are replaced by filled circles whose size depends on the actual value. With manual interaction or automatic permutations, different patterns in the data are made visible.

For the human user, it is not easy to understand the semantics of data based only on raw numbers. Replacing the numbers with colored boxes is one solution to this problem. A slightly modified reorderable matrix method makes use of a color spectrum to transform a matrix of numbers into a matrix of colors [678].

Figure 4.23(b) represents the colored reorderable matrix of the data given in Figure 4.23(a) (for more information see [679,680]). In order to discover patterns in this visualization, columns/rows should be properly ordered. However, the ordering problem is NP-complete. Thus, heuristics, such as Sugiyama algorithm [804] or techniques based on solutions of the Traveling Salesperson Problem (TSP) [413], are used for ordering the reorderable matrix. Figure 4.23(c) is the reordered matrix corresponding to 4.23(b) where similar columns appear near each other.

The same technique can be used to visualize not only raw data as in Figure 4.23, but also proximity data, e.g., distance matrices or any other similarity matrix as Figure 4.24 illustrates. Figure 4.24(a) shows a similarity matrix generated from a clustering process, whereas Figure 4.24(b) shows its reorderable matrix. For

---

[4] The dimension here represents the magnitude of data, in contrast to dimension in the context of visualization used until now.

	r1 K_la	r1 K_lb	r1 K_mS	r1 r_max	r2 K_eq	r2 K_mP	r2 K_mS	r2 r_max	r3 kdiff	r4 K_eq	r4 K_mP	r4 K_mS	r4 r_max	r5 kdiff
A	-0.435	0.42	0.652	-0.076	-0.044	-0.002	0.003	-0.06	-0.042	0	0	0	0	-0.007
P1	-0.617	0.58	0.927	-0.13	0.021	0.001	0.03	-0.429	-0.013	-0.001	0.001		-0.002	-0.028
P1X	0.119	0.058	-0.181	0.262	0.294	0.013	-0.022	0.401	0.417	-0.252	-0.011	0.016	-0.035	-0.026
P2	-0.541	0.541	0.814	-0.07	-0.303	-0.014	0.023	-0.415	-0.292	0.319	0.015	-0.02	0.045	-0.094
P2X	0.166	0.062	-0.251	0.337	-0.449	-0.02	0.034	-0.609	-0.404	0.514	0.023	-0.031	0.07	0.963
S	0.004	-0.005	-0.006	-0.001	-0.001	0	0	-0.001	-0.001	0.001	0	0	0	0

(a) The raw data matrix

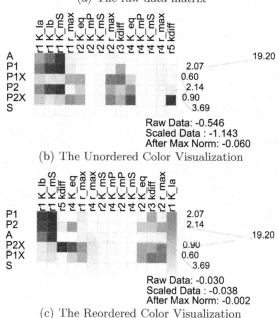

(b) The Unordered Color Visualization

(c) The Reordered Color Visualization

Fig. 4.23. The raw data and its color visualization. The data in (a) represents sensitivity matrices generated during simulation of metabolic models [679, 680]. (b) represents the transformation of the data into a colored reorderable matrix. (c) shows the same data after reordering.

reordering the matrix, the user can either proceed interactively or use heuristics (also in this case the reordering problem is NP-complete) to generate acceptable orderings.

Minnotte et al. [560] use reorderable matrices under another name, *data image*, to explore high-dimensional data. Marchette et al. [543] use data images for outlier detection in data. Corrgrams proposed by Friendly [271] is an approach similar to the reorderable matrix method to visually explore correlation matrices which are important in multivariate statistics. Bezdek and Hathaway [87] use an approach called ODI (Ordered Dissimilarity Image) for visually clustering data. Siirtola [765] combines parallel coordinates with reorderable matrices [84, 85] to visualize multidimensional data.

The biggest challenge encountered with the reorderable matrix is its scaling with growing data size. To solve these problems, techniques, such as sampling or focus+context displays, can be used in order to either reduce the size of datasets or to focus on certain parts of the visualization.

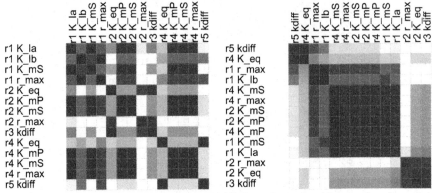

(a) Proximity data

	r1 K_la	r1 K_lb	r1 K_mS	r1 r_max	r2 K_eq	r2 K_mP	r2 K_mS	r2 r_max	r3 kdiff	r4 K_eq	r4 K_mP	r4 K_mS	r4 r_max	r5 kdiff
r1 K_la	1	0.476	0.913	0.505	0.359	0.942	0.942	0.058	0.398	0.175	0.942	0.942	0.942	0.029
r1 K_lb	0.476	1	0.563	0.913	0	0.476	0.476	0	0	0.291	0.476	0.476	0.476	0.437
r1 K_mS	0.913	0.563	1	0.476	0.301	0.913	0.913	0	0.34	0.146	0.913	0.913	0.913	0
r1 r_max	0.505	0.913	0.476	1	0	0.563	0.563	0	0	0.379	0.563	0.563	0.563	0.524
r2 K_eq	0.359	0	0.301	0	1	0.301	0.301	0.699	0.961	0.146	0.301	0.301	0.301	0
r2 K_mP	0.942	0.476	0.913	0.563	0.301	1	1	0	0.34	0.233	1	1	1	0.087
r2 K_mS	0.942	0.476	0.913	0.563	0.301	1	1	0	0.34	0.233	1	1	1	0.087
r2 r_max	0.058	0	0	0	0.699	0	0	1	0.66	0	0	0	0	0
r3 kdiff	0.398	0	0.34	0	0.961	0.34	0.34	0.66	1	0.146	0.34	0.34	0.34	0
r4 K_eq	0.175	0.291	0.146	0.379	0.146	0.233	0.233	0	0.146	1	0.233	0.233	0.233	0.854
r4 K_mP	0.942	0.476	0.913	0.563	0.301	1	1	0	0.34	0.233	1	1	1	0.087
r4 K_mS	0.942	0.476	0.913	0.563	0.301	1	1	0	0.34	0.233	1	1	1	0.087
r4 r_max	0.942	0.476	0.913	0.563	0.301	1	1	0	0.34	0.233	1	1	1	0.087
r5 kdiff	0.029	0.437	0	0.524	0	0.087	0.087	0	0	0.854	0.087	0.087	0.087	1

(b) Colored reorderable matrix of prox-   (c) Sorted reorderable matrix of proxim-
imity data   ity data

Fig. 4.24. Visualization of proximity data. The data in (a) represents accumulation of cluster results for time-varying multidimensional data [680]. (b) represents the transformation of the proximity data into a colored reorderable matrix. (c) shows the same data after reordering.

4.3.3 Usability Issues on Multidimensional Data Visualization

Proper usability studies related to multidimensional visualization techniques are rather scarce. One of the papers focusing on such issues is the one presented by Ward and Theroux [871]. They compared three of the techniques presented above, namely scatterplot matrix, icon based visualizations combined with PCA, and parallel coordinates. The tasks to be performed by the user were related to outlier and cluster detection, tasks which are very important in the context of visualization. On an overall basis, scatterplot matrix performed best followed by star glyphs combined with PCA and lastly by parallel coordinates. However, each of the techniques had its weaknesses, listed below.

- Scatterplot matrices are not effective in the following tasks:
  - Distinguishing overlapping clusters
  - Assessment of the size of large clusters
  - Outlier detection when outliers fall between clusters
- Glyphs are effective for:
  - Outlier detection when outliers fall between clusters
  and moderately effective on:

- Distinguishing overlapping clusters
- Assessment of the size of large clusters
- Assessment of outlier separation
- Differentiating between outlier and non-outliers
- Parallel coordinates are effective for differentiating between outlier and non-outliers.

Lee et al. [501] evaluated empirically the performance of Chernoff faces, star glyphs, and spatial visualizations (which is similar to MDS techniques presented previously) for binary data, i.e., categorical data with only two values. They came to the conclusion that spatial visualizations convey information more effectively than glyph plots. Their conclusions were in accordance with previously published conclusions about the serial processing of information while using Chernoff faces [571]. Regarding the evaluation of other techniques presented above, different measures are used. Thus, the performance of dimension reduction methods is evaluated in two ways, namely how good they approximate the distance matrix of the original data and how good they can recover intrinsic topologies in the data.

Siirtola [766] compares different implementations of the reorderable matrix. Experiments involving the original paper based implementation, a computer based implementation with manual reordering and another one with automatic reordering were conducted. The task to be completed was related to cluster finding and thus related to the finding of similar objects. The three methods had significant differences in performance of different tasks, and the one with automatic ordering performed better than the two others.

4.4   Graphs and Trees

Many real-world data sets are *relational*. Examples include phone calls made among people or the interactions among proteins in bacteria. These data sets can be modeled as graphs (or networks) with nodes representing entities and edges representing the relationships among them. Graph visualization provides a unique way to understand such relational data: By utilizing human perception, it can reveal the overall structure of the data, which is difficult to comprehend otherwise. Graph visualization has been applied successfully as an approach complementary to numerical analysis methods.

Considerable work has been done on graph visualization in the literature. A good survey can be found in the work by Herman et al. [346]. Due to the focus of this book, this section is not a survey of the latest developments of graph visualization, but rather related user studies. Also, not covered in this section are dynamic graph visualization and interaction techniques related to graph visualization to avoid possible overlap with other parts of the book.

Among the various visual elements involved in graph visualization, the emphasis of this section is on *Layout*—the positions of nodes and edges—and related issues, such as labeling. Layout is the key property that distinguishes graph visualization from other fields in information visualization. Proper layout is critical to reveal structure features of graphs, which are the fundamentals of many graph analysis tasks. The problem of finding a "good" graph layout has been well studied in the literature and there are several excellent surveys available [57, 193, 420, 432, 803]. While previous work mainly focuses on the methodology and performance aspects of graph visualization, this section provides an overview of studies on how graph layout and related methods affect people's understanding of graphs which is also known as *graph readability*.

The remainder of this section is organized as follows: Subsection 4.4.1 briefly describes the common applications of graph visualization. The background of graph visualization, including aesthetics and layout algorithms, is covered in Subsection 4.4.2. Subsection 4.4.3 discusses the effect of aesthetics on graph readability. The studies of layout algorithm effectiveness on graph readability are surveyed in Subsection 4.4.4. Visualization of large graphs, which is a problem that challenges the limits of layout algorithms, is discussed in Subsection 4.4.5. Integrated graph visualization and labeling are described in Subsection 4.4.6 and 4.4.7 respectively.

4.4.1 Applications

Early examples of automatic graph visualization applications (opposed to those produced manually) can be found in communication networks [69, 898], in which the nodes are the people and the edges are the phone calls between them. Another early application of graph visualization is VLSI design [628, 737]. Work in this area later led to methods that are important to planar and orthogonal drawing algorithms. Graph visualization has also been widely applied to demonstrate the structure of large software systems, and software visualization has become a relatively independent research field. Another successful application of graph visualization is in trade analysis, in which each node is a country (or region) and the edges between them shows the trade flow.

Recently, graph visualization has been applied to the analysis of biological data, such as phylogenetic trees [17, 148], protein-protein interaction networks [210, 640], and biological pathways [105, 298]. Also, graph visualization has been increasingly applied in social network analysis [108, 109, 268, 567], in which nodes represent people and edges correspond to some relation between them. This is widely accepted as a powerful tool to study the structure within an organization or the spread of epidemic diseases.

4.4.2 Background

In this subsection, we start with *layout conventions* which are the fundamental layout properties. This is followed by *layout aesthetics* which are the criteria layout methods aim to achieve to produce "good" visualizations. Finally, layout methods for different types of graphs are discussed.

Layout Conventions. A layout convention is a basic rule that the drawing of graphs must follow. Common graph layout conventions include [193]:

Polyline drawing: Each edge is drawn as a polygonal chain (Figure 4.25(a)).

Straight-line drawing: Each edge is drawn as a straight line segment (Figure 4.25(b)).

Orthogonal drawing: Each edge is drawn as a polygonal chain of alternating horizontal and vertical segments (Figure 4.25(c)).

Grid drawing: Nodes, crossings, and edge bends have integer coordinates (Figure 4.25(c)).

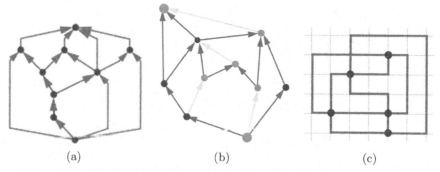

(a) (b) (c)

Fig. 4.25. Examples of various graph layout conventions: (a) Polyline drawing. (b) Straight-line drawing. (c) Orthogonal and grid drawing.

Layout Aesthetics. Aesthetics are quantitative measurements that affect graph readability. Commonly adopted aesthetics include [193]:

Crossings: Minimization of the total number of crossings between edges. Ideally, we would like to have a *planar drawing* (no edge crossing), but not every graph is planar.

Area and aspect ratio: The *area of a drawing* can be defined as the area of the smallest covering rectangle or convex polygon (convex hull). The ability to have area-efficient drawings is essential to save screen space. A closely related aesthetic is the *aspect ratio* which is the ratio between the long and short edge length of its covering rectangle. Ideally, we would like to obtain any aspect ratio in a given range, so the drawing has the flexibility to fit into differently shaped screen space.

Edge length: This includes the minimization of the sum of the edge lengths; minimization of the maximum edge length; and minimization of the variance of the edge lengths.

Bends: Similar to edge length, this includes the minimization of the total number of bends; the minimization of the maximum number of bends on an edge; and the minimization of the variance of the number of bends on the edge. These aesthetics are important for orthogonal drawing, while they are trivially satisfied by straight-line drawing.

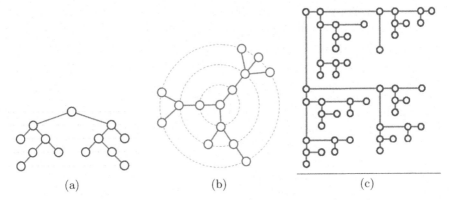

Fig. 4.26. Examples of various tree layout methods. (a) Layered drawing. (b) Radial drawing. (c) HV drawing. *Image courtesy of M. Patrignani.* (Produced by Computer Networks Research Group of the Roma Tre University.)

Angular resolution: Maximization of the smallest angle between two edges incident to the same node. This aesthetic is especially relevant for straight-line drawing.

Symmetry: Display the symmetries of the graph in a drawing. There are many types of symmetry, common ones include *reflective symmetry* (symmetrical along an axis) and *rotational symmetry* (a drawing that matches itself after rotating it by a certain angle). A complete list of symmetries and their definition can be found in [225, 508, 542].

The effectiveness of layout aesthetics on graph readability is detailed in Subsection 4.4.3.

Layout Methods. The aim of layout algorithms is to find positions for nodes and edges so the resulting drawing can facilitate understanding the graph structure. Usually, this is achieved by following one or more of the aesthetics discussed previously. In this section, we provide an overview of fundamental layout algorithms for various types of graphs.

Trees. Trees are one of the simplest and most commonly used graphs. Many real-world data sets have a tree structure, such as a file system and an organization chart. There are many layout algorithms designed specifically for tree visualization. One of the pioneering work is the hierarchical layout [697], where nodes are placed on horizontal layers according to their distance from the root (Figure 4.26(a)). In a radial drawing [226], the layers are mapped to concentric circles (Figure 4.26(b)). The HV drawing[5] [757] places the edges as rightward horizontal or downward vertical segments (Figure 4.26(c)) All these are straight-line drawings.

Hierarchies are usually visualized as node-link diagrams [697] which are not very space efficient. Space-filling visualizations have been developed to make more efficient use of the display area. These systems are characterized by their

---

[5] "HV" stands for "horizontal vertical".

compactness and effectiveness at showing the properties of nodes in a hierarchy through size or color [756]. One of the most common examples of a space-filling technique is the Treemap [758]. In the Treemap, the display is divided into rectangular regions to map an entire hierarchy of nodes and their children. Each node uses an amount of space relative to the weight of the item being represented in the hierarchy (such as the relative size of files in directories or the volume of shares sold on the stock market). More details about Treemap and its variations can be found in Subsection 4.4.4.

Planar Graphs. A graph is planar if it admits a planar drawing, in which no two edges cross. Due to the scope of this section, the details of layout algorithms are not covered here. Please refer to one of the graph drawing surveys previously mentioned on Page 189. Popular planar graph drawing methods include polyline drawing [60] (Figure 4.25(a)), straight-line drawing [189, 739] (Figure 4.25(b)), and orthogonal drawing [816] (Figure 4.25(c)).

Directed Graphs. The edges of a directed graph have a direction pointing from one end node to the other. While methods designed for general graphs (not considering edge direction) can be applied, there are many algorithms designed specifically for directed graphs, and layered drawing [804] is one of them. The method produces polyline drawings with nodes arranged on horizontal layers. The method consists of four steps:

1. *Cycle removal:* If the input graph contains directed cycles, temporarily reverse the direction of a subset of the edges to make the digraph acyclic.
2. *Layer assignment:* Nodes are assigned to horizontal layers which determines their y-coordinate.
3. *Crossing reduction:* Within each layer the nodes are ordered to reduce the number of crossings.
4. *Horizontal coordinate assignment:* The x-coordinate of each node is determined.

An example of the layered drawing of a directed graph is shown in Figure 4.27.

Undirected Graphs. Force-directed algorithms [224] are commonly used to draw general undirected graphs. They use a physical analogy to produce a straight-line drawing. A graph is treated as a system of entities with forces acting between them. These algorithms seek a configuration with locally minimal energy, i.e., a position for every entity such that the sum of the forces on each entity is zero. In general, they all have two parts:

1. *The model:* A force system defined by the nodes and edges which provides a physical model for the graph.
2. *The algorithm:* This is the technique for finding an equilibrium state of the force system.

Force-directed algorithms are very popular for undirected graphs because the physical analogy makes them easy to understand and relatively simple to code; and the resulting drawings are pleasing and can reveal the structural properties of the graph (such as symmetry). Figure 4.28 shows a force-directed drawing produced by GEOMI [10].

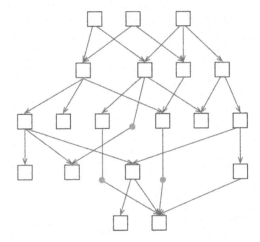

Fig. 4.27. Layered drawing of directed graph. Nodes are placed on horizontal layers and edges are always pointing downwards. The circles are the dummy nodes representing edges that span more than two layers.

Fig. 4.28. Force-directed drawing of an undirected graph.

4.4.3   Aesthetics vs. Graph Readability

Aesthetics are widely used as measurements of drawing qualities produced by different layout methods. It is commonly accepted that a drawing is better if it has fewer crossings or less edge bends. However, the effectiveness of aesthetics on improving graph readability has not been studied systematically until recently.

Aesthetics of Abstract Graphs. The work by Purchase et al. [676, 677] is one of the early attempts to evaluate the effectiveness of graph layout aesthetics on improving graph readability. The experiments focused on three aesthetics:

1. Minimizing edge crossings,
2. Minimizing bends, and
3. Symmetry.

Two planar graphs were used, one with 16 nodes and 18 edges (named "sparse graph" in the paper), the other with 16 nodes and 28 edges (named "dense graph" in the paper). Nine drawings were produced for each graph with three levels (few, some, and many) of bends, crossings, and symmetry respectively. To isolate the effect of each aesthetic, the drawings with different bend levels showed no crossings or symmetry, and it was the same for crossing and symmetry drawings. The two sets of drawings are shown in Figure 4.29. The subjects were asked to answer three questions:

1. How long is the shortest path between two given nodes?
2. What is the minimum number of nodes that must be removed in order to disconnect two given nodes such that there is no path between them?
3. What is the minimum number of arcs that must be removed in order to disconnect two given nodes such that there is no path between them?

The test results show that increasing bend or crossing number decreases graph readability, while the effect of symmetry is not clear because most subjects managed to answer all the questions correctly for all symmetry levels.

The two graphs used in the tests are relatively simple and small compared to those from real-world applications. Also, there is no justification for the chosen tasks, which all seem to focus on paths (or connections) between nodes. This does not cover all the information a graph structure can possibly convey.

A following work [668, 671, 674] studied the relative importance of aesthetics. The number of aesthetics included was increased to five with the addition of "minimum angle" (angular resolution) and "orthogonality". One planar graph with 16 nodes and 28 edges was used in the tests. Ten drawings were created, two for each aesthetics—representing a strong or weak presence of the aesthetic (Figure 4.30). The same three questions as mentioned before were used. The results showed that reducing the number of crossing was the most important aesthetic, while minimizing the number of bends and maximizing symmetry had a lesser effect. This is slightly different from the previous work which found there is no decisive conclusion on symmetry. Other findings included that the effect of maximizing the minimum angle between edges and fixing edges and nodes to an orthogonal grid were not statistically important. Again, it would be interesting to see such tests on real-world graphs with various types of tasks.

The work by Ware et al. [882] studied the effect of layout aesthetics on graph understanding from a cognitive angle. The tests focused on the performance of finding the shortest path between a pair of given nodes in the drawings produced by force-directed layout algorithms. Some additional aesthetics that are only relevant in the context of finding shortest paths were also included:

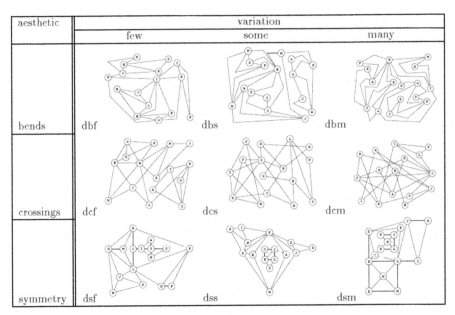

(a) Dense graph

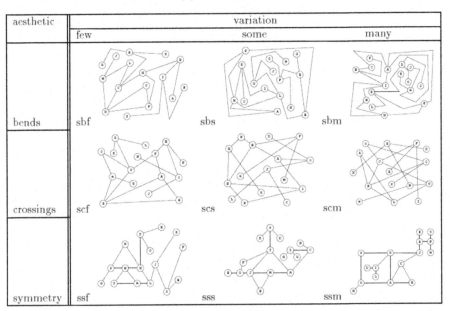

(b) Sparse graph

Fig. 4.29. The drawings used to study the effectiveness of drawing aesthetics. (a) Nine layouts of the same graph following different aesthetics. There are three levels for each aesthetic. (b) Similar to the previous one, except that the graph used here has relatively less edges. *Image courtesy of H. C. Purchase.*

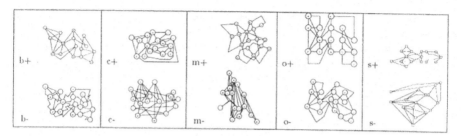

Fig. 4.30. The drawings used to study the relative order of aesthetics. Ten layouts are produced for the same graph. Five aesthetics are considered, and each layout represents either strong or weak presence of one aesthetic. *Image courtesy of H. C. Purchase.*

Continuity (path bendiness): The continuation at a node is defined as the angular deviation from a straight line of the two edges on the shortest path which emanate from the node. To get the total path continuity, the angular deviations were summed at all the nodes on the path.

Number of crossings and average crossing angles: The crossings here are those on the shortest path, as well as the angle of each edge crossing.

Number of branches: For each of the intermediate nodes on the shortest path, the number of edges leaving the node which are not part of the shortest path itself was recorded.

Shortest path length and total edge length: These are self-explanatory.

Each subject was asked to find the shortest path between given nodes in 180 pre-defined drawings. There were 42 nodes in each graph, and the number of edges on one node was randomly varied between one and five.

The data collected was the response time and accuracy. The results suggested that path continuity was an important factor in perceiving shortest paths. It was also found that the total number of edge crossings in the graph drawing is not a significant indicator of response time; it is the number of edges that cross the shortest path that is important. Another important factor is the number of branches emanating from nodes on the path.

Aesthetics of Graphs in Application Domains. The work mentioned so far studies the effect of aesthetics on abstract graph readability. However, for graphs in specific application domains—such as social networks and biological pathways—some required analysis can be considerably different. The work by Blythe et al. [96, 553] is one of the early attempts to understand how aesthetics affect people's understanding of a social network, where usually nodes are persons and edges are some relationship. In the experiments, the subjects were asked to answer the following three questions:

1. How visible or involved is a person based on his/her position in the network (prominence)?
2. How important is a person's position between groups (bridging)?
3. What is the number of groups in the network?

These questions are quite different from those in the previous studies. They focus on the sub-structure in the graph (such as a group or cluster) and its relationship to an individual node. The data they used was a small network with 12 nodes and 24 edges. The two aesthetics considered were reducing the number of crossings and avoiding node-edge overlap. Five drawings were used in the tests (Figure 4.31): Four of them (Arrangement 1-4) were drawn to avoid crossings and node-edge overlap, while the last one (Arrangement 5) used a circular layout (i.e., put all nodes evenly on a circle) which avoided node-edge overlap but could introduce some edge crossings. The results showed that graph layout aesthetics have a significant effect on people's perception on social networks. Besides, there are a few findings regarding the relative node position in the graph that linked to people's perception of its social status:

1. The perceived prominence of a person decreases as the node moves away from the center.
2. A person's bridging importance decreases as it moves away from the center of the bisector of the two groups.
3. The number of groups perceived can be altered by the relative proximity of nodes.

In a following work [552], McGrath et al. studied the effect of graph layout on people's perception of grouping in social networks. The used graph was an interaction network among bank employees (26 nodes and 93 edges); two employees were connected if there is interaction between them. The ethnography of the site suggested that there were two groups, each with their own subculture within the bank. Three layouts were produced for the graph (Figure 4.32). The first layout (Figure 4.32(a)) depicted two spatial groups with two edges connecting the groups. In the second layout (Figure 4.32(b)), a node labeled "N" from the right spatial group was positioned in the left spatial group which introduced four new connections between the groups. The third layout (Figure 4.32(c)) had the nodes clustered in three spatial groups with many edges connecting them.

The subjects were asked to group the nodes into at most five clusters. The results suggested that spatial clustering had a significant effect on viewers' perceptions of the existence of groups in networks. The authors thought one principle to create a clear depiction is that adjacent nodes must be placed near to each other if possible and Euclidean distance should be correlated with path distance. The work by Purchase et al. [672,673,675] evaluated the effect of layout aesthetics on the understanding of UML diagrams. The subjects were asked to rank the aesthetics according to preference. The six aesthetics included were:

1. Minimize bends;
2. Minimize edge crossings;
3. Orthogonality;
4. Width of layout;
5. Text direction; and
6. Font type.

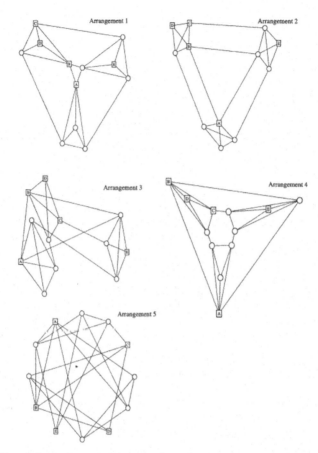

Fig. 4.31. Graph layout vs. social network understanding. Different layouts are used to study their effects on people's perception of the roles of actors (nodes) in a social network. *Image courtesy of J. Blythe, C. McGrath, and D. Krackhardt.*

Note that the last three aesthetics are not commonly considered in abstract graphs, but are important for UML diagrams.

Two types of UML diagrams were used in the tests: *Class diagrams* that provide a static view of a system by describing the types of objects in the system and the relationships between them; *collaboration diagrams* that provide a dynamic view of a system by showing the interactions between objects that send and receive messages. A basic UML class and collaboration diagram were created. The class diagram had 14 classes and 18 relationships, and the collaboration diagram had 12 objects and 17 messages. Each diagram was drawn twice for every aesthetic under consideration to provide a contrast for that particular aesthetic. For example, Figure 4.33(a) was a class diagram with straight-line drawing (no orthogonality); while Figure 4.33(b) is a collaboration diagram drawn orthogonally. The results showed that the priority order of the aesthetics common to both diagram types was: Minimize edge crossings, orthogonality, minimize edge

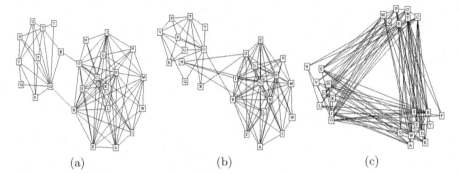

(a)   (b)   (c)

Fig. 4.32. Layout aesthetics vs. grouping perception. The subjects were asked to identify groups in a social network drawn with different aesthetics. (a) The layout shows two groups. (b) One node is moved from right to left, creating more connections between the groups. (c) Nodes were put into three groups with many connections between them. *Image courtesy of J. Blythe, C. McGrath, and D. Krackhardt.*

bends, text direction, width of layout, and font type. It is interesting to note that aesthetics that are not commonly considered for abstract graphs (text direction, width of layout, and font type) were also considered less important in this context.

4.4.4 Layout vs. Graph Readability

Layout algorithms try to improve graph readability by satisfying one or more aesthetics. As we have seen in the last subsection, the effectiveness of aesthetics varies considerably. Some user experiments were performed to verify the effectiveness of layout algorithms on helping people understand graph structure.

Trees and Hierarchies. Hierarchical data possess a tree-like structure. Such data are ubiquitous in biology, e.g., in phylogenetic trees which measure similarities between species or DNA sequences, or in clustering where a hierarchy is created during the clustering process, etc.

Generally, depending on the origin of the data to be visualized, we can distinguish two large groups of hierarchical data visualization:

– Visualization of hierarchies related to numerical/proximity data, i.e., dendrograms generated during clustering;
– Visualization and navigation of ubiquitous hierarchical data, such as file systems, etc.

The natural way of visualizing hierarchical data is using a tree. Figure 4.34 presents such a visualization, representing the tree created in the process of hierarchical clustering of the so-called Iris dataset (cp. Page 179) which is commonly called a *dendrogram*. The hierarchical data to be visualized in this context is the set of embedded clusters created during hierarchical clustering. Two major challenges are distinguished in the context of tree visualization of hierarchical data:

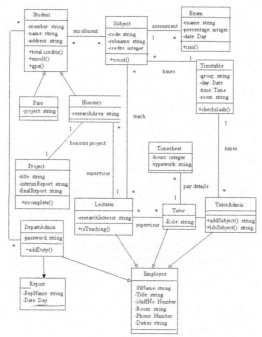

(a) A class diagram.

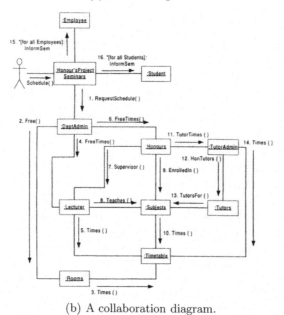

(b) A collaboration diagram.

Fig. 4.33. Examples used to study the effect of layout aesthetics on people's understanding of UML diagrams. *Image courtesy of H. C. Purchase.*

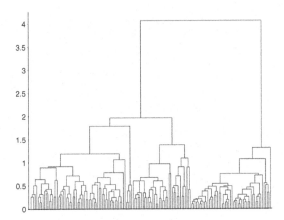

Fig. 4.34. Dendrogram representation of hierarchical clustering results. Similar objects appear near each other in the dendrogram, whereas dissimilar objects appear far from each other.

- Problems related to the ordering of leaves so that similar items are also put near each other [52, 574].
- Problems related to the display space for the visualization and comparison of large hierarchies [583, 719].

Furthermore, in [148] five problems related to phylogenetic tree visualization are distinguished which are important also in the context of other hierarchical visualization techniques, namely:

- Layout
- Labeling and annotation
- Navigation
- Tree Comparison
- Manipulation and editing

Cone tree [712] is another approach for visualizing hierarchical data in 3D. Figure 4.35 presents a cone tree visualization, where parent nodes are at the apex of the cone, whereas child notes are arranged on its base. Figure 4.36 presents an approach based on hyperbolic geometry for visualizing hierarchies [488]. This approach uses a focus+context technique to assign more space to a certain part of the hierarchy which is in the focus of the user. The rest of the hierarchy is also visualized albeit smaller than the focused part.

Another very interesting approach for visualizing hierarchical data is the Treemap approach [73]. Treemaps were first developed at the Human-Computer Interaction Laboratory (HCIL) of the University of Maryland during the 1990s, and they make use of all the available display space, mapping the attributes of the data into the size and color of nested rectangular regions, providing thus a rapid overview of the relative size of nodes. Two examples are provided for illustration:

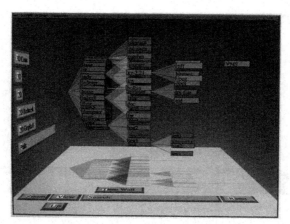

Fig. 4.35. Cone Tree visualization, showing the hierarchical structure of a Unix file system [712]. *Image courtesy of G. G. Robertson et al.*

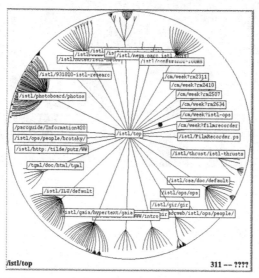

Fig. 4.36. Hyperbolic Browser is based on the Focus+Context paradigm, thus being able to display large tree structures. The current node is displayed enlarged while peripheral nodes are displayed smaller but still provide the context for the current node [488].

the first in Figure 4.37, taken from [603], shows a hierarchical view of news headlines grouped according to their main theme and importance. The second example in Figure 4.38, taken from [545], visualizes stock results by grouping the respective companies according to their field of business. The coloring reflects the stock evolution over a certain period.

A derivative of treemap is presented by the Sequoiaview [855] visualization in Figure 4.39, where the standard treemaps are extended by using shading in

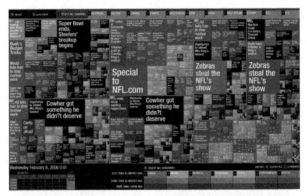

Fig. 4.37. Treemap used to visualize news headlines. The hierarchy of related news is mapped into a Treemap visualization [603]. *Image courtesy of M. Weskamp.*

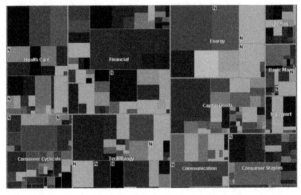

Fig. 4.38. Treemap used to visualize stock results. The stocks are grouped according to their field of business and the color of treemap nodes reflects the stock evolution [545].

order to overcome the difficulties encountered by treemaps in representing the structure of the visualized hierarchy.

Beamtrees [847] are a similar approach, concerned with the structure of hierarchical data which suffer from the occlusion effect.

Usability Studies Related to Tree Visualization Systems. A study of decision tree visualization is reported in [54]. Four different tree visualization methods are included in the tests:

1. *Organization chart,* which is based on the algorithm by Reingold and Tilford [697] with a modification proposed in [345].
2. *Tree ring,* which is a space-filling visualization method. It displays tree topology and nodes sizes. Node size is proportional to the angle swept by a node. The tree ring is similar to the information slices [20].
3. *Icicle plot,* whose node size is proportional to the width of the node. It is similar to the Kleiner and Hartigan's concept of castles [451].
4. *Treemap,* as discussed above.

Fig. 4.39. Sequoiaview uses a visualization technique called *cushion treemaps* to provide a view of the hierarchical structure. In contrast to treemaps, shading is used to improve the perception of the hierarchy in the data [855]. *Image courtesy of J. van Wijk et al.*

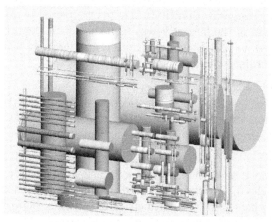

Fig. 4.40. Beamtrees are used for the visualization of large hierarchical data sets with nodes shown as stacked circular beams. Their strength consists in extracting the global information about the hierarchy [847]. *Image courtesy of F. van Ham et al.*

The examples of these four visualization methods are shown in Figure 4.41. Two experiments are conducted. The first one is to test the visualization's ability to communicate simple characteristics of the tree's topology. The subjects were asked to perform the following tasks:

— Decide whether the tree is binary or n-ary.
— Decide whether the tree is balanced or not.
— Find deepest common ancestor of two given nodes.
— Determine how many levels are in the tree (height).
— Find three largest leave nodes.

Eight trees were created for this test. The trees combined three characteristics: number of children (2, more than 2), number of leaves (16, 100), and degree of

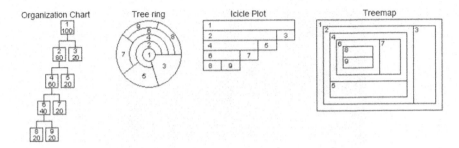

Fig. 4.41. Four visualizations of the same tree.

balance (balanced or unbalanced). Each participant saw each of the four compact views and completed each task four times. The organization chart was included in the study as a control condition. The results showed that the participants' performance with the icicle plot and the tree ring were similar to their performances with the organization chart. The participants' performance with the Treemap was worse in the largest leaves task than with the other views.

The second test included node description and memory tasks. The node description task contained the following:

− Select the shallowest leaf in the tree.
− On level 3, select the ancestor of the deepest leaves in the tree.
− Select the leaf on level k where k was different for each tree.
− Select the deepest common ancestor of the leaves on the two deepest levels in the tree.

In the node memory task, the subjects were asked to identify nodes that were previously highlighted. The results showed that none of the methods was clearly superior to the others in this experiment. Participants' performance depended on a combination of the task and the view. They responded faster in the node description tasks when using the icicle plot and organization chart. In contrast, when performing the node memory task, they were faster when using the tree ring and slowest when using the icicle plot.

In [455] on the other side, six different visualization techniques for trees are compared with each other. The visualization techniques include:

− Treemaps,
− Sequioaview,
− Beamtrees,
− Hyperbolic trees,
− Tree Viewer, and
− Windows Explorer.

A set of 15 tasks was selected to be performed by the users and it included problems such as:

- Finding items (leaves) fulfilling a certain condition, e.g., having a certain name, a certain parent, or a certain property;
- Finding duplicates;
- Estimating the depth of the tree; or
- Determining if the tree is balanced or not?

In the following list, the most important results of this evaluation are summarized shortly.

- Windows Explorer showed the best overall performance, both with regard to correctness, speed of task completion, and user satisfaction. This comes mainly from the fact that users are highly skilled in using Explorer for obvious reasons. However, difficulties are encountered for tasks which require expanding and scanning all directories, such as finding files that do not end with a certain suffix.
- Treemap on the other side had the best performance when compared to the rest (i.e., after Windows Explorer). Difficulties were encountered in date-related tasks such as finding the most recent modified file. Furthermore, no statistically significant differences between Windows Explorer and Treemap were distinguished. Considering that Windows Explorer is a ubiquitous tool, further training with Treemap could possibly reverse the results.
- Sequoiaview, in contrast to expectations and although it was designed to improve the perception of structure of hierarchies, showed an average performance. Except difficulties which were observed when using the original Treemap with attribute related questions, users had also difficulties to answer structure-related questions. The structure perception enhancement was not very useful for hierarchies with few internal nodes (directories) and many leaves (files).
- Beamtrees were the worst performer. However, regarding structure-related tasks, BeamTrees performed comparably to the rest. Difficulties were encountered with tasks such as estimation of how balanced/unbalanced the tree is.
- Star Tree, which is a derivative of the hyperbolic browser, had also an average performance. Tasks that required from the user to rotate the tree, thus changing the focus, introduced inaccuracy in the completion of the task.

Abstract Graphs. Using a setup similar to that of the graph aesthetics evaluation, Purchase [670, 671] tested the effectiveness of graph layout on human perception. A planar graph of 17 nodes and 29 edges was used, the maximum node degree was limited to 4 to make it applicable to the orthogonal drawing algorithm. Three types of graph drawing algorithms were tested:

1. Force-directed approaches, including the algorithm by Fruchterman and Reingold [274] (FD-FR); the algorithm by Kamada and Kawai [426] (FD-K); and the algorithm proposed by Tunkelang [839] (Tu).
2. The planar orthogonal grid drawing algorithm by Tamassia [814] (POGB).
3. Planar grid drawing methods, including the algorithm by Woods [912] (PG); the algorithm by Fraysseix, Pach and Pollack [189] (PGS); and the algorithm by Seisenberger [747] (SEIS).

All these algorithms were implemented in GraphEd [350], and the resulting drawings are shown in Figure 4.42. The average response times for the eight drawings were not significantly different, implying that the subjects did not perceive the drawings to be of varying difficulty. However, the average number of errors for the drawings varied significantly, indicating that there was indeed a difference in interpreting the difficulty of the drawings. The SEIS drawing produced significantly more errors than the rest, which had similar performance. The result that the majority of layout methods have similar effect on graph readability is a bit surprising given that the drawings they produce are considerably different.

For one drawing convention, there are usually many layout algorithms available, but there is little available evaluation on the similarity/difference among the drawings they produce. A user study was performed by Bridgeman et al. [116] to examine the measurements of difference in drawings produced by various orthogonal drawing methods. What makes this work interesting is that the criteria used in many evaluations and comparisons are arbitrary (without justification), whereas in this work the authors tried to find measurements from experimental results. Three fundamental differences in orthogonal drawings needed to be measured:

Rotation: Given 2 drawings D and D'; what is the minimum angle the user thinks D needs to be rotated to be D'?

Ordering: Given 3 drawings D, D', and D''; what makes a user think that D' is more like D than D'' is like D?

Magnitude: Given 3 drawings D, D', and D''; what makes a user think that D' is k times more like D than D'' is like D?

To identify the measurements of these differences, the subjects were asked to complete three types of tasks in the experiments:

1. *Rotation:* In the tests, the user was presented with a screen as shown in Figure 4.43(a). The eight drawings on the right were different orientations of the base drawing on the left. The user chose the orientation that looked most like the base drawing.

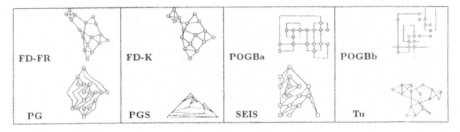

Fig. 4.42. The drawings used to study the effectiveness of graph layout methods. These are eight drawings of the same graph produced by eight different layout methods implement in GraphEd. *Image courtesy of H. C. Purchase.*

2. *Ordering:* In this part, the user was presented with a screen as shown in Figure 4.43(b). The two rightmost drawings were different drawings after modification was applied to the base drawing on the left. The user chose one of the two rightmost drawings that looked most like the base drawing.

3. *Magnitude:* A drawing (left) was presented with its modification (right) in this part (Figure 4.43(c)). The user identifies the node in the right drawing missing from the left drawing. Nodes have random two-letter names, because the task is too difficult with unlabeled nodes. Measured is the response times on a task, with the assumption that the user will complete the task more quickly if the drawings are more similar.

The graphs used were generated from a base set of 20 graphs with 30 nodes each, taken from an 11,582-graph test suite [58]. Each of the 20 base graphs was drawn using a graph drawing package called Giotto [815]. Forty modified drawings were created by adding a degree-two and a degree-four node to separate copies of each base drawing. Four new drawings were produced for each modified drawing using InteractiveGiotto [115]. The new drawings ranged from very similar to the base drawing to significantly different. Seventeen measurements, such as corresponding objects and point set selection, were evaluated.

The results from the rotation and ordering parts showed that there was not a large difference in the performance of the tested measures, among which absolute and relative point positions were better indicators of similarity. It also suggested that point positions were less significant for ordering. The results of the magnitude part suggested that the amount of difference between the drawings that was considered "reasonable" varied greatly with the task: When the users only needed to recognize the graph as familiar, the perimeter of the drawing and the position/shape of few key features were the most important; when trying to find a specific change, however, the drawings needed to look very much alike or some other cues (change in color, more distinctive node names, etc.) were needed to highlight the change.

An interesting work is reported by Huang et al. [373] that used an eye-tracking device to study the eye movement of people reading graphs. Three social networks were used in the tests: Krackhardt's High-tech managers friendship relations (one graph) and Padgett's Florentine families business relations (two graphs) [883]. All graphs are small and simple with around 10 nodes and 15 edges. Four drawings were made from each graph, among them two used a circular layout and the other two used a radial layout. Among the pair of drawings using the same layout, one had more crossings than the other. A pair of drawings with circular layout is shown in Figure 4.44. Two shortest-path questions were used in the tests. For the Florentine family business relations graph, the subjects were asked to find the shortest path length between two highlighted nodes. For the high-tech manager friendship relations graph, the subjects were asked to check if the shortest-path length between two highlighted nodes was two. The analysis showed that a particular graph layout can affect the reading behavior in two ways: Slow down and trigger extra eye movements. In terms of path searching tasks, the edges incident to the nodes concerned, edges going toward to the

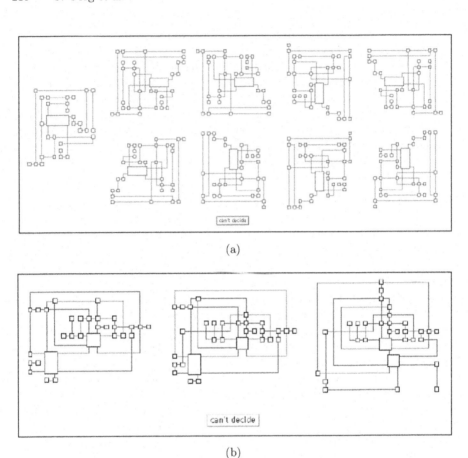

(a)

(b)

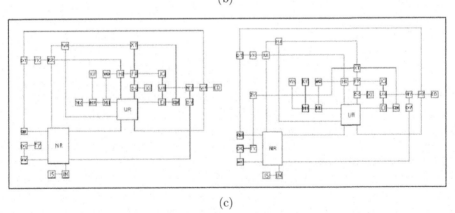

(c)

Fig. 4.43. The tasks used to identify orthogonal layout similarity measurements. (a) *Rotation:* The original drawing is on the very left, and the subject needs to find one out of eight rotated drawings that looks most alike. (b) *Ordering:* The original drawing is on the very left, and the subject needs to find one out of two modified drawings that looks more alike. (c) *Magnitude:* The subject needs to identify the nodes exist in the left drawing but missing in the right one. *Image courtesy of R. Tamassia.*

target node, and the edges alongside the paths affect a drawing's readability and trigger extra eye movements.

Graphs in Application Domains. The tests reported by Huang et al. [374] studied the effects of layout and crossings on people's understanding of social networks (which are called "sociograms" in the paper). Krackhardt's advice network [474] was used in the test, and it had 14 nodes and 23 edges. Five layouts, which were slightly modified for the social networks, were used to produce the drawings:

1. *Circular layout:* All nodes are placed on a circle.
2. *Hierarchical layout:* Nodes are arranged by mapping actors' status scores to the nodes' vertical coordinates.
3. *Radial Layout:* All nodes are laid on circumference of circles in a way that their distances from the center exactly reflect their centrality levels.
4. *Group layout:* Nodes are separated into different groups with nodes in the same group close to one another.
5. *Free layout:* Nodes are arranged without any particular purpose or order.

Two drawings were produced for each layout, where one had more crossings than the other. All the drawings were produced manually. The tasks were:

1. Find the three most important actors and rank them according to their importance levels;
2. Determine how many groups are in the network, and separate the four highlighted actors according to different groups.

The subjects were also asked to give their preference ranking of the following:

1. Preference of the layouts regarding completing the tasks;
2. Preference of the crossings regarding completing the tasks;
3. General preference of the drawings.

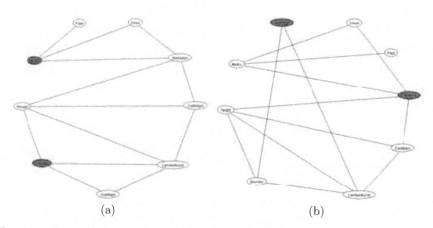

(a)   (b)

Fig. 4.44. Two circular drawings used in the study of eye movement when people were reading a graph. The same graph is used in both drawings. (a) The drawing has fewer crossings. (b) The drawing has more crossings. *Image courtesy of W. Huang.*

The authors found that there was no obvious evidence that either edge crossings or layouts posed significant impact on the performance of the user importance task (task 1). Users generally performed better when they took longer time. Only those tasks which are closely related to edges and involve edge tracing (such as finding groupings) were significantly affected. For communicating information about actor status, the angular resolution and node positioning in a sociogram were more important than drawing conventions and reducing the number of edge crossings.

The work by Huang et al. [375] studied the effect of cognitive load on users' ability to understand social networks. Three factors were tested:

Data complexity: This refers to the amount of the data. It includes objects in the data, attributes of the objects and relationships between them.

Visual complexity: This includes all visual elements and their spatial distributions. A visualization with fewer elements or based on general aesthetics does not necessarily always lead to lower visual complexity.

Task complexity: This determines the load imposed by task demand including the number of objects involved and interactivity of these objects.

The different levels of data complexity were achieved by using social networks with different node number or edge density. The level of visual complexity was varied by using either a *combined display*, in which the network was visualized as a single graph and used colors to represent different relations, or a *separated display*, in which the network was visualized as multiple graphs with each representing one relation. Tasks with three different complexity levels were included in the tests:

1. *Simple:* Find one neighbor of a given actor (node);
2. *Medium:* Find all common neighbors of two given actors; and
3. *Complex:* Find all triangle patterns.

The results indicated that the cognitive load increased with data, visual, and task complexity. When a graph became large and dense, human perception and cognitive systems were quickly overwhelmed, causing errors in tasks such as finding relationship patterns.

4.4.5 Large Graphs

As the graph size grows larger—for instance to thousands of nodes—its layout computation becomes more expensive and its readability decreases quickly. A number of algorithms have been proposed to layout large graphs. Among them are:

1. Methods that are based on the force-directed model, such as the GRIP Method [286, 287], the Fast Multi-Scale Method [331], the Fast Multipole Multilevel Method [321], and the FADE Method [684];
2. Methods that are based on linear algebra techniques, such as the ACE Method [458]; and

3. Methods based on the high-dimensional embedding, such as the one proposed by Harel and Koren [332].

In general, these algorithms sacrifice layout quality for performance. Please refer to the work by Hachul and Jünger [322] for a comparison. Even with slower algorithms, the readability of large graphs is still a serious problem. Figure 4.45 shows a graph with 3200 nodes laid out with a force-directed algorithm [875]; the overall structure is hardly perceivable. It is unlikely that this can be improved by applying another layout algorithm. Therefore, new graph visualization approaches besides layout algorithms are needed to improve the readability of large graphs.

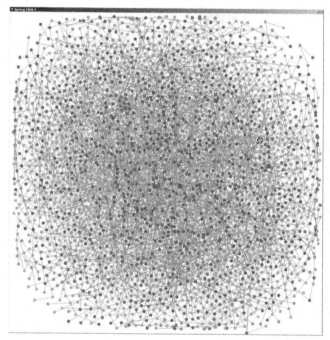

Fig. 4.45. A large graph with 3,200 nodes laid out with a force-directed algorithm. *Image courtesy of C. Ware.* (This is an image similar to the one that appeared in the paper.)

Clustered Graphs. Clustering is one of the common approaches to show the structure of a large graph. Nodes are partitioned into clusters and the connections between clusters reveal the structure of the underlying graph. Clustering can be done according to node connectivity or other criteria. Please refer to the work by Kaufmann et al. [432] for a survey on graph clustering methods. Once a graph is clustered, various methods have been proposed to layout the graph. The methods proposed by Eades et al. [227, 229] are the first straight-line and orthogonal drawing methods for clustered graphs. A multilevel method [228] that produces 2.5D drawings for hierarchically-clustered graphs is shown in Figure

4.46. Clustered graph layout methods based on the force-directed approach include the one by Wang et al. [869], in which each cluster is treated as a node to decide the graph layout and then nodes within a cluster are laid out using spring forces; and the one by Huang et al. [372], in which dummy nodes (invisible) are added to each cluster to keep the nodes within a cluster together and clusters themselves away from each other.

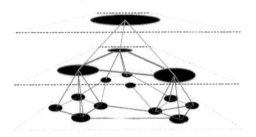

Fig. 4.46. A multi-level drawing of a hierarchically clustered graph. *Image courtesy of P. Eades.*

3D Layout. Another approach to improve the readability of large graphs is to extend traditional layout algorithms from 2D to higher dimensionality. Every class of 2D layout algorithms has a correspondent in 3D. Cone tree [712] is an extension of layered tree drawing in 3D (Figure 4.35). The method proposed by Hong and Murtagh [363] visualizes large hierarchies in 3D by placing subtrees on poly-planes (Figure 4.47(a)). The layered drawing is extended to 3D by placing nodes on the parallel circles on the surface of a cone or cylinder [627] (Figure 4.47(b)) or by placing nodes on parallel layers in vertical planes [364] (Figure 4.47(c)). Orthogonal drawing and force-directed methods can be extended to 3D naturally, and examples of such methods are the work by Di Battista et al. [59] and Ostry [627] respectively. Three dimensional drawing methods are also proposed for clustered graphs [356].

A series of studies have been performed to examine the effectiveness of using 3D drawing to improve graph readability. The experiments conducted by Ware and Franck [877] compared various approaches to visualize a graph in 2D or 3D:

2D: The 3D graph was projected onto a 2D plane using an orthographic projection by removing z-axis information.

Static Perspective: Essentially the same as above, except that a perspective projection is used with depth cues of relative size and overlap/occlusion.

Stereo: This condition made use of a pair of shutter glasses to provide disparity depth cues, so the user can see graphs in 3D (similar to the effect of a 3D movie).

Passive rotation: The scene rotated at a constant angular velocity about a vertical axis.

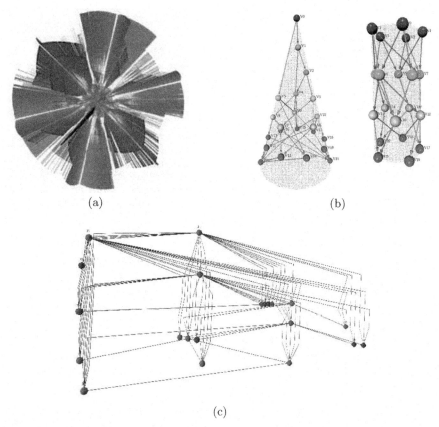

(a)   (b)

(c)

Fig. 4.47. Graph drawing in 3D. (a) Large tree with poly-plane. Each subtree is placed on an individual plane. *Image courtesy of Seok-Hee Hong.* (b) 3D layered drawing on cone and cylinder. The nodes are placed on the horizontal layer on the surface of a cone or cylinder. (c) 3D layered drawing with parallel vertical plane. Nodes are divided into layers in parallel planes to reduce crossings. *Image courtesy of S.-H. Hong.*

Stereo, passive rotation: Same as above, except with stereo.

Hand coupled: Lateral movement of the mouse caused rotation of the scene about a vertical axis.

Stereo, hand coupled: Same as above, except with stereo.

Head coupled perspective: The scene's projection changed continuously according to the subject's head position. The perspective projection was defined by a single viewpoint centered between the eyes.

Stereo, head coupled perspective: Same as above, except with stereo. The correct view was generated for each eye position.

The task was to decide whether there was a path of length two connecting two nodes which were highlighted in a randomly laid out graph. The results suggest the following:

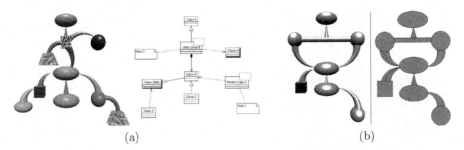

(a)   (b)

Fig. 4.48. Geon diagram. It extends the conventional node-link diagram with color, texture, and 3D shape. (a) A comparison between UML diagram and its geon diagram representation. (b) A comparison between geon diagrams with and without 3D shape and texture. *Image courtesy of P. Irani.* (These are images similar to those that appeared in the paper.)

1. A static perspective image provides little improvement in graph readability in comparison with a 2D diagram.
2. 3D motion and stereo viewing both help in understanding, but the type of motion is not particularly important. All improve performance, and all are more significant than stereo cues.
3. The head-coupled stereo viewing can increase the size of an abstract graph that can be understood by a factor of 3. Using stereo alone provided an increase by a factor of 1.6 and head coupling alone produced an increase by a factor of 2.2.

Given that head-coupled stereo vision is still not universally available, a following work [391, 392] explored other approaches to improve 3D graph readability. Experiments were performed to study the readability of a *geon diagram* which is an extension of the traditional 3D node-link diagram with extra visual elements, such as shape and lighting. Two sets of experiments were conducted. The first set compared geon UML diagrams against 2D UML diagrams (Figure 4.48(a)). The subjects were first shown a structure in either geon or UML form, and were later asked to identify its presence or absence in a series of diagrams. The second set compared a geon diagram against its 2D version (Figure 4.48(b)). The results of the first set of experiments showed that substructures can be identified in geon diagrams with approximately half the errors and significantly faster. The results also showed that geon diagrams can be recalled much more reliably than structurally equivalent UML diagrams. The results of the second set showed that substructures can be identified much more accurately with shaded components than with 2D outline equivalents and remembered more reliably. The authors speculated that geon diagrams provided a better input to the processes that occur in human object recognition and thus they were easier to interpret and remember.

Motion. If we can say 3D layout uses a third dimension to improve graph readability, motion uses the fourth dimension—time—to achieve this goal. Sev-

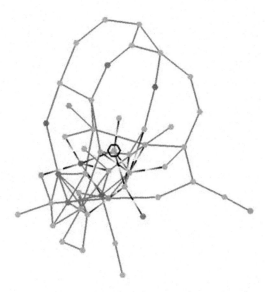

Fig. 4.49. A screen shot of a graph with "crawl" motion highlighting. *Image courtesy of C. Ware.* (This is an image similar to the one that appeared in the paper.)

eral motion highlighting techniques are studied in the work by Ware and Bobrow [874]:

Circular: Nodes and edges take on a circular motion around their static positions obtained from a layout algorithm.

Jolt: Nodes and links move in pulses using the function $sin(t)/t$. The result is similar to the effect of an object being struck briefly and oscillating from the blow.

Crawl: The selected edges show smoothly animated sawtooth patterns radiating out from the selected node (Figure 4.49).

Expanding nodes: The selected nodes grow larger and smaller periodically.

Three tests were performed to evaluate the effectiveness of motion highlighting in various tasks. The graphs used in the test were generated with 50 nodes and 82 edges on average. The graphs were laid out using a force-directed algorithm and nodes were randomly colored to simulate a real application situation. For each task, every subject were given 9 blocks of 12 graphs. For the first experiment, the task was to determine whether or not there were two red nodes within a radius of two links from a node identified by having a circle drawn around it. Besides the motion highlighting techniques previously mentioned, the test also included cases with no highlighting or static highlighting present, i.e. for the latter case, the selected subgraph was not marked with a different color. Recorded data were response time and error rate. The results showed that motion highlighting is faster but has higher error rate than static highlighting. The poor performance of the no-highlighting approach suggests that a graph of this size is unlikely to be useful in the absence of some highlighting method.

In the second test, the subjects were asked to answer if there are at least two red nodes/edges within two links of the highlighted subgraph. The results showed that separate highlighting of nodes and links could be used to pick them out respectively; it was also shown that having both nodes and links move at the same time was just as good or better. In comparison, the static highlighting method was equally effective for revealing links, although not as good as circular motion for revealing nodes.

In the third test, the subjects were asked to identify a more complex pattern which was a chain of three red nodes connected by blue edges. The results showed less of an advantage of motion highlighting over static highlighting relative to the two previous ones. The authors thought this may have been caused by the fact that the pattern was relatively easy to identify, although more complex.

This work was later extended to larger graphs [875]. The graphs used in the experiments had a size of up to 3,200 nodes (Figure 4.45). Four highlighting methods were compared:

1. No highlighting;
2. Static highlighting;
3. Motion highlighting; and
4. Combined static and motion highlighting.

The static highlighting was achieved by increasing the size of nodes and edges and adding a white border to the edges; "expanding nodes" was used in combining static and motion highlighting. Graphs of five different sizes were used: 32, 100, 320, 1,000, and 3,200. The graphs were laid out using a force-directed method.

Two experiments were performed. In the first one, the subjects' task was to determine if there was a red node within two links of a particular node designated by a bold circle drawn around it. The results showed that the interactive highlighting methods support rapid visual queries of nodes in close topological proximity to one another, even for the largest diagrams tested. Without highlighting, error rates were high even for the smallest network that was evaluated. Motion highlighting and static highlighting were equally effective.

The second experiment was to evaluate methods for showing two subsets of a larger network simultaneously in such a way that both were clearly distinct. A large graph containing two highlighted subgraphs with combination of static and various motion highlighting was presented to the subject. The specific task was to determine if the two subsets had nodes in common. The results showed that this task could be performed rapidly and with few errors if one subset was highlighted using motion and the other was highlighted using a static technique.

Matrix Representation. The matrix-based visualization of graphs is based on the fact that a graph can be represented by its *adjacency matrix* whose rows and columns represent the nodes of the graph. The matrix element can be either boolean or a numeric value (for a weighted graph). This representation offers an alternative to the traditional node-link diagrams. One important advantage is that it does not have any edge crossings which can considerably reduce node-link diagrams readability when the graph size is large.

One of the early matrix visualizations of large graphs was used in the work by Becker et al. [69]. The authors show that it is possible to reveal the underlying structure of a network represented by a matrix through successive permutations of its rows and columns. A comparison between node-link and matrix representation is reported by Ghoniem et al. [293]. Seven generic tasks were asked in the tests:

1. Estimating the number of nodes in the graph;
2. Estimating the number of links in the graph;
3. Finding the most connected node;
4. Finding a node with a given label;
5. Finding a link between two specified nodes;
6. Finding a common neighbor between two specified nodes; and
7. Finding a path between two nodes.

The test data sets were generated random graphs of three different sizes (20, 50, and 100 nodes). For each size, graphs with different edge density[6] (0.2, 0.4, and 0.6) were used. An observation from the experiments was that when graphs are larger than twenty nodes, the matrix-based visualization performs better than node-link diagrams on most tasks. Only path finding was consistently in favor of node-link diagrams throughout the evaluation. The conclusions are:

1. For small graphs, node-link diagrams are always more readable than matrices.
2. For larger graphs, the performance of node-link diagrams deteriorates quickly while matrices remain readable for simple tasks with a lead of 30% of correct answers with comparable if not better answer time.
3. For more complex tasks, such as "path finding", an appropriate interaction is always preferable, for example, by selecting a node and displaying all the possible paths starting from it and ending at a pointed node.

Besides graph size, there are other issues that make graph visualization challenging. Examples include visualizing multiple graphs and node/edge attributes. These topics are addressed in the next subsection.

4.4.6 Integrated Graph Drawing

In some applications, it is essential for users to be able to compare different graphs visually. However, well-known techniques, like multiple views or dynamic graph drawing, are not sufficient for this task as they are based on "splitting" the picture. Multiple views use a spatial separation, dynamic graphs a separation in time. Furthermore, a single two-dimensional drawing of a graph must fulfill certain requirements in order to be regarded as "good" [669].

In order to preserve the quality of a graph, it is not a good choice to draw additional visual objects to allow visual comparison. In order to keep the aesthetic quality of a graph representation and to provide a combined picture of more graphs, the third dimension again comes into mind.

---

[6] The portion between edge and node number.

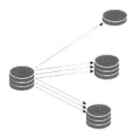

Fig. 4.50. A sketch of a stack of three graphs. The similarity among the three graphs becomes obvious, namely that all three graphs contain three equal nodes and two equal edges. But, it is also visible that one graph has an additional node. This example shows a disadvantage of this method: The user cannot detect the graph that has an additional node. Therefore, a separate view that only displays one graph at a time is needed for example when the user is interested in the exact graphs.

When three-dimensional visualizations are allowed, graphs can be "stacked" [106] such that all graphs are visible at once (Figure 4.50). A user is supported by additional views, the use of transparency, and additional graphical features when exploring such a stack of graphs. This technique is useful when the differences among the graphs are small. One application for this method is the visualization of similar metabolic pathways of related species [107].

However, there are two main challenges that have to be dealt with. The first is to compute drawing layouts for each graph that are as similar as possible. The second is to define a stacking order such that the most similar graphs are adjacent in the stack.

It is clear for a three-dimensional view that the system must provide interaction methods for the user to navigate through the 3D scene. Brandes et al. [106] implemented the rotation of the scene to be able to reveal edge crossings between edges from different levels. Furthermore, they added a special window that displays single graphs of the stack when the user demands it.

In some cases, a combination of graph drawing with the visualization of time-varying data is desired in order to visualize the relations among the data. Examples for that can be found in the area of bioinformatics [121]. Saraiya et al. [729] showed that the choice of the visual metaphor should depend on the desired application: Displaying time-series data inside a graph's node makes it easier to compare different nodes' values. However, accuracy may suffer as the density of information increases (Figure 4.51 (a)). Another technique is to display only the data at one single time point. This can be done using a simple color-mapping of the nodes. In this case, users can compare values at a certain point in time directly, but they are not able to detect trends of the time-series without using further interaction, see Figure 4.51(b).

Borisjuk et al. [121] used a straightforward approach when visualizing experimental data in the context of a metabolic network. Instead of using simple circles or rectangles to represent nodes, they used small visualizations (Figure 4.52).

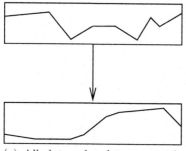 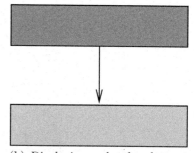

(a) All data related to one node can be displayed using a plot inside the node's rectangle. Outstanding values can be indicated fast while comparing the values of different nodes at a certain point in time is difficult.

(b) Displaying only the data at a certain point in time makes it easy to compare the different values of the different nodes. However, the comparison of trends is not possible without further interaction methods or additional views onto these data.

Fig. 4.51. Different approaches for displaying time-series data inside a node of a graph.

The technique is simple and provides a view to all available information. The immediate visual comparison of the experimental data however is not possible. Although the relations between the experimental data are visible, the user has to move his eyes in order to compare the results. Similar work was done by Jankun-Kelly and Ma [403]. They described how to visualize configurations of proteins inside Moiré graphs which can be considered as a combination of radial graph layout with a set of interaction techniques.

4.4.7 Labeling of Graphs

Annotating graphs by text labels is a large area in graph drawing. While nodes can be labeled with standard text placement techniques (like those presented in [163]), edge labeling needs much more attention by the graph drawing system to preserve layout quality.

Kakoulis and Tollis presented a strategy for computing a placement for text boxes [423] that provided a good trade-off between computational complexity of the algorithm and its results. This algorithm was enhanced to use rotated boxes such that labels have the same orientation as the corresponding edge [424]. A result of this enhanced method is shown in Figure 4.53. The basic idea behind this algorithm is to find a set of label positions that produces no overlaps from a given set of possible positions.

There exist more techniques, for instance the one by Klau and Mutzel [450], and another one by Binucci et al. [91]. They presented algorithms that are able to create orthogonal graph drawings together with labelings. Although both algorithms provide annotated graphs with a high aesthetic quality, they are not widely used as they are based on integer linear programming which requires

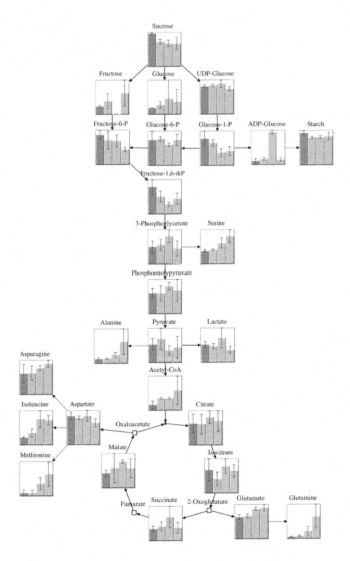

Fig. 4.52. A combination of two kinds of visualization. This picture shows the relative substance levels of different *Vicia narbonensis* lines integrated into the glycolysis and the citric acid cycle. Although all information is present in the picture, a user still needs a long time to compare the experimental data with respect to the network structure. This picture was taken from [121]. *Image courtesy of IPK Gatersleben.*

a very high complexity of computation. This makes them not feasible for interactive graph drawing as the computation may take too long (as described in [234]).

Specialized labeling techniques not only belong to certain algorithms but also to certain metaphors. Wong et al. proposed the so-called *extended labels* [905].

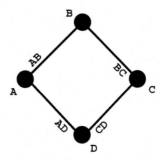

Fig. 4.53. A labeled graph using the label placement strategy described by Kakoulis and Tollis. The similar orientation of label boxes and edges makes it easier to find correspondent label-edge pairs.

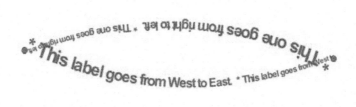

Fig. 4.54. Two nodes (red circles) are connected with to directed edges using extended labels. The shape of an extended label indicates the direction. Edges go from the thick to the thin end. This picture was taken from [905]. *Image courtesy of P. C. Wong.*

Instead of drawing edges as straight or curved lines together with a text box, the label itself represents the edge. The direction of an edge is indicated using a varying thickness (from thick to thin) of the label's shape (Figure 4.54). If the text is too short to fit between the two linked nodes it is repeated. If it is too long, the label is either truncated or animated as sliding text.

The approach of Wong et al. also deals with node labels. A node is represented by a circle and the respective label is arranged around it. This way the number of node-label overlaps decreases.

Replacing the usual geometric shapes by text leads to less overlaps of labels with the elements of the graph. If two edges are crossing in the drawing, the labels still overlap but as the labels are repeated or animated most of the times this problem is mainly resolved. The user can look at the repeated label or wait until the desired part of the text appears while sliding away from the crossing point.

Figure 4.55 shows a comparison of the traditional labeling approach with the extended labels approach. The Figure was part of a user evaluation study that revealed that finding specific nodes or edges can be done much quicker and with less interaction (measured in number of mouse interactions) than in tradition-ally drawn graphs. Detecting the neighborhood of a selected node however took slightly more time when using extended labels.

| (a) The traditional labeling approach. | (b) Drawing using extended labels. |

Fig. 4.55. Comparison of two labeling methods for the same graph. These drawings were part of an evaluation study by Wong et al. This picture was taken from [905]. *Image courtesy of P. C. Wong.*

4.5 Multiple Views

In order to visualize different sorts of data simultaneously, the multiple view technique is often used in visualization environments. Combining several views by simply drawing them close together allows the usage of the most powerful visualization strategies for each specific data source. Furthermore, this approach is easy to implement, as it does not significantly increase the degree of the visualization's complexity. A famous example are graphical system surveillance tools that display data from several data sources simultaneously, see Figure 4.56.

4.5.1 Classification

The multiple view paradigm can be used in different ways, depending on the degree of connection between the separate data sources. The classification consists of three main groups, cp. also Table 4.5.

Coordinated views. This group covers all visualizations where several views provide a different abstract perspective on the same information. This can be useful when dealing with large data sets. The Visualization Mantra [759]—overview first, zoom and filter, details on demand—can be implemented using multiple views. In many applications, there exist views for the visualization of an overview and other views for details. These views are then coupled using an appropriate interaction technique. An example for this class of multiple views is the combined treemap and compound fisheye view by Abello et al. [3]. Every single view shows the same graph: While the treemap view provides information about the hierarchical structure of the graph, the graph view itself allows the inspection of a certain area. Another example for coordinated views is the Information Mural by Jerding and Stasko [406]. Their approach can be used to visualize large documents. It offers an overview window and a detail window whereby the user can explore the document via the overview window (which looks like a mural).

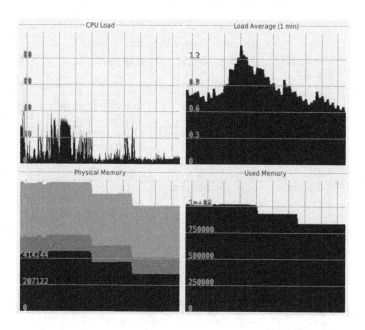

Fig. 4.56. System surveillance using *ksysguard* (part of the *K-Desktop Environment (KDE)*) [435]. This application uses a very simple instance of the multiple view paradigm. The four views are connected using the same time line. Further interaction on the visualizations is not possible. This visualization shows that cleaning up physical memory (decreasing values in the bottom-left view) needs CPU attention (some peaks in the top-left view). The information displayed in the bottom-right view is displayed in the bottom-left view as well (context).

Enhanced views. Visualization techniques that use multiple views to display data of different types simultaneously can be considered enhanced views. Structured data and scalar values then can be visualized using a special view on the structured part (for example, a node-link diagram) and a special view on the scalar part (for example, a parallel-coordinate diagram). Each view can be used separately. The combination of the two views results in a much more expressive visualization. The EPOSee-system [132] makes use of enhanced views, see Figure 4.57.

Multiple views. Multiple view systems are visualizations where each view can be used separately without any loss of information. An example is shown in Figure 4.56: It could be sufficient to show the CPU load without any further information—it would remain readable and understandable as there is only an indirect connection among the views. All views display data with the same timebase, but there is no direct a-priori relation between usage of memory and the CPU load.

Table 4.5. Overview about the three classes of multiple views.

Class	Separation of views	Interaction	Remarks	Example
Coordinated views	In general, destroys readability	Required	Often used for overview and detail visualizations	Information Mural
Enhanced views	Views remain readable, loss of expressivity	Recommended	Often used for simultaneous visualization of different types of data	EPOSee
Multiple views	Possible	Not necessary	Often used for the visualization of complex systems containing several information sources	ksysguard

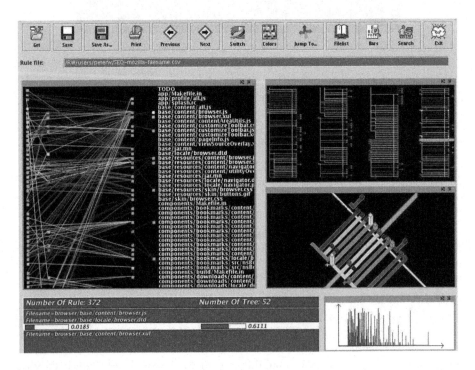

Fig. 4.57. Screenshot of EPOSee. EPOSee visualizes the evolution of a software archive and uses a mixture of coordinated and enhanced views. While the user selects an area of interest in the overview in the upper right part, all other views switch their view on the information about the selected area (coordinated views). The histogram view in the lower right part presents additional information about the parallel-coordinates view in the left area (enhanced views). *Image courtesy of M. Burch.*

4.5.2   The Design of Multiple Views

Multiple views, especially enhanced views, require a sophisticated design in order to be regarded as good. According to Baldonado et al. [44], there exist different design issues for the multiple views paradigm that should be paid attention to:

1. *Diversity:* Multiple views should be used when there is a diversity of attributes, models or levels of abstraction. The number of views should be as small as possible to give the user an impression of the different meanings of the views.

2. *Complementarity:* Different views may offer the user a greater insight in correlations and disparities. This rule is the counter-part of the rule of diversity: The number of views should be as high as needed.

3. *Decomposition:* Complex data can be displayed in multiple views to offer insight into the relations between the different dimensions of data. The designer of a visualization environment should not try to create an all-in-one view on one information source.

4. *Parsimony:* Multiple views should be used minimally as a user switching the views needs time to acquire the new context. When designing, it is not always best to remove the complexity of the information inside one view by splitting it up into multiple views.

5. *Space/Time resource optimization:* There should be a balance between the spatial and temporal costs as well as the spatial and temporal benefits of using multiple views. For example, when increasing the number of views, the spatial costs of the splitting should be compensated by a faster cognition by the user.

6. *Self-evidence:* Perceptual cues make relationships among the views much more apparent. Interaction through linking and brushing makes use of this rule.

7. *Consistency:* All views should display the same state of data to prevent the user from getting false impressions. For example, Figure 4.56 displays the information items that belong together at the same time. If the CPU meter would show values only from a few seconds earlier, the user would need a lot of effort to put the values in relation.

8. *Attention management:* The user's attention must be focused on the right view at the right time.

Some of these guidelines appear to be obvious. It should be clear that the multiple view approach should only be used when visualizing different types of data. However, each of the mentioned aspects should be kept in mind when developing visualization systems for complex applications. Ignoring only one aspect might cause the system to be worthless. It should be noted that the work by Baldonado et al. proposes the only currently known high-level guidelines for multiple views.

Another aspect is described by Kosslyn [469]: He recommends to separate views if there would be more than four chunks to be displayed in one view. The information sources then should be grouped according to their semantics to increase the homogeneity inside each single view.

4.5.3 Interaction

Multiple views can be connected through interaction techniques. This way, a user can discover connections between the data displayed in different views. In today's applications, the interaction methods used most often are *linking* and *brushing*.

Linking: Linking denotes that selecting a certain area of interest in one view forces all connected views to display this area as well. This method is mainly used for connection inside coordinated views. When selecting a region in the overview, the detail view updates itself to show a detailed picture of the selected region.

Brushing: Interaction through brushing means that connected items of different views are either drawn in the same color or are highlighted with a frame. It is also possible to draw a link from one item to another to indicate their connection. Brushing is usually used for visualizations of discrete data, where each data item is clearly separated from the others. Table rows or columns and nodes in node-link-diagrams are objects which are suitable for brushing techniques.

It should be noted that it does not matter how linking or brushing are triggered. As each view itself may implement a different interaction method, the interaction technique used to connect the views may vary among visualizations.

4.5.4 Comparison with Integrated Views

Multiple views can be merged into one view which then is called an *integrated view*. Integrated views can save space on a display and may decrease the time a user needs to find out relations; all data is displayed in one place. However, these facts heavily depend on the visualized data's structure and the design of the integrated view.

Yost and North compared a multiple view visualization of scalar attributes with an integrated view in order to measure understandability [919]. The result of their evaluation was that using one separate view for each attribute is more effective than showing all attributes in one picture. This result, however, cannot be generalized. Other integrated visualization designs may have fared better than the chosen one.

Another user study by Saraiya et al. [729] revealed that multiple views can be more useful when displaying graphs with associated scalar data compared to integrated drawings. When displaying a graph in one view and a time series in a separate view, the behavior of one node's data can be compared with that from other nodes. This result can only be generalized to a certain extent. The study also validated that a visualization required to facilitate visual comparison between values at a specific point in time should make use of an integrated view.

4.6 Chapter Notes

At the beginning of this chapter, some fundamental basics for the development
of visual representations are introduced: the different steps in the visualization
process, data types and attributes, as well as knowledge on perceptual and cognitive issues, such as preattentive processing.

The next Section 4.2 on criteria in information visualization and metaphors
provided a brief overview on the most important questions: how to make sense of
the (abstract) data, how to use it in the decision making, how to avoid to be overwhelmed. etc. Metaphors play a fundamental role in answering these questions.
Their importance is exemplified by means of the PeopleGarden metaphor.

Section 4.3 presented different visualization techniques for visualizing multidimensional data. The general impression in this subfield of information visualization is, however, that there is no visualization technique that is best suited
for exploring every kind of high-dimensional data. The common problems encountered in different visualization techniques include:

- Clutter/occlusion
- Scalability with massive data sets
- Computational issues

Furthermore, visualization—if used improperly—can create false impressions
about the data as Figure 4.58 illustrates, where the values 5.2, 4.9, 5.1, 5, and 4.8
are visualized. The difference between values cannot be distinguished in Figure
4.58(a), in contrast to Figure 4.58(b).

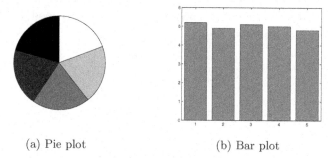

(a) Pie plot   (b) Bar plot

Fig. 4.58. Comparison of two different visualization techniques. The bar plot offers a
clearer view of the data.

A good visualization framework should offer several visualization techniques and
at least some of them should be as "orthogonal" as possible to each other in
order to bring different perspectives of data to the user. For instance, combining
parallel coordinates with Andrews plot would not bring additional insight to the
user as the techniques are quite similar to each other, whereas combining the
reorderable matrix with MDS or parallel coordinates could possibly be applied
well to different datasets [678, 765].

In Section 4.4, we discussed the effect of various visualization techniques on graph readability. We started with graph aesthetics and showed they indeed have an impact on graph readability. However, not all the aesthetics have the same level of effectiveness, and this also depends on the application domains. This is followed by a discussion on graph layout methods which are also shown to affect graph readability. But, the relative effectiveness order between different layout methods is not clear. Various techniques aim to improve the readability of large graphs are also covered. These include using 3D visualization, motion highlighting, and matrix representation. The user studies showed their improvements over previous graph visualization techniques. Also covered are the advanced topics, such as integrated graph visualization and labeling.

Many of the user studies are still based on graphs of very small size and tested with relatively simple tasks. Experimenting with larger dataset and more complex tasks will provide new insights that are more applicable to real-world applications. Lacking of a graph visualization task taxonomy makes it difficult to systematically study the effectiveness of various techniques. Applying the research results to related fields, such as cognitive psychology, will also provide improvements to existing methods.

Section 4.5 covered the technique of multiple views. Examples for multiple view-based visualization systems can be found throughout this book. We described a classification of multiple views in three different groups as well as important design issues when using multiple views. Although there are many applications that make use of this technique to generate visualizations, only a few general studies on multiple views exist. Two user-studies were presented that showed that there is no general answer to the question whether integrated views are more useful than multiple views or vice versa. Their impact heavily depends on the type of visualizations employed and whether there are a good match with the purpose of the visual presentation.

5 Challenges and Unsolved Problems

Robert S. Laramee and Robert Kosara

Self-criticism, evaluation, solved and unsolved problems, and future directions are wide-spread themes pervading the visualization community today. The top unsolved problems in both scientific and information visualization was the subject of an IEEE Visualization Conference panel in 2004 [706]. The future of graphics hardware was another important topic of discussion the same year [414]. A critical evaluation of usability and utility of visualization software was also the focus of a recent panel discussion [307]. The topic of how to evaluate visualization came up again two years later [370, 852]. Chris Johnson recently published his list of top problems in scientific visualization research [409]. This was followed up by report of both past achievements and future challenges in visualization research as well as financial support recommendations to the National Science Foundation (NSF) and National Institute of Health (NIH) [410]. That report is the result of two workshops that took place in the Fall of 2004 and Spring of 2005 on visualization research challenges and also includes input from the larger visualization community. C. Chen recently published the first list of top unsolved information visualization problems [154]. Future research directions of topology-based visualization was also a major theme of a workshop on topology-based methods [341, 736].

These pervasive themes are the result of shift in visualization research. They coincide roughly with the 20th anniversary of what is often recognized as the start of visualization in computing as a distinct field of research [550]. Consensus is growing that some fundamental problems have been solved and a re-alignment including new directions is sought. This shift is characterized by rapid increases in computing power with respect to both the CPU and the GPU as well as swift decreases in the cost of computing hardware. Advances in display technology and networking have also made visual computing more ubiquitous. Cell phones, personal digital assistants (PDAs), other hand-held devices, as well as flat panel displays are now commonplace.

In accordance to this redirection, we present a more comprehensive list of top unsolved problems and future challenges in visualization with an emphasis on human-centered visualization. Our list draws upon and summarizes previous related literature, previous chapters, discussions in the visualization community, as well as our own first hand experiences. We recognize the subjective nature of the topic and thus our presentation aims to survey and complement previous related research as well as introduce some of our own personal view points. Our

A. Kerren et al. (Eds.): Human-Centered Visualization Environments 2006, LNCS 4417, pp. 231–254, 2007.

survey of related literature identifies several future challenges and then classifies each into one of three categories: human-centered, technical, and financial, as follows:

Human-Centered Challenges

- *Interdisciplinary Collaboration*: Communication and knowledge transfer between the visualization community and application domain experts is very important (and currently lacking, Section 5.1.1).
- *Evaluation of Usability*: Human-centered evaluation of interfaces, metaphors, and abstractions that appeal best from an HCI perspective will play an important role (Section 5.1.1).
- *Finding Effective Visual Metaphors*: Assigning an intuitive geometry to non-spatial data promises to remain an important challenge (Section 5.1.1).
- *Choosing Optimal Levels of Abstraction*: From an implementation point of view, choosing an optimal level of data abstraction is arbitrary. Finding the optimal level of abstraction from a user's point of view is non-trivial (Section 5.1.1).
- *Collaborative Visualization*: The art and science of sharing interaction and visualization between multiple user simultaneously is still in its infancy, rich with unsolved problems and future challenges (Section 5.1.1).
- *Effective Interaction*: Much work still remains in developing intuitive interaction techniques, especially in the field of virtual reality.
- *Representing Data Quality*: Not all data is equal. The quality of data can vary according to several different factors. Such variance provokes several research challenges (Section 5.1.1).

Technical Challenges

- *Scalability and Large Data Management*: The size of data sets continues to grow faster than the software used to handle it, a trend that promises to continue in the future (Section 5.1.2).
- *High Data Dimensionality and Time-Dependent Data*: The complexity posed by data with many attributes is a challenge that every visualization researcher is familiar with (Section 5.1.2).
- *Data Filtering*: Ever growing data sets demand more methods and technologies needed to filter out subsets of the data that are deemed interesting by the user (Section 5.1.2).
- *Platform Independent Visualization*: Although we may want to show the same image to several different people, very rarely do two users have the exact same hardware and software setup (Section 5.1.2).

Financial Challenges

- *Evaluating Effectiveness and Utility*: Not all visualizations and interaction methodologies are equally effective and useful. Deciding in which technologies to invest both time and money will certainly challenge researchers in the future (Section 5.1.3).
- *Introducing Standards and Benchmarks*: While many other branches of computer science feature standards, e.g., networking protocols and database designs, visualization is still lacking standards at many different levels (Section 5.1.3).
- *Transforming Research Into Practice*: In order to contribute to society at large, successful research results must find their way into practical applications (Section 5.1.3).

This is the first such list in visualization to present financial challenges in such an explicit manner–in a category on their own. Our survey of top unsolved problems attempts to provide more depth than previous, related articles. We also do not abide by the common, arbitrary restriction of limiting the number of unsolved problems and future challenges based on the number of fingers we have.

5.1   Classification of Future Challenges and Unsolved Problems in Human-Centered Visualization

Before going into depth with respect to related research on the topics of unsolved problems and future challenges in information visualization, we provide a brief overview of important and influential related literature and events.

For a look back at human-centered visualization research, we refer the reader to Tory and Möller [830]. Related literature describing unsolved problems dates back over 100 years in other disciplines. David Hilbert's list of unsolved problems in mathematics[1] was presented at the Second International Congress in Paris on August 8, 1900. Lists of unsolved problems more closely related to visualization date back to 1966 with Ivan Sutherland's list of unsolved problems in computer graphics [808]. Another list of unsolved problems in computer graphics was presented by Jim Blinn at the ACM SIGGRAPH conference in 1998 [95].

In 1994, Al Globus and Eric Raible published one of the first self-criticisms of the visualization community [296]. We feel that such criticism is closely related to challenges and unsolved problems because common visualization flaws are highlighted. The identification of non-ideal practices must occur before such problems can be corrected. Multiple themes occurring in this list serve as precursors to material that later appears in visualization challenges literature. Self-criticism is also presented by Bill Lorensen [515].

The first list of future challenges in visualization specifically, was published in 1999 by Bill Hibbard [349]. In fact, Hibbard's list is very human-centered. The

---

[1] Available online at: `http://mathworld.wolfram.com/HilbertsProblems.html`

two major themes throughout his presentation are: (1) the interface between computer and people and (2) the interface between people and other people created by a combination of computer networking and visualization. Challenges are based on adapting computer capabilities to correspond as closely as possible to human capabilities and perception.

Fifteen years later, Chris Johnson published his list of top visualization research problems in scientific visualization [409]. His work includes topics such as: more interdisciplinary knowledge transfer, quantifying effectiveness, representing error, perception, utilizing novel hardware, global vs. local visualization, multi-field visualization, feature extraction, time-dependent visualization, distributed visualization, visual abstractions, and visualization theory. These themes are brought up again and elaborated on in the follow-up NIH/NSF Visualization Research Challenges report [410] published in 2005 and 2006.

Chaomei Chen published the first list (to our knowledge) of top unsolved information visualization problems [154] in 2005. Themes include: usability, knowledge of other domains, education, evaluation of quality, scalability, aesthetics, and changing trends. Many of these topics are discussed in more detail in a book by the same author [153].

Thomas and Cook have also recently published a book describing the future agenda in the emerging field of visual analytics [826]. Chapter one presents the *"Grand Challenges"* for researchers in visual analytics. Themes include: data filtering, large data sets, multiple levels of scale, cross-platform visualization, collaborative visualization, visual metaphors, evaluation, and system interoperability. These grand challenges were presented in Jim Thomas' Keynote Address: *"Visual Analytics: a Grand Challenge in Science–Turning Information Overload into the Opportunity of the Decade"*, at the IEEE Information Visualization Conference 2005 in Minneapolis, Minnesota.

For completeness, we also note that University of North Carolina, Charlotte is hosting a *"Symposium on the Future of Visualization"*, which took place 1–2 May, 2006.

Each literature source or event mentioned here influences our survey of future challenges and unsolved problems. Many issues pervade each list however terminology may differ. We incorporate not only previously published literature but also our personal experiences, view points, discussions with other researchers, and reviewer feedback. Indeed our list of grand challenges both overlaps and diverges from previous view points. Diverging on some topics serves to spark further discussion and thought.

5.1.1 Human-Centered Challenges

Here, we elaborate on the literature and events addressing top future challenges and unsolved problems in visualization research, starting with those focused on human-centered themes. The literature survey is organized by the future challenges and unsolved problems themselves. For each topic, the reader can find references to previous literature that addresses it. We note that most of the future challenges contain elements from all three categories we have chosen for

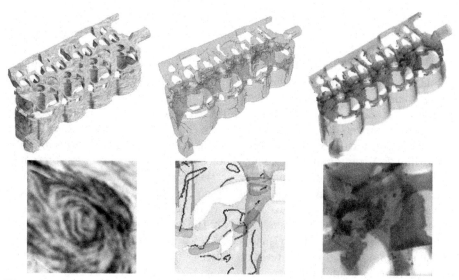

Fig. 5.1. The visualization of CFD simulation data from a cooling jacket: (left) texture-based flow visualization applied to the surface, (middle) semi-automatic extraction and visualization of vortex core lines using the moving cutting plane method [833], and (right) a feature-based, focus+context visualization showing regions of near-stagnant flow, specified interactively. Each snap-shot is accompanied by a close-up. This work was the result of a collaboration between visualization researchers and mechanical engineers [492].

our grouping: (1) human-centered with a focus on people, (2) technical with a focus on computing, and (3) financial with a focus on money. Thus, we have classified the top unsolved problems where we feel the challenge mainly lies.

Challenge #1: Interdisciplinary Collaboration. Visualization research is not for the sake of visualization itself. In other words, visualization is ultimately meant to help a user, i.e., someone normally outside the visualization community, gain insight into the problem they are trying to solve or the goal being sought after. Thus, visualization researchers must communicate with practitioners in other disciplines such as business, engineering, or medicine in order to understand the problems that other professionals are trying to solve. This requires communication across more than one discipline. The disciplines may even be closely related, e.g., information and scientific visualization. Johnson called this problem *"thinking about the science"* [409]. It is also an opinion expressed strongly by Bill Lorensen [515]. As a concrete example, if a visualization researcher is writing software to visualize computational fluid dynamics (CFD) simulation results, it is best if the researcher collaborates with a CFD expert or a mechanical engineer. A CFD practitioner generally has a set of expectations from their CFD simulation results. Understanding these expectations requires interdisciplinary communication (Figure 5.1).

Any researcher who has attempted to collaborate with a practitioner in another discipline knows how difficult this challenge can be. Engineers, doctors, business people, etc., are neither paid nor required to communicate with a visualization researcher. If a professional is not interested in visualization, they may lack motivation to collaborate. Also, differences in domain-specific terminology must be overcome. Researchers at the VRVis Research Center have a considerable amount of experience with this problem. The VRVis Research Center, conceptually, acts as a transfer-of-knowledge bridge between the university and industry sectors in Austria. The vision of their research center is to bridge the gap between universities and industry by sharing knowledge and collaborating. Recently, they have been conducting interdisciplinary research with engineers from the CFD community [492, 496]. The results of their work were presented to both the visualization community at the IEEE Visualization Conferences and to the CFD and engineering analysis community at the NAFEMS World Congress [493]. When talking to the engineers at the NAFEMS conference, the attendees they spoke with were not aware of the existence of a visualization community. There were no other visualization researchers that they were aware of at the conference. And we see few practitioners visiting the IEEE Visualization of IEEE InfoVis Conferences.

Interdisciplinary collaboration can be very challenging. Generally, the motivation for such communication with practitioners could be strengthened. However, we do see signs of progress in this area. More quality, application-track papers have been published in recent years. We also note the emergence of the first Applied Visualization Conference (AppliedVis 2005) that took place in Asheville, North Carolina in April of 2005 (more information available at http://www.appliedvis.org). This topic was also a subject discussed in a recent panel discussion [825] as well as a recent research paper [852]. The Topology-Based Methods in Visualization Workshop 2005, (more information can be found at http://www.VRVis.at/topo-in-vis) had participants from both industry and academia.

Challenge #2: Evaluation of Usability. Software usability is a top challenge on most lists of future research directions, e.g., see Chen, challenge number 1–"Usability" [154] and Johnson, challenge number 2–"Quantify Effectiveness" [409], including Ivan Sutherland's list from 1966 [808]. Usability and evaluation are themes featured on virtually every visualization conferences' call for participation (CFP). Evaluation, perception, and usability are often topics featured in visualization conference panels [285, 307, 370, 557]. The ACM conference on Human Factors in Computing Systems (CHI) is well known and attracts thousands of visitors every year. Yet, the vast majority of visualization research literature does not the address human-computer interaction. New visualization techniques and systems rarely undergo any usability studies. But user-centered software design is central to the wide-spread use and success of any application (Figure 5.2).

In our experience, visualization researchers are often skeptical with respect to the topic of human-centered evaluation. Some factors contributing to this perception may include:

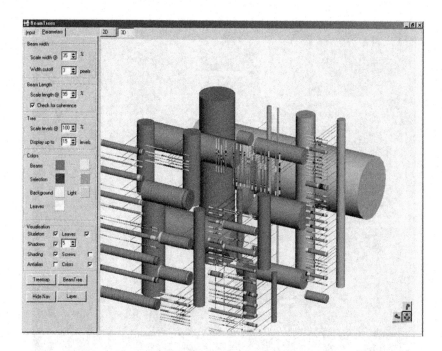

Fig. 5.2. BeamTrees were evaluated for along side other tree visualization systems [455]. *Image courtesy of A. Kobsa.*

– *Time Consumption*: User studies are viewed as very time consuming and error prone.
– *Design Challenges*: Those with experience can agree that designing an effective user study can be very challenging [463,495]. Visualization systems can be very complex and designing a user-study that isolates individual interactions and variables in an effective manner is difficult.
– *Design Literature*: Literature addressing effective user study design, although exists [463,873], is generally lacking, especially in visualization.
– *Implementation*: Visualization techniques are generally difficult to implement. Thus, implementing more than one algorithm in order to evaluate multiple approaches is problematic.

The usability challenge has a long history and promises to remain an unsolved problem for the foreseeable future. Thus, we consider this area to be rich with future research.

Challenge #3: Finding the Most Effective Visual Metaphors. Assigning a geometry to inherently non-spatial, abstract data can be problematic (see Figure 5.3). (See also challenge number 9 on Hibbard's list [349], challenge number 14, *"Visual Abstractions"* on Johnson's list [409], and Chapter 3–"Visual Representations and Interaction Techniques from Thomas and Cook [826]) A wide range of information visualization techniques have been introduced over the years to address this challenge. Some examples include: focus+context methods like

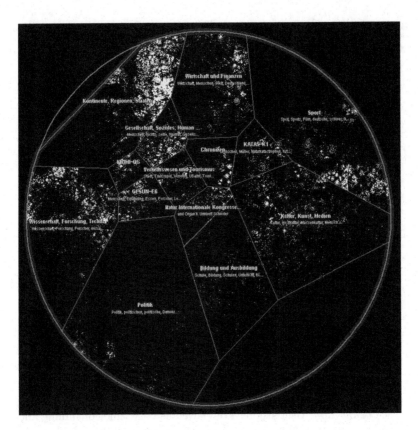

Fig. 5.3. The InfoSky system uses the night sky as a visual metaphor for visualizing large numbers of documents [303]. It was also the subject of a usability study. *Image courtesy of M. Granitzer et al.*

fisheye views [279], the use of hyperbolic trees [487,488], perspective walls [535], table lenses [691], parallel coordinates [389], cone and cam trees [712], collapsible, cylindrical trees [186], treemaps [758], and Beamtrees [847]. For a more comprehensive overview, see Kosara et al. [462]. In fact, one could argue that the entire field of information visualization is the pursuit of this challenge. Obstacles to overcoming this problem include:

- *Cognition*: creating visual metaphors that are intuitive from a user-perspective,
- *Scalability*: engineering abstract geometries that can represent large amounts of data,
- *High Dimensionality*: discovering visualizations that are able to encode multi-dimensional data in an intuitive manner.

It is difficult to imagine one visual metaphor that is able to handle all of these aspects. Thus, we expect a range of tools and visual metaphors in information applications. One important point to note with this challenge is that the choice of most effective visual metaphors may depend on user expectations and goals.

Challenge #4: Choosing Optimal Levels of Visual Abstraction. This is very closely related to the challenge of finding effective visual metaphors. Bill Hibbard also stressed the importance of defining, *"effective abstractions for the visualization and user interaction process"* [349]. Thomas and Cook also describe this challenge in Chapter 4–"Data Representations and Transformations" [826]. Essentially, all visualizations that assign a geometry to abstract, non-spatial data are forced to choose some level of abstraction in order to represent the underlying information. What exactly the optimal level of abstraction is requires serious consideration. Scatter plots are an example of a fine level of abstraction. There is a one-to-one correspondence between data sample and visual representation. However, representing data sets with hundreds of thousands or millions of data samples causes problems with perception and technical difficulties. Many data samples may overlap in image space and using a one-to-one mapping of points to data samples implies that the finest resolution that can represented faithfully is bound to the resolution of the display being used. Raising the level of abstraction to something coarser is required to represent so many data samples effectively. This could be accomplished with a clustering technique for example. Tree data structures are a natural choice for arbitrary levels of abstraction since parent nodes may represent multiple child nodes and trees may contain a more-or-less arbitrary number of levels. However, the higher the level of abstraction, the more difficult cognition and interpretation can be.

One of the central, fundamental challenges implicit with optimal levels of visual abstraction is the fact that *optimal* depends on the user. Some users want a simple, high-level of abstraction with maximal ease-of-use. Other users desire, as-closely-as possible, a direct representation of the underlying data, with as many options as possible for interaction, exploration, and analysis of the data. Implied here is the ability to provide a smooth and intuitive transition between multiple layers of abstraction either with one visual metaphor or with multiple views of the data at different levels of abstraction. Another popular viewpoint is that users follow a general path in the visualization process: (1) start with an overview of the data, (2) select a region of interest, (3) focus on the region of interest by showing more details (overview first, zoom and filter, then details-on-demand [759]). In other words, optimal levels of abstraction must show details on demand. These are tasks that focus+context visualizations address as well as software systems using multiple, linked views [203, 204].

In the end, finding the optimal level of visual abstraction encompasses several other challenges–the solutions to which promise to remain elusive for years to come.

Challenge #5: Collaborative Visualization. This challenge is identified by Hibbard [349] (see challenge number 8 under *"Interactions"*) and discussed again in detail by Thomas and Cook [826], see the topic *"Collaborative Visual Analytics"*. As hardware becomes less expensive, as display technologies advance, and as computing devices become more and more ubiquitous, the demand for collaborative visualization (both co-located and distributed visualization) technology will also increase. The idea is simple, one user investigating some data would like to share their visualization with another user(s)–in a different location. The practice, however, is difficult and full of challenges. If the visualization is static, then the problem reduces to simply sending an image(s) from one location to another–a problem already solved. The future work lies in interaction.

What happens if multiple users in disparate locations would like to explore, analyze, or present their data in an interactive, collaborative manner? There are many related questions that require consideration here:

- *Control*: Who steers the visualization? In other words, who controls the interaction and visualization parameters?
- *Coordination*: How is control passed from one person to another during collaborative visualization? Can multiple users share control simultaneously?
- *Communication*: What is the best way for viewers to communicate observations with each other during synchronized visualization?
- *Network Latency*: What are the bottlenecks introduced by network latency? How can network latency be minimized? What is the best way to handle multiple users, each with different network bandwidth?
- *Display Technology*: Chances are, each user will have different display technology. How can we ensure that each user is actually seeing the same thing?
- *Security*: Should the visualization environment have permissions associated with it? Are some subsets of the visualization private? Or public? What is the best way to establish viewing permissions?

Many questions provoked by collaborative visualization suggest a large amount of future research is needed to solve this problem. Protocols need to be engineered that establish coordination during synchronized visualization. In other words, modification of visualization parameters must be done in some coordinated fashion, with pre-established rules. Presumably, each user should be able to speak or at least send messages to each other during the collaboration. What is the best way to establish verbal or written communication with multiple users during the visualization?

Although the speed of networks continues to increased rapidly–it seems it can never be fast enough. And certainly each viewer cannot be expected to have exactly the same network bandwidth. Should the visualization parameters be determined by the lowest common denominator, i.e., the person with the slowest network connection? Users cannot be expected to have the exact same set of hardware, including display technology. The choice of display technology, in theory, should not prevent a user gaining the same insight into the data as the other users. Of course, there are many technical issues associated with this that we discuss in another challenge. In fact, the list of open questions is so long that it is almost daunting. Bill Hibbard was also concerned about this topic in 1999 [349]. Thomas and Cook describe this topic again in 2005 as a grand (future) challenge [826]. How much progress have we made in this area since 1999? We refer the reader to Brodlie et al. [119] as well as the chapter on collaborative visualization for a comprehensive overview of distributed and collaborative visualization research.

Challenge #6: Effective Interaction. The challenge of interaction is mentioned several times in related research literature including Hibbard's list, item number 7 under *"Interactions"* [349], in the future work section of Kosara et al. [462], Johnson's list, item number 6, *"HCI"* [409], as well as by Van Dam [842, 843]. Two classes of interactions are important here: interaction using the traditional keyboard and mouse and interaction techniques that go beyond the keyboard and mouse.

We mention the first class of interaction techniques because the keyboard and mouse have been around for many, many years now without significant evolution and we believe they are here to stay for many years to come because users are familiar with them. Nonetheless, much work remains in providing *more* interaction to the user of visualization tools and *intuitive* interaction. It seems that no matter how much interaction is provided to the user, the user will always want more with the passage of time and experience. This has been our first-hand experience working in software development alongside mechanical engineers. It is also a theme echoed by many researchers in our field. And with the coming of new visual metaphors come new interaction techniques. Providing intuitive interaction techniques will be a challenge as long as new visual metaphors are introduced. For example, it is not obvious what the most effective interaction tools are for those wishing to control the visual parameters of a BeamTree [455].

In the other class of interaction, those techniques which reach beyond the keyboard and mouse, developing intuitive interaction techniques is still in the early stages. Direct interaction will be central for users immersed in a virtual world. Much work needs to be done in the areas of voice recognition, gesture recognition, and 3D user interfaces. Clearly, communication with the voice and physical gesture is much more natural and intuitive from a human-centered point of view than using a mouse and keyboard to interact with an arbitrary 2D GUI. Users want to work with their hands as they do in the physical world. Many questions remain to be answered in this growing field. For example, what is the most effective way of drawing a line in 3D?

Challenge #7: Representing Data Quality. This topic comes up often in the visualization community and hence is often cited as a top future challenge [154, 409, 826]. In the scientific visualization literature, this topic is often described using the terms *"error"* and *"uncertainty"* visualization [409, 412]. Statisticians may use the term *"probability"*. Information visualization literature may address this theme as assessing the *"intrinsic quality"* of data [154]. Whatever the term(s) used, there is a common notion being described. Not all data is equal. Data has varying accuracy, reliability, probability of correctness, confidence, or quality.

In scientific visualization, most data sets have an associated measure of error or uncertainty. This error can come from various sources, but it is often associated with the hardware device that generates the data, e.g., a magnetic resonance imaging (MRI) scanner or some other 3D scanning device. However, this error is only very rarely represented in subsequent visualization [705]. Also in the context of scientific visualization, particle tracing integration algorithms

Fig. 5.4. The visualization of uncertainty in fluid flow resulting from different streamline tracing algorithms [510]. Different streamline integration schemes result in different paths, even in the same vector field. *Image courtesy of A. Pang et al.*

have a certain amount of error associated with them [494], however this uncertainty is normally not represented in the visualization [510] (Figure 5.4). Other examples come from multiresolution (MR) and adaptive resolution (AR) visualization [491]. Each resolution in an MR hierarchy has some measure of error associated with it since a coarser approximation can normally not be as authentic as original, fine resolution data. AR visualizations also normally contain uncertainty in regions of coarser resolution. In both the MR and AR cases, this uncertainty is usually not included in subsequent visualizations.

Other measures of data quality are not difficult to imagine. In an information visualization context, imagine a census collected from two distinct time periods, separated by 10 years. Presumably, the more recent census data is more accurate and thus of higher quality than its older counterpart. Does the newer census data render the old data no longer useful? Not necessarily. The older census may represent a slightly different geographic coverage than the latter. In other words, the physical domain is slightly different for each case. This example brings up two more important factors when considering data quality: namely *temporal factors* and *coverage*. The age of data may influence its quality. More recent data may be considered more reliable. *Incomplete* data is also a problem arising very frequently. In the case of the census data, the more recent census may be considered incomplete if it does not maintain the same geographic coverage of its predecessor.

Erroneous and incomplete data is often discussed in the context of databases. Any database derived from manual data entry is assumed to have both (human) errors and missing items, i.e., incomplete records, sparse fields. And although the data in virtually every database contains some amount of error, this error is more often than not left out in subsequent visualization(s). In fact, so careful are visualization researchers at abstracting away problems with sources of data, that they have developed terms specifically for this purpose: data *smoothing* or sometimes *preprocessing*. We have even heard the term: to *massage* the data (before visualization).

Regardless, the challenge of assessing data quality promises to remain a top unsolved problem for years to come. And we regard this a mainly a human-centered problem. Once an intelligent decision has been made on how to measure or evaluate the quality of a certain data source, we believe technical solutions already exist to incorporate this information into resulting visualizations, e.g., using error bars, standard deviations, confidence intervals, color-coding, etc. Essentially any multi-dimensional visualization technique could potentially incorporate this as an additional data dimension.

5.1.2 Technical Challenges

Here we describe the challenges we claim are centered on technical issues like the development of novel, innovative algorithms or challenges closely coupled with hardware.

Challenge #8: Scalability and Large Data Management. A challenge identified by Chen [154] (see problem number 6– "*Scalability*"), Kosara et al. [462] and Thomas and Cook [826], see the topic– "*Visual Scalability*", most researchers agree that the rate of data growth always exceeds our capacity develop software tools that visualize it. At the very heart of visualization research is the rapid growth of data set sizes and information. The primary motivation for visualization research is to gain insight into large data sets. Software programs are often composed of thousands of files and millions of lines of code. Simulation results are often several gigabytes in size. Databases often store data on the terabyte scale. A popular example of data management on the terabyte scale–generated daily, comes from the field of astrophysics [811]. Very large databases are the focus of their own conferences like VLDB–the annual Very Large Data Base conference, now meeting for over 30 years. Technical problems that form the core challenges are:

- *Designing Scalable Visualizations*: Visualization algorithms that are capable of handling very large data sets and scale correspondingly to ever-increasing data sets sizes (Figure 5.5).
- *Limited Processing Speed*: Even with Moore's law describing the growth rate of processing power, software growth seems to exceed the rate of hardware growth.
- *Limited Memory and Storage Space*: Visualization technology that makes efficient use of limited storage capacity, e.g., out-of-core algorithms.
- *Limited Network Bandwidth*: Visualization algorithms that make efficient use of limited network bandwidth.

Fig. 5.5. The visualization of a large graph containing 15,606 vertices and 45,87
edges at different scales: (top,left) at the original scale, (top,right) with 4,393 vertices
(bottom,left) with 1,223 vertices, and (bottom,right) with 341 vertices [288]. *Imag
courtesy of E. R. Gansner.*

Scalability and large data visualization were themes in the IEEE InfoVis 200
Contest. The winner of the InfoVis 2003 contest, TreeJuxtaposer [583], was abl
to visualize a tree with about 500,000 elements. Clearly, there is still a non-trivia
gap between the larger data set sizes and visualization algorithms designed fo
large data sets. Ideally, visualization algorithms can realize interactive or rea
time frame rates. But this is generally not true when data set sizes exceed
certain threshold size. Effective visualization will face the challenge of ever-large
data set sizes and limited processing speed for many years to come.

Note how we have used the term *limited* to describe memory, storage spac
and network bandwidth. The cost of memory and storage space has droppe
dramatically in recent years and availability has increased correspondingly. Bu
the growth of data still exceeds the growth of both memory and storage spac
and we do not expect this trend to change in the near future. Every practitione
working on a daily basis has had the experience of running out of disk space, e.g
see Figure 5.6. And virtually everyone has gone through the process of findin
data to delete in order to free up more space–a task aided by various softwar
programs. In short, data is collected to meet disk storage capacity.

Fig. 5.6. Sequoia View is a very effective tool for visualizing disk space usage [856]. Each file is represented by a rectangle in the image. As of January 2006, it has been downloaded over 500,000 times. *Image courtesy of of J. J. van Wijk et al.*

Analogous statements hold true regarding network bandwidth. Network speed has increased rapidly over the last 20 years, but seemingly it can never be fast enough. As an example, the VRVis Research Center participated in the IEEE Visualization Contest in 2004, another contest focused at visualizing large data sets. It took two days to download the 60 gigabyte contest data set–the visualization of hurricane Isabel. Furthermore, how many copies of a such data set can be made? Future visualization algorithms must make effective use of both limited storage space and limited network bandwidth if they are to enjoy long term success.

Challenge #9: High Data Dimensionality and Time-Dependent Data. The challenges of high data dimensionality (also called multi-field, multi-attribute, or multi-variate data) and time-dependent data are continuous themes throughout the visualization community and appear often in the literature (See Hibbard's challenge number 5 on information [349] and Johnson's problem number 9 on multi-field visualization [409]).

The VRVis Research Center develops tools to visualize CFD simulation data [490]. Typical CFD simulation data attributes that describe the flow through a geometry include: velocity, temperature, pressure, kinetic energy, dissipation rate, and more. Plus the data sets are time-dependent with possibly hundreds or even thousands of time steps. And this is a description of single phase data. The number of attributes multiplies with each phase in a multi-phase simulation.

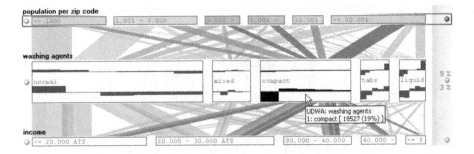

Fig. 5.7. Parallel sets are targeted specifically at the visualization of high-dimensional, abstract data [76]. Parallel sets can be considered an extension of parallel coordinates. This visualization shows the relationships between different questions in the survey. *Image courtesy of H. Hauser.*

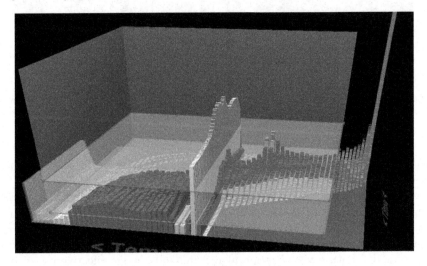

Fig. 5.8. Time Histograms are able to visualize time-dependent data in a still image [461]. Time is given a spatial dimension along one histogram axis.

With categorical data the problem becomes even worse. If each category is treated as a data dimension, then it's possible to have hundreds of dimensions. An example is described by Bendix et al. [76] who apply parallel sets–an extension of parallel coordinates–to an application with 99 dimensions (Figure 5.7). The case stems from a questionnaire containing information from about 94,000 households attempting to assess living standards. A particularly difficult challenge stems from the objective of trying to understand the relationships between multiple attributes (or dimensions) in the data.

Although time can be considered as another data dimension or attribute, it is treated separately here since time normally adds motion to a visualization. Effective, time-dependent visualization techniques promise to remain a future research challenge for several years to come. Watching objects in motion gener-

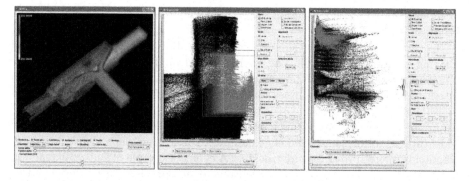

Fig. 5.9. Multiple, linked views are used in combination with brushing (middle) in order to filter out data in areas of interest (left) [205]. On the left is the scientific (or geometric view) of the data while the scatter plot view is on the right. Here, CFD simulation data is being analyzed. *Image courtesy of H. Doleisch et al.*

ally provides more insight than static images, but also requires more cognition on behalf of the viewer. The transient nature of a dynamic visualization can make some things not only easier to see, but also more difficult to see, e.g., fast moving phenomena. Also, representing motion in a static image generated from a time varying data set can be very challenging and relatively few methods have been presented on this topic [461] (Figure 5.8). One of the fundamental challenges with representing time in a static image lies in the length of time to be shown–both in the past and in the future. Ultimately, the needs of the user will play a large role in deciding this.

Challenge #10: Data Filtering. As mentioned in our top future research challenge in regards to assessing data quality: not all data is equal. Not only is not all data of equal quality but not all data is of equal interest or importance. Most would agree that one of the central problems of the current digital age and perhaps even of the twenty first century centers around the fact that we have too much information. In a 2003 study[2] lead by P. Lyman and H.R. Varian entitled *"How Much Information"*, it is estimated that five exabytes (5×10^{18} bytes) of data were produced world wide. And the rate of storage is growing each year at a rate of more than 30%. Consequently, developing tools that filter the data, namely, techniques that separate the data into interesting and uninteresting subsets is one of the major research challenges of the future (Figure 5.9).

As an example, consider the AT&T long-distance telephone network. AT&T maintains a database of all calls made using this network for a time period of one year [410]. The network connects 250 million telephones from which hundreds of millions of calls are made each day. Analyzing and visualizing this data in order to find fraudulent phone calls is a serious undertaking. Developing visualization tools to filter out the important information from such data sets is challenging for at least two reasons. Firstly, the size of the data set makes searching more difficult and time-consuming. Secondly, filtering the data based on importance

---

[2] Available at: http://www.sims.berkely.edu/how-much-info

or interest measures is a function of the user. Different users will filter the data based on different criteria.

In fact, one could view the new field of visual analytics from a pure visual filtering point of view [826]. The goal of visual analytics tools is to separate interesting data from non-interesting data. Visual analytics tools allow users to interactively search data sources for features of interest, special patterns, and unusual activity.

In scientific visualization, such filtering is often called feature extraction [660] or feature detection [409] (challenge number 11) and time-dependent feature extraction is referred to as feature tracking. A typical example of feature extraction can be found in flow visualization. Various algorithms have been developed to extract vortices from vector fields either automatically or semi-automatically. Another approach is to interactively extract features of interest using a combination of multiple, linked information and scientific visualization views [206] (Figure 5.9).

Regardless of the terminology used, software that helps a practitioner search and find those subsets of the data deemed most interesting will be in very high demand in the future. And visualization software is particularly suited for this challenge because it takes advantage of the high bandwidth channel between our visual and cognitive systems.

Challenge #11: Cross-Platform Visualization. This problem is identified multiple times previously [349, 409] and described in detail in Thomas and Cook [826] in the section on *"Collaborative Visual Analytics"*. Two users rarely have the exact same set of hardware. If we consider both the hardware and the software configurations of a user, the probability of an exact match is highly unlikely. For a long time, advances in display technology were fairly slow. However, flat panel display technology has made rapid advances in recent years. The cost of display technology has also fallen, making display technology virtually ubiquitous in many countries. If we consider the range of possible hardware configurations: from desktops and laptop computers with various combinations of graphic cards and monitors, to handheld devices like cell phones, PDAs, and other electronic hand-held devices, to large displays using digital projectors, and we throw in various operating systems and memory resources for each of those devices then we are left with a vast array of possible hardware and software combinations. And the range of different possibilities is expanding, yet each user will demand advanced visualization functionality. Consequently, visualization tools that are able to cross inter-platform bridges will remain a serious challenge in the future just from a technical point of view (and also from a human-centered point of view as mentioned in the challenge concerning collaborative visualization).

Currently, we are witnessing an explosion in research literature related to the topic of programmable graphic card capabilities [239]. Many visualization algorithms have been written that are tied to an individual graphics card and the set of programming language capabilities that it supports. We see a rather negative aspect of this trend and we are not in full support of this as a research direction. In fact, this trend works against the goal of cross-platform visualiza-

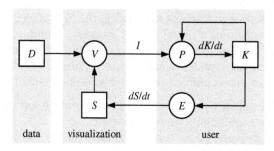

Fig. 5.10. A simple model to assess the value of a visualization [852]. D = data, V = visualization, I = image, P = perception, K = knowledge, S = specification, E = exploration. *Image courtesy of J. J. van Wijk.*

tion. Have you ever asked a practitioner, e.g., an engineer, what kind of graphics card their workstation has? Tying an application to a specific graphics card has some negative implications: one of which is a sharp increase in cost. Imagine requiring specific hardware and application software to be sold together. That would imply that a user would have to buy a special workstation just for one visualization application. The scenario quickly becomes infeasible if we ask a user to buy a separate set of hardware for each software application. It is rather the job of the operating system software to be tied to the hardware and not necessarily the application software. The exception to this is when cross-platform standards, like OpenGL, are introduced–another future research challenge found on our list.

5.1.3 Financial Challenges

Here, we separate out literature on the topic of financial challenges facing visualization researchers. Seldom are financial challenges address explicitly in related literature. Financial challenges certainly abound however. This is especially true when one equates investments of time with money–something reasonable since time is costly. Note that this group of related work and challenges could also be re-formulated under the theme of transforming research into practice.

Challenge #12: Evaluating Effectiveness and Utility in Practice. Also identified as a future problem by Chen [154] (see unsolved problem number 5 "*Intrinsic quality measures*"), human-centered evaluation of visualization software is a common and old theme. Evaluation of visualization tools from an economic standpoint is a relatively new topic. Nonetheless it is very important. Are all research directions of equal worth? Probably not. Can all research directions be pursued? Again, this is most unlikely. Certainly, problems that are considered by many to be solved, like volume rendering of medical data [515], deserve less attention than unsolved problems. We also consider the problem of 2D flow visualization, both steady and unsteady, to be solved [851]. How do we as researchers decide where to invest our time and money?

Jarke van Wijk presents, to our knowledge, the first attempt at assessing the value of visualization from a practical and economic standpoint [852]. A model is presented that summarizes the requirements and processes associated with creating and evaluating visualization software (Figure 5.10). Several cost factors are identified. From an economic point of view, costs include:

- An initial development cost: This includes one or more software engineers and may include the acquisition of new hardware.
- An initial cost per user: The user must learn how to generate a visualization result using the developed software. In the CFD community, this process may take weeks, even months since simulation result may take a long time to compute and CFD software can be complex and feature-rich.
- Costs per session/use: This includes the time it takes the user to generate the required visualization from a given algorithm or method each time of use.
- The cost of cognition: This is the time the user needs to understand and explore the visualization result and thus gaining knowledge or insight into the underlying phenomenon.

The costs identified in this list must be multiplied by the number of developers and users respectively. In short, the cost of development and use is expensive. The take away? Careful consideration is required if we would like to invest our time and money properly.

Can visualization survive without customer demand? This was an important question raised by Bill Lorensen [515]. Lorensen argues that the success of research in computer graphics owes to the fact that there is a large customer demand–the computer gaming industry. In order to succeed the visualization community must establish better contact with potential customers–a challenge discussed here previously. Part of this must include the assessment of value. We must be able to offer something of value to potential practitioners. In order to do this, we need a way to assess value of visualization from an economic standpoint. This promises to remain a central challenge for visualization researchers for the foreseeable future.

Challenge #13: Introducing Standards and Benchmarks. Other areas of computer science have developed standards and benchmarks. Databases have standard normal forms. Networking is full of standard protocols. Many standard sorting algorithms are used. Standards represent progress in the field and are important to future, widespread use and success. Visualization lacks standards and benchmarks. (See also Thomas and Cook [826]) This encompasses several different aspects:

- *Standard Data File Formats:* The field of visualization is lacking standard data file formats. In CFD alone, several different data file formats exist. In medical visualization, much work has been done in order to establish a standard file format [786]. In information visualization, perhaps the closest thing to a standard file format is XML.

- *Standard Visualizations:* The closest thing we have now to standard visualizations are pie charts, bar graphs, and 2D scatter plots. However, these are already quite old, generally restricted to 2D, and are generally not interactive.
- *Standard Interaction Techniques:* Scaling (or zooming), rotation, and translation (or panning) are simple, standard interactions in a visualization application. However, from a users perspective their use is certainly not standard. Each application has its own way of rotating an object.
- *Standard Interfaces:* Standard interfaces, like OpenGL, are a great contribution to the field. Continued development of such interfaces is very important in order to enable cross-application interaction.
- *Standard Benchmarks:* Benchmark tests and data sets are used in industry before a software release. Standard benchmarks, including standard data sets, could also be used to demonstrate and compare new algorithms to their predecessors.

Lacking standard data file formats makes the problems of sharing data and comparing algorithms more difficult. It also generates more work thus slowing progress. One of the major problems is finding the proper trade-off between usability and compactness for large data sets. Identifying standard, up-to-date visualizations which have proven to be effective would help in comparing and evaluating novel visualizations. Trying to identify both standard visualizations and standard interaction techniques is difficult because of the large variety that have been introduced by the research community. Volume rendering with typical transfer functions like maximum intensity projection is established enough now that perhaps that could be considered a standard visualization. Panning, rotation and zooming are standard interaction techniques but each application has its own set of additional interaction capabilities.

Standard hardware and software interfaces are the key to system interoperability. System interoperability is one of the grand challenges identified by Thomas and Cook [826]. Teams will be deployed to develop disparate applications in disparate locations, yet interoperability standards must be developed if different groups are to work together and benefit from one another's implementation work.

We consider establishing benchmarks mainly as a financial challenge because of the financial and temporal investments that must be carried out for success. For example, who is willing to pay for a web server that hosts a collection of large data sets? Who is willing to invest the time it takes to maintain a web site or other hardware and web pages that describe and distribute standard, benchmark data sets? The importance of standard benchmarks and data sets is now fully recognized by the visualization community with the introduction of the IEEE InfoVis and IEEE Visualization contests. The motivation behind these contests is to introduce community-wide availability to challenging data sets that can be used to test any visualization technique. Further development of standards and benchmarks will certainly remain a financial challenge for a long time to come because developing such standards requires a long-term investment of time and labor.

Challenge #14: From Research Into Practice. As mentioned previously, visualization research is not for visualization's sake itself just as research in general is not for research's sake. The long term goal of research is to make a useful and important contribution to society at large. Transforming research ideas and prototypes into real applications will play a central role if we are to make a contribution to society as a whole. This challenge also pervades the visualization community. It's discussed by Thomas and Cook [826] (See the chapter entitled, *"Moving Research into Practice"*.) and was the topic of multiple, recent, discussion panels [763, 825]. We save this future challenge for last because it encompasses so many other challenges described previously:

- *Interdisciplinary Communication*: Turning research into practice will require collaboration with professionals from other disciplines (Section 5.1.1).
- *Evaluation of Usability*: Building software that supports a wider user audience (Section 5.1.1).
- *Scalability and Large Data Management*: Building software that is supports a wide variety of real-world, multi-scale, possibly incomplete or sparse data sets (Section 5.1.2).
- *Cross-Platform Visualization*: Deploying applications that run on more than one software and hardware platform (Section 5.1.2).

Another area key to the success of bringing research into practice includes educating users. That means more pedagogic literature needs to be published. Bringing knowledge to public both written and verbally will play a vital role.

We consider this mainly a financial challenge because the knowledge necessary for building an industry-grade software product is already available. The main question is finding the required man-power, e.g., the time and money necessary to build a real-world software application. Considerable progress has already been made in this area. Many commercial applications have been built using the VTK [743]. Advantage Windows from GE and Vitrea from Vital Images are also examples of successful visualization applications used in industry [515]. However, visualization applications are still not generally known as success stories. The gap between researchers and the needs of application scientists is well known. Bringing more research prototypes into the hands of real users will remain a challenge for the foreseeable future.

5.2 Chapter Notes

We have presented a literature survey of selected future challenges and unsolved research problems in visualization, with an emphasis on human-centered aspects. We note that our survey did not cover every single topic mentioned in the literature, but concentrated on those themes that were mentioned in multiple sources and where some (at least minimal) level of consensus was reached. Some of the unsolved problems and future challenges that we did not list specifically include:

- **Improving Visual Quality:** Producing hardware displays which are indistinguishable from physical reality (see challenge number 1 on Visual Quality from Hibbard [349]).
- **Integrating Virtual with Physical Reality:** Solving this problem would involve eliminating head mounted displays, special gloves or glasses, and embedding displays directly into the physical environment (see challenge number 2 on Visual Quality from Hibbard [349]).
- **Integrating Problem Solving Environments:** This is also sometimes referred to as computational steering and means allowing the user to interactively steer a computation in progress (see challenge number 8, *"Integrated Problem Solving Environments (PSEs)"* from Johnson [409]).
- **Developing a Theory of Visualization:** Some researchers feel that visualization as a discipline does not contain enough fundamental theory on which the premise itself (see challenge number 15, *"Theory of Visualization"* from Johnson [409]).
- *A Priori* **Knowledge:** Building visualization tools that take into account the already existing amount of application domain knowledge the user may have. (see challenge number 3, *"Prior Knowledge"* of Chen [154]).
- **Improving Aesthetics:** Improving the resulting appearance of a visualization is an important future problem identified by Chen [154] (see challenge number 7, *"Aesthetics"* [154]).
- **Privacy and Security:** Producing software which is capable of data anonymization, audit trails, and access controls to protect privacy or provide information security is a grand challenge identified by Thomas and Cook [826] (see Chapter 6, *"Moving Research into Practice"*).
- **Reducing Complexity:** Although this problem is not stated and described explicitly in the related literature, we feel that tools and techniques that focus on reducing complexity, especially from an implementation point of view, will be important and pose a difficult challenge to future visualization researchers.

Comments on the Future

Concerning the future of future challenges and unsolved problems in human-centered visualization, an outlook is difficult to predict. Perhaps 20 years from now the visualization community will again go through a similar phase of evaluation, self-criticism, and retrospection–seeking new directions. What brand new problems researchers will face is intriguing. We can, with caution and some margin of error, however, guess what problems here might be solved 20 years from now:

Solved Challenges in 20 Years

- *Interdisciplinary Collaboration*: We think this is a solvable problem within (less than) the next 20 years.
- *Finding Effective Visual Metaphors*: This problem also has the potential to be solved before the next phase shift.

- *Representing Data Quality*: We are optimistic and believe this will fall under the list of solved problems.
- *Transforming Research Into Practice*: The knowledge necessary to solve this problem already exists.

(Still) Unsolved Challenges in 20 Years

- *Evaluation of Usability*: Research in this area is still in the early stages. We think it will be only partially solved in 20 years.
- *Choosing Optimal Levels of Abstraction*: This problem is complex enough that we think it will still require more work in 20 years.
- *Collaborative Visualization*: The complexity here combined with the lack of progress in the last five years makes us confident that this problem will still remain unsolved in 20 years.
- *Effective Interaction*: We expect effective interaction to be solved in the traditional desktop environment, but not in environments beyond the desktop, e.g., virtual reality environments.
- *Scalability and Large Data Management*: This problem has been around for more than 20 years. Maybe this problem will be even worse in 20 years.
- *High Data Dimensionality and Time-Dependent Data*: This one is difficult to predict. We error on the side of caution and categorize it as unsolved in 20 years.
- *Data Filtering*: Again, the complexity here combined with the ever-expanding data set sizes leads us to believe that this problem will not be solved by then.
- *Platform Independent Visualization*: Will remain unsolved.
- *Evaluating Effectiveness and Utility*: It is not clear that this problem can ever be solved given its subjective nature.
- *Introducing Standards and Benchmarks*: We predict that this will be a partially solved problem in 20 years.

The list of solved problems is shorter than the list of unsolved problems. However, the list of unsolved problems contains partially solved challenges.

We recognize the subjective nature of the topic and realize that no such list will appeal entirely to all readers. Hopefully, our description will provide readers with a starting point and overview of both solved and unsolved problems in visualization. We also aim at sparking thought provoking discussion. We trust the reader will conclude that many unsolved problems and thus much future research remains. Correspondence is solicited. To contribute feedback to this survey of future challenges and unsolved problems in visualization research, please contact Robert S. Laramee[3].

---

[3]   The authors thank all those who have supported to this work including AVL (http://www.avl.com) and the Austrian research program Kplus (http://www.kplus.at). The first author may be contacted at: r.s.laramee@swansea.ac.uk.

Part II:

Domain-Specific Visualization

6 Geographic Visualization

Martin Nöllenburg

Geographic visualizations always played an important role in human history, especially in the earth sciences, long before computer visualizations became popular. The earliest examples of geographic visualization even date back to the stone age with map-like wall paintings depicting the surroundings of our ancestors. Since then cartography, the art and science of map-making, has evolved continuously until today. This is why computer-based geographic visualization can build upon a large base of established cartographic knowledge. Well-known examples of static visualizations beyond geographic maps are thematic maps that display the spatial pattern of a theme such as climate characteristics or population density. Moreover, the use of modern visualization technology offers many new possibilities for geographical visualization tasks. These visualizations may help to explore, understand, and communicate spatial phenomena.

Many readers will already have some preconceived ideas of what geographic visualization is about. Nonetheless, to avoid misconceptions, the most common definitions of the term *geovisualization* (short for geographic visualization) will be given. The following explanation according to the 2001 research agenda of the International Cartographic Association (ICA) Commission on Visualization and Virtual Environments is most widely accepted today: *"Geovisualization integrates approaches from visualization in scientific computing (ViSC), cartography, image analysis, information visualization, exploratory data analysis (EDA), and geographic information systems (GISystems) to provide theory, methods and tools for visual exploration, analysis, synthesis, and presentation of geospatial data"* [528]. Others take a more human-centered view and describe geovisualization as *"the creation and use of visual representations to facilitate thinking, understanding, and knowledge construction about geospatial data"* [513] or as *"the use of visual geospatial displays to explore data and through that exploration to generate hypotheses, develop problem solutions and construct knowledge"* [473]. There are a few immediate observations from these definitions. It is clear that geovisualization research is a multidisciplinary task. Since it is the human who uses visualizations to explore data and construct knowledge, effective geovisualization techniques must above all take the user needs into account.

The chapter is structured as follows. First, the range of possible goals of geovisualization and its driving forces are described in Sections 6.1 and 6.2, respectively. Then, Section 6.3 looks at some perceptual issues and theoretical results in geovisualization. The main part of the survey, Section 6.4, covers a va-

A. Kerren et al. (Eds.): Human-Centered Visualization Environments 2006, LNCS 4417, pp. 257–294, 2007.

riety of suitable visualization methods from map-based and abstract techniques to animation. It also deals with interaction techniques and combined visual and computational mining of geospatial data. A number of existing geovisualization environments and tools are described in Section 6.5. Usability issues in the context of geovisualization, namely user-centered design, results from user studies, and geovisualization that supports group work, are reported in Section 6.6. The final part of this chapter looks at current and future challenges in geovisualization.

6.1 Goals of Geovisualization

The goals of geovisualization are manifold. The *map use cube* (Figure 6.1) by MacEachren and Kraak [528] models the space of visualization goals with respect to three dimensions:

- the *task* can range from revealing unknowns and constructing new knowledge to sharing existing knowledge;
- the *interaction with the visualization interface* can range from a rather passive low level to a high level where users actively influence what they see;
- finally, the *visualization use* ranges from a single, private user to a large, public audience.

The four visualization goals *exploration, analysis, synthesis*, and *presentation*, as identified in the International Cartographic Association's research agenda [528], are placed on a diagonal in this map-use space. On the one extreme, exploration can be found as a private, highly interactive task to prompt thinking and to generate hypotheses and ultimately new scientific insight. The other extreme is formed by presenting knowledge in low-interaction visualizations to a wide audience, e.g., on a professional conference or in a publication. DiBiase et al. [196] described these two extremes as *visual thinking* which creates and interprets graphic representations, and *visual communication* which aims at distributing knowledge in an easy-to-read graphic form. The former task is exploratory, while the latter one is explanatory.

In the beginning of the 1990s, geovisualization research focused on exploratory methods and tools. Communication was the realm of traditional cartography. Every map communicates a message by stressing certain aspects of the underlying data. Cartographers, due to the lack of interaction in paper maps, had the goal of finding an optimal map for the intended message. In exploration, where the 'message' is yet to be discovered, there is no optimal map in the beginning. The early focus on exploration has expanded recently to include the whole range of visualization tasks as Dykes [221] observed. The reason is that sophisticated interactive geovisualization methods are now recognized as useful not only for exploration but also for presentation of knowledge through *guided discovery*. The *visualization experience* [221] offers great benefits for understanding and learning as it enables both experienced scientists and students to (re)discover knowledge through interaction. The map is now frequently seen as an interactive

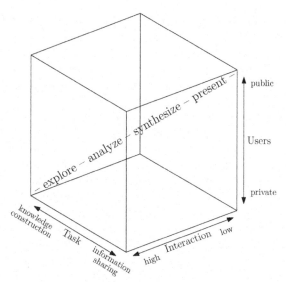

Fig. 6.1. The map use cube after MacEachren and Kraak [528] characterizing geovisualization objectives in a three-dimensional space by their level of interaction, their audience, and the addressed tasks.

interface to access and explore geospatial data while it still retains its traditional role as a presentational device [473]. Dykes argued that interaction appears to be the key defining characteristic of geovisualization today and MacEachren and Kraak [528] stated that geovisualization is characterized by interaction and dynamics. Concerning previously private tasks such as exploration, a shift from individual use towards support of group work has been demanded in the ICA agenda [528]. So recently, in terms of the map use cube, more research efforts have been attracted by the high-interaction and group-use (or public) parts of the geovisualization space.

6.2   Driving Forces of Geovisualization

So what is the reason for the increasing interest in geovisualization over the last 15 years? There are three driving forces for geovisualization.

The first is the rapid advances that have been made in *graphics and display technology*. The availability of both low-cost 3D graphics hardware in personal computers and the development of highly immersive 3D virtual environments resulted in investigating the potential that these technologies have for visualizing geospatial data. However, this emphasis on realism contrasts with the history of cartography that points to centuries of successful abstraction making the world easier to understand according to MacEachren [520]. Indeed, maps filter out unnecessary details of the environment in order to highlight interesting information. For example, a road map based on satellite images would be extremely hard to use. The challenge is to study the relative advantages and disadvantages of realism and abstraction in geovisualization and then, depending on the problem context, potentially integrate both abstract and realistic displays in a single geovisualization environment.

The second driving force for geovisualization is the need to analyze and explore a dramatically *increasing amount of geospatial data* that are routinely collected these days by a multitude of scientific and governmental institutions, private companies, and individuals. This is due to an increasing availability and decreasing cost of technology to acquire, store, and process these data. For example, the location of a credit card purchase or a mobile phone call is recorded by computers. A majority of the data, MacEachren and Kraak [528] estimated up to 80 percent, contain geospatial references, e.g., coordinates of environmental measurements, census data, positions of vehicles, ships, planes, and parcels, addresses of customers, etc. These data, often characterized by a high dimensionality, are a vast source of potentially valuable information for research and decision making, e.g., in studying disease incidence patterns, traffic flows, credit card fraud, or climate change. Privacy issues with these data are an important concern but they are out of the scope of this chapter. The large volume of many data sets poses challenging problems for their exploration. While computers are well suited for processing large amounts of data or finding well-known patterns, they perform rather poorly in detecting and interpreting unknown patterns in noisy data—at least in comparison to the human brain [400]. On the other hand, with increasing data volume and complexity humans quickly reach the limit of their capacities in analyzing raw numeric and textual data. The goal of geovisualization is to combine the strengths of human vision, creativity, and general knowledge with the storage capacity and the computational power of modern computers in order to explore large geospatial data sets. One way of doing this is by presenting a multitude of graphic representations of the data to the user, which allow him or her to interact with the data and change the views in order to gain insight and to draw conclusions, see Keim et al. [438].

Finally, the third driving force for geovisualization is the *rise of the Internet* and its development into the prominent medium to disseminate geospatial data and maps [473]. On the one hand, the Internet facilitates collaboration of expert users at different places, which is one of the ICA Commission's research challenges [528], and, on the other hand, it enables geovisualization applications to address the public. Reaching the public is an important aspect both for governmental agencies and for business companies who provide and sell services based on geospatial information, see for example Steiner et al. [792] who developed web-based tools to publish census data.

In general, there has been a shift away from technology-driven visualization towards more human-centered approaches that base on usability engineering principles and apply theoretical results from cognitive research as demanded by Slocum et al. [772]. To exploit the full potential of geospatial data, geovisualization tools need to adapt to their users. The question of what is a suitable map or visualization method depends not only on the visualization task at hand but also on the user's background. According to Griffin [305], there are different types of map readers who use geovisualization systems differently and who bring different knowledge to the map reading process. Hence, this chapter will not only present different methods and techniques applied in geovisualization, but also focus on usability testing and user-centered design of geovisualization systems.

6.3 Cognitive Aspects

This short section describes a cognitive framework for visualization in general and geovisualization in specific. The first part discusses visual thinking, i.e., how human vision perceives maps and images and how it finds patterns. The second part describes Bertin's concept of graphic variables for traditional paper maps and extensions for dynamic visualization techniques.

6.3.1 Visual Thinking

Visual thinking describes mental information processing through images instead of words. DiBiase [195] saw the origins of the potential power of visual thinking in the biological evolution where individuals with a quick reaction to visual cues survived. While we communicate mostly through words, we are connected to our environment primarily through vision. Hence, our visual perception has evolved into a powerful system that actively seeks meaningful patterns in what we see, sometimes even imposing them where they do not exist. Visual thinking often does not follow a logical train of thought and hence has not been appreciated for a long time in science. However, in 1990, MacEachren and Ganter [527] reported a renewal of interest in human vision as a tool of advancing science.

Prominent examples of successful visual thinking are Wegener's theory of continental drift prompted by the similar shapes of the facing coasts of Africa and South America, Kekulé's ring-shaped model of the benzene structure, or the discovery of the double helix structure of DNA by Watson and Crick stimulated by an x-ray photograph of DNA.

MacEachren and Ganter [527] developed a cognitive approach to geovisualization. They concentrated on the explorative side of visualization and thus on gaining new scientific insight through visual thinking. In their article visualization is seen in the first instance as a mental process rather than generating images using computer graphics. Nonetheless, computer graphics are a valuable tool to stimulate this mental process by creating graphics that facilitate visual identification of patterns or anomalies in the data. Visualization should not primarily focus on generating images but on using images to generate new ideas [195]. This also means that elaborate and highly realistic images are not necessarily required to generate valid hypotheses. Instead it is often abstraction, in the past achieved with pencil and paper, that helps to distinguish pattern from noise and thus makes a map or some other graphic useful. One key aspect in visual data exploration is to view a data set in a number of alternative ways to prompt both hypotheses and their critical reflection.

Fig. 6.2. John Snow's map of cholera deaths in London 1854. Deaths are marked by dots and water pumps by crosses. Version of Gilbert [295]. © *1958 Blackwell Publishing. Reprinted with permission.*

An early example of how a cartographic picture was used to gain new insight comes from medicine. In 1854 the London physician John Snow mapped cholera cases to a district map and made the link between cholera and a specific water pump that was used by the infected persons who 'clustered' around that pump on the map, see Figure 6.2. In fact, it was reported [456] that an anomaly of that pattern finally prompted his insight, namely the case of a workhouse with very few infections in the center of the cholera outbreak: it had an independent water source.

In order to successfully facilitate visual thinking it is necessary to understand how the human mind processes visual information. MacEachren and Ganter [527] and MacEachren [519] described visual information processing. Essentially, human vision produces abstractions from the complex input on the retina and these abstractions are matched to the mind's vast collection of patterns (or schemata) from experience.

MacEachren and Ganter [527] proposed a two-stage model for interacting with geovisualization tools in scientific exploration. At the first stage, called *seeing-that*, the analyst searches for patterns in the visual input. They distinguished two types of pattern-matches: a pattern is *recognized* if it is expected in the context; *noticing*, however, means detecting unexpected patterns that might lead to new insight. Once a pattern is recognized or noticed the analyst enters the second stage called *reasoning-why*, also known as the confirmatory stage of scientific inquiry. At this stage, the judgment made before is carefully examined to identify errors or to explain a pattern or anomaly. These two steps are iterated to collect more evidence for or to modify a judgment.

Finally, when the scientist has confirmed a hypothesis, he or she will usually want to share his insight with scientific peers through presentations and publications. Now, the goal is to lead fellow scientists to the same insight by invoking their seeing-that and reasoning-why process through well-designed graphics. If fellow scientists discover the patterns themselves the author's arguments will be much more convincing [527].

The model of MacEachren and Ganter implies that the success of a geovisualization tool in scientific inquiry depends primarily on its ability of displaying patterns that can be identified and analyzed by a human viewer [527]. However, individual users recognize and notice patterns differently based on their individual experience. Hence, explorative geovisualization tools must be interactive and permit a wide range of modifications to the visual display of the data. In the reasoning-why process, a key to insight or error detection is examining a judgment from different perspectives. Errors in pattern identification are divided into two categories: Type I errors mean seeing-wrong, i.e., to see patterns where they do not exist. Type II errors, on the contrary, denote not-seeing, i.e., missing patterns that are really there. Since human perception is adapted to seeing patterns all the time humans are susceptible to Type I errors (e.g., seeing shapes in clouds). Conversely, there is an effect known as *scientific blindness*, a phenomenon describing the tendency to overlook what one is not actively searching for. Consistency of patterns across multiple perspectives and modes is a cue to a valid pattern while inconsistencies demand reconsidering or rejecting the pattern [527].

6.3.2 Graphic Variables

On a map, information is usually represented by symbols, points, lines, and areas with different properties such as color, shape, etc. Bertin's concept of fundamental graphic variables for map and graphic design and rules for their use, published as "Sémiologie graphique" [85] in 1967, has proposed a basic typology for map design. This work was based on his experience as geographer and cartographer. For a discussion of Bertin's graphic variables see also Section 4.1 in this book. Since then his original set of variables has been modified and extended, see MacEachren [519, 520]. Bertin's fundamental graphic variables, namely *location, size, density/size of texture elements, color hue, color saturation, color value, orientation*, and *shape*, are means of communicating data to a map reader. Especially the different variables of color have been studied with regard to their efficiency in representing different kinds of data (categorical, sequential, binary, etc.). See Brewer [113] for detailed guidelines on how to represent data by colors. Variables can also be combined to represent the same information redundantly, for example using both size and color value. This provides better selectivity and facilitates the judgment of quantitative differences on a map in comparison to using just one variable.

Originally, Bertin's variables have been designed to describe information visualization on paper maps. Today, advances in graphics display technology provide a set of new graphic variables that can be utilized in geovisualization. Transparency and crispness are regarded as static graphic variables, the latter for example is suitable to represent uncertainty of some classification on a map [520]. However, geovisualization goes beyond static maps and therefore sets of tactile, dynamic, and sonic variables have been proposed, e.g., loudness, pitch, duration, temporal position, rate-of-change, etc. Most of these variables are analogs of graphic variables in another dimension, e.g., duration corresponds to size and temporal position to spatial location. However, both dynamic and sonic variables need to be observed over time and thus require more user attention than static representations.

6.4 Visualization Methods and Techniques

A number of techniques and methods adapted from cartography and scientific visualization are studied and applied in geovisualization. This section first introduces geospatial data and their unique properties. Sections 6.4.2 and 6.4.3 discuss 2D and 3D map-based visualization techniques, respectively. A selection of different techniques to display abstract multivariate attributes of geospatial data is covered in Section 6.4.4. Animation as a dynamic visualization technique that utilizes time as a visual dimension is the focus of Section 6.4.5. Spatial data often contain temporal attributes and hence Section 6.4.6 discusses the display of time, using animation as well as graphic variables like space or color. Interaction is considered as one of the key characteristics of geovisualization. Interactive methods and interfaces that control and link different visual representations are introduced in Section 6.4.7. Finally, Section 6.4.8 deals with the combination of visual and computational data mining techniques to explore very large data sets.

6.4.1 Geospatial Data

In contrast to information visualization displaying any abstract data, geovisualization deals specifically with geospatial data, i.e., data that contain georeferencing. This is a unique feature and special methods and tools are needed to take full advantage of it. Haining [323] decomposed geospatial data into an abstract attribute space and a geographic space with two or three dimensions. According to MacEachren and Kraak [528] geospatial data and information are fundamentally different from other kinds of data since they are inherently spatially structured in two or three dimensions (latitude, longitude, and possibly altitude). In case of spatio-temporal data, time can be seen as a fourth dimension. Remaining dimensions are often unstructured and there are various visualization methods for these abstract data, compare Section 4.3. Note also that distances and directions have an immediate meaning in those dimensions in contrast to distances computed on abstract data. While general visualization methods may be applied to spatial data as well, they do not take into account the special characteristics of the attributes. The georeference is usually either to a single point or to a whole area. Whether geospatial data are defined as a point or as an area obviously depends on the geographic scale at which they are examined. For example, a village can be represented as an area on a large scale map, as a point on a map of its province, and not at all on a country level.

6.4.2 2D Cartographic Visualization

The most common visualization method for geospatial data is a cartographic display of some form, i.e., a map where the area under consideration is depicted, and onto which the data of interest are plotted at their corresponding coordinates. *Space* is used to depict *space* by mapping latitude and longitude to the coordinate axes of the map drawing area. This might seem to be the most natural way of using this graphic variable. However, there are good reasons of linking for example population to space resulting in a *cartogram*[1] where area on the map is not proportional to a certain geographic area but in this case to the number of people living in that very area. Still, cartograms usually try to preserve the users' mental map by keeping similar shapes and by preserving the adjacencies between the depicted areas. An example of a world population cartogram is shown in Figure 6.3. Tobler [827] gave an overview of algorithms to automatically create contiguous value-by-area cartograms and van Kreveld and Speckmann [848] studied drawing rectangular cartograms. Especially when the focus of a map is on social, economic, or political issues, cartograms help to draw the users' attention to population as the map's theme while avoiding to emphasize large but sparsely inhabited regions. MacEachren [519] described space as an indispensable graphic variable with a large influence on what the user of a map sees. He argued that therefore space should represent the map theme.

For both cartograms and geographic maps the interesting aspect is of course how to depict abstract attributes of the data or at least a subset of them. Among the most popular methods to represent categorical but also numerical data are *choropleth*[2] maps. A choropleth map uses the graphic variables describing properties of color or texture to show properties of non-overlapping areas, such as provinces, districts, or other units of territory division. A number of categories is mapped to distinct colors or textures which are used to fill the areas accordingly. Examples are land cover/use with categories like forest, crop land, housing, etc. or election results per district, e.g., displaying the percentage of

---

[1] Among the most widely used cartograms are schematic maps of public transport systems, e.g., the London Tube map [289] which emphasize the topology of the transport network.

[2] Greek from *choros* place and *plethos* magnitude.

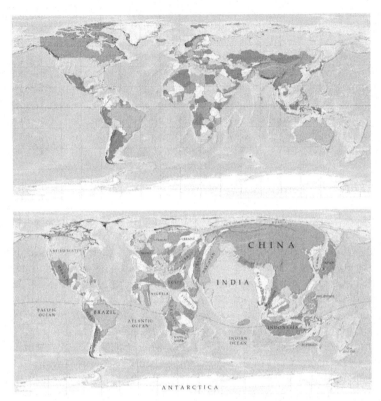

Fig. 6.3. Geographical world map (top) and world population cartogram (bottom). In the cartogram the size of a country is proportional to the size of its population. *Image courtesy of M. Newman. http://www-personal.umich.edu/~mejn/cartograms/*

votes for a certain party or the voter turnout as in Figure 6.4. For unordered data well-distinguishable colors are needed while for ordered data it is important to find a lightness or hue scale that represents the original range of numbers efficiently, i.e., that the user can estimate values and differences from the colors. Alternatively, a continuous range of attribute values is mapped to a continuous color range without assigning values to a fixed number of classes. While choropleth maps help to show general trends in the data there is certainly a loss of information because the user cannot map a certain color to its exact numerical value. Furthermore, a choropleth map can only express one or two attributes of the data (by using a two-dimensional color scheme or by combining color and texture). Andrienko and Andrienko [21] described a selection of methods to represent single and multiple attributes in a map. Depending on the type of the attributes (logical, numeric, or nominal), they used bar and pie diagrams common in statistic visualization. Similarly, glyph-based techniques from visual data mining can also be combined with map displays. These techniques, described in more detail in Section 6.4.4, use compound glyphs to represent the values of multiple abstract attributes. Using their geospatial reference, glyphs or statisti-

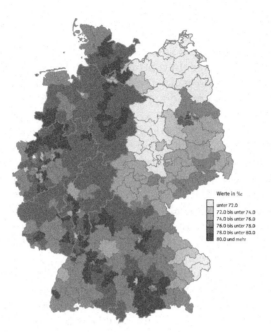

Fig. 6.4. A choropleth map showing turnout of voters in the 2005 federal elections in Germany [129]. *Image courtesy of Statistisches Bundesamt, Wiesbaden.*

cal diagrams are placed on the map and thus both spatial and multidimensional abstract attributes are represented on a single map. However, if the number of symbols or attributes exceeds a certain limit the symbols become hard to compare and other non-map based techniques from visual data mining should be applied in addition to the display of a map or cartogram, see Section 6.4.4.

Other approaches for displaying high-dimensional data reduce the dimensionality of the data, e.g., by applying statistical techniques like principal component analysis or by calculating compound indices representing, for example, the socioeconomic development of a region. The disadvantage, especially for explorative visualization, is that through the loss of information potential patterns of some attributes might get lost.

6.4.3 3D Cartographic Visualization

In contrast to traditional paper maps and two-dimensional visualization methods, geovisualization can go one step further and use the potential of increasingly experiential representation technologies. 3D visualization includes the full range from regular 3D graphics hardware in desktop computers to immersive 3D displays, CAVEs (Cave Automatic Virtual Environments), and Power Walls providing stereoscopic views. For an overview on display technology, the reader is referred to Section 3.2. Since humans live in a three-dimensional environment our perception and cognition is adapted to processing 3D visual stimuli. But there is still little known about when 3D visualization is appropriate and how it can effectively enhance visual thinking.

Cartography has a long and successful tradition using abstraction to depict a wide range of data on maps. In contrast, the focus of computer graphics technology is on producing increasingly realistic images and virtual environments. Virtual reality techniques are widespread, for example, in architecture and landscape planning where realism is very important. Depending on the geovisualization task, realism can be a distraction and insight is more likely when using abstract visual symbolism. But as MacEachren et al. [525] pointed out, there had been only few efforts exploring abstract visualizations of geospatial data in 3D.

In terms of the 3D representation of the data, MacEachren et al. [525] distinguished between using the three dimensions of the representation to display the three dimensions of physical space, using one or two dimensions for nonspatial data, e.g., income or time, and using all three dimensions for abstract data. Representing time as the third dimension is common and will be discussed in Section 6.4.6 on spatio-temporal visualization.

Today, the most widespread use of 3D is at the level of visual representation while the display is a 2D screen. It is important to be aware of the implications that the projection of a 3D representation onto a 2D plane has. Depth cues such as perspective and occlusion also cause problems because distances are harder to estimate, and occlusion hides objects depending on the viewpoint. Ware and Plumlee [881] observed that due to occlusion humans cannot perceive much information in the depth direction while the x- and y-directions, orthogonal to the line of sight, can convey complex patterns. A set of interactive navigational controls are necessary to move within the 3D representation, e.g., zooming or flying, cf. Section 3.1 of this book or Bowman et al. [104]. As Wood et al. [908] pointed out the effectiveness of the virtual environment metaphor relies to some extent on navigational realism. While moving (e.g., walking or flying) slowly through the visual space maintains a sense of orientation, faster modes of movement such as teleporting lose the context and the user has to reorientate.

6.4.4 Visual Data Mining Tools

Visual data mining, also denoted as Exploratory Data Analysis (EDA) in statistics by Tukey [838], is a human-centered task that aims at *visually* analyzing data and gaining new insights. This contrasts computational data mining techniques which use algorithms to detect patterns in the data. Effective visual data mining tools need to display multivariate data in a way that the human viewer can easily perceive patterns and relationships in the data. Visual data mining in general is not tailored specifically for geospatial data. See Section 4.3 for a general discussion of visualizing multivariate data. Since geospatial data usually have many abstract attributes (cf. Section 6.4.1) these general techniques can be applied for displaying non-spatial attributes of the data. Visualization techniques for multivariate data were broadly classified as geometric, glyph- or icon-based, pixel-oriented, and hierarchical by Schroeder [742] and Keim and Kriegel [437]. In a geovisualization context, geometric and glyph-based techniques are most

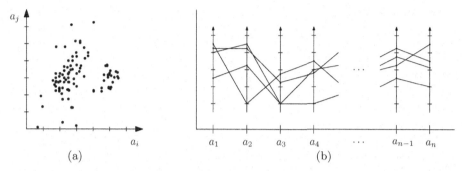

Fig. 6.5. Example of a 2D scatter plot in subfigure (a) and a parallel coordinate plot in subfigure (b).

common. Graph-drawing techniques that depict relationships between individual data items are also covered in this section.

Geometric Techniques. Two geometric techniques commonly used in geovisualization are scatter plots and parallel coordinate plots. Scatter plots in their basic two-dimensional form depict objects as points in a coordinate system where the axes correspond to two selected attributes, see Figure 6.5(a) for an example. Elements in the data set with similar values in these attributes form visual clusters in the scatter plot. The idea of a scatter plot can be extended to three dimensions but then phenomena as occlusion and different perception of depth as described in Section 6.4.3 may occur. The extension to more than three dimensions is often implemented by drawing a scatter-plot matrix containing one scatter plot for each pair of attributes. This, however, makes the identification of multidimensional patterns difficult because many plots in the matrix need to be linked mentally.

Parallel coordinate plots (PCP) [389] are a means of displaying high-dimensional data in a single plot. In a PCP, one dimension is used to place multiple parallel axes, each of which represents one attribute of the data. Each element of the data set is then characterized by the values of its attributes which are connected along the axes and thus build a geometric profile of that element as depicted in Figure 6.5(b). Since all elements are plotted in this way, the user can identify similar objects by comparing the geometric shape of their profiles. However, depending on the number of profiles, overplotting occurs and may result in poor legibility. Keim and Kriegel [437] estimated that about 1,000 items could be displayed at the same time. Moreover it becomes difficult to compare profiles based on an increasing number of attribute axes. Another important aspect of PCPs is the order of the attributes plotted along the parallel axes since this order has a strong influence on the shapes of the profiles. Hence, a user should be able to rearrange the attributes manually or based on sorting algorithms.

Glyph-Based Techniques. Glyph-based or icon-based techniques use a mapping of multiple attribute values to a set of different visual features of a glyph which in turn represents one data object. Two examples of such techniques are

Chernoff faces [156] and star plots [254]. In a Chernoff face, different variables of the data are related to facial features of an iconic face, such as size and shape of mouth, eyes, ears, etc., see Figure 6.6(a). The motivation of using faces to depict multidimensional data is that human mind is used to recognize and compare faces. However, different features, e.g., shape of the eyes and area of the face, are hard to compare and Chernoff faces are, in contrast to human faces, not perceived pre-attentively [572] such that there is no advantage over other types of glyphs.

Star plots depict the value of a set of attributes by the length of rays emanating from the center of the glyph. The endpoints of the rays are connected to create a closed shape as depicted in Figure 6.6(b). While the maximum number of facial features in Chernoff faces is reached quickly, star plots can display data with higher dimension by increasing the number of rays. Again, as for parallel coordinate plots, the order of the attributes influences the shape of the star plots.

A nice property of glyph-based techniques is that they can be easily combined with map displays described in Section 6.4.2 by placing each glyph according to its geospatial coordinates on the map. However, with an increasing number of symbols or attributes glyph-based techniques are of limited use due to the difficulty of visually recognizing patterns and distinguishing features on a display with too many glyphs or glyphs with too many features.

Graph-Drawing Techniques. Geospatial data often contain links between related elements, e.g., routes, trade connections, etc. Exploring such data sets includes the search for patterns in the link structure between items. Data containing relationships between elements are mathematically modeled as a graph consisting of a set of nodes, the data elements, and a set of (weighted) edges, the links between elements. The research area of graph drawing provides a multitude of algorithms for visualizing such graphs, see di Battista et al. [193]. Section 4.4 discusses visualization of graphs from a human-centered perspective and Rodgers [714] gives an overview of graph drawing methods and their application to geovisualization. In general, for graph drawing the emphasis is on finding a layout, i.e., positions of nodes and edges of a given graph that satisfies certain aesthetic criteria, e.g., few edge crossings. In geovisualization, there are usually certain constraints on such a layout since nodes already have a spatial location. In that case, finding a legible layout for the edges is of interest, for example in schematizing road networks [139]. In other cases, such as drawing metro maps [362, 615, 799], the network topology is more important and node positions are only required to satisfy certain relative positions (e.g., left, right, above, below) in order to preserve the user's mental map. Finally, some data is best analyzed by putting no restrictions to node positions and using a general algorithm to find a graph layout in which link patterns can be identified visually. Such methods are applied in visual social network analysis, see for example Brandes and Wagner [110]. In the latter cases, where node positions are modified, a map display of the true geography in combination with a graph layout focusing on the link topology is helpful for identifying both spatial and link-based patterns. An example by Rodgers [714] visualizing trade volume between regions of

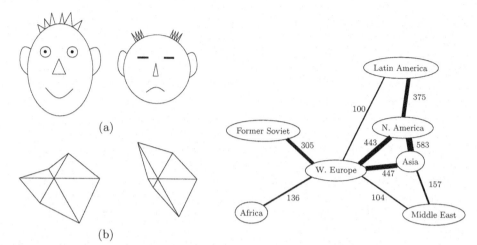

Fig. 6.6. Two examples of glyph-based techniques: subfigure (a) shows two Chernoff faces and subfigure (b) shows two star plots on six attributes.

Fig. 6.7. A graph showing trade relationships. Edges are weighted by trade volume and drawn shorter and thicker with increasing weight. Only edges with at least 100 billion dollars trade volume are shown.

the world as a graph is shown in Figure 6.7. The stronger a trade relationship between two regions the more they attract each other in the graph layout.

6.4.5   Animation

The methods described so far are primarily static displays of geospatial data. They can all be printed and studied on paper. In geovisualization, however, dynamic and interactive displays are core concepts today. Since the 1930s cartographers are experimenting with map movies and animated maps. Leaving interaction aside, which is covered in Section 6.4.7, animated maps are using time to add another visual dimension to the display. It is intuitive to relate time to time, just as space depicts space in most maps [333]. In this case, the time period of the data is mapped to the animation time. Each scene or frame of the animation shows the state of the data at one moment accordingly. Thus, the temporal change of the attributes becomes visible. It may be necessary to smooth the animation using interpolation to generate intermediate frames. Scenes can also be reordered from chronological order to an order based on attribute values. This may be helpful for studying at what points of time events with similar properties took place. For example, earthquake data can be ordered by the number of human fatalities in such a way that the beginning of the animation shows the least and the end the most catastrophic earthquakes [196]. Animation can also be used to display spatial features, e.g., animations of flights over the terrain. In other cases, the temporal dimension is used to display quantitative attributes by mapping their values to the blinking frequency of symbols or to highlight classes in a choropleth map by blinking. The presence of the temporal dimension in dynamic visualizations also introduces the potential to use acoustic variables. Although visualization is mostly concerned with visual aspects, using sound to complement dynamic graphics expands the possibilities of visualization. Krygier [479] summarized the role of sound in geovisualization from attracting attention over narrative voice and representing quantitative attributes (e.g., using the variable pitch) to sound maps for visually impaired.

Bertin's notion of visual variables [85], as introduced in Section 6.3.2, has been extended to dynamic animated displays, see MacEachren [520] and Chapter 6 of MacEachren [519]. Six dynamic variables are suggested: (1) temporal position, i.e., *when* something is displayed, (2) duration, i.e., how long something is displayed, (3) order, i.e., the temporal sequence of events, (4) rate of change, e.g., the magnitude of change per time unit, (5) frequency, i.e., the speed of the animation, and (6) synchronization, e.g., the temporal correspondence of two events.

Animation and its set of additional visual variables represents a powerful tool for map designers. However, animation should not be used carelessly and it is always worth asking *"why do I need to animate these data?"* [334]. From a user's perspective, things that change on a map attract more attention than the static background and moving objects attract more attention than objects that appear and disappear. The fact that animated displays change over time has an important disadvantage, especially if there are no interactive controls: there is always the risk that the user will miss important information. While a static display can be analyzed at an individual speed, an animation has to be followed at the predefined pace. Therefore, it is hard to compare data displayed at different points of time as the human brain usually forgets most details of previous frames of an animation. A study by Rensink et al. [702] showed how difficult perceiving changes in an animation can be.

Harrower [334] gave some guidelines for designing effective animated maps. Because dynamic variables attract more attention than static variables the information conveyed by static variables should be kept simple, e.g., by using a choropleth map with only few data classes (*high*, *medium*, and *low*) and a rather low level of detail. Details are often more effectively displayed using static visualization techniques. Temporal exaggeration, i.e., displaying durations not to scale, is often necessary since otherwise a short event, e.g., an earthquake, in an animation spanning several decades will be missed by the viewer. Directing the user's attention to critical events can be done for example by initially flashing new symbols on the map. In general, animated maps are better suited to depicting geographic *patterns*, e.g., growth or shrinkage of an area, rather than specific *rates of change* according to Harrower [334]. Finally, he observed that people are less confident with animated maps than with static maps, due to less experience and training.

Many of the above problems can be avoided by giving the control of the animation to the user. In interactive animations, where the user can control the displayed level of detail and the speed of the animation, information is less likely to be missed and users feel more confident with the animation. Still, the study of dynamic displays with regard to their geospatial expressiveness is identified as one of the challenges in the ICA research agenda [528] and further usability studies are required, see Section 6.6.

6.4.6 Spatio-Temporal Visualization

Spatio-temporal data are very common in the earth sciences and related disciplines. The goal of many studies is to reveal, analyze, and understand patterns of temporal change of phenomena, such as global warming, population development, or spread of diseases. The previous section has presented animation as a means of displaying temporal data. Animation works well in displaying patterns if they are based on the same temporal sequence as the animation itself, e.g., showing trends like urban growth over time. However, Andrienko et al. [26] criticized that for less evident patterns it is necessary to compare the data at different points in time which involves memorizing a large number of states in an animated display, even if interactive controls allow to pause, jump, and step through specific points in time. Thus it might be more effective to statically display selected moments in time simultaneously using small multiples. Then, an analyst can directly compare attribute properties of different points in time at his or her own speed. However, the number of simultaneous images on the screen is limited and long time series have to be evaluated piecewise. Andrienko et al. argue that, for all these reasons, spatio-temporal data exploration must be supported by a variety of techniques, possibly in combination with an animated display [26].

Andrienko et al. [25, 26] classified spatio-temporal data according to the type of temporal changes: (1) existential changes, i.e., appearance and disappearance of features, (2) changes of spatial properties, i.e., change of location, shape, size, etc., and (3) changes of thematic properties, i.e., qualitative and quantitative changes of attributes. Following this classification, they presented corresponding visualization techniques. All techniques involved a map display to visualize the spatial attributes of the data.

Data of existential changes usually consist of events or observations at specific moments or time periods during which a certain property holds, e.g., road congestion data. Hence a map showing these data always considers a selected time interval. If data items are represented by glyphs, one way to display the time associated with them is by using textual labels. Another possibility is using a color scheme to represent the age of the data. A 3D representation of space and time is a third and common method [519]. In such a *space-time cube*, the third dimension corresponds to time while two dimensions represent geographical space. The reference map is usually displayed in the coordinate plane corresponding to time 0 and data items are positioned above the map depending on their spatial locations and their times of appearance. An example of a space-time cube is shown in Figure 6.8. It shows the trajectory of Napoleon's troops during the French campaign against Russia in 1812.

For data that contain moving objects, comparing object trajectories is of interest. Static 2D maps are able to show the trajectories of a small number of

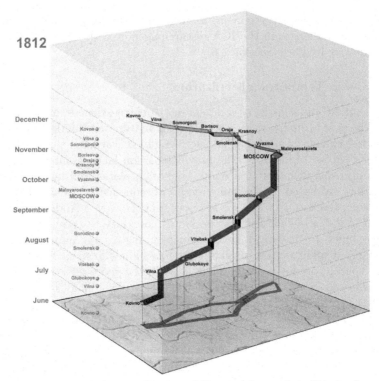

Fig. 6.8. A space-time cube visualization of Napoleon's march in Russia. *Image courtesy of M.-J. Kraak.*

objects but in this simple form it is not possible to evaluate aspects like speed or whether two objects met at a crossing or just visited at different points in time. Andrienko et al. [25] suggested animating object movements, either as a sequence of snapshots in time in which at each moment objects are shown at their current positions or using the movement history and showing the trajectories up to the current point in time. Movement history can optionally be limited to a specified time interval. It was found that the snapshot technique was suited for a single object while several objects were better observed displaying also the movement history. MacEachren [519] suggested using the space-time cube to display trajectories which avoids the disadvantages of 2D trajectories mentioned above as it shows *when* and not just *if* an object visited a point.

There are several methods of displaying thematic attributes on a map. A very effective and common method is the choropleth map, see Section 6.4.2. Animating a choropleth map is able to give a good overview of the values in a selected attribute. However, it is difficult to estimate trends in a particular area on the map or to compare trends between different areas [26]. *Change maps* [25], adapted from conventional cartography, use the choropleth map to show the differences of an attribute between two selected points in time. Mapping increase and decrease in attribute value to shades of two different colors allows

Fig. 6.9. Cartographic representation of the spatial distribution of the burglary rates in the USA. *Image courtesy of G. Andrienko.*

to evaluate regional changes for two moments. Such a map is restricted to two points in time and the map can be misleading because information on the actual attribute values is lost, e.g., concerning crime data two areas can have very different burglary rates but still be colored the same if the rates both decrease by the same value. Andrienko and Andrienko [23] combined time-series graphs with maps to avoid these disadvantages. A time-series graph is a two-dimensional plot of the temporal variation of attribute values, where time is represented on the x-axis and attribute values on the y-axis. Plotting all data in the same time graph gives an overview of the dynamics of the whole data set. To assess local behaviors, Andrienko and Andrienko plotted the time-series data individually for each area on the map and used the closed shape of the plot as a symbol superimposed on each area similarly to the glyph-based techniques in Section 6.4.4, see Figure 6.9 for an example. This technique allows to evaluate changes and actual values of an attribute for the whole time period under consideration. The user can explore both spatial patterns and patterns in the attribute space in the same view.

Shanbhag et al. [753] presented three techniques that modify choropleth maps in order to display temporal attribute data. They did not color each district area in the map uniformly but partitioned it into several regions, each representing one point of time in the data. Their first technique builds on a cyclical, clock-like metaphor for perceiving time and partitions the area polygon into wedges. The second technique draws from the metaphor of annual rings of a tree trunk and assigns time points to 'rings' of the polygon. Finally, they suggested time slices for a linear perception of time, i.e., polygons were partitioned into vertical slices. Using any of the three techniques, temporal trends in each area could be detected by observing the variation (e.g., brightness) of the different regions of the district area. However, for an effective visualization the number of simultaneously displayed time points must be limited with respect to the size of the polygons in order to avoid clutter [753].

For detecting periodic temporal patterns, Hewagamage et al. [348] suggested using spirals to depict time in a 3D representation similar to MacEachren's space-time cube [519]. They used this technique to display events, i.e., data with existential changes like the sight of a bird at a specific time and place. Depending

on the semantics of the data, events often show some periodic appearance patterns, e.g., bird migration depends on the season and observed birds may rest at
a certain place every year. Hewagamage et al. took a linear time line and coiled
it such that one loop of the resulting three-dimensional spiral corresponded to
a user-specified time interval, e.g., a year or month. At each location of interest such a spiral was positioned, and the events at that position were placed as
small icons along the spiral. Thus, points in time whose temporal distance was a
multiple of the selected time period were vertically aligned on the spirals. Since
parts of the spirals were occluded the display needed to have interactive controls
for zooming and panning, as well as for changing the period of the spirals.

6.4.7 Interactive User Interfaces

Interaction is paramount in geovisualization, especially for visual exploration,
recall the map-use cube in Figure 6.1. The communication aspect of geovisualization is also shifting towards higher levels of interaction. Dykes introduced
guided discovery as a communication task [221]. For example, consider a student
who is learning by interactively (re-)discovering known relationships in a data
set. Dykes saw interaction as the key defining characteristic of visualization early
in the 21st century and according to MacEachren [520] interaction is a key factor
distinguishing geovisualization from traditional cartography. He continued that
geovisualization *"is an active process in which an individual engages in sorting,
highlighting, filtering, and otherwise transforming data in a search for patterns
and relationships"* [520]. In this sense, the present section focuses on common
interaction principles and interactive user interfaces in current geovisualization
systems.

Map use in traditional cartography, too, has been benefiting from interaction
albeit to a far lesser degree than current geovisualization. For example, drawing
with a pencil or using colored pins to mark spots on a paper map is a way of
interactively changing the map. For centuries using these and similar techniques
were the only way of exploring geospatial data. However, such manual interaction
techniques are time consuming and often give only very limited insight into
the data. Generating individual maps on demand had to be done manually by
cartographers and at a prohibitive cost for most explorative purposes. This has
changed drastically in computer-based geovisualization.

Buja et al. [128] introduced a taxonomy for general interactive multivariate data visualization. In the following, interactive visualization techniques are
grouped using this taxonomy. Their two main classes are *focusing individual
views* and *linking multiple views*. For a detailed description of interaction methods see Chapter 3 of this book.

Focusing. By focusing Buja et al. [128] mean any interactive modification that
selects what to see in a single display and how it is seen. They compared focusing
to operating a camera: choosing a perspective, deciding about magnification
and detail, etc. The individual visualization methods introduced in the previous
sections all profit from one or the other form of interaction—as static displays

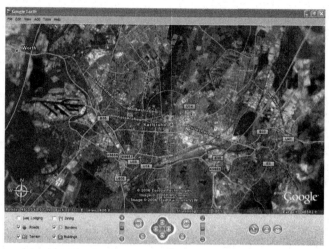

Fig. 6.10. Screenshot of Google Earth [300].

most of them are of very limited use. Two- and three-dimensional maps (see Section 6.4.2 and 6.4.3) usually come along with a set of navigational controls to move within the map space either by scrolling, shifting, or rotating a map or by walking or flying through a virtual 3D environment. Further controls allow users to zoom in or out of the map and thus to increase or decrease the level of detail and the amount of generalization of the underlying geographic features (rivers, cities, lakes, etc.). Once a perspective on the map is chosen, its appearance can be modified further, depending on the type of map. The display of geographic background features such as rivers, mountains, roads, etc. can be switched on or off. Depending on the user's task such surface details may be informative or distracting. In Figure 6.10, a screenshot of the satellite image viewer Google Earth[3] [300] is shown. With the navigational controls in the bottom of the figure the user can move around and change the scale. The check boxes on the left can be used to hide or show information like roads or borders.

The next mode of interaction concerns the way that the actual data items are displayed. For the general case of multivariate data the user must be able to select the attributes of interest and the type of their visualization, such as choropleth map or glyph-based map. Deselected attributes as well as the actual numeric values of selected attributes should be accessible, e.g., as tool tip information when moving the mouse over a symbol or area on the map. *Dynamic isolation* was used by Andrienko and Andrienko [21] to highlight a subset of data items in maps that use different symbols to depict different classes of data items, e.g., to select only coal mines in a map of natural resources. Spatial patterns may be cluttered in a map of all resources while they become evident once dynamically isolated.

---

[3] http://earth.google.com

Modification of the color scheme in a choropleth map is another important aspect. Assigning colors to classes or color ranges to numerical ranges is a very simple way of interacting with choropleth maps. While traditional paper maps use well-established color schemes that are suitable for the majority of map users these schemes may still not be optimal for an individual analyst and hence should be adaptable. In an *unclassed* map, i.e., numbers are mapped to color shades directly, Andrienko and Andrienko [21] used *dynamic visual comparison* to display attribute values with respect to a number N in the value range. To this end they applied a diverging color scheme which maps N to a neutral color, e.g., white, values lower than N to shades of red, and values higher than N to shades of green. The greater the difference the darker the color. This is a way to visually split the areas on a choropleth map. The reference value N can be selected by clicking on an object in the map to select its value or by using a slider unit representing the value and color range. Statistic values like mean, median, or quantiles are typically used as reference value. In *classed* maps the value range of an attribute is partitioned into a set of intervals and a distinct color is assigned to each interval. Here *dynamic classification* was applied, i.e., interactive modification of the underlying classes by shifting interval boundaries or changing the number of classes.

Finally, the mapping of a numeric value range to color shades in a choropleth map or to height in bar maps can be modified. This mapping is usually a linear function and hence outliers in the value distribution may cause a poor color resolution for the bulk of values. To reduce this effect Andrienko and Andrienko [21] used *dynamic focusing* to map the full scale of colors to a subrange of values with the outliers removed. Values to the left or right of the subrange are simply colored by the minimum or maximum color value. Using non-linear functions to map values to colors, as it is common for statistical graphics, is undesirable for choropleth maps as visual analysis greatly depends on the immediate expression [21]. Similar colors would no longer necessarily reflect numeric closeness of values. For scatter plots, however, non-linear transformations (e.g., logarithmic scale) are acceptable if the goal is to find a functional relationship between two attributes.

As mentioned in Section 6.4.4, visual tools like the parallel coordinate plot (PCP) or glyph-based techniques depend on an order of the attributes. Ordering the axes in a PCP or star plot and assigning facial features to attributes in Chernoff faces has an important effect on the geometric shape of PCP profiles and glyphs. Giving users the opportunity to change these properties allows them to see the same data from multiple perspectives. Concerning outliers and visual resolution, similar arguments and solutions as for mapping a value range to a color range in choropleth maps apply for the scale of PCP axes.

For animated maps there is a need to give control of the animation to the user. Even simple animations have VCR-like interfaces to control the animation speed, to pause the animation, or to select individual scenes. Harrower [334] described these abilities to navigate in time as equivalent to navigating in space, i.e., zooming and panning on static maps. Tools to navigate in time vary from linear time lines with sliders, which the user can move to select points or intervals in time, to more sophisticated devices like the time wheel[4]. The time wheel supports a cyclic view of time and consists of three concentric circles, the innermost representing hours, the next one days, and the outer circle represents months. In each circle, the respective time units can be marked and thus it enables to select recurring periods in time, e.g., the hours between 7 and 9 p.m. on the first five days of January, April, and May.

Linking and Brushing. The full potential of interaction in geovisualization lies in linking multiple views of the same data on the screen which is the defining criterion of the second class of Buja et al.'s taxonomy of interactive multivariate visualization [128]. See also Section 4.5 which discusses multiple and integrated views from a more general perspective. *Linking* basically means simultaneous highlighting of data items in multiple views. It is usually combined with *brushing*, i.e., selecting display objects by pointing on them or encircling them on the screen. Brushing was originally used for scatter-plot matrices, where points highlighted in one scatter plot are simultaneously highlighted in the other plots of the matrix to evaluate for example whether a relationship in two attributes also holds for other pairs of attributes. Monmonier [566] extended this idea as *geographic brushing* and links a map with scatter plots or other visual data mining tools. An example of linking and brushing is shown in Figure 6.11, where an outlier point in the scatter plot of per-capita income and percentage of poor is selected. The map shows the geographic location of the corresponding county New York, which has the highest average income in the USA. The PCP in the bottom of the screenshot allows to evaluate the remaining statistical attributes of New York.

Different views should be linked in a geovisualization system. Highlighting a point cluster in a scatter plot or a cluster of PCP profiles thus shows the spatial pattern of the corresponding objects in the associated map view. If there is, for example, a set of objects that are visually similar in a PCP the analyst might ask whether these object are located in the same region on the map or whether they are spread over the whole country but only in rural areas etc. Consequently, outliers that deviate from a general pattern can be located and examined more thoroughly. Similarly, one can select spatial object clusters on the map and subsequently analyze their behavior in attribute space using the remaining views. If the map is a choropleth map then linking and brushing can be done automatically using the same color scheme for the representations of objects in all views. Then, the analyst can mentally connect multiple views because the classes of the choropleth map are marked identically in all views. Changing the class assignment in the choropleth map immediately updates the linked displays. Conversely a scatter plot can be used to define new class boundaries for the map. A very simple example is the *cross map* [519]. It divides the value ranges of both attributes in a scatter plot into a lower and upper range thus defining four classes, each of which is represented with a distinct color on the map. Changing

---

[4] Demonstration applet by Rob Edsall available at http://www.geovista.psu.edu/products/demos/edsall/Tclets072799/cyclicaltime.htm.

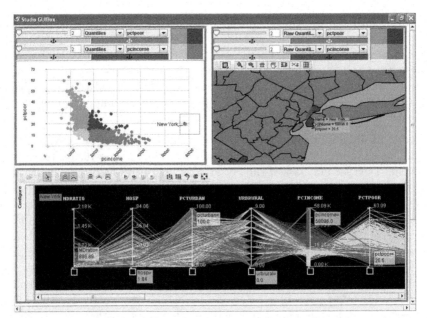

Fig. 6.11. Screenshot of GeoVISTA Studio showing linking and brushing between a scatter plot, a map view, and a PCP. The red item marked in the scatter plot is simultaneously highlighted in the other views.

the class assignment is as simple as moving the class-break point, i.e., the center of the cross separating the four classes in the scatter plot.

The possibilities of interacting with multiple linked views through highlighting and brushing are numerous. The number, type, and arrangement of the views depend on the specific geovisualization task, the individual user, and the available space on the screen. In any case, it is linking and brushing that make the use of multiple views more than simply the sum of its parts. The interactive principles introduced in this section all concern a core aspect of geovisualization: stimulate visual thinking by presenting the data in different ways and from a large number of perspectives. This is a key aspect of avoiding both Type I (seeing-wrong) and Type II (not-seeing) errors as false patterns are unlikely to be visible from many perspectives and patterns hard to see in a single view are more likely to be discovered in other views.

6.4.8 Combining Visual and Computational Exploration

The visualization and interaction techniques described so far seem most successful for data exploration tasks in small and medium-sized data sets, i.e., up to a few hundred items and a few tens of attributes. Geospatial data sets in practice, however, are continuously growing in size and are often characterized by a high number of dimensions as a report by the US National Research Council observed [598]. In such large data volumes with high-dimensional attributes human vision cannot be successful in isolating patterns [528]. Visualizing large data sets result in maps and other displays that are cluttered with overlapping items and small symbols such that properties of data items are hardly visible. Zooming is no remedy to these problems: it does help to avoid information overload and magnifies small symbols but at the cost of losing the overall view of the data which is just as important.

On the other hand, computational methods have been developed in areas like machine learning and data mining that can analyze large data volumes and automatically extract knowledge. But data mining methods have limited pattern interpretation abilities. They are susceptible to missing patterns with unusual, non-linear shapes. Interpreting potential patterns is also extremely difficult for computational methods which do not have the domain knowledge of a human expert.

With their strengths and weaknesses, computational methods and visual approaches complement each other. The integration of both approaches to combine their advantages promises further advances in the exploration of geospatial data. MacEachren and Kraak [528] reported *"integrating advantages of computational and visual approaches for knowledge discovery"* as one of the four primary themes on the ICA research agenda. Data exploration with tools that integrate both approaches is an iterative process. Results of the initial computational analysis are displayed graphically for further examination by an analyst. Using visual tools the patterns detected automatically need to be explored and interpreted. Questioning the results of a single run is very important. The user must be able to verify patterns and their stability by interactively changing the parameters of the data mining methods.

Examples of this integrative approach comprise the use of self-organizing maps (SOM) as a form of neural networks by Guo et al. [315] and Koua and Kraak [471] as well as applying k-means clustering by Andrienko and Andrienko [22]. Both methods are used for detecting *clusters* in a data set. A cluster denotes a subset of data items that are similar to each other and different from items in other clusters. This implies the need for a similarity measure on the attribute space, e.g., based on the Euclidean distance. In an explorative environment, where the goal is to discover unknown relationships, patterns have no predefined shape. Therefore, it is important to apply computational methods that do not impose a-priori hypotheses about the shape of patterns and instead let the data speak for themselves [315]. Kohonen's SOM is an example of such a method. The basic idea is to project high-dimensional data to a given grid of nodes on a two-dimensional surface such that (potentially non-linear) similarities are preserved and transformed into spatial proximity: data items within the same node are most similar, and the similarity between an item in one node and items in other nodes decreases with increasing grid distances to these nodes. A detailed description of SOMs can be found in Hastie et al. [340].

A SOM for geospatial data by itself is missing some important information. First, the geographic locations of clustered items cannot be extracted from the SOM view and second, the attribute values representative for a node cannot be

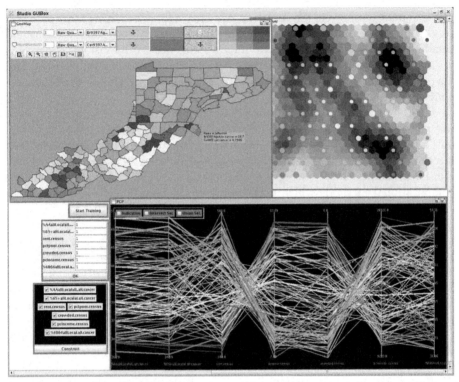

Fig. 6.12. Visualization of a cancer data set with a choropleth map, a parallel coordinate plot, and a SOM view. Screenshot of an application built with GeoVISTA Studio [812].

displayed. Guo et al. [315] solved this problem by linking a view of the SOM with a map and a PCP view which provided the missing information. A screenshot of their tool is shown in Figure 6.12. The map depicts 156 counties in the US states Kentucky, Pennsylvania, and West Virginia. They used an appropriate (user-adjustable) 2D color scheme to color SOM nodes such that nearby nodes have similar colors. This can be seen in the upper right window in Figure 6.12. The hexagons in this windows colored with shades of grey depict the distance in attribute space between adjacent SOM nodes. In the choropleth map view, each county is colored according to the SOM node it belongs to. This enables the user to compare proximity in attribute space with proximity in geographic space in a single view. A PCP is used to display the summarized attribute values of all SOM nodes. Summarizing data items in the same node avoids overplotting in the PCP since the number of SOM nodes (e.g., 10 × 10) is usually much smaller than the number of data items. The profile of each node is again colored identically and the line thickness is adapted to the number of items in that node. Brushing and linking of the three views are supported and the user can select either counties on the map, profiles in the PCP, or nodes in the SOM. The corresponding objects in the other displays are immediately highlighted.

The example of Guo et al. [315] shows that the integration of a computational data-mining technique into a geovisualization system allows the exploration of large geospatial data sets. The visual information load is reduced by automatically clustering the data and only displaying summary information while details are still available on demand. Users can explore the data and generate hypotheses by interacting with the system and by bringing in their expertise.

6.5   Geovisualization Tools

In the previous section, a wide range of methods and techniques used in geovisualization have been presented. However, the challenge for designers of geovisualization tools is to put these methods together effectively in order to help users solving their respective tasks. It has become clear that both users and tasks vary considerably. Hence, there cannot be a universal tool that fits all users and tasks. Instead, tools need to be flexible and easily configurable by users in order to be applicable to more than just a tightly defined problem. Users should be able to select freely from the methods discussed in the previous section and to link multiple views. In the following, five examples of geovisualization systems are briefly described to show how multiple views are combined and linked in practice.

ArcView. ArcView[5] is a commercial tool for visualizing and analyzing geographic data. It is a component of ArcGIS, one of the world's leading geographic information systems. ArcView offers a range of methods for creating customized thematic maps and analyzing spatial data. It is primarily used in administrative and industrial settings, e.g., for emergency planning, site planning, or marketing.

XGobi. XGobi [810], initially released in 1996, is a general data visualization system supporting linked scatter-plot matrices and parallel coordinate plots. XGobi is a freely available tool, and it can also be linked to ArcView.

Cartographic Data Visualizer. The Cartographic Data Visualizer (CDV) [220] integrates the mapping and abstract data visualization components into a single application. Its latest release is from 2000, and it is freely available on the Internet. CDV offers dynamic choropleth maps, population cartograms, and statistical graphics like PCPs. Graphic symbols serve as interface elements to access detailed information or to select subsets of items. The views are linked such that highlighting items in one view is passed on to the other views.

CommonGIS. CommonGIS [24] is another integrated geovisualization environment developed at Fraunhofer AIS which is in practical use in academic, administrative, and commercial settings. It combines a multitude of geovisualization techniques from (multiple) dynamic choropleth maps, optionally combined with bar plots and pie plots, over animated maps, time-series diagrams, and space-time cubes to multivariate visualizations like PCPs or scatter plots, see

---

[5] More information at `http://www.esri.com/software/arcgis/arcview`.

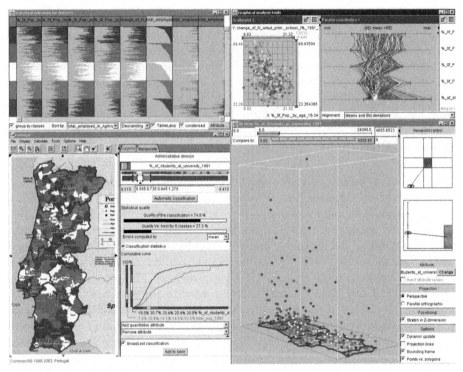

Fig. 6.13. Screenshot of CommonGIS. *Image courtesy of G. Andrienko.*

Figure 6.13. The user interface of CommonGIS supports interaction through focusing, brushing, linking of multiple views, and dynamic range selection for attributes. It is also possible to complement the visual data analysis by computational data-mining techniques. One focus in the development of CommonGIS was that it could be used even by users with no expertise in cartography and geosciences. The tool is commercially distributed, but it is free of charge for academic users.

GeoVISTA Studio. The approach taken by GeoVISTA Studio [812] is different. It is an open source software development environment for geovisualization rather than a static application. It is a component-oriented system with the goal to integrate a wide range of both computational and visual analysis activities and ultimately to improve geoscience research. Creating custom applications is done via a visual programming user interface that allows to connect different geovisualization components, provided as Java Beans, according to the desired data and control flow. Visual programming is a key aspect according to Takatsuka and Gahegan [812] because it allows geoscientists with little computational background to rapidly create prototypes when they are searching for useful insight. GeoVISTA Studio comes with a range of standard components, such as choropleth maps, 3D renderers, PCPs, scatter plots, color maps, spreadsheet views, and computational tools as k-means clustering and self-organizing maps.

Additionally, Java Beans created by third-party developers can easily be plugged in. Once a specific application or applet has been designed, its deployment over the Internet, for example to students for educational purposes, is supported. Sample applications can be downloaded from the project web site[6]. One example is the SOM-based tool by Guo et al. [315] described in Section 6.4.8 and shown in Figure 6.12 which is built using GeoVISTA Studio.

6.6   Usability of Geovisualization Systems

In the early days of geovisualization, the development of new tools was mainly technology-driven. New features of computer hardware had to be used extensively just because they were available. The tools were often seen as proofs of concept or designed for personal use and not really intended to be utilized in practice by geoscientists and other professionals. Currently, this scope is shifting away from innovators and early adopters towards a broader audience of pragmatic and conservative users [275]. Hence, it becomes increasingly important to provide geovisualization systems that are useful and usable for their target users. As Slocum et al. [772] put it, *"the most sophisticated technology will be of little use if people cannot utilize it effectively"*. In other words, considering cognitive and usability issues throughout the whole development process of a geovisualization tool is highly important for its success with the users. Cartography has a long tradition of applying perceptual and cognitive principles to map design, e.g., devising color schemes [113]. However, the cognitive theory for static maps does not easily generalize to current geovisualization systems. Slocum et al. [772] argued that cognitive and usability issues had to be considered in the context of (1) dynamic interactive maps, (2) immersive geovisualization environments, (3) interface design, (4) individual and group differences, (5) collaborative visualization, and (6) the effectiveness of geovisualization methods.

Usability issues and evaluation of visualizations are covered in depth in Chapter 2 of this book. Here, only the most important aspects with respect to geovisualization are discussed. Usability and usefulness are terms originating from the field of human-computer interaction (HCI) which are increasingly influencing geovisualization research after being put on the 2001 ICA research agenda [528]. Usability in the HCI community refers to the *effectiveness, efficiency*, and *satisfaction* with which specified users can achieve specified goals in a software system. This is not to be confused with usefulness which denotes the system's ability to achieve the specified goal in principle. A tool can be useful for some spatial analysis task (it provides all necessary information) but still not be usable e.g., because of poorly designed interfaces or because users don't understand its intended usage. Usability engineering in HCI refers to a human-centered design process in which the usability of the system at different stages is evaluated, see Nielsen [606] for a comprehensive introduction. Quantitative usability evaluation, as introduced in Section 2.4 of this book, is successfully applied for tasks

---

[6] http://www.geovistastudio.psu.edu

that are well defined. However, in geovisualization well-defined tasks are hard to identify when it comes to data exploration and knowledge discovery. These scenarios are inherently poorly defined and goal achievement becomes difficult to assess. Fuhrmann et al. [275] gave an overview on how principles of usability engineering could be modified to take the characteristics of geovisualization into account. Common quantitative measures like the required time to complete a task or the number of correctly answered questions are often not directly applicable. Rather are system developers interested in whether their tool supports the user's abilities to understand the data and to uncover hidden patterns. Therefore, qualitative assessment methods using various interview and discussion techniques, participant observations, or thinking-aloud protocols proved to be suitable for evaluating geovisualization tools, see the results reported in Section 6.6.2.

One difficulty of usability testing in geovisualization, reported by Andrienko et al. [27], is that often the goal is to evaluate a concept, e.g., a parallel coordinate plot, but the actual test must be performed with an implementation of that concept. A positive result provides evidence in favor of the concept (and the implementation), but a negative result does not imply the failure of the concept. It could simply mean that this implementation of the concept is not appropriate. It is therefore important to evaluate preliminary prototypes qualitatively to reduce the risk of poor implementations of a concept.

A user group that may not be forgotten—and one of the most challenging according to Plaisant [651]—is the general public. Problems that need to be addressed in this context mainly deal with the diversity of users. But reaching every citizen is becoming important for governmental agencies and companies offering geospatial services for end users. Such services need to be distributed to a wide audience, most likely over the Internet. However, users range from children to senior citizens, have different levels of education, speak different languages, and—not to forget—may have visual disabilities like color blindness. Additionally, they use different technology in terms of network bandwidth, processor speed, screen size, etc. Scientific visualization methods such as scatter plots or PCPs are hard to understand for the average user. Simple interfaces and displays are paramount to keep the required training as low as possible. In general it is important that the visualizations are adjustable for the needs of the specific user group. All these challenges are subsumed in the term *universal usability* by Shneiderman [760].

6.6.1 Involving Users in the Design of Geovisualizations

Evaluating a geovisualization tool according to usability principles right before its release should only be one of the final stages of usability testing in a human-centered design process. Fuhrmann et al. [275] reported that carrying out 'last-minute' evaluations often revealed major flaws and thus caused timely and costly repairs. In order to avoid this, user participation should take place right from the early stages of tool development as discussed in Section 2.4 of this book. Fuhrmann et al. identified setting an early focus on users and tasks involving

their participation and empirical testing iteratively during the whole design process as common principles in the literature on user-centered design approaches.
Determining the characteristics of the target user group in a user analysis is one
of the first steps. Variables that are important range from cultural background
and sex over domain expertise and education to computer literacy and potential
disabilities. Learning about users and their needs is usually done in individual
interviews, user observations, or group discussions (called *focus groups*). Narrative story telling is another method to gain insight into a user's subjective view
on a problem by listening to users' reports of critical incidents and personal
experiences. These methods usually require that users have already been using
a similar geovisualization system. For novel technologies like virtual environments or highly dynamic geovisualization systems this is, according to Slocum
et al. [772], often not the case. Hence, users cannot be interviewed about or
observed during analogous situations.

During later stages, such as concept development and prototyping, domain
experts' feedback gives valuable hints about the usefulness of the system. In
the beginning, this comprises discussing drafts and paper and pencil prototypes.
Later on, prototypes with still limited functionality can, for example, be tested in
a situation where one of the designers acts as the interface to the tool for expert
users who perform their actions verbally. Once the desired level of usability for
all parts of the product can be ensured, the final implementation takes place. If
similar systems are available comparative evaluations are common in practice.
Otherwise the tool is evaluated on its own by users interacting directly with the
full product or with certain components individually. Depending on the specific
visualization goal the tool is built for, a set of representative user tasks may be
defined and subsequently be solved by the test participants. In this case, results
can be measured quantitatively. Alternatively, users are asked to explore a data
set and report on their findings using methods like interviews, focus groups, etc.
as described in Chapter 2 of this book.

The procedure described above is still vague and actual usability studies
in geovisualization fill in the details differently. The reason for this is that the
ideas of usability testing and user-centered design from HCI research are novel
in geovisualization. The need for a comprehensive user-centered design approach
and formal methods for usability assessment in geovisualization was expressed by
MacEachren and Kraak [528]. A theoretical cognitive framework providing the
basis for novel geovisualization methods and user interfaces is needed as well as
the development of usability engineering principles for designing geovisualization
tools [772]. Slocum et al. [772] also observed that authors of geovisualization tools
often claimed that their methods facilitated science and decision making without
providing empirical support for their claims. In the following section, some results
from user studies that were inspired by these challenges are reported.

6.6.2   Results from User Studies

Griffin [305] studied how experts use geovisualization to explore epidemiological
data with a tool using three types of displays: maps, scatter plots, and time-series

graphs. The thinking-aloud method was used to generate protocols of the system usage of 18 experts from epidemiology and related domains. Participants were asked to use the model for exploring the data set and generating hypotheses after an introduction to the user interface. The main finding matches the intuition that users attending a greater diversity of displays also generated more complex and diverse hypotheses. Since facilitating hypotheses generation is an important goal of explorative geovisualization, Griffin's results provide evidence for including a wide range of different display types in such tools.

A study by MacEachren et al. [522] reported on the use of a single manipulable map by nine experts for the analysis of health data. The authors analyzed mortality rates and risk factors for three types of cancer between 1979 and 1993. The map display supported selection of up to two attributes represented in the choropleth map. Interactive controls comprised dynamic classifiers and a cross map to compare two attributes. Additionally VCR-like temporal controls were offered to analyze changes over time. Verbal protocols from participants were recorded as well as interaction logs during thinking-aloud sessions. Unlike in the study described above [305], participants were given six explorative tasks involving locating areas with certain properties, examining temporal trends, and making space-time comparisons. Depending on how users interacted with the tool they noticed or missed certain patterns. This study provides evidence that users who animated time-series data noticed trends missed by others, who used manual stepping to navigate through time.

Animations in comparison to static graphics, as examined in the previous study, have been the focus of several other studies. Koussoulakou and Kraak [472] compared the communicative expressiveness of animated maps versus static maps. In a study with 39 geodesy students using quantitative evaluation, they found that the correctness of answers was not influenced by the map type. However, spatio-temporal phenomena were perceived more quickly on animated maps. They also stated that using the full potential of animated maps requires an interactive user interface, which was not available in their study.

Harrower et al. [335] studied two interactive controls for animated maps: temporal brushing and focusing with temporal legends (linear and time wheel). In their test setting, 34 undergraduate students were using the interactive learning environment EarthSystemVisualizer. The advanced interaction methods had little impact on the students' performance. The reason is that many students were confused by the new interactive controls and hence did worse than students who did not use brushing and focusing. However, those students who understood the tools performed best in answering a series of objective questions. In contrast to the results from the main evaluation, a preliminary focus group using EarthSystemVisualizer gave mainly positive feedback about the interactive tools. This example of a useful but not very usable system clearly indicates the importance of sufficient user training, especially for novel techniques. A visualization system that is too complex for its users has rather negative than positive effects.

Perceptual salience[7] of dynamic displays was studied by Fabrikant and Golds-berry [243]. They applied a neural-net based and neurobiologically plausible computational model by Itti et al. [396] to predict the most salient locations on either static or animated maps. They found that the most salient locations determined by the vision model differ between static small multiples and non-interactive animations. Future plans include comparing these predicted results with empirical eye-movement measurements in a user study and exploring the perceptual differences of dynamic displays between expert and novice users.

Morrison et al. [579] compared several studies on the efficacy of animations in general. They observed that animation was not superior to static displays in studies where both displays provide equivalent information. Studies reporting positive effects of animation were using non-equivalent static displays, e.g., with the microsteps of an animation not being shown in the static graphics. So, these microsteps might be the power of animations. Slocum et al. [772] pointed out that the methodology of Morrison et al. [579] was limited by comparing only non-interactive animations to static graphics. However, just as users can control (in a sense interactively) the focus location in a static graphic, they should be able to do the same with respect to the temporal dimension of an animation.

Andrienko et al. [27] reported on an experimental usability study of inter-active techniques in CommonGIS assessing tool learnability, memorability, and user satisfaction. Since they primarily wanted to test whether users are able to handle the tools and not whether the tools facilitate knowledge construction, users had to solve well-defined tasks and answer multiple-choice questions. In a first round, the authors gave a tutorial lesson to nine participants before the test which was repeated a month later with the same group to assess memorability of the tool usage. The third web-based test was taken by 102 students who did not receive the introduction to the tools. However, they could read illustrated explanations for each task series. Overall, the performance in the web-based test was much worse in comparison to the first two rounds. This confirms the find-ings of Harrower et al. [335] that demonstrating and teaching the novel tools is very important. Teaching users to interact with web-based tools is a challenging task. Many participants did not read the instructions thoroughly and interactive online tutorials were suggested instead. Positive results were reported for some of the tested techniques, such as visual comparison of values in choropleth maps and dynamic linking of map, scatter plot, and PCP. Negative results were ob-tained for the dynamic query technique. This technique allows to specify value ranges for attributes. Objects with values outside these ranges are removed from the display.

Edsall et al. [232] assessed and compared the effectiveness of a map dynam-ically linked to a PCP with a map linked to a scatter plot. At first, the 37 participants of the study had to use either of the tools to accomplish a series of well-defined tasks. In the second step, participants were observed during unre-stricted exploration of a new data set with all available tools. They did not find

---

[7] An object in a graphic is said to be *perceptually salient* if it can be detected quickly with respect to its surrounding objects.

a statistically significant advantage of one method over the other. However, scatter plots were slightly ahead for studying bivariate patterns while PCPs seem to be more suitable for multivariate data. In the second test, those participants were most successful in finding patterns who made extensive use of a variety of visualization tools and thus taking multiple perspectives on the data.

A software tool to visualize uncertainties of global water balance due to climate change on a wall-size display was described by Slocum et al. [773]. Their goal was to communicate scientific results to decision makers, e.g., to politicians or executives. They followed usability engineering principles and first built a prototype which was evaluated by domain experts. The prototype was followed by two software revisions, the first one evaluated by usability experts and the final version evaluated by decision makers. This approach clearly improved the software, however Slocum et al. recognized that decision makers, the actual users of the system, were involved too late in the design process. Their comments would have been of greatest value in evaluation of the prototype [773].

Another example of a system designed according to usability engineering principles is ESTAT (Exploratory Spatio-Temporal Analysis Toolkit) by Robinson et al. [713]. It was developed in a cooperation of geovisualizers and epidemiologists to facilitate cancer epidemiology research. ESTAT is built in GeoVISTA Studio, and it combines and dynamically links a bivariate choropleth map, a scatter plot, a time series plot, and a PCP. At all stages of the development end-users were involved to assess the usability of the system. A prototype of the PCP module was evaluated in a thinking-aloud study with a group of students and resulted in reorganizing the PCP interface. Then, a refined version of ESTAT was evaluated with a group of epidemiologists in a tutorial and task session and a focus group discussion. Participants expressed the need for more training with the PCP and the time series plot and the desire to see descriptive statistics of the data. it was decided to perform an in-depth case study with an epidemiologist to understand how users would like to work with a geovisualization tool. This case study emerged as a particular beneficial way of gaining a deeper understanding of an expert's analysis strategies and directed attention to previously neglected issues like loading and sorting data and interface icons and controls. All parts of usability evaluation resulted in redesigning significant parts of ESTAT, e.g., the scatter plot was enhanced by a number of descriptive statistics and regression methods. The study clearly demonstrates how important it is to adapt innovative methods to the needs of real users doing real work.

6.6.3 Geovisualization to Support Group Work

Another aspect of human-centered geovisualization is the design of systems that support collaborative use. While many potential applications of geovisualization require coordinated efforts by groups, most geovisualization methods are primarily designed for single users at a workstation. Technological advances such as large screen displays or high-bandwidth communication enable both same-place and different-place multi-user systems but current geovisualization systems often do not use these capabilities. MacEachren and Kraak [528] listed geovisualization methods that support group work as a fundamental multidisciplinary research challenge. Section 3.4 of this book discusses distributed collaborative visualization in general. Here, both same- and different-place collaboration is covered in the context of geovisualization.

Scenarios in which small groups collaborate can be found in scientific research, environmental and urban planning, education, or economic decision making. Commonly, group work is classified by same- or different-place and same- or different-time collaboration as described by Applegate [32], see also the discussion in Section 3.4.1 of this book. Current geovisualization research on group work focuses on both same-place/same-time and different-place/same-time collaboration. Same-place collaboration certainly provides the most natural mode of interaction between humans but in certain situations groups of experts with various backgrounds need to be consulted and it is often impossible to convene at a single place, particularly for time-critical tasks such as emergency management. Same-place collaboration often utilizes wall- or desk-based large screen displays and multimodal user interfaces. In contrast, different-place collaboration introduces the problem of synchronizing and linking the visualizations at multiple places. Brodlie [118] described three models of distributed visualization systems. A *single, shared* application runs on a single machine and the user interface is replicated to different displays, i.o., all collaborators see exactly the same image. Either a single user controls the application, e.g., for a demonstration, or control of the application is passed between users. A *single, replicated* application is executed at each location and parameter settings are shared. This is a more flexible approach, e.g., users can change their personal screen layout or language settings. Finally, *multiple, linked* applications allow the highest degree of flexibility. Users can work individually and share data and parameters as they wish. However, flexibility is also the disadvantage of this approach as it is hard for a user to get a feeling of what others are doing and that makes coordinated work difficult. MacEachren [521] suggested a *participant watcher* as a tool that shows each user's screen layout and currently active windows as well as activity displays that show for example the amount of time each user was in control of the joint display. Such a tool arises concerns about privacy and therefore its acceptance by users but it was not yet evaluated in a user study. Video conferencing is a another common mode of human-human interaction in such applications [118, 521].

Being the object of collaboration is not necessarily the role of geovisualization. MacEachren [521] listed supporting dialogue and supporting coordinated activity as alternative roles. In supporting dialogue, the display can be used, for example, to depict an argument directly or to serve as a framework for arguments. Geovisualization can support coordinated activity, for example, in an emergency response situation, where the command center staff needs to communicate with individuals in the field. The visualization environment serves to guide navigation, to input data and to provide an overall view for assessing the situation.

Collaborative geovisualization systems make different demands on usability and user-centered design in comparison to the single-user case discussed before in Section 6.6.1. Users, such as experts from different fields, are no longer homogeneous and tasks that support and mediate dialogue have not been considered before in single-user systems. MacEachren and Brewer [523] identified several research challenges for geocollaboration. For example, working with a large screen display requires more natural, multimodal user interfaces, such as speech and gestures, to support group work. See Section 3.3 of this book for a survey on multimodal interaction techniques. Furthermore, a theoretical understanding of cognitive and social aspects of collaboration must be developed as a basis for usability studies. In the following, two prototype systems designed for collaborative geovisualization tasks are described.

Brewer et al. [114] developed a prototype system to support same time/different place collaboration of a team of environmental scientists. The system was designed to mediate and enhance knowledge construction in a sample climatic time-series data set. A focus of their study was on usability and human-centered design aspects and they reported the results of a user-task analysis. They interviewed six domain experts and demonstrated their prototype to prompt discussion. The prototype presented a 3D map-based view of precipitation and temperature. The temporal dimension is controlled by a time wheel interface and the map can be animated accordingly. The environment can be displayed on regular displays as well as on an ImmersaDesk virtual reality system. In their user-task analysis, Brewer et al. found that drawing the attention of others is a crucial task [114]. Participants frequently used gestures to draw attention to features on the display. Joint interface controls were endorsed but users added that conflict avoidance is necessary, e.g., with a turn-based approach or separate windows for each user. Alternatively they suggested a single user to be in control. Concerning the display a workbench-like display was preferred over a wall-mounted solution. In terms of different place collaboration, the experts favored voice and video for communication. They expressed the need for a private workspace and for the ability to see what others are doing to the joint workspace, not just the outcome. Again, drawing attention, e.g., with the mouse cursor, was regarded as very important.

A second prototype system is DAVE_G (Dialogue-Assisted Visual Environment for Geoinformation) by MacEachren et al. [524]. DAVE_G was designed for a map-mediated crisis management scenario where decision makers need to coordinate the emergency response. Geoinformation systems (GIS) are used in practice today but they are operated by GIS technicians in response to requests from decision makers. Valuable time is often lost due to this indirect GIS usage. Hence, the goal of MacEachren et al. was to develop a multimodal, dialogue-assisted tool that uses speech and gesture recognition to enhance human-human collaboration around a large screen map display. In this approach, human-computer and human-human interaction use the same modalities which is an important aspect for user acceptance. An initial work-domain analysis with four emergency managers identified a set of required map functionality, e.g., zoom, pan, buffer, select data, and free-hand drawing. Challenges for the user interface include recognition of implicit commands ("we needed to view this in more detail") and sloppy speech. Speech and gestures are fused, i.e., a spoken command, e.g., "zoom in to this area", is associated with a pointing gesture. A dialogue manager requests missing parameters for incomplete commands. Technical details of the user interface can be found in MacEachren et al. [524]. Fuhrmann et al. [276] evaluated the usability and performance of DAVE_G in a user study with ten graduate students. The system was unknown to the participants. In the beginning, they set up individual voice profiles and completed a DAVE_G learning session of about ten minutes after which they felt comfortable with the system. They solved two unguided tasks where they had to load data, zoom, pan, and identify certain objects. About 70% of the requests were successful and 90% of the gestures were correctly recognized. In a subsequent interview, participants were positively describing their experience with DAVE_G and emphasized quick learnability. Fuhrmann et al. [276] reported that hand tracking sometimes lost the cursor and that the dialogue capabilities of DAVE_G needed to be improved.

6.7 Chapter Notes

This chapter aimed to give a comprehensive overview of the state of the art in geovisualization research. However, the abundance of developments and results in this lively research field cannot be covered completely within this book. A good starting point for further reading is "Exploring Geovisualization" [223], a book that contains the results of a cross-disciplinary workshop with the same title held in 2002 at City University, London.

Future Trends

How will geovisualization develop over the next years? In the future, Dykes et al. [222] still see the map as the primary tool to present, use, interpret, and understand geospatial data. However, it has become apparent in the past that the map can and will take a variety of forms, some of which quite astonishing. The map has evolved from its traditional role as a presentational device to an interactive and highly dynamic interface to access and explore geospatial data.

Another common feature of current geovisualization tools is that they consist of multiple linked displays, each depicting an alternative representation of the data under examination to stimulate visual thinking. This will certainly remain a central aspect in geovisualization.

Concerning the tasks and users of geovisualization tools a transition from explorative, individual use by experts towards the whole range of tasks from exploration to presentation and heterogeneous groups of users is taking place. While individual expert tools will continue to develop, there will be an increasing number of applications designed for the public and disseminated over the web. It is clear that the usability requirements differ significantly between research tools for specialists and public applications for the mass of non-expert users. Human-centered aspects need to play a key role in the design of future tools in order to make them fit the needs of their audience. The goal of universal usability, i.e., creating applications for wide ranges of users from children to senior citizens in different languages and respecting visually disabled users, remains a big challenge.

Advances in hardware technology will also have a strong influence on geovisualization. On the one hand, large 2D and 3D displays and virtual environments will be used for geovisualization tasks, especially for collaborative use by a group of experts and decision makers. Usability studies for these new technologies will have to investigate their advantages and disadvantages over traditional visualization methods as well as possible cognitive and social impacts. In particular, the right balance between abstraction and realism needs to be determined for 3D displays. On the other hand, portable devices like PDAs or mobile phones will provide location-based services, e.g., route finding in foreign places which build on some sort of map display. This means additional challenges for application developers in terms of efficient memory and bandwidth use as well as in terms of visualization design for multi-platform, small-size displays.

A last point that is raised by Gahegan [284] is the need for interoperability of geovisualization components. Following the efforts of the Open Geospatial Consortium[8] to define open standards for geospatial information systems, Gahegan promotes a similar initiative for geovisualization. Visualization components should define standard interfaces in order to be reused and integrated into a variety of geovisualization tools. A lack of interoperability means that for developing a new tool too much effort is spent on re-implementing basic functionality and too little effort can be invested in developing new methods.

The coming years will show what directions geovisualization research will take and how it will influence both research in the earth sciences and related disciplines and our everyday handling of geospatial information.

---

[8] See http://www.opengeospatial.org.

7 Algorithm Animation

Andrés Moreno

In the past years, *Software Visualization (SV)* has become an important area in computer science. The ever growing software system complexity is the main reason for this phenomenon. Many software visualization tools are developed to help to understand, improve, test and debug programs. Several extensive anthologies on Software Visualization providing overviews of the field were published, cp. [197, 230, 789]. In general, Software Visualization is used for

- visualizing algorithms and programs;
- visualizing the structure, the behaviour, and the evolution of software;
- visualizing of artifacts related to software and the development of it.

This chapter is dedicated to *algorithm animation* and *program animation*, which are two of the subfields in Software Visualization that focus primarily on education. Both of them convey information about programs and algorithms through the use of animated text and images that helps students in creating mental models how programs and algorithms work. *Program animations* consist of direct representations of programming constructs, e.g., object instances or method frames, whose values or positions change over time. *Algorithm animation* deals with the representation of the program at a more abstract level, see for example [440]. Algorithms use advanced data structures to solve problems that contain clear semantic values and follow certain rules. Such data structures can be graphically represented in different ways, and operations on these structures require special animations. In spite of the differences, we are going to consider both approaches as the same in this section and name them as *algorithm animation*.

The chapter starts with a short overview of the field, and in Section 7.2, we distinguish the two groups of users of algorithm animation. The field of Software Visualization, and specially algorithm animation, has been subject of several classifications and taxonomies. Section 7.3 summarizes the most important taxonomies from a human-centered point of view. In Section 7.4, a set of algorithm animation tools are reviewed. These reviews summarize the way users, either teachers or students, can work with the tools, how these tools have been evaluated, and which results have been reported.

A. Kerren et al. (Eds.): Human-Centered Visualization Environments 2006, LNCS 4417, pp. 295–309, 2007.
© Springer-Verlag Berlin Heidelberg 2007

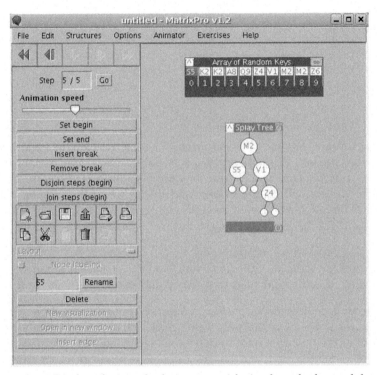

Fig. 7.1. MatrixPro lets the user freely interact with simple and advanced data structures [429].

7.1 Overview

Algorithm animation tools include both the algorithm animation tools themselves and the available precompiled packages with animations of specific algorithms. An example of an interactive algorithm animation tool in action is shown in Figure 7.1, where users can build their animations by dragging keys from the table to a tree. Another example is a graphical representation of a data structure automatically created with an algorithm animation library, see Figure 7.2.

Baecker, with his famous "Sorting out Sorting" video [38], defined a new and promising field of research, namely algorithm animation. Since then, the beauty of animation has attracted many researchers from computer science and education departments; they expect students to understand programming and algorithms better when learning with animations. However, the acceptance of these animations and tools has been lower than expected, the evaluations of these tools have not shown a significant impact of these tools in the learning outcomes.

Developers and researchers of algorithm animation tools are aware of the fact that their tools are not as widely used as they have hoped for. They have convened in several working groups [593, 595] to address the causes behind the low adoption of algorithm animation tools. Naps et al. [595] presented the result

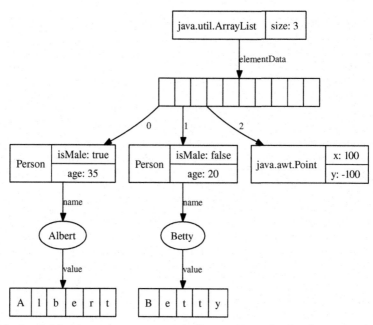

Fig. 7.2. Available libraries can automatically create static visualizations of complex data structures.

of a survey carried out to find out the common problems that educators have with existing visualization tools. Most of the complaints are related to the time they need in order to use algorithm animation tools in their lectures. Using algorithm animation tools in a lecture requires many time-consuming steps, e.g., find the right tool or adapt it to course contents.

7.2   Users of Algorithm Animation

The users of algorithm animation are divided into two groups, namely *educators* and *students*. Educators are those involved in teaching a topic in any of the possible roles involved. Lecturers, teachers, teacher assistants, and policy makers of the educational institutions are the main roles. The ITiCSE[1] working group reports [593, 595] identified the effort required to create an animation as one of the most common complaints given by educators; Ihantola et al. [384] developed a *taxonomy of effortless creation of algorithm animations*. They aim at classifying algorithm animation tools according to the effort needed to create animations. They propose three main aspects:

Scope describes how long the tool can be used in a course on data structures, whether it is just suitable for one lesson, or for the whole duration of the course.

---

[1] Conference on Innovation and Technology in Computer Science Education

Integrability defines how easy the algorithm animation tool can be adapted to different learning scenarios.

Interaction Techniques describe how educators and students can interact with the tool. For example, this category reflects the possibility to create new animations with the tool and the time it requires.

Ihantola et al. wanted to show which features were of interest to educators, and which opportunities they had to implement these features. They demonstrated the taxonomy by classifying four algorithm animation systems. The classification showed the correlation between scope and integrability: as the scope of the tool increased, the amount of effort needed to use the tool in an educational setting increases as well.

Each *Introduction to Programming* or *Algorithms and Data Structures* course is different from any other, but it is expected from teachers or educators to use one or more of the tools designed to foster learning. Before educators consider adopting an algorithm animation tool, the tool's pedagogical effectiveness needs to be proved [379]. Then, the tool needs to be integrated in the course effortlessly [384].

Students face another type of problem when using algorithm animation tools. They have to develop an understanding of the visualization at the same time they learn the concept involved in the visualizations. Thus, the cognitive load required to comprehend the visualization should match the student's abilities. Despite these difficulties, students are satisfied with current algorithm animation tools, and they feel tools are an improvement over previous teaching methods. Section 7.4 will present the tools and the main findings from the tool's user studies.

7.3   Taxonomies for Algorithm Animation Tools

Researchers from different backgrounds have produced many software tools to create animations. Big efforts have been carried out in classifying the results of such research in an organized way. Many different taxonomies have been proposed for the field of software visualization and algorithm animation. They aim at sorting the field and opening new directions for research.

Myers outlined the first taxonomy of software visualization tools in 1986 [586] and revised it in 1990 [587]. He classified Software Visualization tools under two simple dimensions:

Aspect or what they animate: code, data or algorithms.
Display Style or how they animate it: statically or dynamically.

This was the seminal work for future taxonomies. Brown's taxonomy [124] was more oriented into algorithm animation and the visual properties of the generated animations as it was used to introduce his algorithm animation tool, Balsa [123]. Brown classified algorithm animation tools under three *axes*:

Content: It describes the objects displayed by the tool in the screen, e.g., from source code to visual metaphors of the algorithm.

Persistence: It characterizes the ability to display the story of the algorithm execution or just the current state.

Transformation: It describes how the tool shows the changes, either as discrete steps or as smooth animation.

Brown's taxonomy was focused on the implementation of algorithm animation tools. Later, Stasko and Patterson [790] and Price et al. [666] extended Myers' taxonomy. Stasko and Patterson were also focused on the implementation characteristics of algorithm animation tools, but they started to take into account the *user's* role. Stasko and Patterson added two more properties to Myers' taxonomy:

Abstractness: It describes how close the visual representation of an algorithm concept is to that concept, like Brown's *content* category. For example, if a boolean variable is represented as a string of characters (`true` or `false`), its abstractness is low. If the same boolean variable is represented as a switch, with `on` and `off` states, its abstractness is high.

Automation: It describes the degree of effort the user needs to produce a visualization.

Price developed a taxonomy [666] in a more structured way than previous works. Its six main categories are deduced by reducing every SV tool to a black box, where the focus is in the interactions with the tools rather than the internal details of these tools. Further subcategories are derived from these six main categories in a hierarchical way, to sum up a total of 53 subcategories. The taxonomy was tested against twelve systems that were different enough to cover as many subcategories as possible. The six main categories describe the capabilities of the SV tools:

Scope describes what kind of software can be accepted by the tool—the input to the black box. For example, some systems can be useful for only one programming language or only for small toy programs.

Content refers to the subset of the scope that is actually visualized. For example, one tool will focus only in method calls, while another one can only visualize the data containers.

Form describes the properties of the visualization—the output of the black box. The output can be displayed in paper, video, or a graphical workstation. Each medium can have different properties, such as animation, position, or sound.

Method describes how the visualization tool works, how the animation and visualization are produced—the internals of the black box.

Interaction describes the way user interact with the system, and how the user can modify its behavior. It will enumerate some used techniques as zooming, selectivity, and abstraction.

Effectiveness measures how close the proposed goals and basic properties (e.g., clarity and goodness) are met. It also reports the evaluation and actual usage of the tool.

In his taxonomy, Price defined three groups of people involved in the life cycle of the tools:

1. *Programmers*, who implements the software system visualized; in our case a program or a concrete algorithm.
2. *SV Software Developers*, who implement the tool used to visualize the software system.
3. *Users*, who use the tools to comprehend the system.

The programmers and software developers can be seen as source of input into the black-box. The users are at the other side of the black box, receiving its output. For the purpose of algorithm animation tools, an important role needs to be added: the *educator*. He or she takes an active role in presenting and facilitating the use of the tool to the student. Price's taxonomy is closer to the educators' needs than the previous ones as it . All categories, excepting *Method*, are of interest when choosing a tool. The *Effectiveness* category can be considered as the most important one; it contains the *purpose* and *empirical evaluations* subcategories. Unfortunately, due to the wide range of tools considered in the taxonomy, a common framework to compare the purpose of the tools was not developed.

All these taxonomies have been of help to classify new tools and relate them to the existing ones. But, despite being around for a long time, most of the open questions and problems presented by the authors remain unsolved. For example, Price et al. [666] mentioned that formal empirical evaluations are missing in current visualization tools. The reviews of tools (Section 7.4) show the latest user studies in algorithm animation. The number of these studies is low compared to the number of tools that have been developed recently in the algorithm animation.

Urquiza-Fuentes and Velázquez-Iturbide [840] conducted a *"Survey of Program Visualizations for the Functional Paradigm"*. They reviewed sixteen tools and categorized them under two of Price's subcategories: *Program*, or what the tools can animate, and *Purpose*, the goal of the tool (e.g., debugging or programming). Thus, their survey concentrated on the animation capabilities of Program Visualization tools, but did not address how the tools could be used in an educational setting. Only two formal studies were found when reviewing the systems' evaluations. One of them was carried out with students who were developing an animation [555] using WinHipe (see Subsection 7.4.7). The other one was a comparison of three visualization tools based on criteria such as readability of expressions and the process of locating an error.

The survey carried out by Pollack and Ben-Ari [657] is more relevant to educators than the one mentioned in the last paragraph. They reviewed three algorithm animation tools from the point of view of a teacher deciding which tool to choose for his/her lecture. They made the decision upon three criteria: *usability*, *visualization properties*, and *pedagogy interest*. These criteria were subdivided in second level criteria to properly address the needs of the specific learning institution (support for concrete abstract data types) and to address educators' practical needs, e.g., ease of installation.

The following review of tools will basically focus on the characteristics educators and students are more interested in. However, this review will not to be as deep as the review described in Pollack and Ben-Ari [657]. The tools reviewed here introduce a wider set of aims that make inappropriate to compare them according to specific educational requirements. Instead, the review will focus on the user studies and experiments evaluating and assessing the tools.

7.4   Review of Tools and Their Evaluations

The review of the educational tools described in this section summarizes the latest efforts made by researchers in this field. It comprises different publications and studies about the tools in order to provide a clear picture of them and their features. Furthermore, it only shows a set of algorithm animation tools and techniques that have gone at least through some empirical testing and their results have been published. Most of the tools are the outcome of several development iterations motivated by the performed user studies. A summary of the users studies can be found at the end of this section.

7.4.1   Concept Keyboards for Algorithm Visualization

Concept keyboards for algorithm visualization represent a novel combination that brings together developments in usability and visualization. A *concept keyboard* is basically a keyboard where keys can be defined in function, shape, and size. Concept keyboards are meant to be used in education, where students have special motor and cognitive needs [51]. Usually, functions defined in concept keyboards have a smaller number of keys than a normal keyboard, and the keys are clearly labeled. Concept keyboards can be either physical or simulated on a screen. Physical keyboards can have keys drawn on a touch screen or printed on a paper which is placed over a touch sensitive pane (more on such interaction technologies in Subsection 3.2.3).

Algorithms and data structures usually have a small set of operations defined on them. Baloian et al. [50] have investigated the benefits of mapping these common operations onto concept keyboards. They claimed that students' comprehension of algorithms and data structures would be enhanced by building concept keyboards that reflected the *"inherent logical structures"* of algorithms.

They created specially arranged concept keyboards for different algorithms (Quicksort, Prim's, Dijkstra's, and Kruskal's algorithms) and data structures (AVL trees and binary heap trees). Keys on the keyboard represented the operations that the students needed to complete the algorithm or to add elements to the structure. Educators can then select the level of understanding of the algorithm by choosing those methods that the student has to use; the other methods will be activated without student intervention. Educators need also to select a meaningful arrangement of the buttons, e.g., place moveRight on the right. However, advanced students can also design their own concept keyboards as a learning task.

Baloian et al. [50] have evaluated concept keyboards in two different settings. In the first setting, students had to work with web-based visualization, i.e., JHAVÉ (see below), "alongside the concept keyboard software". Participants mentioned *usability* and *interactivity* as the reasons why they liked the concept keyboards. However, while the interactivity of web-based animations was mostly *Play* and *Rewind*, visualizations using concept keyboard allowed students to take part in the animation by deciding what the next step should be.

In the second experiment, students used a "step-by-step interface" to visualize one group of algorithms, and a concept keyboard to visualize another group of algorithms. Authors gathered statistical data and observations from the students. From these observations, they noted that students with less knowledge preferred the "step-by-step interface". On the other hand, using the concept keyboard required better understanding and led to better results in problem solving tasks.

7.4.2   Matrix and MatrixPro

Matrix [459] is a framework that provides libraries to build visual applications that manipulate data structures. MatrixPro [429] is a graphical tool built using the Matrix framework that is freely distributed as Java application. It is designed to create animated simulations of algorithms on data structures.

Creating animations is straightforward with MatrixPro (see Figure 7.1). First, the user needs to select one or more data structures to work with, and the initial set of items, i.e., keys or nodes in a tree. Available data structures range from basic ones such as trees and graphs, to *conceptual data structures*. Conceptual data types are normal data types that follow certain rules and have special properties, e.g., red-black trees [313]. The user generates animations as the data structure is constructed by adding the keys one by one. For example, adding a key to a balanced tree will automatically rebalance the tree after the key is added, and thus, it will keep the structure valid. Once the keys have been inserted, the animation can be edited and saved for later use.

Finally, MatrixPro includes a set of predefined exercises. These exercises ask the student to simulate an algorithm by modifying the structures provided. Steps are again recorded, but the tool will check their correctness after the student has finished the simulation. The list of available exercises in MatrixPro is quite large and contains exercises about sorting algorithms, graph algorithms and others to cover the most important topics in a typical course on Data Structures and Algorithms.

Trakla2 [541] is another tool for visual algorithm simulations derived from Matrix. It provides a framework to create automatically assessed exercises that resemble the ones created with MatrixPro. With Trakla2, students can complete and submit their exercises for automatic grading. However, this requires advanced knowledge on programming, while MatrixPro does not need any programming from the educator to create the animation.

Evaluations of the platform have concentrated on the Trakla2 system, and its application in different settings. Laakso et al. [486] conducted three different studies on Trakla2 focusing on learning outcomes, usability, and acceptance. Results were encouraging:

1. Trakla2 increased the number of students who passed the course on data structure and algorithms;
2. students learned how to use the tool within few minutes;
3. students were positive about using an online tool to complete and submit the assignments.

Thus, it complies with three of the usability aspects defined in Section 2.2: effectiveness, learnability, and user's satisfaction.

7.4.3 Alvis and Alvis Live!

Alvis Live! [377] is the current stage of development of the Alvis [380] visualization tool. Alvis was designed to provide a "low-fidelity" approach to create algorithm animations. Students using Alvis draw the sketches using the tool and animate them using the SALSA scripting language [378]. Alvis Live! features an innovative *edit-mode* visualization called *"What You See Is What You Code"* (WYSIWYC).

Alvis Live! is oriented to help students in writing their first programs and algorithms using a pseudo-code like programming language. This language provides only arrays, variables, and array indexes as data types. The Alvis Live! interface is divided into two vertical panes. Every single new line of code written at the left pane is animated on the right pane. This allows for immediate feedback on the code. Moreover, Alvis Live! provides an error checker that reports errors while the code is being written. These two features help novices to correctly create and understand their code. Students can program their algorithm with Alvis Live! visually. They can add arrays, variables and control structures by using the graphical user interface.

Alvis and Alvis Live! are the result of iterative evaluations [377]. The current stage of Alvis was motivated by an ethnographic study. Students in the study were asked to implement an algorithm in pseudo-code using a text editor and to create their own animations using craft techniques, e.g., paper and scissors. This led to students not being confident in their programs, because they could not test the program either for syntactic errors nor for semantic ones. This resulted in students being "stuck" and not progressing in their tasks. Researchers discussed the opportunity of an immediate visualization supporting students to create code confidently and, at the same time, semantically correct. This resulted in Alvis Live!.

Alvis Live! went through another empirical evaluation: a usability study with 21 novice programmers [377]. They were asked to debug an incorrect program and to implement a simple algorithm using Alvis Live!. Students used the animation to identify and correct a bug presented in an incorrect assignment. Implementing an algorithm with Alvis Live! proved to be successful; 13 out of 14 pairs of students implemented it correctly. Unfortunately, the study report did not mention whether the "stuck" moments were reduced because of the use of the tool or not. Nonetheless, they mentioned that students did not notice the feedback on syntactic errors that occur in real time.

7.4.4   Alice

Alice is a 3D environment, where students can create attractive *"movies"* and *"games"* by programming in an object-oriented fashion. Alice is aimed at students with no prior knowledge in programming, although it has been reported [187] that students at Carnegie Mellon University have used it to write 3000-lines programs. Alice provides students with a large set of objects that have a visual representation, like a bunny or a guitar. These objects can be manipulated by calling methods. Objects can be moved around and their relationship with other objects in the animation can be accessed and modified.

Animations are coded using a special source editor. Programming statements are *dragged-and-dropped* into the source. The system only allows to add syntactically correct statements. Thus, built programs will be free of syntax errors. The Alice programming language supports most of the common concepts in programming such as methods, loops, conditions, and so on. Arrays are the only data structure available, and they are mostly used to group a collection of objects, e.g., to create an army out of soldiers.

Moskal et al. [580] describe an interesting study on the effects of Alice. They considered first year CS students without prior programming experience that were regarded to be *at risk* of dropping out of the major. Students were invited to an introductory course to CS (CS0) where fundamental concepts of programming were *gently* introduced using Alice and supportive material. Those who took the course (the treatment group) obtained higher grades in an introductory course to programming (CS1) than those students at risk who did not. Moreover, the retention rates were significantly better in the treatment group. Change in attitudes towards CS was also measured. The attitude's score of the treatment group in *confidence, liking,* and *creativity* increased more after CS1. It is not known what would have happened if the CS0 course would have taken a more traditional approach. However, the results of the study show the importance of introducing programming in a soft way, before the actual programming courses takes place.

7.4.5   Jeliot 3/Jeliot 2000

Jeliot 3 [569] is a Java tool and part of the Jeliot family [568]. In its current form, it automatically animates most of the Java programs novice students can

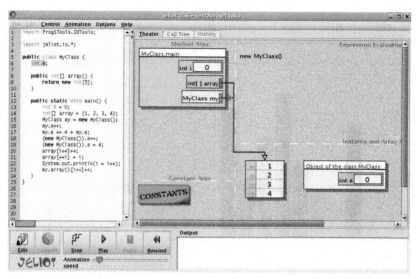

Fig. 7.3. Jeliot 3 provides simple animations of how an object-oriented program is executed.

implement (see Figure 7.3). Its animation tries to be a faithful representation of what happens in a virtual machine: objects are allocated, method frames are created, and expressions are visually evaluated.

The application is divided into two main parts. First, students can modify or implement their own programs using the Java programming language in the integrated editor. When finished, students can visualize the execution in the *theater* by compiling the program and playing the animation. The animation will show method calls, variable declarations, condition evaluations, and flow control, step by step.

Jeliot 3 is an update of Jeliot 2000 [75]. The graphical features are basically the same, but Jeliot 3 incorporates support for object-oriented programming and can be started through the web via Java Web Start. Moreover, BlueJ [457], the integrated development environment for novices, can be extended with Jeliot 3 animation capabilities.

Jeliot 2000 was evaluated by Ben-Bassat et al. [75] in a year-long study that compared the performance of two groups of students. One of them used Jeliot 2000 in the lab sessions; the other used TurboPascal as a debugger. The experiment concluded that mediocre students were the ones who benefited most from the use of the tool. Weaker students found the Jeliot 2000 animations too complicated, and better students did not need the tool to understand the program.

Kannusmäki et al. [428] carried out a small qualitative study with students that took a second course on programming (CS2) course. In the course, Jeliot 3 was required to solve their assignments. Jeliot 3 was found to be an obstacle for some students as they were used to more advanced IDEs (e.g., Eclipse). However,

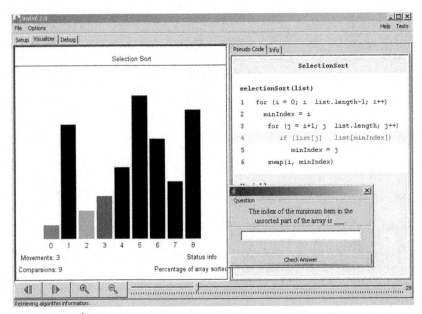

Fig. 7.4. JHAVÉ displays animations of algorithms, along with the corresponding pseudocode, and questions related to the algorithm execution.

some students found positives points in Jeliot 3: animation of concepts like loops and object creation were helpful; Jeliot 3 was convenient to use as it eased the process of compiling and debugging.

7.4.6 JHAVÉ

JHAVÉ [591] can be seen as an animation broker, it can display animations produced with other animation systems; Animal [718], JSamba [219], and GAIGS [592] animations are supported. JHAVÉ's biggest contribution to the previous systems are the *stop and think* questions and explanations that can appear at any time during the animations (see Figure 7.4). The content of the questions and explanations is directly related to what is being animated. Questions usually ask for what will happen next in the animation and can have different answer formats (true-false, fill-in-the-blank, multiple-choice). Answers given by the students are checked for correctness, and feedback is given to them.

JHAVÉ is distributed as a Java application and can also be started through a Java Web Start launcher. Creating new animations for JHAVÉ consists of modifying previously created animation scripts in any of the above animation systems by adding special tags related to the questions and explanations one wants JHAVÉ to display. Unfortunately, creating or modifying JHAVÉ animations is not trivial for educators. Luckily, JHAVÉ application can directly connect to a central repository and retrieve available animations from there.

Grissom et al. [308] studied the effect that interactive questions had on students' engagement. Three groups of student took part in the study: one group

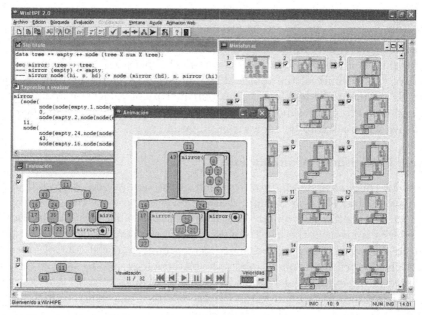

Fig. 7.5. Animation of functional programs using WinHipe. Notice that you can build the animation by selecting the desired frames.

was not using any form of visualization, a second group used the animations provided by JHAVÉ but not the questions, and a third group used both the animation and the questions. Results showed that the third group learned more than the other groups.

Another study [594] analyzed the importance of introducing the animation tool to the students in the course in advance. It was shown that the effect on learning one algorithm with JHAVÉ was higher when the students had been exposed to the tool previously.

7.4.7   WinHipe

WinHipe [858] is a graphical IDE (see Figure 7.5) for the functional programming paradigm. Programs can be directly animated within the IDE. Functional expressions are expanded as they are interpreted, and reduced as their actual value is evaluated. Thus, animations are comprehensive and can involve a large number of steps. Fortunately, WinHipe incorporates an animation editor. The editor displays all the single steps of the visualization in a single window and let the user select the steps which will be part of the animation. WinHipe is unable to perform smooth transitions from state to state; instead, it highlights the next part of the functional expression to be evaluated and displays the previous graphical state and the current one. So, students can interpret the reason of the new state. Selecting the steps to animate enables the possibility to use WinHipe animations for large programs. Thus, students can concentrate in those parts of the algorithm they are interested in. In addition to visualize lists in a graphical way, WinHipe also provides automatic visualizations of trees. This allows the visualization of a wide range of trees and lists algorithms.

Medina et al. [555] conducted an empirical experiment regarding some aspects of the usability of the tool and its animations. They found the attitude towards the tool to be highly positive: a great share of students found it easy to use and useful to understand. Finally, students used the animation on their own initiative when asked to debug a given program.

7.4.8 User Studies Compilation

Table 7.1 contains a summary description of the user studies discussed in the previous section. The first column, *Evaluation*, refers to what kind of study was conducted using the *Tool* reported in the *Referenced* publication. A summary of the studies is given in the last columns. # lists the number of subjects taking part in the study either in the experiment group or in the control group (if any). The *Methodology* column report the methodology used to analyze the data gathered in the experiment (qualitative, quantitative, or mixed). The source of the gathered data is listed in the *Materials* column. And finally, a brief note on the results obtained is given in the *Findings* column.

7.5 Chapter Notes

In this chapter, a wide range of tools and techniques in Software Visualization were presented that have been developed and researched over the last 30 years.

Computer science teachers and software developers, as the first professionals that were involved with software systems, have been the earliest adopters of visual representations for their code. However, they were more interested in solving problems and developing new tools than studying the cognitive aspects of the developed tools.

Currently, most of the available tools have not gone through desirable empirical evaluation. Often, maybe because it requires much less effort, the researchers try to prove the usefulness of a tool rather than its usability. For example, the importance of properly teaching how to use a visualization tool is reported in the few usability and usefulness studies. As more data is to be visualized, known graphical interfaces (e.g., VCR interfaces) are not powerful enough. Moreover, different evaluations state that newly developed interfaces or tools usually require longer training time before their effects can be best captured in user studies.

Animations are actively used in software visualization and, while there are well known techniques for static visualization, studies on the cognitive properties of animations are scarce. Jones and Scaife [418] conducted two studies on the effects of animations and warned about the possible overconfidence in the learned materials. Nonetheless, animations provided better cues on where to focus and in which order to process the information. However, more user studies are needed to prepare a set of guidelines that can be of interest to researchers when developing new software visualization tools.

Table 7.1. Summary of User Studies

Evaluation	Tool	Ref.	#	Methodology	Materials	Findings
Exploratory Study	Concept Keyboards	[50]	17	Qualitative	Questionnaires.	Students found visualization software necessary.
Usability	Concept Keyboards	[50]	18	Qualitative	Questionnaires, solutions to exercises.	Explanatory hints about the algorithm should be given when using the software.
Effectiveness Study	Trakla2	[486]	351	Quantitative	Course grades and attendance statistics.	More passed attendants when Trakla2 was deployed.
Satisfaction Survey	Trakla2	[486]	280	Mixed	Three Web based surveys during the course.	High suitability of web-based exercises at Data Structure course.
Usability Test	Trakla2	[486]	5	Qualitative	Observations, tests, and questionnaire.	The system is easy to learn, and promotes learning.
Usability Study	Alvis Live!	[377]	21	Qualitative	Observations, debugging outcome.	Students detected the bug, but were not aware of all the tool features.
Effectiveness Study	Alice	[580]	36	Quantitative	Surveys, pre- and post-tests.	Learners who used the tool got better grades and were more likely to not "drop out".
Effectiveness Study	Jeliot 2000	[75]	38	Mixed	Interviews, observations, course grades.	Mediocre students benefit the most from the tool.
Usability Study	Jeliot 3	[428]	35	Qualitative	Course exercises with results and comments.	Advanced students reject simple animation tools.
Effectiveness Study	JHAVÉ	[594]	50	Quantitative	Survey, exam grades.	The longer exposure to the tool the better acceptance of it.
Usability Study	WinHipe	[555]	52	Quantitative	Questionnaires.	Animations are easy to use and to understand. Animations are also used to debug programs.

8 Biomedical Information Visualization

Mircea Lungu and Kai Xu

The ongoing developments in the fields of molecular biology, genetics, and medical sciences have recently generated an explosion of information collected from living organisms. For the scientist who analyzes these huge amounts of data, information visualization can be a very useful tool[1].

Because an exhaustive survey of the use of information visualization in the molecular biology, genetics and medical science is beyond the scope or space of this chapter, the chapter will present several highlights on the use of information visualization in the aforementioned domains.

The reader is not expected to be an expert in any of the analyzed fields, in fact, the material is organized in such a way that it does not make any assumptions on reader's domain knowledge. This means that for the domain expert, the level of discourse might be superficial, but one can always refer to the original papers for more details. The assumption that the reader is not an expert has also determined our organization of the material: the analyzed tools are grouped according to problem domains, and each section begins by providing a brief introduction to the domain before presenting the tools and techniques. The problem domains that are addressed are the following:

- Phylogenetic Tree Visualization (Section 8.1)
- Sequence Alignment (Section 8.2)
- Biochemical Network Analysis (Section 8.3)
- Microarray Data Visualization (Section 8.4)
- Medical Records Visualization (Section 8.5)

The analysis of each tool described in this chapter is based on several of the following information visualization issues which are partially inspired by the work of Card et al. [145]:

Space and Colors. The most basic decision to be taken for the design of a visual representation is how to use the spatial axes. Some data is inherently linear (e.g., DNA sequences), and the reader will see that this has a strong effect on the associated visualizations. Other data are naturally represented using two

---

[1] The publication of a special issue of the Information Visualization Journal [617] dedicated to applications of visualization in Bioinformatics stands as a proof that the efforts in the domain are acknowledged by the larger information visualization community.

A. Kerren et al. (Eds.): Human-Centered Visualization Environments 2006, LNCS 4417, pp. 311–342, 2007.
© Springer-Verlag Berlin Heidelberg 2007

or three dimensions. Is the space used in an adequate way for the given data? How do the colors provide feedback? Do they reinforce spatial information?

Data Magnitude. The magnitude of the visualized data is important for the techniques that are used. For the same type of data, different magnitudes might enforce the use of different visualization techniques, as the reader will see in Section 8.1.

Interaction. Most of the times, interaction plays a critical role in the process of visual analysis. Some of the analyzed tools employ specific and sometimes innovative interaction modes while others provide only the traditional navigation primitives (e.g., navigating in 3D space).

Limitations. Where limitations of the techniques are apparent (e.g., the visualization does not scale, the tool can be used only in a particular context, ...) they are mentioned together with possible improvements.

8.1 Phylogenetic Tree Visualization

The Swedish botanist Carl Linnaeus is credited with pioneering *systematics*[2], the field of science which attempts to classify nature in a hierarchical way based on the similarities between organisms. Since the times of Linnaeus, the classification mechanisms have evolved and scientists realized that, beyond being a taxonomy, systematics was an insight into the evolution of the various organisms.

Although evolution is an abstract phenomenon, scientists can benefit from representations of it, and one of the most used representations is the *phylogenetic tree* (also called phylogeny or cladogram). In a phylogenetic tree each node represents a species and each branch, or node, denotes a relation between two neighboring species in terms of ancestry. However, when the analyzed trees become larger, the need for better visual representations increases.

Request for a better representation is directed to solving several problems. Some of the most challenging problems are: finding adequate layouts for large trees, optimally labeling the nodes in a tree, providing navigation and interaction facilities and supporting the comparison operations between alternative trees [148]. This section discusses several ways of addressing the layout problem.

Different types of analyses work with phylogenetic trees of different magnitudes and for each magnitude different visualizations are desirable and applicable. In this section, the applications are classified based on the magnitude of the displayed trees.

8.1.1 Small Trees – Working in Euclidean Space

Applications that visualize trees with several hundreds of nodes can afford to represent them in such a way that the lengths of the edges have evolutionary meaning. This means that the resulting tree respects the following property:

---

[2] More about systematics and phylogenetic trees at http://www.ncbi.nlm.nih.gov/About/primer/phylo.html.

(P1): The length of an edge should represent the evolutionary distance between species. Moreover, the length of a path should be proportional with the evolutionary distance between the corresponding species. [162]

The second problem that has to be addressed when drawing phylogenetic trees is labeling the nodes and edges. Graph labeling is a well-known graph drawing problem and, in the case of phylogenetic trees, it is accentuated by the long latin names that are usually associated with the represented entities. The final factor that has to be taken into consideration that the edges of the tree should not intersect one another.

Drawing phylogenetic trees which respects the (P1)-property is theoretically very difficult, and the solution is usually reduced to an energy minimization problem where the quantity to minimize is a function of the deviations of the nodes from the ideal positions. This approach is the one used by the PhyloDraw application [162].

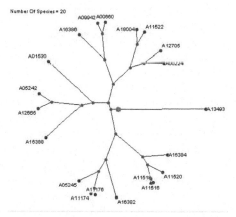

Fig. 8.1. PhyloDraw rendering a phylogenetic tree for 20 species. *Image courtesy of J. H. Choi.*

Figure 8.1 shows PhyloDraw displaying a phylogenetic tree with 20 nodes. Each node of the tree is positioned such that the distance between two nodes approximates the phylogenetic distance between the represented species. The visualization provides insights into the evolutionary relations and phylogenetic distances between the species. The interaction with the application is limited to moving the nodes of the tree. The user also has the choice of choosing the representation of the trees from several predefined possibilities: rooted tree, radial tree, rectangular tree, etc.

PhyloDraw was designed to work with trees with up to 100 nodes [162]. However, once the number of nodes exceeds several hundreds the view becomes too clogged, and algorithms that respect property (P1) do not yield acceptable results anymore.

8.1.2   Large Trees – Using Focus and Context

For trees with thousands of nodes, the types of visualizations that work for small trees are not effective anymore. Instead, an overview of the entire data set provides a starting point from which the user can further explore the data and select details that he/she wishes to see. One particular type of refinement is the change of focus as employed in *focus+context* techniques.

Hypertree [90] is an application which exploits the focus+context techniques by displaying a tree using a 2D hyperbolic space. This representation is useful because it provides both a global overview of the structure and local detail for the part of the tree which is under focus. The visualization technique allows for the representation of much larger hierarchies than the ones represented in euclidean space. However, as a result of the distortion introduced by hyperbolic space, the property (P1) does not hold anymore.

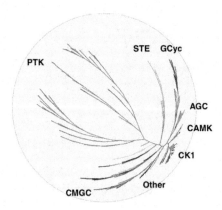

Fig. 8.2. Hypertree displaying the 492 protein kinases in C.elegans.

Another application which uses focus and context techniques is TreeJuxtaposer [583]. The tool introduces the concept of *guaranteed visibility*, meaning that areas that the user designates are guaranteed to remain visible on the screen independent of subsequent navigation operations. In TreeJuxtaposer, the complete tree is displayed as an orthogonal tree and zooming works by expanding vertically a focus region and shrinking other out of focus regions. The authors named the technique the *accordeon drawing technique*. Besides representing single phylogenetic trees, TreeJuxtaposer also supports the comparison of multiple trees.

Rost and Bronberg-Bauer propose the TreeWiz application [719] which is also aimed at visualizing very large trees and puts heavy accent on interaction. The application can handle trees with tens of thousands of leafs and implements filtering mechanisms that are specific to the biological data. One of the mechanisms that enables the display of such large amounts of information is called the *restricted view*, a dynamic layout algorithm that shows nodes only up to a certain depth in such a way that it still preserves the overall structure of the tree. The interaction mechanisms provided by TreeWiz are collapsing and expanding nodes, zooming and filtering.

8.1.3 Very Large Trees – Hyperbolic 3D Space

While the life scientists have discovered more than 1.7 million species to this day, only 80,000 species have been placed in their corresponding phylogenetic trees [645]. Classifying the remaining species is one of the tasks that will receive attention in the future, and together with it, the representation of very large phylogenetic trees.

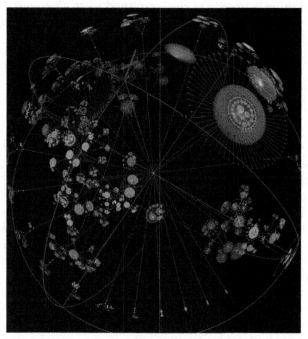

Fig. 8.3. 3D hyperbolic representation of taxonomy which comprises about 180,000 species. *Image courtesy of T. Hughes.*

As a solution to the scalability problem, Hughes et al. [376] propose visualizing phylogenetic trees in 3D hyperbolic space. Instead of developing a new tool for the purpose, they use Walrus [585], a general-purpose visualization tool. The only thing that they need to do in order to obtain the visualization is to convert the data from the standard phylogenetic tree format to the format which is specific to Walrus. With Walrus, it becomes possible to visualize and navigate phylogenetic trees with more than 100,000 nodes. Figure 8.3 shows the visual representation of an entire NCBI[3] taxonomy which comprises about 180,000 species.

The hyperbolic 3D space provided by Walrus is useful for providing a focus and context type of visualization and allowing the visualization of very large trees. However, the type of information that it presents is totally different than the one presented using the euclidean space trees. While the distances between the individual species can not be observed anymore, the distances between families and the properties of the families themselves become visible.

8.1.4 Discussion and Further Reading

One good indicator of the acceptance of a tool is its number of users. At the time of writing this book, one of the oldest and most widely used phylogenetic tree drawing packages is PHYLIP [252], an application which exists since 1980. The online documentation of the tool mentions over 15,000 registered users. The associated website also contains a very rich collection of pointers to other phylogenetic tree drawing applications[4].

In a recent survey on phylogenetic tree drawing applications, Carizzo [148] presents the results of a questionnaire carried out with users of the phylogenetic tree drawing tools. The results show that users are still not satisfied with the actual tools. For a domain which is older than 25 years, this is a sign that the problem is not trivial. Maybe the lack of complete user satisfaction is one sign of the need for a user centered development method.

Some authors provide anecdotal evidence of the user satisfaction with the phylogenetic tree drawing tools. Although less formal than the controlled experiments, anecdotal evidence can be considered as an estimation of a tool usefulness and acceptance. One such example is TreeJuxtaposer, an application designed for drawing large phylogenetic trees. The application provides guaranteed frame rate for browsing trees larger than 500,000 nodes. The authors report that the users found the application *"useful even for trees of smaller sizes"* [583].

An interesting fact about TreeJuxtaposer is that the application was designed to work with and tested on large desktop displays of up to 9 megapixel. The display and comparison of phylogenetic trees seems to be indeed a good application for a large screen displays (see Section 3.2).

8.2 Sequence Alignment

For nearly 20 years, three leading public repositories for DNA and RNA sequence data [386] have collaborated to provide access to the increasing amount of genetic data produced by institutions around the world. The three repositories

---

[3] National Center for Biotechnology Information (http://www.ncbi.nlm.nih.gov)
[4] http://evolution.genetics.washington.edu/phylip/software.html

have reached a significant milestone by collecting and disseminating 100 giga-bases of sequence data [613][5]. Scientists analyze this data in order to associate DNA sequences with corresponding biological functions hoping that once these associations are discovered, they will be valuable in improving the health of individuals and society [330].

Very simplified, the two principles that form the foundation of sequence align-ment are: (1) Common features of two organisms encoded in their DNA are pre-served between the species, and (2) DNA sequences that are responsible for the differences between species are themselves different.

From the two previously mentioned principles follows that various informa-tion can be inferred by analyzing the differences and similarities of different genomes[6] of different species. However, as the genome of diverse species has changed over time by many insertions, mutations, or deletions of individual po-sitions in the DNA, aligning two or more genomes for comparison is not an easy task. In fact, the task can not be completely automated, and for the fine tun-ing process, scientists need to manually process the data. This section presents visualization techniques that support sequence alignment.

8.2.1 Sequence Logos

DNA sequences are represented as strings created with the alphabet {A,C,G,T} where each individual letter stands for one of the four nucleotides: A = Adenine, C = Cytosine, G = Guanine, T = Tymine. Sequence alignment is the process of arranging two or more DNA sequences in such a way that the nucleotides in one sequence are mapped onto corresponding nucleotides in the other sequence[7]. In order to maximize the number of matching nucleotides between two strings, the sequences can be padded with gaps. It is possible to align several sequences of DNA. Figure 8.4 shows an example of alignment for five toy DNA sequences.

$$
\begin{array}{l}
\texttt{TATACA-} \\
\texttt{TATACGT} \\
\texttt{TATACGT} \\
\texttt{TAT-CGT} \\
\texttt{TTTCCAT}
\end{array}
$$

Fig. 8.4. Alignment of five simple DNA sequences. Dashes represent gaps in the se-quences.

---

[5] In molecular biology, two nucleotides on opposite complementary DNA or RNA strands that are connected are called a *base pair*. A base pair can also be referred as a base for brevity.

[6] In biology, the genome of an organism is the whole hereditary information of an organism that is encoded in the DNA.

[7] Also protein sequences can be aligned. The difference is that they have a larger alphabet.

However, as in reality the size of the compared sequences and the number of compared sequences are high, biochemists and bioinformaticians need ways to summarize the results of an alignment process. The simplest summary representation of an alignment is a *consensus sequence*. A consensus sequence is a sequence which has at each position a set with the distinct nucleotides that appear at that position in the compared sequences. An example of a consensus sequence is presented in Figure 8.5:

$$T[AT]T[AC]C[AG]T$$

Fig. 8.5. A consensus sequence which summarizes the alignment from Figure 8.4. The notation [AG] means that on the respective position there can be either an A or a G.

One major drawback of the consensus sequence notation is that, as the example shows, the information regarding the frequency of a given element at a given position is lost in this representation.

To address this problem, Schneider [738] proposes another technique for the representation of sequence alignment result, called a *sequence logo*. A sequence logo is a graphical representation in which the nucleotides that occur in the aligned sequences at a given position are represented stacked one on top of the other at the corresponding position. Colors reinforce the information provided by the initial letters of the nucleotide names. Every nucleotide in the stack has it's height proportional with its frequency of occurrence at that position in the aligned sequences. The stacked nucleotides are sorted from bottom to top based on their frequency of occurrence. Figure 8.6 presents a sequence logo taken from Shaner et al. [754].

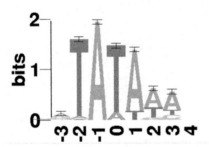

Fig. 8.6. A *sequence logo* generated from 40 yeast genetic sequences showing what is called a *TATA site*, an evolutionary conserved sequence. *Image courtesy of T. Schneider.*

Figure 8.6 shows that on position 0 element T is more frequent than element A. Beyond showing the relative frequency of the letters at that position, the entire stack of letters is scaled to show the sequence conservation at a given position in the aligned sequences. The sequence conservation is measured in bits of information and corresponds to the information theory concept of *information* [738].

It is interesting to see how a simple visual representation can become the standard representation in a domain, because it efficiently conveys the needed information. The visualization supports the process of pattern discovery during the sequence alignment analysis. It is also commonly used as a standard notation in scientific articles.

One disadvantage of sequence logos is their reduced scalability; although they could be printed on several lines per page, and even on several pages, a user will have a hard time handling all the represented detail. For a better scalability, one can quit using the letters and display only color-coded bars but the essential problem remains.

8.2.2 Editing and Visualizing Sequence Alignment: Jalview

Analyzing the results of multiple sequence alignments is a basic method for understanding the function of groups of DNA and protein sequences. However, it is known that, most of the times, the automatic alignment of multiple sequences can be improved by manual editing [164]. The Jalview multiple alignment editor [164, 401] enables the viewing and editing of alignments of large sequences.

Figure 8.7 presents a snapshot of the Jalview tool. The interaction with the application consists of inserting, deleting and modifying bases in the sequences presented in the upper part of the figure. By altering the sequence structure, the user can be seen as simulating the natural selection process. However, the user's goal is to discover the best alignment of the given sequences. To visually assist

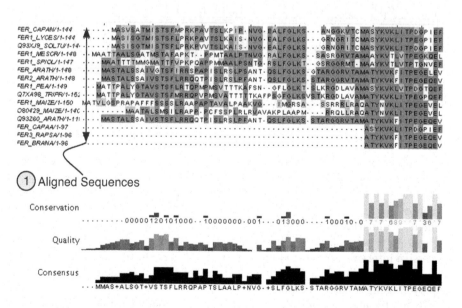

Fig. 8.7. Sequence alignment of 15 protein sequences in Jalview. The upper part of the window presents the aligned sequences while the bottom part presents various graphs that express sequence consensus.

the user in detecting an optimal alignment, the application provides feedback by
several visual means:

- The background color of each element of the aligned sequences is a measure
  of the consensus between the analyzed sequences for the respective position.
- The height of a consensus bar chart on the bottom of the display (Figure 8.7)
  expresses consensus for the given position.

One drawback of the presented visualization type is that for a sequence which
can not fit on the screen there is no way to say what the influence of a change is
at the global level. A solution would be to provide a focus and context technique
or an overview of the whole analyzed sequence.

8.2.3   Vista: Online Visualization of DNA Alignment

Vista is an online tool that displays global DNA sequence alignments of arbitrary length [549]. The goal of the application is to visualize the results of
multiple DNA sequence alignment. The alignment analysis is done a-priori, as
processing the large amounts of data would take too much time. Moreover, once
the alignment is created, there is no need to recompute it for each visualization
session.

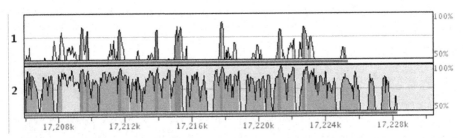

Fig. 8.8. The applet version of Vista displaying the alignment of two sequences of
20,000 bases in length.

The application provides a visual perspective of the results of aligning and comparing two or more DNA sequences (Figure 8.8). As the sequences are an inherently linear data type, the visualization is also linear: the main information is
presented as a function graph. The x-axis represent the positions in the aligned
sequences, and the y-axis represents the conservation between the aligned sequences (as a percent value). In order to make a better use of the screen space,
successive intervals are plotted one below the other. On top of the conservation
plot, further informations regarding the types of regions inside the sequences are
displayed using a color mapping.

Given the high magnitude of data and the inherently linear properties of
it, zooming is a natural interaction need in Vista. In fact, zooming spans several orders of magnitude, possible views ranging from whole genomes down to

nucleotide level. Zooming can be performed by holding down the left mouse button while moving the mouse over the region of interest. Beyond zooming, the application provides searching facilities and a history of the user's navigation.

8.2.4 Sequence Walkers

Sequence Walkers are graphical, interactive visualization techniques ways of exploring how binding proteins and other macromolecules interact with individual bases of nucleotide sequences. The walkers are represented using similar visual conventions as the sequence logos (Subsection 8.2.1). However, while the sequence logos present an overview of the result of aligning multiple DNA sequences, the Sequence Walkers present information about a single sequence's interaction with other molecules.

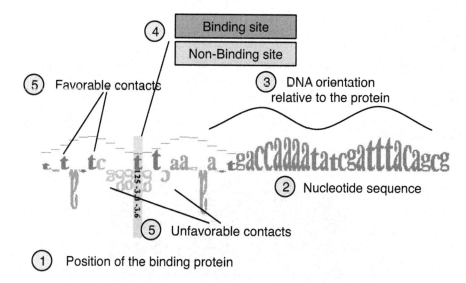

Fig. 8.9. The various types of information displayed by the Sequence Walkers application are useful for finding binding sites. *Image courtesy of T. Schneider.*

The Sequence Walkers can be stepped along raw sequence data to visually search for binding sites. Many walkers, for the same or different proteins, can be simultaneously placed next to a sequence to create a quantitative map of a complex genetic region. One can alter the sequence to quantitatively engineer binding sites.

Figure 8.9 shows that, although simple, the Sequence Walkers visualization is rich in information. The display emphasizes the following:

1. *Position of the binding protein:* this can be modified by the user by moving the window to the left or right.
2. *Nucleotide Sequence:* presents the structure of the DNA strand under analysis.

3. *DNA Orientation*: The spatial orientation of the DNA.
4. *Binding site*: The goal of the exploration is finding a binding site. If the current site is one, the green colour of the marker shows it.
5. *Contacts*: Characters representing a sequence are either oriented normally and placed above a line indicating favorable contact, or upside-down and placed below the line indicating unfavorable contact. The positive or negative height of each letter shows the contribution of that base to the average sequence conservation of the binding site, as represented by a sequence logo.

The simple interaction mechanism of the walkers (moving the position of the binding proteins from left to right) coupled with the rich dimensionality of displayed information make it a technique which can be used effectively to solve the problem at hand. The application emphasizes that there is no need for stunning graphics to make a useful visualization tool, or as Tufte expresses this: *"A visualization is as interesting as the data it represents"* [837].

8.2.5 Dot Plots

A special kind of sequence alignment is the intrasequence duplication. Detecting patterns in the case of intrasequence duplication is a good candidate for visual data mining. Dot plots are one of the first representations used for displaying the commonalities between two sequences. The sequences to be compared are arranged along the margins of a matrix.

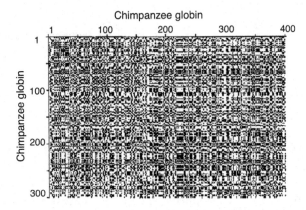

Fig. 8.10. Duplication inside a DNA sequence represented using a dot plot. The main drawback of the representation is the large amount of noise which results from the reduced alphabet out of which the sequences are built.

A point is placed in the matrix for the points for which the column and row symbols are the same. A diagonal stretch of dots will indicate regions where the two sequences are similar.

Figure 8.10 shows a dot plot of the globin intergenic region in chimpanzees plotted against itself (bases 1 to 400 vs. 1 to 300). The solid line on the main diagonal is a reflection that every base of the sequence is trivially identical to itself. As Figure 8.10 reveals, a dot plot is not very useful when displaying duplication in DNA sequences because of the strong noise introduced by random matches between nucleotides. The situation is better when dot plots are applied to protein sequences since the larger alphabet decreases the amount of background noise [294].

One advantage of the dot plot is that, in its simplicity, reading and understanding it is straightforward. The biggest drawback is the lack of scalability. Indeed, given the way the dot plot is defined, the size of the sequences which are analyzed is limited by the resolution of the screen. Zooming techniques might be useful but the authors are not aware of tools which use such techniques for DNA duplication detection. A second drawback is that the technique is limited to visualizing duplications between at most two sequences. A final disadvantage is specific to DNA duplication detection: the characteristics of the data set make the analysis harder as the reduced diversity of the sequence components (the 4 bases) increases the probability of a match by chance. To address this problem, some techniques preprocess the data to filter out the noise [538].

8.2.6 Arc Diagrams

An *arc diagram* [885] is a visually effective way of displaying complex patterns of intrasequence duplication in string data. Initially used for musical score pattern visualization which remains their most compelling application, they have also been used to display the structural repetition in DNA strands. Figure 8.11(b) shows a diagram representing duplications in a DNA sequence of a particular yeast gene.

(a)   (b)

Fig. 8.11. Arc diagrams: (a) used for displaying a visual summary of the duplications in a musical score and, (b) used for representing duplication inside a DNA sequence. *Image courtesy of M. Wattenberg.*

Arc diagrams plot the analyzed string on the horizontal axis. An algorithm is used to detect the minimum set of substrings that can represent all the duplications in the analyzed string, and these duplications are represented as arcs between the corresponding duplicated regions.

Wattenberg [885] mentions that when applied to DNA the arc diagrams are visually poor in information, and Figure 8.11(b) is a good example. The reason is that exact string matching techniques to preprocess the data are not appropriate to DNA analysis. In an attempt to address this issue, the Bard (Biological Arc Diagrams) tool [782] adapts the technique of arc diagrams to better fit the specifics of bioinformatics. One of the contributions of the approach is that it considers new types of matching between substrings which are better suited for genetic data:

Inexact matches. Sometimes, in genetics, an analyst is interested also in inexact matches. Algorithms can compute the degree of conformity of two matches. And when they are above a given threshold, they can be considered matches and represented. Problems appear because transitivity does not always hold for these matches [885].

Reverse matches. Since DNA is formed by two paired strands of nucleotides, and the nucleotides always pair in the same way (Adenine with Thymine and Cytosine with Guanine), a single-stranded sequence of DNA can be considered equal with its complementary sequence. This means that strings, which are not typographically equal, can be still detected as duplicates which is called complemented palindrome matching. Another type of match is when the second sequence is also reversed: this is called a reverse complemented palindrome matching.

The original arc diagrams are modified such that the reversed matches are mapped on bottom arcs.

The arc diagrams are able to present the same information in a more intuitive way and with less visual elements[8] than a dot plot. While n repetitions of a substring in a string, would require $n \times n$ lines in a dot plot, an arc diagram can represent all the duplications with only $n - 1$ arcs between the duplicated regions. Moreover, another advantage of the arc diagrams is that they can also be used to visualize duplication between multiple sequences.

In the dot plot diagrams, the user had the task of discovering the duplication. In the arc diagrams instead, the duplications are already computed and the user uses them only to visualize the places in the sequences where the duplications occur.

8.2.7 Discussion and Further Reading

The large amount of linear data analyzed during sequence alignment is a good candidate for visual data mining. The goal of visualization in all the applications surveyed in this chapter is to provide means for the users to gain new insight into the data sets.

There are many other tools and techniques that use information visualization to support sequence alignment. For multiple alignment of sequences, Shah et al. [752] propose a volume-based visualization technique that utilizes 3D space

---

[8] Tufte would say: with less ink!

to represent the results of sequence alignment and use more effectively screen real estate. Slank et al. [770] introduce Sequence Juxtaposer, a tool which uses focus and context techniques to provide interactive navigation of sequences.

Although there is a lot of work being done in the domain of sequence alignment there still is need for more comparative studies that would show which techniques are the most useful to the users.

8.3   Biochemical Network Analysis

Many biochemical systems can be modeled as graphs or networks. One example is "protein-protein interaction network", where nodes are proteins and edges are interactions between them. Such networks provide an overview of the biochemical mechanism in a living organism (such as bacteria). Another example is "gene regulatory network", where nodes are genes and there is a directed edge from gene g_1 to g_2 if the status of g_2 is controlled by g_1. Such networks can help biologists find cure for genetic-related disease by targeting genes that controls the status of the disease-causing genes. Many tools have been developed to visualize biochemical networks.

8.3.1   Cytoscape

Cytoscape [755] is one of the most popular tools for generic biochemical network visualization (Figure 8.12). It supports a number of graph layout algorithms (please refer to Section 4.4 "Graphs and Trees" for the details on layout algorithms). Filtering functions are provided to reduce network complexity. For instance, users can select nodes and edges according to name and other attributes. More complex filtering are also possible: Examples include "Minimum Neighbors" filter which selects nodes having a minimum number of neighbors within a specified distance in the network, and "Local Distance" filter which selects nodes within a specified distance of a group of pre-selected nodes.

Cytoscape allows the mapping of data attributes to visual elements of nodes and edges. For instance, different node shapes are used to indicate different types of molecules in the network on the left of Figure 8.12. A user can also load a protein-protein interaction network and its gene expression data (showing how active a gene is) and color the proteins by gene expression values in a continuous manner from green, signifying under expressed compared to a control experiment, to red, signifying over expressed. This shows the gene expression data in the biological context of the interaction network, where it can be examined for patterns that are not obvious in each individual dataset.

Finally, Cytoscape can be extended by its "plug-in" architecture. New functions, such as additional layout algorithm and statistical analysis method, can be added to the system as plug-ins. This reduces the efforts required to develop a new biochemical visualization tool by utilizing the existing functions and makes it possible to customize the tool for specific research purposes.

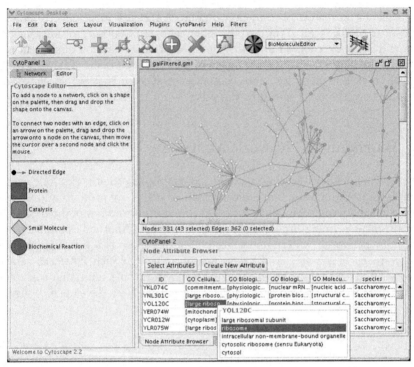

Fig. 8.12. Cytoscape is a visualization tool designed for various biological networks. It allows the mapping of data attributes to visual elements of nodes and edges. *Image courtesy of T. G. Ideker.*

8.3.2 Biochemical Pathway Analysis

Certain type of biochemical networks are also known as *pathways* which is a complex network of chemical reactions that biochemistry experts are familiar with and often need to use. A pathway usually includes a series of reactions that results in some biochemical function. For instance, *metabolic pathways* describe various reaction series that either cause the formation of some metabolic product or trigger another metabolic pathways. Sometimes pathways are used interchangeably with biochemical network, but in this section we treat it as a subset of biochemical networks that focuses on certain functions.

Biochemical pathways are usually drawn manually (see Figure 8.13), and the results are published in biochemistry textbooks or as posters. All these situations represent occurrences of what is called *static visualization* of pathway diagrams. There are several disadvantages of the static creation of the diagrams:

– Their generation is very time-consuming (the design of a poster can take up many months);
– They are hard to update;
– They lack flexibility, e.g., information can not be filtered and the substances can not be represented in alternate ways.

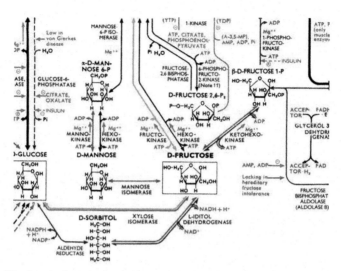

Fig. 8.13. Biochemical pathways are usually drawn manually and the results are published as posters. *Image courtesy of G. Michal.*

Considerable work has been done to automatically produce pathway visualizations.

BioPath. BioPath [741] is a web-based application designed specifically for pathway visualization.

Traditional graph layout algorithms are not adequate for the drawing of biochemical pathways as the resulting graphs are far from the conventions that the specialists in biochemistry are used to. In order to address this, the authors proposed a set of requirements for biochemical pathway drawings to make the resulting diagrams acceptable for the experts. Some of the requirements are:

– The way the substances are labeled (e.g. by name, by formula, by abbreviation);
– The sizes of the vertices in the final graph;
– To make sure that the temporal order of the reactants is visible and;
– To make sure that the general orientation of the reactions conforms with the traditional conventions.

The layout method that the authors proposed for drawing biochemical pathways is a modification of the traditional Sugyiama layout [804] (see the "layout" part in Subsection 4.4.4). The modifications are made in such a way that the resulting image respects the conventions commonly used in the hand-made diagrams that the biologists are accustomed with. The differences between the presented layout and the Sugyiama layout are:

– The algorithm is adapted to various vertex sizes and leads to more compact placements.
– The algorithm clusters subgraphs in higher level nodes.

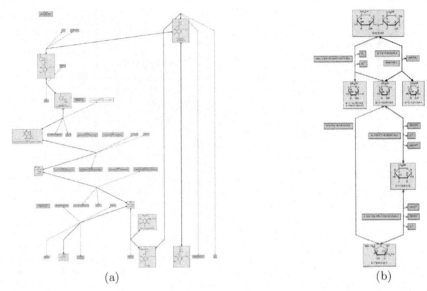

(a)   (b)

Fig. 8.14. Biopath modifies the Sugyiama algorithm so that it respects drawing conventions with which the domain experts are accustomed. The figure shows (a) a diagram rendered with the Sugyiama layout and (b) a diagram rendered with Biopath's modified layout. Note that the two diagrams are similar but not exactly the same. *Image courtesy of F. Schreiber.*

– Layout constraints are specific to the application: top-bottom, left-right constraints that regulate the relative positioning of the nodes. Horizontal and vertical constraints to regulate the x and y coordinates of nodes.

PathBank. PathBank [357] is a web-based 3D pathway visualization system with a database back end that integrates data from various sources. It has an intuitive "Google-like" search interface (Figure 8.15(a)) which allows for simple and fast keyword-based searches. PathBank supports complex boolean queries, and the web interface provides a search assistant to help construct such complex queries. It also features filtering functions that allow to hide commonly occurring small molecules (such as H_2O, $H+$, and ATP) to reduce the visual complexity.

Pathways can be automatically visualized in two or three dimensions in Path-Bank (Figure 8.15(b)). This is coupled with interactions that allow user to zoom, pan, rotate, and drag. A number of layout algorithms are available, but they are mainly based on traditional methods that do not consider pathway conventions. New visualizations can be added easily due to its plug-in framework.

PathBank can integrate pathway data from different sources automatically. Its storage approach automatically convert pathway data, given in BioPAX format—an XML format designed to store pathway data—into a corresponding relational schema. This approach is very generic and is capable of mapping any format similar to BioPAX into a human readable relational schema. The relational database back end also makes it possible to ask most searches with with simple and hence fast SQL queries which provides quick interactive response time.

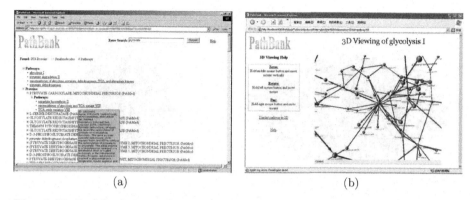

(a)   (b)

Fig. 8.15. PathBank is a web-based 3D pathway visualization system: (a) "Google-like" search interface. (b) 3D pathway visualization.

8.3.3 Layout for Large Biochemical Networks: LGL

The tools discussed so far are designed for biochemical networks with up to hundreds of nodes. However, many networks occur in biochemical study have hundreds of thousands of vertices and millions of edges. At this scale, the time requirement to compute layout and the visual complexity of the resulting visualization become serious problems. Special layout methods, such as the *Large Graph Layout* technique [6] (LGL), have been developed to address these problems.

The LGL algorithm first computes a Minimal Spanning Tree (MST) of the network and then lays it out. This approach is also used in the H3 Layout algorithm [584] which is used for drawing large directed graphs as node-link diagrams in 3D hyperbolic space. The relatively simple tree structure of MST speed ups the layout process considerably. It is interesting to observe that the algorithm does not try to minimize edge crossings which is a very important criterion for traditional graph visualization. The authors argue that doing this for the size of the analyzed graphs would be of no benefit as the information is presented at a much higher abstraction level. The version of the layout that is presented here works in two-dimensional space, but the authors mention also that it would be possible to use 3D space.

The LGL is applied to data obtained from more than 140,000 proteins from 50 complete genomes and more than 20 billion comparisons between the given proteins [6]. The network contains a node for every analyzed protein and an edge between every two proteins that have a similarity above a given threshold. Because of the MST, proteins that show strong structural similarity are laid out first and these proteins spatially grouped together. The authors assumed that proteins similar in structure are also similar in functionality, and they were able to characterize 23 previously uncharacterized protein families in this way [6]. A subset of this network is used in Figure 8.16 to show the difference between LGL and traditional spring layout algorithm.

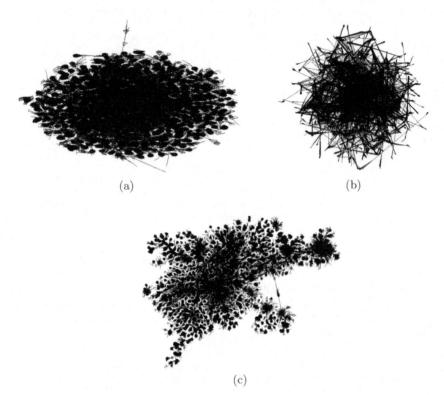

Fig. 8.16. A network containing more than 32,000 proteins and their similarities (represented as edges) laid out with three different techniques: (a) simple spring layout, (b) spring layout after equivalent nodes were collapsed (c) LGL layout. *Image courtesy of E. Marcotte.*

8.3.4 Discussion and Further Reading

Besides Cytoscape, there are a large number of tools available for biochemical network visualization. While some of them are designed to support generic biochemical networks, the others aim for specific networks such as gene regulatory network.

Among these tools, Osprey [112] provides functions similar to those of Cytoscape: it can visualize biochemical networks with a few layout methods, allows text search such as gene names, and uses color to map data attributes to nodes and edges of the network. It also support network comparison: users can load a few networks simultaneously, and then performance analysis such as comparing the structural differences among them.

VisANT [371] is another system designed to visualize generic biochemical networks. Besides the functions similar to previous systems, it also provides a few statistical analysis tools such as the node degree and clustering coefficients distribution, the results of which can be shown in separate scatter plots. Also,

VisANT is web-based system (implemented as a JavaApplet) which makes it more accessible by removing the requirement of installing a local client.

BioTapestry [512] is a visualization tool designed for study of genetic regulatory networks in developmental biology. Because of this specific purpose, some unique functions are provided in BioTapestry. Examples include an interactive graphical network editor and a tool for highlighting multiple direct and indirect paths between any two genes in a network.

Saraiya et al. [732] summarized the requirements of pathway visualization systems collected from interviews with biologists. The initial requirement list was distributed among biologists to gain feedback. From the feedback, they compiled a list of five requirements that are important for biologists working on pathway analysis, but still not fully developed in the existing visualization systems. These requirements are:

- Automated construction and updating of pathways by searching literature databases;
- Overlaying information on pathways in a biologically relevant format;
- Linking pathways to multi-dimensional data from high-throughput experiments, such as microarrays;
- Overviewing multiple pathways simultaneously with interconnections between them;
- Scaling pathways to higher levels of abstraction to analyze effects of complex molecular interactions at higher levels of biological organization.

Six pathway visualization systems are evaluated according to these requirements. The results suggest that biologists are usually reluctant to use these systems, because the absence of the previously listed functionalities makes the efforts required to learn a system not worth the possible benefit the users can obtain. Also, biologists like visualizations that are similar to those in the text books which currently can only be produced manually.

8.4   Microarray Data Visualization

Microarray is a recent breakthrough in genetic experiment technology. It makes it possible to measure thousands of genes in one experiment which reduces the test time by several orders of magnitude and makes new types of experiments possible. As defined by Schena et al. [735], a *microarray* is an ordered array of nucleic acids that enables parallel analysis of complex biochemical samples. The most common microarray is *DNA microarray* which is essentially a large array of genes (DNA segments) attached to a solid surface (such as silicon chip). A DNA microarray chip measures the expression levels of these genes in an experiment. An example of a microarray chip is shown in Figure 8.17.

8.4.1   TreeView

One of the most important tasks in analyzing microarray data is *gene clustering*, i.e., the identification of groups of genes that share a similar active level

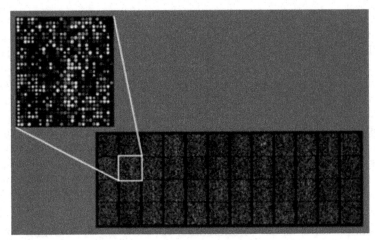

Fig. 8.17. An example of Microarray. The upper-left part shows a enlarged view of part of the microarray chip. Each dot on is a gene and the color of the dot indicates its active level.

(also known as *expression level*). In many cases, biologists also want to find genes that have similar expression level in a number of microarray experiments. It is often the case that genes with similar expression level—especially in a series experiments—have similar functions. This makes it possible to predict the function of unknown genes by using known genes with similar expression profile.

Gene clustering can be achieved using numerical analysis, or visualization, or the combination of the two. One of the first tools that provides the visualization and analysis of microarray data is the TreeView [236] (Figure 8.18). The main function of TreeView is to provide a hierarchical gene clustering according to the results of a series of microarray tests. The results are visualized as a matrix, where each column is the result of one microarray and each row is a gene. Increased gene-expression values are highlighted with a red brightness scale, decreased gene-expression values are highlighted with a green brightness scale, and the unchanged gene expression values are colored in black. Genes are clustered according to their expression level similarity across the experiments. The problem is that the number of genes in a microarray chip (usually thousands) is much larger than number of tests which results in a long-and-thin matrix (left part of Figure 8.18). In TreeView, users can select a small part to study in more detail (right part of Figure 8.18). The results of hierarchical clustering is shown as a dendrogram.

A different visualization approach is used by TimeSearcher [358] which is based on the idea of parallel coordinates. The fact that a microarray dataset is usually composed of the expression level of a gene at different times of one experiment turns it essentially into multivariate data, and thus suitable for parallel coordinates. In TimeSearcher, each line represents expression levels of a gene in the series experiments. Genes with similar expression profiles have their line close to each other (Figure 8.19). The advantage of TimeSearcher is that it

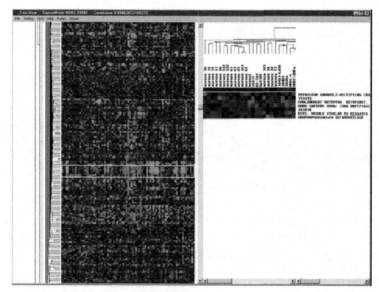

Fig. 8.18. A screen shot of TreeView. The left part shows a section of the entire data set, and the hierarchical clustering is shown as the dendrogram on its left. The right part shows the details of the highlighted part on the left.

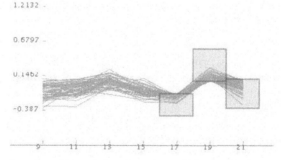

Fig. 8.19. TimeSearcher follows the idea of parallel coordinates, and the expression profile of each gene is visualized as a polyline.

clearly shows the expression value bound of each clusters, i.e., the minimal and maximal expression level in every experiment. A single gene can be highlighted by with different color to help identify it in a cluster. However, a microarray dataset usually contains thousands of genes and even with color highlight it quickly becomes difficult to see the details of genes as their number increases.

8.4.2 Hierarchical Clustering Explorer

While clustering is important knowledge of microarray data, there is also other information that is essential for microarray data analysis, such the functions of the genes used in the experiments. Biologists need all the information to help

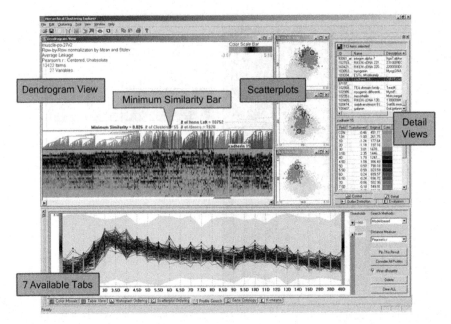

Fig. 8.20. Hierarchical Clustering Explorer provides multiple visualizations of microarray data. This screen shot shows the dendrogram, heatmap, and parallel coordinate views of the hierarchical clustering results. *Image courtesy of University of Maryland – Human-Computer Interaction Lab.*

them identify the biological principles underpins the microarray test results. This means multiple perspectives of the microarray data are required. Also, biologists need to use different visual representation for various analysis. For instance, biologists may want to compare clustering results in dendrogram and parallel coordinates. This means multiple perspectives on the same data are also required. Hierarchical Clustering Explorer (HCE) [749, 750] is a tool that provides multiple visualization of multiple perspectives of the microarray data (Figure 8.20). It provides dendrogram, heatmap and parallel coordinate views of the clustering results. Gene information is listed in tables, and its distribution is shown in scatter plots. Information displayed in different views is linked together using "brushing" techniques: selecting a cluster in one view automatically highlights the related information in the other view. It is also possible to filter out unwanted information according to user-defined conditions. All these functions make HCE a powerful tool for microarray data visualization.

8.4.3   Evaluation of Microarray Visualization Tools

The ultimate goal of visualization is to help biologists gain insights into microarray data. An evaluation focusing on the ability of revealing biological insights was performed by Saraiya et al. [730, 731]. Five microarray data visualization tools were included; besides the TreeView, TimeSearcher, and HCE discussed earlier, it also added two commercial packages: Spotfire[9] and GeneSpring[10]. Similar to HCE, these two packages provide a large range of visualization tools to facilitate microarray visualization. Visualizations offered by Spotfire includes: scatter plots, bar graphs, histograms, line charts, pie charts, parallel coordinates, heat maps, and spreadsheet views. It presents clustering results in multiple views and places each cluster in a separate parallel coordinate view. GeneSpring has a even larger selection of visualizations for microarray data analysis: parallel coordinates, heat-maps, scatter plots, histograms, bar charts, block views, physical position on genomes, array layouts, pathways, ontologies, spreadsheet views, and gene-to-gene comparison.

The authors tried to evaluate how much biological insight each tool can bring to a biologist. A *insight* is defined as *"an individual observation about the data made by the participant, a unit of discovery"*. Insight was identified using *"think-aloud"* protocol as subjects reported their observations during evaluation. The authors also proposed a list of characteristics to quantify the measurement of insight. These are: observation count, required time, domain value, hypotheses count, directed vs. unexpected, correctness, breadth vs depth, and category. Most of these characteristics are self-explanatory, but the reader is encouraged to consult the paper for the details. Three microarray data sets were used, and each user was assigned to analyze one data set with one tool. Users first listed some analysis questions they would typically asked about such a data set. Then, they started to examine the data with the tool until they felt that they would not gain any additional insight. Also, users were asked to estimate how much of the total potential insight they felt they had obtained so far about the data every 10-15 minutes.

The authors found that the choice of visualization tool clearly influences the interpretation of the data and insight gained. Some tools work more effectively with certain types of data: TreeView, TimeSearcher, and HCE each performed better with a different one of three data sets, but provided below average results for the other data sets. Larger software packages, like Spotfire and GeneSpring, work consistently across different data sets. If a researcher needs to work with just one kind of data, more focused tools can provide better results in a shorter time.

8.5 Medical Records Visualization

Clinical information is usually represented by multidimensional data extracted from patient examinations. The analysis of this data is an important activity to the clinical practitioner and to him/her, visualization is an important asset in the process of visual data mining.

8.5.1 LifeLines: Visualizing Patient Temporal Data

Time-based personal histories are important in the medical applications as together with examinations they form the basis for a physician's decision making
process. LifeLines is one of the first applications and techniques that was proposed for visualizing personal histories [654]. Although initially proposed as a
general visualization tool for viewing personal historical data, this section analyzes its relevance to the medical domain. The basic principle of the tool is that
the overview of the data should fit in one screen (see Figure 8.21(b)), and details
can be obtained by applying filters on the data. In this way, an user can have
access to both overview and in-depth knowledge about the analyzed record.

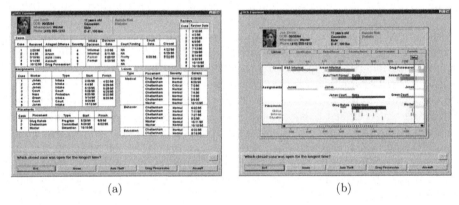

       (a)   (b)

Fig. 8.21. The two interfaces analyzed in a user study by Lindwarm Alonso et al. [15]:
(a) a tabular based interface (b) the visual interface offered by the LifeLines tool.

LifeLines was used in a study where thirty-six participants used a static version of either LifeLines or a tabular representation to answer questions about
a database of temporal personal history information [15]. Results suggest that
overall the LifeLines representation led to much faster response times, primarily
for questions which involved interval comparisons and making intercategorical
connections. Moreover, the authors relate that a post-experimental memory test
led to significantly higher recall for LifeLines.

8.5.2 The Cube: Multidimensional Analysis of Medical Records

More recently, a tool called The Cube [245, 246] was proposed as one of the
results of an interdisciplinary project between computer science and medical
experts. The project had the goal to develop tools that could support clinicians
in their daily diagnostic work. The purpose of The Cube is to visualize medical
examination records, and the typical question that the tool aims to support
answering is: "How does a set of attributes relate to each other from the available
data?". The tool proposes a technique called 3D parallel diagrams which is an

Drug	=	Levaxin
Smoking	=	Four cigarettes a day
Allergy	=	Oranges
Diagnosis	=	Gingival problems

Fig. 8.22. An example of patient examination data represented as attribute-value pairs.

extension of the traditional parallel coordinates technique [388]. It is similar to the casement displays used by Tukey [838].

The data to be visualized is represented by multiple patient examinations where each examination can be seen as an attribute-value pair (see Figure 8.22 for an example). The Cube is composed of a number of planes; each plane corresponding to an attribute that is part of the analysis. In this plane, one axis represents possible values of the associated attribute and the other axis represents time. For each examination, a line connects individual values in the different planes.

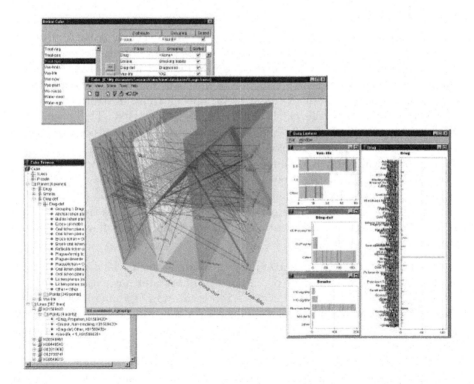

Fig. 8.23. The Cube is a complete environment for exploratory data analysis. The window in the center of the figure presents a 3D parallel diagram, an extension of the parallel coordinates technique. The lower right window is the Data Explorer which shows statistics about a given plane. *Image courtesy of G. Falkman.*

Figure 8.23 presents a screenshot of The Cube during an analysis of drug and smoking habits of patients. The tool presents raw data that the user has to scan for patterns and features of interest. The user interacts with the data using the main window of the cube by zooming, rotating and translating the cube. Because the tool is basically used in the process of visual data mining, it is important to obtain multiple perspectives to support the analysis process. Individual perspectives can be provided on the analyzed data by using the Data Explorer which shows statistics about a given plane.

Once an interesting pattern is found, the user has to perform statistical evaluations and investigations to understand the nature of the observations. The authors report that the tool has been successfully tested on a knowledge base of 1500 examinations and that the clinical practitioners preferred the 3D parallel coordinates visualization to other available 2D visualizations.

8.5.3 Visualizing Medical Practice Guidelines and Protocols

Computer support in protocol-based care is a relatively new field of medical informatics. Its core entity, medical treatment plans, are complex documents, currently mostly in the form of prose text including tables and figures. Standardized and widely-accepted health care procedures encourage the health care organizations to share and reuse such treatment plans in order to benefit from the experience of other organizations, to critique and improve existing procedures, and also to support the reduction of the costs associated with the clinical treatment. In order to formally describe the specifications of treatment plans, a plan specification language, called *Asbru*, was developed [468]. The specification language is too complex to be handled by the practitioners directly; so, visual representations have been developed.

The most widely used visual representation of clinical guidelines are so-called *flowchart algorithms*. There is even a standard for drawing this kind of flowchart diagrams proposed by a committee of the *Society for Medical Decision Making* [468]. However, some of the particular characteristics of the treatment plans (e.g., the existence of concurrent tasks or complex conditions), flowcharts proved to be inadequate.

AsbruView. One tool that attempts to address the problems, AsbruView, makes heavy use of a variety of visual metaphors and navigation techniques to represent plans. Figure 8.24 shows a representation of a plan in AsbruView. AsbruView utilizes metaphors of running tracks and traffic control to communicate important concepts and uses glyphs to depict the complex time annotations used in Asbru. The interface consists basically of two major parts: one captures the topology of plans, whereas the second one shows the temporal dimension of plans but no depiction of plan and patient data is possible. The intention of AsbruView is to support plan creation and manipulation.

The advantages of AsbruView over flowcharts are that the associated visualization is able to capture: (1) the hierarchical decomposition of plans, (2) time-oriented plans, (3) sequential, concurrent and cyclical execution of plans,

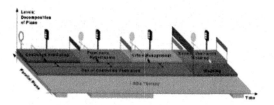

Fig. 8.24. AsbruView representation of a clinical treatment plan specified in Asbru.

(4) high-level goals that would allow the medical personnel flexibility in implementing the plans, and (5) conditions that need to hold on particular steps.

CareVis. Aigner and Miksch [11] propose CareVis, a tool which represents a step further in visualizing medical plans. The tool uses multiple coupled perspectives on the data. One perspective is dedicated to the plan specification—here the user can interact and explore a plan using *focus+context* techniques. Plans can be expanded and collapsed. One interesting feature of the navigation is that, to denote plan containment, the tool uses well-known visual cues like the small triangle which is oriented right when a plan is folded and oriented down when the plan is expanded[11] [11].

The other perspective is dedicated to patient data and is based on the idea of LifeLines (Subsection 8.5.1). The original concept has been extended to enable the display of hierarchical decomposition, complex time annotations and temporal uncertainties.

While AsbruView was not involved in user studies, CareVis was built based on user-centered principles. The authors organized guided interviews and a user study with eight physicians. As soon as the first prototype of the tool was available, the authors organized another review session for early feedback. A final evaluation was conducted with five of the eight physicians interviewed initially which *"considered the two coupled displays very helpful in working with and exploring treatment plans as well as patient data"* [11].

Further Reading. For a general survey on the use of information visualization techniques in medicine, see the survey by Chitarro [161]. A more specific survey is presented by Kosara and Miksch [465]; in their work they analyze existing techniques for visualizing preponderantly time-based clinical data.

8.6 Chapter Notes

The goal of this chapter was to assist the reader in developing an understanding of some of the biomedical problems which have visualization as part of the solution. The presented applications represent starting points for further analysis of the domains and, in the same time, provide the possibility of several conclusions on the application of information visualization in the biomedical domain.

---

[11] This technique is familiar to the users of Finder—the file system explorer for OS X operating system.

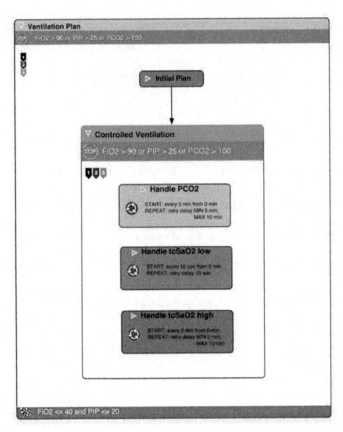

Fig. 8.25. To denote plan containment, CareVis uses well-known visual cues like the small triangle which is oriented right when a plan is folded and oriented down when the plan is expanded.

Space. It is interesting to see that few applications use complex graphic representations. Most of the applications use 2D space but there are also few which use 3D. On the other hand, the choice of applications is in a way arbitrary, so one should not generalize easily. Nevertheless, the chapter has shown that useful applications of information visualization can be implemented using simple concepts.

Another observation referring to the space usage is that the type of data has a very strong influence on the associated visualization possibilities. For example, all but one approach to DNA sequence visualization have represented the sequences as a horizontal axis in a 2D plane. It was only the work by Shah et al. [752] that proposed a 3D visualization of an inherently linear type of data.

Data Magnitude. The magnitude of the visualized data is important and has a strong influence on the techniques that can be used. For the same type of data, different magnitudes might need different visualization techniques. This was observed for sequence alignment (Section 8.2) as well as for phylogenetic trees (Section 8.1). In fact, not only the techniques change based on the data magnitude but also the user goals and possible insight: if for small phylogenetic trees the user goal was to see the evolutionary distance between species, for huge phylogenetic trees, the goal can be merely obtaining an overview. One might even wonder if the problem stays the same or not.

Interaction. Most of the applications use basic interaction techniques: navigating in 3D space, filtering data, and requesting more detail on specific subsets of the data. However, for some applications, interaction lays at their very core. This is the case for applications like Sequence Walkers or Jalview where the user's goal is to interactively generate hypotheses and test them.

Using Visualization to Think. The analyzed applications can be divided in the ones where the user tries to solve a specific problem (e.g., sequence walkers) and the ones in which the user is a simple viewer (e.g., the 3D hyperbolic tree of life). Usually, the ones where the user is a simple viewer employ more complex graphics. The applications which need interaction from the user are usually simpler. Also 3D might be an issue as many users actually have problems in navigating 3D space on a computer.

Validation. In most cases, the only way to prove that a particular tool or technique makes a task easier for the users is to conduct user studies. Unfortunately, few of the articles that introduces novel visualization techniques do so. Most of the articles provide anecdotal evidence about the way the users perceived the tool. On the other hand, Subsection 8.5.3 showed that researchers start applying user-centered principles (see Section 2.4) when developing their tools.

This chapter also mentioned some comparative evaluations where users were asked to grade the usability of multiple tools. Unfortunately, the general conclusion in the mentioned cases is that the users are not yet satisfied with the state of the art of the analyzed tools. One of the main problems was the difference between the expectations of the users and the facilities provided by the applications. One noteworthy application here is Biopath (see Section 8.3.2) which makes a step towards user-centered visualization by trying to implement the layouts in such a way that they resemble the ones that the domain experts are used with.

One special kind of validation is exemplified by the LGL protein similarity graph. In a way, it is the simplest possible validation: showing the domain experts that some insight was possible by using visualization and the result is as valid as when alternative techniques were used. On the other hand, not all tools can provide this kind of insight. In fact, some tools do not aim at providing the user with new insight, but rather supporting her in performing a task. In these cases, controlled experiments could be useful in assessing the best way in which the goal can be achieved.

Flexibility. Few of the presented applications offer the user the possibility of adjusting the visual representation of the data. The user is provided with predefined visualizations and he/she can at most change some visual parameters or change the type of representation (e.g., from 2D to 3D). But if a more serious customization of the visualization is needed, the user needs to request it from the developer. However, as the number of users of information visualization tools will increase and as the computer literacy of the users will also increase, they will eventually become able to perform part of the responsibilities of the programmers.

This increased flexibility would be especially useful for scientists who use tools for visual data mining. For this purpose, the possibility of drafting a totally new visualization or customizing an existing one in a short time might be valuable. One possible solution is represented by domain-oriented visual programming languages such as the ones that are proposed by Repenning and Summer [703]. It would not be surprising if, in the future, such environments would be provided for the researchers in the domains that were studied in this chapter.

Another domain where one needs flexibility is the automatic layout generation for biochemical pathways. Generic layout techniques need to be adapted to meet the particular requirements of the domain experts.

Future Trends. We expect that visualization will continue to play an important role in the biomedical domains as more information that is gathered and needs to be analyzed. One tendency that can be currently observed is moving visualizations towards the web. This is a natural result as the research in the biochemical domain is advancing fast and the old ways of disseminating information can not keep up with it. We have seen one clear example of the inefficiency of the old dissemination mechanisms in the biochemical pathways visualization.

Another reason for the migration of visualization applications towards the web is determined by the characteristics of the target audience of the domain-specific visualization environments. If one researcher wants to give visibility to his work, it is easier to provide it through a web-interface which introduces lower cognitive challenges to the users.

Together with the increase in computer literacy some users will request more power in defining their own customized visualizations. For these users, tools will need to provide flexible ways of customizing existing visualizations and easy ways of generating new ones.

Acknowledgments. The authors of this chapter would like to express their appreciation for observations and suggestions on previous drafts to Wim Fikkert, Olga Kulyk, Andrés Moreno, Martin Nöllenburg, Mathias Pohl, Ermir Qeli, Riccardo Mazza, and Ingo Wassink.

Bibliography

1. 3D Connection: SpaceBall, SpacePilot, and SpaceMouse, http://www.3dconnexion.de (2006)
2. 5DT (Fifth Dimension Technologies) Inc.: 5DT Data Glove 5 Ultra (2006)
3. Abello, J., Kobourov, S.G., Yusufov, R.: Visualizing Large Graphs with Compound-Fisheye Views and Treemaps. In: Proceedings of the 12th International Graph Drawing Symposium, pp. 431–441 (2004)
4. Abram, G., Treinish, L.: An Extended Data-Flow Architecture for Data Analysis and Visualization. In: VIS '95: Proceedings of the 6th conference on Visualization '95, p. 263. IEEE Computer Society Press, Los Alamitos (1995)
5. ABTIM: Braille displays, http://www.abtim.de/ (2006)
6. Adai, A.T., Date, S.V., Wieland, S., Marcotte, E.M.: LGL: creating a map of protein function with an algorithm for visualizing very large biological networks. Journal of Molecular Biology 340(1), 179–190 (2004)
7. Ahlberg, C., Shneiderman, B.: Visual Information Seeking: Tight coupling of dynamic query filters with starfield displays. In: Summary of the ACM Conference on Human Factors in Computing Systems (CHI'94), pp. 313–317. ACM Press, New York (1994)
8. Ahlberg, C., Wistrand, E.: IVEE: an Information Visualization and Exploration Environment. In: Proceedings Information Visualization, pp. 66–73. IEEE Computer Society Press, Los Alamitos (1995)
9. Ahlborn, B.A., Thompson, D., Kreylos, O., Hamann, B., Staadt, O.G.: A practical system for laser pointer interaction on large displays. In: VRST: Proceedings of the ACM Symposium on Virtual Reality Software and Technology, pp. 106–109 (2005)
10. Ahmed, A., Dwyer, T., Forster, M., Fu, X., Ho, J., Hong, S.-H., Koschützki, D., Murray, C., Nikolov, N.S., Taib, R., Tarassov, A., Xu, K.: GEOMI: GEOmetry for Maximum Insight. In: Proceedings of the 13th International Symposium on Graph Drawing, pp. 468–479 (2005)
11. Aigner, W., Miksch, S.: Supporting Protocol-Based Care in Medicine via Multiple Coordinated Views. In: Proceedings of the Second International Conference on Coordinated and Multiple Views in Exploratory Visualization (CMV '04), pp. 118–129. IEEE Computer Society Press, Los Alamitos (2004)
12. Albinsson, P.-A., Zhai, S.: High precision touch screen interaction. In: CHI '03: Proceedings of the SIGCHI conference on Human factors in computing systems, pp. 105–112. ACM Press (2003)
13. Allendoerfer, K., Aluker, S., Panjwani, G., Proctor, J., Sturtz, D., Vukovic, M., Chen, C.: Adapting the Cognitive Walkthrough Method to Assess the Usability of a Knowledge Domain Visualization. In: IEEE Symposium on Information Visualization (InfoVis'05), IEEE Computer Society Press, Los Alamitos (2005)
14. Allwood, J.: Cooperation and Flexibility in Multimodal Communication. In: Cooperative Multimodal Communication, Second International Conference, CMC'98, Tilburg, The Netherlands, January 28-30, 1998, Revised Papers (1998)

15. Alonso, D., Rose, A., Plaisant, C., Norman, K.: Viewing Personal History Records: A Comparison of Tabular Format and Graphical Presentation Using LifeLines. Behaviour and Information Technology 17, 249–262 (1998)

16. Amar, R., Stasko, J.: A Knowledge Task-Based Framework for Design and Evaluation of Information Visualizations. In: IEEE Symposium on Information Visualization (InfoVis'04), pp. 143–150. IEEE Computer Society Press, Los Alamitos, CA (2004)

17. Amenta, N., Klingner, J.: Case Study: Visualizing Sets of Evolutionary Trees. In: IEEE Symposium on Information Visualization, pp. 71–74 (2002)

18. André, E.: Natural language in multimedia/multimodal systems. In: Handbook of Computational Linguistics, pp. 650–669. Oxford University Press, Oxford (2003)

19. Andrews, D.: Plots of High Dimensional Data. Biometrics 28, 125–136 (1972)

20. Andrews, K., Heidegger, H.: Information Slices: Visualising and Exploring Large Hierarchies using Cascading, Semi-Circular Discs. In: IEEE Symposium on Information Visualization, Late Breaking Hot Topic Proceedings, pp. 9–12 (1998)

21. Andrienko, G., Andrienko, N.: Interactive Maps for Visual Data Exploration. International Journal of Geographical Information Science 13(4), 355–374 (1999)

22. Andrienko, G., Andrienko, N.: Geo-Visualization Support for Multidimensional Clustering. In: Proceedings 12th International Conference on Geoinformatics, pp. 329–335 (2004)

23. Andrienko, G., Andrienko, N.: Visual Exploration of the Spatial Distribution of Temporal Behaviors. In: Proceedings of the Ninth International Conference on Information Visualisation (IV '05), pp. 799–806 (2005)

24. Andrienko, G., Andrienko, N., Voss, H.: GIS for Everyone: The CommonGIS Project and Beyond. In: Peterson, M. (ed.) Maps and the Internet, pp. 131–146. Elsevier, Amsterdam (2003)

25. Andrienko, N., Andrienko, G., Gatalsky, P.: Exploratory Spatio-Temporal Visualization: an Analytical Review. Journal of Visual Languages and Computing 14(6), 503–541 (2003)

26. Andrienko, N., Andrienko, G., Gatalsky, P.: Impact of Data and Task Characteristics on Design of Spatio-Temporal Data Visualization Tools. In: Dykes, J., MacEachren, A.M., Kraak, M.-J. (eds.) Exploring Geovisualization, pp. 201–222. Elsevier, Amsterdam (2005)

27. Andrienko, N., Andrienko, G., Voss, H., Bernardo, F., Hipolito, J., Kretchmer, U.: Testing the Usability of Interactive Maps in CommonGIS. Cartography and Geographic Information Science 29(4), 325–342 (2002)

28. Animazoo: GypsyGyro-18, Gypsy5, and Gypsy-Hybrid, http://www.animazoo.com (2006)

29. Anupam, V., Bajaj, C.L.: Collaborative multimedia scientific design in SHASTRA. In: MULTIMEDIA '93: Proceedings of the first ACM international conference on Multimedia, pp. 447–456. ACM Press, New York (1993)

30. Anupam, V., Bajaj, C.L., Schikore, D., Schikore, M.: Distributed and Collaborative Visualization. IEEE Computer Society Press 27(7), 37–43 (1994)

31. Apple Computer: Exposé, http://www.apple.com/macosx/features/expose (2006)

32. Applegate, L.M.: Technology Support for Cooperative Work: A Framework for Studying Introduction and Assimilation in Organizations. Journal of Organizational Computing 1, 11–39 (1991)

33. Archer, L.B.: A View of the Nature of the Design Research. Design: Science: Methods. Westbury House, Guildford, UK (1981)

34. Ascension: Various Interaction Devices, http://www.ascension-tech.com (2006)

35. AVS: AVS 5 and Express, http://www.avs.com/ (2006)

36. Bachvarova, Y.: Survey on the knowledge representation formalisms underlying multimedia and multimodal presentations. Under review (2006)
37. Baecker, R.: Towards Animating Computer Programs: A First Progress Report. In: Proceedings of the Third NRC Man-Computer Communications Conference (1973)
38. Baecker, R.: Sorting Out Sorting (video). SIGGraph Video Review 7 (1981)
39. Baecker, R.: Sorting Out Sorting: A Case Study of Software Visualization for Teaching Computer Science. In: Stasko, J., Domingue, J., Brown, M.H., Price, B.A. (eds.) Software Visualization: Programming as a Multimedia Experience, pp. 369–381. MIT Press, Cambridge, MA (1998)
40. Bailey, R.W.: Performance vs. preference. In: Proceedings of the Human Factors and Ergonomics Society 37th Annual Meeting, pp. 282–285 (1993)
41. Baillie, L., Kunczier, H., Anegg, H.: Rolling, rotating and imagining in a virtual mobile world. In: MobileHCI '05: Proceedings of the 7th international conference on Human computer interaction with mobile devices & services, pp. 283–286. ACM Press, New York (2005)
42. Bajaj, C., Cutchin, S.: Web Based Collaborative Visualization Of Distributed And Parallel Simulation. In: Proceedings of the 1999 IEEE Parallel Visualization and Graphics Symposium (PVG'99), pp. 47–54. IEEE Computer Society Press, Los Alamitos (1999)
43. Balakrishnan, R., Hinckley, K.: The role of kinesthetic reference frames in two-handed input performance. In: UIST '99: Proceedings of the 12th annual ACM symposium on User interface software and technology, pp. 171–178. ACM Press, New York (1999)
44. Baldonado, M.Q.W., Woodruff, A., Kuchinsky, A.: Guidelines for Using Multiple Views in Information Visualization. In: Proceedings of the working conference on Advanced visual interfaces, pp. 110–119 (2000)
45. Ball, R., North, C.: Analysis of User Behavior on High-Resolution Tiled Displays. In: Costabile, M.F., Paternó, F. (eds.) INTERACT 2005. LNCS, vol. 3585, pp. 12–16. Springer, Berlin Heidelberg (2005)
46. Ball, R., North, C.: Effects of tiled high-resolution display on basic visualization and navigation tasks. In: CHI '05: CHI '05 extended abstracts on Human factors in computing systems, pp. 1196–1199. ACM Press, New York (2005)
47. Ballagas, R., Rohs, M., Sheridan, J., Borchers, J.: BYOD: Bring Your Own Device. In: UBICOMP Workshop on Ubiquitous Display Environments (September 2004)
48. Ballagas, R., Rohs, M., Sheridan, J., Borchers, J.: Sweep and Point & Shoot: Phonecam-Based Interactions for Large Public Displays. In: CHI '05: CHI '05 extended abstracts on Human factors in computing systems, pp. 1200–1203. ACM Press, New York (2005)
49. Ballagas, R., Rohs, M., Sheridan, J., Borchers, J.: The Smart Phone: A Ubiquitous Input Device. In: IEEE Pervasive Computing, pp. 70–77 (2006)
50. Baloian, N., Breuer, H., Luther, W.: Algorithm visualization using concept keyboards. In: SoftVis '05: Proceedings of the ACM symposium on Software visualization, pp. 7–16. ACM Press, New York (2005)
51. Baloian, N., Luther, W., Sánchez, J.: Modeling educational software for people with disabilities: theory and practice. In: Assets '02: Proceedings of the fifth international ACM conference on Assistive technologies, pp. 111–118. ACM Press, New York (2002)
52. Bar-Joseph, Z., Gifford, D.K., Jaakkola, T.: Fast optimal leaf ordering for hierarchical clustering. In: ISMB (Supplement of Bioinformatics), pp. 22–29 (2001)
53. Baratloo, A., Karaul, M., Karl, H., Kedem, Z.M.: KnittingFactory: An Infrastructure for Distributed Web Applications. Technical report, New York University (1997)

54. Barlow, T., Neville, P.: A Comparison of 2-D Visualizations of Hierarchies. In: Proceedings of the IEEE Symposium on Information Visualization (InfoVis'01), pp. 131–138. IEEE Computer Society Press, Los Alamitos (2001)

55. Bartlett, J.C., Topms, G.E.: Developing a protocol for bioinformatics analysis: an integrated information behavior and task analysis approach. Journal of the American Society for Information Science and Technology 56(5), 469–482 (2005)

56. Bartram, L., Ware, C., Calvert, T.: Moticons: Detection, distraction and task. International Journal of Human-Computer Studies 58(5), 515–545 (2003)

57. Battista, G.D., Eades, P., Tamassia, R., Tollis, I.G.: Algorithms for drawing graphs: an annotated bibliography. Computational Geometry: Theory and Applications 4(5), 235–282 (1994)

58. Battista, G.D., Garg, A., Liotta, G., Tamassia, R., Tassinari, E., Vargiu, F.: An experimental comparison of four graph drawing algorithms. Computational Geometry: Theory and Applications 7(5–6), 303–325 (1997)

59. Battista, G.D., Patrignani, M., Vargiu, F.: A Split and Push Approach to 3D Orthogonal Drawing. In: Whitesides, S.H. (ed.) GD 1998. LNCS, vol. 1547, pp. 87–101. Springer, Berlin Heidelberg (1999)

60. Battista, G.D., Tamassia, R.: Algorithms for plane representations of acyclic digraphs. Theoretical Computer Science 61(2-3), 175–198 (1988)

61. Baudisch, P., Cutrell, E., Hinckley, K., Gruen, R.: Mouse ether: Accelerating the acquisition of targets across multi-monitor displays. In: CHI '04: CHI '04 extended abstracts on Human factors in computing systems, pp. 1379–1382. ACM Press, New York (2004)

62. Baudisch, P., Cutrell, E., Robbins, D., Czerwinski, M., Tandler, P., Bederson, B., Zierlinger, A.: Drag-and-Pop and Drag-and-Pick: Techniques for Accessing Remote Screen Content on Touch- and Pen-Operated Systems. In: Proceedings of IFIP INTERACT'03: Human-Computer Interaction, vol. 2: UI design, p. 65 (2003)

63. Baudisch, P., Cutrell, E., Robertson, G.G.: High-Density Cursor: A Visualization Technique that Helps Users Keep Track of Fast-moving Mouse Cursors. In: Proceedings of IFIP INTERACT'03: Human-Computer Interaction, vol. 2: Display I/O, p. 236 (2003)

64. Baudisch, P., DeCarlo, D., Duchowski, A.T., Geisler, W.S.: Focusing on the essential: considering attention in display design. Communications of the ACM 46(3), 60–66 (2003)

65. Bavoil, L., Callahan, S.P., Crossno, P.J., Freire, J., Scheidegger, C.E., Silva, C.T., Vo, H.T.: VisTrails: Enabling Interactive Multiple-View Visualizations. In: Proceedings of the 16th IEEE Conference on Visualization (Vis '05), pp. 135–142 (2005)

66. Beard, D.B., Walker, J.Q.: Navigational Techniques to Improve the Display of Large Two-Dimensional Spaces. Behaviour and Information Technology 9(6), 451–466 (1990)

67. Beca, L., Cheng, G., Fox, G., Jurga, T., Olszewski, K., Podgorny, M., Sokolowski, P., Stachowiak, T., Walczak, K.: TANGO – A collaborative environment for the World Wide Web (1997)

68. Beca, L., Cheng, G., Fox, G., Jurga, T., Olszewski, K., Podgorny, M., Sokolwski, P., Walczak, K.: Web Technologies for Collaborative Visualization and Simulation (1997)

69. Becker, R., Eick, S., Wilks, A.: Visualizing network data. IEEE Transactions on Visualization and Computer Graphics 1, 16–28 (1995)

70. Bederson, B.B., Boltman, A.: Does Animation Help Users Build Mental Maps of Spatial Information? In: IEEE Symposium on Information Visualization (InfoVis 1999), pp. 28–35. IEEE Computer Society Press, Los Alamitos (1999)

71. Bederson, B.B., Clamage, A., Czerwinski, M.P., Robertson, G.G.: DateLens: A fisheye calendar interface for PDAs. ACM Trans. Comput.-Hum. Interact. 11(1), 90–119 (2004)

72. Bederson, B.B., Meyer, J., Good, L.: Jazz: An Extensible Zoomable User Interface Graphics ToolKit in Java. In: Proceedings of the 13th Annual ACM Symposium on User Interface Software and Technology (UIST'00), pp. 171–180. ACM Press, New York (2000)

73. Bederson, B.B., Shneiderman, B., Wattenberg, M.: Ordered and quantum treemaps: Making effective use of 2D space to display hierarchies. ACM Transactions on Graphics 21(4), 833–854 (2002)

74. Bellik, Y.: Media integration in multimodal interfaces. In: Multimedia Signal Processing, pp. 31–36. IEEE, LIMSI, CNRS, Orsay, June 1997. ISBN 0-7803-3780-8 (1997)

75. Ben-Bassat Levy, R., Ben-Ari, M., Uronen, P.A.: The Jeliot 2000 program animation system. Computers & Education 40(1), 1–15 (2003)

76. Bendix, F., Kosara, R., Hauser, H.: Parallel Sets: Visual Analysis of Categorical Data. In: Proceedings of the Symposium on Information Visualization (InfoVis 2005), pp. 133–140 (Oct. 2005)

77. Bennet, J.: Managing to meet usability requirements. In: Bennet, J., Case, D., Sandelin, J., Smith, M. (eds.) Visual Display Terminals: Usability Issues and Health concerns, Prentice-Hall, Englewood Cliffs (1984)

78. Benyon, D., Turner, P., Turner, S.: Designing Interactive Systems:People, Activities, Contexts, Technologies. Addison-Wesley, Reading, MA (2005)

79. Bergman, E.: Information Appliances and Beyond. Morgan Kaufmann, San Francisco, CA (2000)

80. Berkelman, P., Butler, Z., Hollis, R.: Design of a hemispherical magnetic levitation haptic interface device (1996)

81. Berkelman, P., Hollis, R.: Interacting with virtual environments using a magnetic levitation haptic interface. In: IROS '95: Proceedings of the International Conference on Intelligent Robots and Systems, vol. 1, IEEE Computer Society Press, Los Alamitos, CA (1995)

82. Bernsen, N.: Multimodality in Language and Speech Systems - From Theory to Design Support Tool. In: Multimodality in Language and Speech Systems, Kluwer, Dordrecht (2001)

83. Berry, B., Smith, J., Wahid, S.: Visualizing Case Studies. Technical Report TR-04-12, Virginia Tech (2003)

84. Bertin, J.: Graphics and Graphic Information Processing. Walter de Gruyter, Berlin New York (1981)

85. Bertin, J.: Semiology of Graphics: Diagrams, Networks, Maps (original French edition: (1967)). University of Wisconsin Press, Madison (1983)

86. Beyer, H.: Contextual Design: Defining Customer-Centered Systems. Morgan Kaufmann Publishers Inc., San Francisco (1997)

87. Bezdek, J., Hathaway, R.: VAT: A Tool for Visual Assessment of (Cluster) Tendency. In: Proceedings of the International Joint Conference on Neural Networks(IJCNN), pp. 2225–2230. IEEE Computer Society Press, Los Alamitos, CA (2002)

88. Bezerianos, A., Balakrishnan, R.: The vacuum: facilitating the manipulation of distant objects. In: CHI '05: Proceedings of the SIGCHI conference on Human factors in computing systems, pp. 361–370. ACM Press, New York, NY (2005)

89. Bezerianos, A., Balakrishnan, R.: View and Space Management on Large Displays. IEEE Computer Graphics and Applications 25(4), 34–43 (2005)

90. Bingham, J., Sudarsanam, S.: Visualizing large hierarchical clusters in hyperbolic space. Bioinformatics 16(7), 660–661 (2000)

91. Binucci, C., Didimo, W., Liotta, G., Nonato, M.: Computing Labeled Orthogonal Drawings. In: Proceedings of the 10 International Symposium on Graph Drawing, pp. 139–153 (2002)
92. Bjork, S.: Flip Zooming. The Development of an Information Visualization Technique. PhD thesis, Goteborg University, Dept. of Informatics (2000)
93. Björk, S., Holmquist, L.E., Ljungstrand, P., Redström, J.: PowerView: Structured access to integrated information on small screens. In *CHI '00: CHI '00 extended abstracts on Human factors in computing systems*, pp. 265–266. ACM Press, New York, NY (2000)
94. Blanch, R., Guiard, Y., Beaudouin-Lafon, M.: Semantic pointing: Improving target acquisition with control-display ratio adaptation. In: CHI '04: Proceedings of the SIGCHI conference on Human factors in computing systems, pp. 519–526. ACM Press, New York, NY (2004)
95. Blinn, J.: SIGGRAPH 1998 Keynote Address (Transcribed by J. M. Fijii). Computer Graphics 33(1), 43–47 (1999)
96. Blythe, J., McGrath, C., Krackhardt, D.: The Effect of Graph Layout on Inference from Social Network Data. In: Brandenburg, F.J. (ed.) GD 1995. LNCS, vol. 1027, pp. 40–51. Springer, Berlin Heidelberg (1996)
97. Boehm, B.: A spiral model of software development and enhancement. IEEE Computer 21(5), 61–72 (1988)
98. Böhme, D., Sotoodeh, M.: Haptik, http://www.informatik.uni-bremen.de/~nostromo/haptik/ (2006)
99. Bolt, R.A.: "Put-that-there": Voice and gesture at the graphics interface. SIGGRAPH Computer Graphics 14(3), 262–270 (1980)
100. Bourguet, M.-L.: Towards a Taxonomy of Error Handling Strategies in Recognition-Based Multimodal Human-Computer Interfaces. Signal Processing (2006)
101. Bowman, D.A., Hodges, L.F.: User Interface Constraints for Immersive Virtual Environment Applications. Technical Report 95-26, Virginia Polytechnic Institute and State University (1995)
102. Bowman, D.A., Johnson, D.B., Hodges, L.F.: Testbed evaluation of virtual environment interaction techniques. In: VRST '99: Proceedings of the ACM symposium on Virtual reality software and technology, pp. 26–33. ACM Press, New York, NY (1999)
103. Bowman, D.A., Koller, D., Hodges, L.F.: Travel in Immersive Virtual Environments: An Evaluation of Viewpoint Motion Control Techniques. In: VRAIS '97: Proceedings of the 1997 Virtual Reality Annual International Symposium (VRAIS '97), IEEE Computer Society Press, Los Alamitos, CA (1997)
104. Bowman, D.A., Kruijff, E., LaViola, J.J., Poupyrev, I.: 3D User Interfaces: Theory and Practice. Addison-Wesley, Reading, MA (2004)
105. Brandenburg, F.J., Forster, M., Pick, A., Raitner, M., Schreiber, F.: BioPath – Exploration and Visualization of Biochemical Pathways. In: Jünger, M., Mutzel, P. (eds.) Graph Drawing Software, pp. 215–236. Springer, Berlin Heidelberg New York (2004)
106. Brandes, U., Corman, S.R.: Visual Unrolling of Network Evolution and the Analysis of Dynamic Discourse. In: Proceedings of the 2005 IEEE Symposium on Information Visualization, pp. 145–151. IEEE Computer Society Press, Los Alamitos, CA (2001)
107. Brandes, U., Dwyer, T., Schreiber, F.: Visualizing Related Metabolic Pathways in Two and a Half Dimensions. In: Proceedings of the International Symposium on Graph Drawing, pp. 111–122 (2003)
108. Brandes, U., Raab, J., Wagner, D.: Exploratory Network Visualization: Simultaneous Display of Actor Status and Connections. Journal of Social Structure 2 (2001)

109. Brandes, U., Wagner, D.: Contextual visualization of actor status in social networks. In: Proceedings of the 2nd Joint Eurographics and IEEE TCVG Symposium on Visualization, pp. 13–22 (2000)
110. Brandes, U., Wagner, D.: visone—Analysis and Visualization of Social Networks. In: Juenger, M., Mutzel, P. (eds.) Special Issue on Graph Drawing Software. Springer Series in Mathematics and Visualization, pp. 321–340. Springer, Berlin Heidelberg New York (2003)
111. Brandstein, M., Ward, D.: Microphone Arrays: Signal Processing Techniques and Applications (Digital Signal Processing), 1st edn. Springer, Berlin Heidelberg New York (2001)
112. Breitkreutz, B.-J., Stark, C., Tyers, M.: Osprey: a network visualization system. Genome Biology 4, R22 (2003)
113. Brewer, C.A.: Color Use Guidelines for Mapping and Visualization. In: MacEachren, A.M., Taylor, D.F. (eds.) Visualization in Modern Cartography, pp. 123–147. Pergamon Press, Oxford (1994)
114. Brewer, I., MacEachren, A.M., Abdo, H., Gundrum, J., Otto, G.: Collaborative Geographic Visualization: Enabling Shared Understanding of Environmental Processes. In: IEEE Symposium on Information Visualization, 2000 (InfoVis 2000), pp. 137–141. IEEE Computer Society Press, Los Alamitos, CA (2000)
115. Bridgeman, S.S., Fanto, J., Garg, A., Tamassia, R., Vismara, L.: InteractiveGiotto: An Algorithm for Interactive Orthogonal Graph Drawing. In: DiBattista, G. (ed.) GD 1997. LNCS, vol. 1353, pp. 303–308. Springer, Berlin Heidelberg (1997)
116. Bridgeman, S.S., Tamassia, R.: A User Study in Similarity Measures for Graph Drawing. In: Marks, J. (ed.) GD 2000. LNCS, vol. 1984, pp. 19–30. Springer, Berlin Heidelberg (2001)
117. Brodlie, K.W.: Visualization over the World Wide Web. Dagstuhl, 00:23 (1997)
118. Brodlie, K.W.: Models of Collaborative Visualization. In: Dykes, J. et al. (ed.) Exploring Geovisualization, pp. 463–475. Elsevier, Amsterdam (2005)
119. Brodlie, K.W., Duce, D.A., Gallop, J.R., Walton, J.P.R.B., Wood, J.D.: Distributed and Collaborative Visualization. Computer Graphics Forum 23(2), 223–251 (2004)
120. Brodlie, K.W., Duce, D.A., Gallop, J.R., Wood, J.D.: Distributed Cooperative Visualization. In: Eurographics'98: STAR State of The Art Report, pp. 27–50. Eurographics (1998)
121. Broisjuk, L., Hajirezaei, M.-R., Klukas, C., Rolletschek, H., Schreiber, F.: Integrating Data from Biological Experiments into Metabolic Networks with the DBE Information System. In: Silico Biology 5(0011), 2004. Special Issue: Dagstuhl Seminar "Integrative Bioinformatics"
122. Brønsted, T., Dalsgaard, P., Larsen, L.B., Manthey, M., Kevitt, P.M., Moeslund, T.B., Olesen, K.G.: The IntelliMedia WorkBench - An Environment for Building Multimodal Systems. In: Cooperative Multimodal Communication, Second International Conference, CMC'98, Tilburg, The Netherlands, January 28-30, 1998, Revised Papers (1998)
123. Brown, M.H.: Exploring Algorithms Using Balsa-II. Computer 21(5), 14–36 (1988)
124. Brown, M.H.: Perspectives on algorithm animation. In: Proceedings of the SIGCHI conference on Human factors in computing systems, pp. 33–38. ACM Press, New York, NY (1988)
125. BSIK. The Netherlands Bioinformatics Centre (NBIC) BioRange project 4.2.1, http://www.nbic.nl/ (2006)
126. BSIK. Virtual Laboratory for e-Science, http://www.vl-e.nl/ (2006)

127. Bui, T.D.: Creating Emotions and Facial Expressions for Embodied Agents. Phd thesis, University of Twente, July 2004. Publisher: Taaluitgeverij Neslia Paniculata, Publisher location: Enschede, ISSN: 1381-3617; No. 04-63 (CTIT Ph.D), ISBN: 90-75296-10-X

128. Buja, A., Cook, D., Swayne, D.F.: Interactive High-Dimensional Data Visualization. Journal of Computational and Graphical Statistics 5(1), 78–99 (1996)

129. Bundeswahlleiter, Statistisches Bundesamt, Wiesbaden: Wahlkreiskarte für die Wahl zum 16. Deutschen Bundestag. In: Wahl zum 16. Deutschen Bundestag am 18. September 2005, Heft 3: Endgültige Ergebnisse nach Wahlkreisen, p. 281. Statistisches Bundesamt, Quelle der Verwaltungsdaten: VG 1000, Bundesamt für Kartographie und Geodäsie (2005)

130. Bunt, H.: Issues in Multimodal Human-Computer Communication. In: Multimodal Human-Computer Communication, Systems, Techniques, and Experiments, pp. 1–12. Springer, Berlin Heidelberg New York (1998)

131. Bunt, H., Kipp, M., Maybury, M., Wahlster, W.: Fusion and coordination for multimodal interactive information presentation. In: Algorithms in Ambient Intelligence. Philips Research Book Series, vol. 2, pp. 21–53. Kluwer, Dordrecht (2003)

132. Burch, M., Weissgerber, P., Diehl, S.: EPOSee - A Tool for Visualizing Software Evolution. In: Proc. of the 3rd IEEE Int. Workshop on Visualizing Software for Program Understanding and Analysis, pp. 127–128. IEEE Computer Society Press, Los Alamitos, CA (2005)

133. Burdea, G.C.: Haptics Issues in Virtual Environments. In: Computer Graphics International, pp. 295–302 (2000)

134. Burdea, G.C.: Introduction to VR Technology. In: VR, p. 265. IEEE Computer Society Press, Los Alamitos, CA (2004)

135. Burigat, S., Chittaro, L.: Location-aware visualization of VRML models in GPS-based mobile guides. In: Web3D '05: Proceedings of the tenth international conference on 3D Web technology, pp. 57–64. ACM Press, New York, NY (2005)

136. Burtnyk, N., Khan, A., Fitzmaurice, G., Balakrishnan, R., Kurtenbach, G.: StyleCam: interactive stylized 3D navigation using integrated spatial & temporal controls. In: UIST '02: Proceedings of the 15th annual ACM symposium on User interface software and technology, pp. 101–110. ACM Press, New York, NY (2002)

137. Butler, D., Almond, J., Bergeron, R., Brodlie, K.W., Haber, R.: Panel: Visualization Reference Models. In: Proceedings of 4th IEEE Visualization Conference, pp. 337–342. IEEE Computer Society Press, Los Alamitos, CA (1993)

138. Bystrom, K.-E., Barfield, W., Hendrix, C.M.: A Conceptual Model of the Sense of Presence in Virtual Environments. Presence 8(2), 241–244 (1999)

139. Cabello, S., d. Berg, M., van Dijk, S., van Kreveld, M., Strijk, T.: Schematization of Road Networks. In: Proc. 17th Annual Symposium on Computational Geometry (SoCG'01), pp. 33–39. ACM Press, New York, NY (2001)

140. Cabral, M.C., Morimoto, C.H., Zuffo, M.K.: On the usability of gesture interfaces in virtual reality environments. In: CLIHC '05: Proceedings of the 2005 Latin American conference on Human-computer interaction, pp. 100–108. ACM Press, New York, NY (2005)

141. Caldwell, D.G., Lawther, S., Wardle, A.: Tactile Perception and its Application to the Design of Multi-modal Cutaneous Feedback Systems. In: Proceedings of the 1996 IEEE International Conference on Robotics and Automation, pp. 3215–3221. IEEE Computer Society Press, Los Alamitos, CA (1996)

142. Cao, X., Balakrishnan, R.: VisionWand: Interaction techniques for large displays using a passive wand tracked in 3D. In: Proceedings of the 16th annual ACM symposium on User interface software and technology, pp. 173–182. ACM Press, New York, NY (2003)

143. Card, S.K., Hong, L., Mackinlay, J.D., Chi, E.H.: 3Book: a 3D electronic smart book. In: AVI '04: Proceedings of the working conference on Advanced visual interfaces, pp. 303–307. ACM Press, New York, NY (2004)

144. Card, S.K., Mackinlay, J.: The structure of the information visualization design space. In: IEEE Symposium on Information Visualization (InfoVis '97), pp. 92–100. IEEE Computer Society Press, Los Alamitos, CA (1997)

145. Card, S.K., MacKinlay, J.D., Shneiderman, B. (eds.): Readings in Information Visualization: Using Vision to Think. Morgan Kaufmann, San Francisco, CA (1999)

146. Carpendale, M., Montagnese, C.: A framework for unifying presentation space. In: Symposium on User Interface Software and Technology, pp. 61–70. ACM Press, New York, NY (2001)

147. Carranza, J., Theobalt, C., Magnor, M.A., Seidel, H.-P.: Free-viewpoint video of human actors. ACM Trans. Graph. 22(3), 569–577 (2003)

148. Carrizo, S.F.: Phylogenetic Trees: An Information Visualisation Perspective. In: CRPIT '04: Proceedings of the second conference on Asia-Pacific bioinformatics, pp. 315–320. Australian Computer Society, Inc (2004)

149. Carroll, J., Rosson, M.: Usability specifications as a tool in iterative development. Advances in Human-Computer Interaction 1, 1–28 (1985)

150. CEI. Collaborate with EnSight Gold, http://www.ensight.com/products/collab.html (2006)

151. Chabert, A., Grossman, E., Jackson, L.S., Pietrowiz, S.R., Seguin, C.: Java object-sharing in Habanero. j-CACM 41(6), 69–76 (1998)

152. Chen, C.: Empirical Studies of Information Visualization. In: Information Visualization: Beyond the Horizon, pp. 173–210. Springer, Berlin Heidelberg New York (2004)

153. Chen, C.: Information Visualization: Beyond the Horizon, 2nd edn. Springer, Berlin Heidelberg New York (2004)

154. Chen, C.: Top 10 Unsolved Information Visualization Problems. IEEE Computer Graphics and Applications 25(4), 12–16 (2005)

155. Chen, H., Sun, H.: Real-time haptic sculpting in virtual volume space. In: VRST '02: Proceedings of the ACM symposium on Virtual reality software and technology, pp. 81–88. ACM Press, New York, NY (2002)

156. Chernoff, H.: The Use of Faces to Represent Points in k-Dimensional Space Graphically. Journal of the American Statistical Association 68, 361–368 (1973)

157. Chewar, C.M., McCrickard, D.S., Ndiwalana, A., North, C., Pryor, J., Tessendorf, D.: Secondary Task Display Attributes – Optimizing Visualizations for Cognitive Task Suitability and Interference Avoidance. In: Proceedings of the Joint Eurographics - IEEE TCVG Symposium on Visualization 2002 (VisSym'02), pp. 165–171. IEEE Computer Society Press, Los Alamitos, CA (2002)

158. Chi, E.H.: A Taxonomy of Visualization Techniques using the Data State Reference Model. In: Proceedings of IEEE Symposium on Information Visualization (InfoVis'00), pp. 69–75. IEEE Computer Society Press, Los Alamitos, CA (2000)

159. Chi, E.H., Riedl, J., Barry, P., Konstan, J.A.: Principles For Information Visualization Spreadsheets. IEEE Computer Graphics and Applications 18(4), 30–38 (1998)

160. Chien, J.-T., Lai, J.-R.: Use of Microphone Array and Model Adaptation for Hands-Free Speech Acquisition and Recognition. The Journal of VLSI Signal Processing, Special Issue on Real World Speech Processing 36(2–3), 141–151 (2004)

161. Chittaro, L.: Information visualization and its application to medicine. Artificial Intelligence in Medicine 22(2), 81–88 (2001)

162. Choi, J.-H., Jung, H.-Y., Kim, H.-S., Cho, H.-G.: PhyloDraw: a phylogenetic tree drawing system. Bioinformatics 16(11), 1056–1058 (2000)

163. Christensen, J., Marks, J., Shieber, S.: An Empiriclal Study of Algorithms for Point-Feature Label Placement. ACM Transactions on Graphics 14(3), 203–232 (1995)
164. Clamp, M., Cuff, J., Searle, S.M., Barton, G.J.: The Jalview Java alignment editor. Bioinformatics 20(3), 426–427 (2004)
165. Cleveland, W.C., McGill, M.E.: Dynamic Graphics for Statistics. CRC Press, Inc., Boca Raton, FL, USA (1988)
166. CMC Cooperative: Multimodal Communication. In: Bunt, H., Beun, R.-J. (eds.) CMC 1998. LNCS, vol. 2155, pp. 28–30. Springer, Berlin Heidelberg (2001)
167. Cockburn, A., Firth, A.: Improving the Acquisition of Small Targets. In: Proceedings of HCI 2003, pp. 181–196 (2003)
168. Cockburn, A., McKenzie, B.: An Evaluation of Cone Trees. In: People and Computers XIV: British Computer Society Conference on Human Computer Interaction, pp. 425–436. Springer, Berlin Heidelberg New York (2000)
169. Cockburn, A., McKenzie, B.: 3D or not 3D?: evaluating the effect of the third dimension in a document management system. In: Proceedings of the SIGCHI conference on Human factors in computing systems, pp. 434–441. ACM Press, New York, NY (2001)
170. Cockburn, A., McKenzie, B.: Evaluating the Effectiveness of Spatial Memory in 2D and 3D Physical and Virtual Environments. In: Proceedings of ACM CHI' Conference on Human Factors in Computing Systems, pp. 203–210. ACM Press, New York, NY (2002)
171. Cohen, P.R., Cheyer, A., Wang, M., Baeg, S.C.: An open agent architecture. Readings in agents, pp. 197–204 (1998)
172. Cohen, P.R., Johnston, M., McGee, D., Oviatt, S.L., Pittman, J., Smith, I., Chen, L., Clow, J.: QuickSet: multimodal interaction for distributed applications. In: MULTIMEDIA '97: Proceedings of the fifth ACM international conference on Multimedia, pp. 31–40. ACM Press, New York, NY (1997)
173. Cohen, P.R., McGee, D., Oviatt, S.L., Wu, L., Clow, J., King, R., Julier, S., Rosenblum, L.: Multimodal Interaction for 2D and 3D Environments. IEEE Computer Graphics and Applications 19(4), 10–13 (1999)
174. Cohen, P.R., Oviatt, S.L.: The Role of Voice Input for Human-Machine Communication. Proceedings of the National Academy of Sciences 92(22), 9921–9927 (1995)
175. Collomb, M., Hascoet, M., Baudisch, P., Lee, B.: Improving drag-and-drop on wall-size displays. In: GI '05: Proceedings of the 2005 conference on Graphics interface, pp. 25–32. Canadian Human-Computer Communications Society (2005)
176. Constantine, L., Lockwood, L.: Software for Use: A Practical Guide to the Models and Methods of Usage-Centred Design. ACM Press, New York, NY (1999)
177. Cooper, A.: The inmates are running the asylum. Sams, 1 edn. (1999)
178. I. Corporation: CyberGrasp(TM) Exoskeleton, http://www.immersion.com/ (2006)
179. Corradini, A., Cohen, P.R.: Multimodal speech-gesture interface for hands-free painting on virtual paper using partial recurrent neural networks for gesture recognition. In: Proceedings of the International Joint Conference on Neural Networks, vol. III, pp. 2293–2298 (2002)
180. COVISE: COllaborative VIsualization and Simulation Environment – Homepage, http://www.hlrs.de/organization/vis/covise/ (2006)
181. Crowley, J.L., Coutaz, J., Berard, F.: Things That See. Communications of the ACM 43(3), 54–64 (2000)

182. Cruz-Neira, C., Sandin, D.J., DeFanti, T.A.: Surround-screen projection-based virtual reality: The design and implementation of the CAVE. In: SIGGRAPH '93: Proceedings of the 20th annual conference on Computer graphics and interactive techniques, pp. 135–142. ACM Press, New York, NY (1993)

183. Cruz-Neira, C., Sandin, D.J., DeFanti, T.A., Kenyon, R.V., Hart, J.C.: The CAVE: audio visual experience automatic virtual environment. Commun. ACM 35(6), 64–72 (1992)

184. Cutting, J.E.: How the Eye Measures Reality and Virtual Reality. Behavior Research Methods, Instrumentation, and Computers 29, 29–36 (1997)

185. Newman, C.B.D.J., Hettich, S., Merz, C.: UCI Repository of machine learning databases (1998)

186. Dachselt, R., Ebert, J.: Collapsible Cylindrical Trees: A Fast Hierarchical Navigation Technique. In: Proceedings of the Symposium on Information Visualization (InfoVis 2001), pp. 79–86 (2001)

187. Dann, W., Cooper, S., Pausch, R.: Learning to Program with Alice. Prentice-Hall, Englewood Cliffs (2006)

188. Davis, J., Chen, X.: LumiPoint: Multi-User Laser-Based Interaction on Large Tiled Displays. Displays 23(5) (2002)

189. de Fraysseix, H., Pach, J., Pollack, R.: How to Draw a Planar Graph on a Grid. Combinatorica 10, 41–51 (1990)

190. de Jong, H., Rip, A.: The computer revolution in science: steps toward the realization of computer-supported discovery environments. Artificial Intelligence 91, 225–256 (1997)

191. DeCarlo, D., Santella, A.: Stylization and abstraction of photographs. In: SIGGRAPH '02: Proceedings of the 29th annual conference on Computer graphics and interactive techniques, pp. 769–776. ACM Press, New York, NY (2002)

192. Deng, L., Wang, Y., Wang, K., Acero, A., Hon, H., Droppo, J., Boulis, C., Mahajan, M., Huang, X.D.: Speech and Language Processing for Multimodal Human-Computer Interaction. J. VLSI Signal Process. Syst. 36(2-3), 161–187 (2004)

193. di Battista, G., Eades, P., Tamassia, R., Tollis, I.G.: Graph Drawing: Algorithms for the Visualization of Graphs. Prentice-Hall, Englewood Cliffs (1999)

194. Diamondbullet. Usability first: Usability Glossary, http://www.usabilityfirst.com/glossary/ (2006)

195. DiBiase, D.: Visualization in the Earth Sciences. In: Earth and Mineral Sciences, Bulletin of the College of Earth and Mineral Sciences, vol. 59, pp. 13–18. Penn State University (1990)

196. DiBiase, D., MacEachren, A.M., Krygier, J.B., Reeves, C.: Animation and the Role of Map Design in Scientific Visualization. Cartography and Geographic Information Systems 19(4), 201–214 (1992)

197. Diehl, S. (ed.): Software Visualization. LNCS, vol. 2269. Springer, Berlin Heidelberg (2002)

198. Diehl, S., Görg, C., Kerren, A.: Animating Algorithms Live and Post Mortem. In: Diehl, S. (ed.) Software Visualization. LNCS, vol. 2269, pp. 46–57. Springer, Berlin Heidelberg (2002)

199. Dietz, P., Leigh, D.: DiamondTouch: A Multi-User Touch Technology. In: UIST '01: Proceedings of the 14th annual ACM symposium on User interface software and technology, pp. 219–226. ACM Press, New York, NY (2001)

200. Dietz, P., Raskar, R., Booth, S., v. Baar, J., Wittenburg, K., Knep, B.: Multiprojectors and implicit interaction in persuasive public displays. In: Working Conference on Advanced Visual Interfaces (AVI '4), pp. 209–217. ACM Press, New York, NY (2004)

201. Dinse, H.R., Kalisch, T., Ragert, P., Pleger, B., Schwenkreis, P., Tegenthoff, M.: Improving human haptic performance in normal and impaired human populations through unattended activation-based learning. ACM Trans. Appl. Percept. 2(2), 71–88 (2005)
202. Dodgson, N.A.: Autostereoscopic 3D Displays. IEEE Computer Society Press 38(8), 31–36 (2005)
203. Doleisch, H., Gasser, M., Hauser, H.: Interactive Feature Specification for Focus+Context Visualization of Complex Simulation Data. In: Data Visualization, Proceedings of the 5th Joint IEEE TCVG–EUROGRAPHICS Symposium on Visualization (VisSym 2003), pp. 239–248 (2003)
204. Doleisch, H., Hauser, H.: Smooth Brushing For Focus and Context Visualization of Simulation Data in 3D. In: WSCG 2002 Conference Proceedings, pp. 147–151, (February 2002)
205. Doleisch, H., Mayer, M., Gasser, M., Priesching, P., Hauser, H.: Interactive Feature Specification for Simulation Data on Time-Varying Grids. In: Conference on Simulation and Visualization 2005 (SimVis 2005), pp. 291–304 (2005)
206. Doleisch, H., Mayer, M., Gasser, M., Wanker, R., Hauser, H.: Case Study: Visual Analysis of Complex, Time-Dependent Simulation Results of a Diesel Exhaust System. In: Data Visualization, Proceedings of the 6th Joint IEEE TCVG–EUROGRAPHICS Symposium on Visualization (VisSym 2004), pp. 91–96, (May 2004)
207. Donath, J., Karahalios, K., Viegas, F.: Visualizing Conversation. In: Proceedings of the 32nd Hawaii International Conference on System Sciences, IEEE Computer Society Press, Los Alamitos, CA (1999)
208. Donoho, A.W., Donoho, D.L., Gasko, M.: MacSpin: Dynamic Graphics on a Desktop Computer. IEEE Computer Graphics and Applications 08(4), 51–58 (1988)
209. Donoho, D., Ramos, E.: PRIMDATA: Data Sets for Use With PRIM-H. In: American Statistical Association (ASA) Second Exposition of Statistical Graphics Technology (1983)
210. Drabkin, H., Hollenbeck, C., Hill, D., Blake, J.: Ontological visualization of protein-protein interactions. BMC Bioinformatics 6, 29 (2005)
211. Drury, C.G., Clement, N.R.: The Effect of Area, Density, and Number of Background Characters on Visual Search. Human Factors 20, 597–603 (1979)
212. DSDM. Dynamic Systems Development Method, http://www.dsdm.org (2006)
213. Duce, D.A., Gallop, J.R., Johnson, I.J., Robinson, K., Seelig, C.D., Cooper, C.S.: Distributed Cooperative Visualization – The MANICORAL Approach. In: Proceedings of the Eurographics Workshop on Visualization in Scientific Computing, pp. 69–85 (March 1998)
214. Duce, D.A., Giorgetti, D., Cooper, C.S., Gallop, J.R., Johnson, I.J., Robinson, E., Seelig, C.D.: Reference Models for Distributed Cooperative Visualization. Computer Graphics Forum 17(4), 219–233 (1998)
215. Duchowski, A.T.: Eye Tracking Methodology: Theory and Practice. Springer, New York (2003)
216. Dumas, F.: Joseph and C. Greenwood, Westport, CT (1993)
217. Dunbar, K.: How scientists really reason: Scientific reasoning in real-world laboratories. In: Sternberg, R., Davidson, J. (eds.) The nature of Insight, pp. 365–395. MIT Press, Cambridge, MA (1995)
218. Dunbar, K.: How Scientists Think: On-Line Creativity and Conceptual Change in Science. In: Creative Thought: An Investigation of Conceptual Structures and Processes (2001)
219. Duskis, S.: JSamba, http://www-static.cc.gatech.edu/gvu/softviz/algoanim/jsamba/ (2006)

220. Dykes, J.: cdv: A Flexible Approach to ESDA with Free Demonstration Software. In: Proceedings British Cartographic Society 34th Annual Symposium, pp. 100–107 (1997)

221. Dykes, J.: Facilitating Interaction for Geovisualization. In: Dykes, J. et al. (ed.) Exploring Geovisualization, pp. 265–291. Elsevier, Amsterdam (2005)

222. Dykes, J., MacEachren, A.M., Kraak, M.-J.: Advancing Geovisualization. In: Dykes, J. et al. (ed.) Exploring Geovisualization, pp. 693–703. Elsevier, Amsterdam (2005)

223. Dykes, J., MacEachren, A.M., Kraak, M.-J. (eds.): Exploring Geovisualization. Elsevier, Amsterdam (2005)

224. Eades, P.: A Heuristic for Graph Drawing. Congressus Numerantium 42, 149–160 (1984)

225. Eades, P.: Computational Morphology, chapter Symmetry finding algorithms, pp. 41–51. North-Holland, Amsterdam (1988)

226. Eades, P.: Drawing free trees. Bulletin of the institute for Combinaiorics and its Applications 5, 10–36 (1992)

227. Eades, P., Feng, Q.-W.: Drawing Clustered Graphs on an Orthogonal Grid. In: DiBattista, G. (ed.) GD 1997. LNCS, vol. 1353, pp. 146–157. Springer, Berlin Heidelberg (1997)

228. Eades, P., Feng, Q.-W.: Multilevel Visualization of Clustered Graphs. In: DiBattista, G. (ed.) GD 1997. LNCS, vol. 1353, pp. 101–112. Springer, Berlin Heidelberg (1997)

229. Eades, P., Feng, Q.-W., Lin, X.: Straight-Line Drawing Algorithms for Hierarchical Graphs and Clustered Graphs. In: DiBattista, G. (ed.) GD 1997. LNCS, vol. 1353, pp. 113–128. Springer, Berlin Heidelberg (1997)

230. Eades, P., Zhang, K. (eds.): Software Visualization. World Scientific Pub., Singapore (1996)

231. Ebert, D.S., Shaw, C.D., Zwa, A., Starr, C.: Two-handed interactive stereoscopic visualization. In: VIS '96: Proceedings of the 7th conference on Visualization '96, IEEE Computer Society Press, Los Alamitos, CA (1996)

232. Edsall, R.M., MacEachren, A.M., Pickle, L.: Case study: Design and Assessment of an Enhanced Geographic Information System for Exploration of Multivariate Health Statistics. In: Proceedings IEEE Symposium on Information Visualization (InfoVis), pp. 159–162. IEEE Computer Society Press, Los Alamitos, CA (2001)

233. Eick, S.G., Steffen, J.L., Sumner, E.E.: Seesoft-A Tool for Visualizing Line Oriented Software Statistics. IEEE Transactions on Software Engineering 18(11), 957–968 (1992)

234. Eiglsperger, M., Kaufmann, M., Siebenhaller, M.: A Topology-Shape-Metrics Approach for the Automatic Layout of UML Class Diagrams. In: Proceedings of ACM Symposium on Software Visualization, pp. 189–198. ACM Press, New York, NY (2003)

235. Einsfeld, K., Ebert, A., Agne, S., Klein, B.: DocuWorld - A 3-D User Interface to the Semantic Desktop. In: 1st Workshop on The Semantic Desktop - Next Generation Personal Information Management and Collaboration Infrastructure at the International Semantic Web Conference (2005)

236. Eisen, M.B., Spellman, P.T., Brown, P.O., Botstein, D.: Cluster analysis and display of genome-wide expression patterns. Proc Natl Acad Sci. U. S. A. 95(25), 14863–14868 (1998)

237. Elrod, S., Bruce, R., Gold, R., Goldberg, D., Halasz, F., Janssen, W., Lee, D., McCall, K., Pedersen, E., Pier, K., Tang, J., Welch, B.: Liveboard: A large interactive display supporting group meetings, presentations, and remote collaboration. In: CHI '92: Proceedings of the SIGCHI conference on Human factors in computing systems, pp. 599–607. ACM Press, New York, NY (1992)

238. Engel, K., Ertl, T.: Texture-based Volume Visualization for Multiple Users on the World Wide Web. In: Virtual Environments '99. Proceedings of the Eurographics Workshop, pp. 115–124 (1999)

239. Engel, K., Ertl, T.: Interactive High-Quality Volume Rendering with Flexible Consumer Graphics Hardware. In: Proceedings of Eurographics 2002, State of the Art Reports, (Sept 2002)

240. Eslambolchilar, P., Murray-Smith, R.: Tilt-Based Automatic Zooming and Scaling in Mobile Devices - A State-Space Implementation. In: Brewster, S., Dunlop, M.D. (eds.) Mobile Human-Computer Interaction – MobileHCI 2004. LNCS, vol. 3160, pp. 120–131. Springer, Berlin Heidelberg (2004)

241. Espinosa, O., Hendrickson, C., Garrett, J.: Domain Analysis: A Technique to Design a User-Centered Visualization Framework. In: INFOVIS '99: Proceedings of the 1999 IEEE Symposium on Information Visualization, IEEE Computer Society Press, Los Alamitos, CA (1999)

242. Essential Reality: P5 Glove, http://www.essentialreality.com (2006)

243. Fabrikant, S.I., Goldsberry, K.: Thematic Relevance and Perceptual Salience of Dynamic Geovisualization Displays. In: Proceedings, 22nd ICS/ACI International Cartographic Conference, (July 9–16 2005)

244. Fakespace Systems Inc.: Advanced Visualization Solutions, http://www.fakespace.com (2006)

245. Falkman, G.: Information Visualization in Clinical Odontology: Multidimensional Analysis and Data Exploration. Artificial Intelligence in Medicine 22, 133–158 (2001)

246. Falkman, G.: Issues in structured knowledge representation: Adefinitional approach with application to case-based reasoning and medical informatics. PhD thesis, Department of Computing Science, Chalmers University of Technology, Göteborg, Sweden (2003)

247. Fallman, D.: Design-orientend Human-Computer Interaction. In: Proceedings of the SIGCHI conference on Human factors in computing systems, pp. 225–232. ACM Press, New York, NY (2003)

248. Favalora, G.E.: Volumetric 3D Displays and Application Infrastructure. IEEE Computer Society Press 38(8), 37–44 (2005)

249. FCS Robotics: HapticMASTER, http://www.fcs-cs.com (2006)

250. Fekete, J.-D., Greinstein, G., Plaisant, C.: InfoVis Contest, 2004, http://www.cs.umd.edu/hcil/iv04contest. Retrieved 27-01-2006

251. Fekete, J.-D., Plaisant, C.: Information Visualization Benchmark Repository, 2004, http://www.cs.umd.edu/hcil/InfovisRepository Retrieved 27-01-2006

252. Felsenstein, J.: PHYLIP: Phylogeny Inference Package, http://www.nih.go.jp/~jun/doc/phylip/main.html (1995)

253. Ferber, J.: Multi-Agent Systems: An Introduction to Distributed Artificial Intelligence. Addison-Wesley Longman, Amsterdam (1999)

254. Fienberg, S.E.: Graphical Methods in Statistics. American Statisticians 33, 165–178 (1979)

255. Figueroa, P., Bischof, W.F., Boulanger, P., Hoover, H.J.: Efficient comparison of platform alternatives in interactive virtual reality applications. International Journal of Human-Computer Studies 62(1), 73–103 (2005)

256. Fikkert, W., Heylen, D., van Dijk, B., Nijholt, A.: Estimating the Gaze Point of a Student in a Driving Simulator. In: Sixth International Conference on Advanced Learning Technologies (ICALT) - Technologies for Life-Long Learning, pp. 497–501. IEEE Computer Society Press, Los Alamitos, CA (2006)

257. Fineman, B.: Computers as people: human interaction metaphors in human-computer interaction. Master's thesis, The School of Design - Carnegie Mellon University (2004)

258. Fisher, R.A.: The use of multiple measurements in taxonomic problems. Annals of Eugenics 7(2), 179–188 (1936)

259. Fitts, P.M.: The Information Capacity of the Human Motor System in Controlling Amplitude of Movement. Journal of Experimental Psychology 47, 381–391 (1954)

260. Fitzmaurice, G., Khan, A.A., Kurtenbach, A.G., Binks, A.G. et al.: Cinematic Meeting Facilities Using Large Displays. IEEE Computer Graphics and Applications 25(4), 17–21 (2005)

261. Fitzmaurice, G.W.: Situated information spaces and spatially aware palmtop computers. Communications of the ACM 36(7), 39–49 (1993)

262. Fitzmaurice, G.W., Zhai, S., Chignell, M.H.: Virtual reality for palmtop computers. ACM Tranactions on Information Systems 11(3), 197–218 (1993)

263. Force Dimension. 6-DOF DELTA, 2006, http://www.forcedimension.com

264. Foster, M.E., White, M., Setzer, A., Catizone, R.: Multimodal Generation in the COMIC Dialogue System. In: Proceedings of the ACL Interactive Poster and Demonstration Sessions, pp. 45–48. Association for Computational Linguistics (June 2005)

265. Foulser, D.: IRIS Explorer: A Framework for Investigation. SIGGRAPH Comput. Graph. 29(2), 13–16 (1995)

266. Foxlin, E.: Motion tracking requirements and technologies. In: In Handbook of Virtual Environments – Design, Implementation, and Applications. Human Factors and Ergonomics Series, pp. 163–210. Lawrence Erlbaum Associates, Mahwah, NJ (2002)

267. Frank, A., Timpf, S.: Multiple Representations for Cartographic Objects in a Multi-Scale Tree-An Intelligent Graphical Zoom. Computers and Graphics 18(6), 823–829 (1994)

268. Freeman, L.: Visualizing Social Networks. Journal of Social Structure 1(1) (2000)

269. Freeman, W.T., Anderson, D.B., Beardsley, P.A., Dodge, C.N., Roth, M., Weissman, C.D., Yerazunis, W.S., Kage, H., Kyuma, K., Miyake, Y., Tanaka, K.i.: Computer Vision for Interactive Computer Graphics. IEEE Computer Graphics and Applications 18(3), 42–53 (1998)

270. Freeman, W.T., Beardsley, P.A., Kage, H., Tanaka, K.-I., Kyuma, K., Weissman, C.D.: Computer vision for computer interaction. Computer Graphics 33(4), 65–68 (1999)

271. Friendly, M.: Corrgrams: Exploratory Displays for Correlation Matrices. In: The American Statistician, pp. 316–324 (2002)

272. Fröhlich, B., Plate, J., Wind, J., Wesche, G., Göbel, M.: Cubic-Mouse-Based Interaction in Virtual Environments. IEEE Computer Graphics and Applications 20(4), 12–15 (2000)

273. Frokjaer, E., Hertzum, M., Hornbaek, K.: Measuring Usability: Are Effectiveness, Efficiency, and Satisfaction Really Correlated? In Proceedings of ACM Conference on Human Factors in Computing Systems (CHI'00), pp. 345–352. ACM Press, New York, NY (2000)

274. Fruchterman, T.M.J., Reingold, E.M.: Graph drawing by force-directed placement. Software-Practice & Experience 21(11), 1129–1164 (1991)

275. Fuhrmann, S., Ahonen-Rainio, P., Edsall, R.M., Fabrikant, S.I., Koua, E.L., Tobón, C., Ware, C., Wilson, S.: Making Useful and Usable Geovisualization: Design and Evaluation Issues. In: Dykes, J. et al. (ed.) Exploring Geovisualization, pp. 553–566. Elsevier, Amsterdam (2005)

276. Fuhrmann, S., MacEachren, A.M., Dou, J., Wang, K., Cox, A.: Gesture and Speech-Based Maps to Support Use of GIS for Crisis Management: A User Study. In: Proceedings AutoCarto 2005 (2005)

277. Fung, J.: GPU Gems 2: Programming Techniques for High-Performance Graphics and General-Purpose Computation (Gpu Gems). Addison-Wesley, Reading, MA (2005)
278. Fung, J., Mann, S.: OpenVIDIA: parallel GPU computer vision. In: MULTI-MEDIA '05: Proceedings of the 13th annual ACM international conference on Multimedia, pp. 849–852. ACM Press, New York, NY (2005)
279. Furnas, G.W.: Generalized Fisheye Views. In: Proceedings of the Conference on Human Factors in Computing Systems (CHI'86), pp. 16–23 (1986)
280. Furnas, G.W.: Effective view navigation. In: Conference Proceedings on Human Factors in Computing Systems (CHI'97), pp. 367–374. ACM SIGCHI, ACM Press, New York, NY (1997)
281. Furnas, G.W.: The FISHEYE View: A New Look at Structured Files. In: Card, S., Mackinlay, J., Shneiderman, B. (eds.) Information Visualization: Using Vision to Think, pp. 145–152. Morgan Kaufmann, San Francisco, CA (1999)
282. Furnas, G.W., Bederson, B.B.: Space-Scale Diagrams: Understanding Multi-scale Interfaces. In: Proceedings of the ACM Conference on Human Factors in Computing Systems (CHI'95), pp. 234–241. ACM Press, New York, NY (1995)
283. Furnas, G.W., Zhang, X.: MuSE: a multiscale editor. In: Proceedings of the 11th Annual ACM Symposium on User Interface Software and Technology (UIST'98), pp. 107–116. ACM Press, New York, NY (1998)
284. Gahegan, M.: Beyond Tools: Visual Support for the Entire Process of GIScience. In: Dykes, J. et al. (ed.) Exploring Geovisualization, pp. 83–99. Elsevier, Amsterdam (2005)
285. Gaither, K., Ebert, D., Geisler, B., Laidlaw, D.: Panel: In the Eye of the Beholder: The Role of Perception in Scientific Visualization. In: Proceedings IEEE Visualization 2004, pp. 567–568. IEEE Computer Society Press, Los Alamitos, CA (2004)
286. Gajer, P., Goodrich, M.T., Kobourov, S.G.: A Multi-dimensional Approach to Force-Directed Layouts of Large Graphs. In: Marks, J. (ed.) GD 2000. LNCS, vol. 1984, pp. 211–221. Springer, Berlin Heidelberg (2001)
287. Gajer, P., Kobourov, S.G.: GRIP: Graph dRawing with Intelligent Placement. In: Marks, J. (ed.) GD 2000. LNCS, vol. 1984, pp. 222–228. Springer, Berlin Heidelberg (2001)
288. Gansner, E., Koren, Y., North, S.: Topological Fisheye Views for Visualizing Large Graphs. In: Proceedings of the Symposium on Information Visualization (InfoVis 2004), pp. 175–182 (2004)
289. Garland, K.: Mr Beck's Underground Map. Capital Transport Publishing (1994)
290. Gaver, B., Dunne, T., Pacenti, E.: Design: Cultural probes. Interactions 6(1), 21–29 (1999)
291. Gaver, W., Beaver, J., Benford, S.: Ambiguity as a resource for design. In: SIGCHI conference on Human factors in computing systems, pp. 233–240. ACM Press, New York, NY (2003)
292. Gerald-Yamasaki, M.J.: Cooperative visualization of computational fluid dynamics. In: PDIS '91: Proceedings of the first international conference on Parallel and distributed information systems, p. 169. IEEE Computer Society Press, Los Alamitos, CA (1991)
293. Ghoniem, M., Fekete, J.-D., Castagliola, P.: A Comparison of the Readability of Graphs Using Node-Link and Matrix-Based Representations. In: IEEE Symposium on Information Visualization, pp. 17–24. IEEE Computer Society Press, Los Alamitos, CA (2004)
294. Gibbs, A., McIntyre, G.: The Diagram, a Method for Comparing Sequences. Eur. J. Biochem 16, 1–11 (1970)
295. Gilbert, E.W.: Pioneer Maps of Health and Disease in England. Geographical Journal 124(2), 172–183 (1958)

296. Globus, A., Raible, E.: Fourteen Ways to Say Nothing with Scientific Visualization. IEEE Computer (July 1994), 86–88 (1994)

297. Goble, J.C., Hinckley, K., Pausch, R., Snell, J.W., Kassell, N.F.: Two-Handed Spatial Interface Tools for Neurosurgical Planning. Computer 28(7), 20–26 (1995)

298. Goesmann, A., Haubrock, M., Meyer, F., Kalinowski, J., Giegerich, R.: PathFinder: reconstruction and dynamic visualization of metabolic pathways. Bioinformatics 18, 124–129 (2002)

299. Gonzales, R.C., Woods, R.E.: Digital Image Processing. Prentice-Hall, Englewood Cliffs (2001)

300. Google Inc.: Google Earth. http://earth.google.com (2005)

301. Gould, J.D., Lewis, C.: Designing for usability: key principles and what designers think. Commun. ACM 28(3), 300–311 (1985)

302. Graham, M., Kennedy, J., Benyon, D.: Towards a methodology for developing visualizations. International Journal of Human-Computer Studies 53(5), 789–807 (2000)

303. Granitzer, M., Kienreich, W., Sabol, V., Andrews, K., Klieber, W.: Evaluating a System for Interactive Exploration of Large, Hierarchically Structured Document Repositories. In: Proceedings of the Symposium on Information Visualization (InfoVis 2004), pp. 127–134 (2004)

304. Grave, M.: Shared Data Spaces for Distributed Computing and Parallelism in Scientific Visualization Systems. CWI Quarterly 7(2), 175–185 (1994)

305. Griffin, A.L.: Understanding How Scientists Use Data-Display Devices for Interactive Visual Computing with Geographical Models. PhD thesis, The Pennsylvania State University (2004)

306. Grinstein, G.G., Hoffman, P.E., Laskowski, S.J., Pickett, R.M.: Benchmark Development for the Evaluation of Visualization for Data Mining. In: Fayyad, U., Grinstein, G.G., Wierse, A. (eds.) Information Visualization in Data Mining and Knowledge Discovery, pp. 129–176. Academic Press, San Francisco (2002)

307. Grinstein, G.G., Kobsa, A., Plaisant, C., Shneiderman, B., Stasko, J.T.: Panel: The Future Visualization Platform. In: Proceedings IEEE Visualization 2003, pp. 605–606 (2003)

308. Grissom, S., McNally, M.F., Naps, T.L.: Algorithm visualization in CS education: comparing levels of student engagement. In: SoftVis '03: Proceedings of the 2003 ACM symposium on Software visualization, pp. 87–94. ACM Press, New York, NY (2003)

309. Grossman, T., Balakrishnan, R.: The bubble cursor: enhancing target acquisition by dynamic resizing of the cursor's activation area. In: CHI '05: Proceedings of the SIGCHI conference on Human factors in computing systems, pp. 281–290. ACM Press, New York, NY (2005)

310. Grossman, T., Balakrishnan, R., Kurtenbach, G., Fitzmaurice, G., Khan, A., Buxton, B.: Interaction Techniques for 3D Modeling on Large Displays. In: SI3D '01: Proceedings of the 2001 symposium on Interactive 3D graphics, pp. 17–23. ACM Press, New York, NY (2001)

311. Grossman, T., Wigdor, D., Balakrishnan, R.: Multi-finger gestural interaction with 3d volumetric displays. In: UIST '04: Proceedings of the 17th annual ACM symposium on User interface software and technology, pp. 61–70. ACM Press, New York, NY (2004)

312. Grudin, J.: Partitioning digital worlds: focal and peripheral awareness in multiple monitor use. In: CHI '01: Proceedings of the SIGCHI conference on Human factors in computing systems, pp. 458–465. ACM Press, New York, NY (2001)

313. Guibas, L.J., Sedgewick, R.: A dichromatic framework for balanced trees. In: Proceedings of the 19th Annual IEEE Symposium on Foundations of Computer Science, pp. 8–21. IEEE Computer Society Press, Los Alamitos, CA (1978)

314. Guimbretière, F., Stone, M.C., Winograd, T.: Fluid interaction with high-resolution wall-size displays. In: UIST '01: Proceedings of the 14th annual ACM symposium on User interface software and technology, pp. 21–30. ACM Press, New York, NY (2001)

315. Guo, D., Gahegan, M., MacEachren, A.M., Zhou, B.: Multivariate Analysis and Geovisualization with an Integrated Geographic Knowledge Discovery Approach. Cartography and Geographic Information Science 32(2), 113–132 (2005)

316. Guo, H., Zhang, W., Wu, J.: The Effect of Zooming Speed in a Zoomable User Interface. Report from Student HCI Online Research Experiments (SHORE), http://otal.umd.edu/SHORE2000/zoom/, 2006 (2000)

317. Haber, R., McNabb, D.: Visualization Idioms: A Conceptual Model for Scientific Visualization Systems, pp. 74–93. IEEE Computer Society Press, Los Alamitos, CA (1990)

318. Hachet, M., Guitton, P., Reuter, P.: The CAT for efficient 2D and 3D interaction as an alternative to mouse adaptations. In: VRST '03: Proceedings of the ACM symposium on Virtual reality software and technology, p. 225. ACM Press, New York, NY (2003)

319. Hachet, M., Pouderoux, J., Guitton, P.: A camera-based interface for interaction with mobile handheld computers. In: SI3D '05: Proceedings of the 2005 symposium on Interactive 3D graphics and games, pp. 65–72. ACM Press, New York, NY (2005)

320. Hachet, M., Pouderoux, J., Guitton, P., Gonzato, J.-C.: TangiMap: a tangible interface for visualization of large documents on handheld computers. In: GI '05: Proceedings of the 2005 conference on Graphics interface, pp. 9–15. Canadian Human-Computer Communications Society (2005)

321. Hachul, S., Jünger, M.: Drawing Large Graphs with a Potential-Field-Based Multilevel Algorithm. In: Pach, J. (ed.) GD 2004. LNCS, vol. 3383, pp. 285–295. Springer, Berlin Heidelberg (2005)

322. Hachul, S., Jünger, M.: An Experimental Comparison of Fast Algorithms for Drawing General Large Graphs. In: Healy, P., Nikolov, N.S. (eds.) GD 2005. LNCS, vol. 3843, pp. 235–250. Springer, Berlin Heidelberg (2006)

323. Haining, R.P.: Spatial Data Analysis: Theory and Practice. Cambridge University Press, Cambridge (2003)

324. Hakala, T., Lehikoinen, J., Aaltonen, A.: Spatial interactive visualization on small screen. In: MobileHCI '05: Proceedings of the 7th international conference on Human computer interaction with mobile devices & services, pp. 137–144. ACM Press, New York, NY (2005)

325. Hall, E.T.: The Hidden Dimension: Man's Use of Space in Public and Private. Doubleday (1966)

326. Han, J.Y.: Low-cost multi-touch sensing through frustrated total internal reflection. In: UIST '05: Proceedings of the 18th annual ACM symposium on User interface software and technology, pp. 115–118. ACM Press, New York, NY (2005)

327. Hand, C.: Survey of 3D Interaction Techniques. Computer Graphics Forum (December 1997)

328. Hansen, D.: Committing Eye Tracking. PhD thesis, IT University of Copenhagen (July 2003)

329. Hardenberg, C., Brard, F.: Bare-Hand Human-Computer Interaction. In: Proceedings of the ACM Workshop on Perceptive User Interfaces, ACM Press, New York, NY (2001)

330. Hardison, R.C.: Comparative Genomics. PLoS Biology 1(2), 156–160 (2003)

331. Harel, D., Koren, Y.: A fast multi-scale method for drawing large graphs. In: Proceedings of the working conference on Advanced visual interfaces, pp. 282–285. ACM Press, New York, NY (2000)

332. Harel, D., Koren, Y.: Graph Drawing by High-Dimensional Embedding. In: Goodrich, M.T., Kobourov, S.G. (eds.) GD 2002. LNCS, vol. 2528, pp. 207–219. Springer, Berlin Heidelberg (2002)

333. Harrower, M.: Visualizing Change: Using Cartographic Animation to Explore Remotely-Sensed Data. Cartographic Perspectives 39, 30–42 (2002)

334. Harrower, M.: Tips for Designing Effective Animated Maps. Cartographic Perspectives 44, 63–65 (2003)

335. Harrower, M., MacEachren, A., Griffin, A.L.: Design, Implementation, and Assessment of Geographic Visualization Tools to Support Earth Science Education. Cartography and Geographic Information Science 27, 279–293 (2000)

336. Hartson, H., Hix, D.: Toward empirically derived methodologies and tools for human computer interface development. International Journal of Man.-Machine Studies 31, 477–494 (1989)

337. Hascoët, M.: Throwing Models for Large Displays. In: HCI 2003, vol. 2, pp. 73–77 (2003)

338. Hascoët, M., Sackx, F.: Exploring Interaction Strategies with Wall-Screen: A New Dual-Display Device for Managing Collections of Web Pages (2002)

339. Hasler, A.F., Palaniappan, K., Manyin, M.: A High Performance Interactive Image Spreadsheet (IISS). Computers in Physics 8, 325–342 (1994)

340. Hastie, T., Tibshirani, R., Friedman, J.: The Elements of Statistical Learning. Springer, Berlin Heidelberg New York (2001)

341. Hauser, H., Bremer, P., Theisel, H., Trener, M., Tricoche, X.: Panel: What are the most demanding and critical problems, and what are the most promising research directions in Topology-Based Flow Visualization In: Topology-Based Methods in Visualization Workshop, September 2005. Held in Budmerice, Slovakia (2005)

342. Hauser, H., Ledermann, F., Doleisch, H.: Angular brushing for extended parallel coordinates. In: Proceedings of the IEEE Symposium on Information Visualization, pp. 127–130. IEEE Computer Society Press, Los Alamitos, CA (2002)

343. Hawkey, K., Kellar, M., Reilly, D., Whalen, T., Inkpen, K.M.: The proximity factor: Impact of distance on co-located collaboration. In: GROUP '05: Proceedings of the 2005 international ACM SIGGROUP conference on Supporting group work, pp. 31–40. ACM Press, New York, NY (2005)

344. Healey, C.G., Enns, J.T.: Large Datasets at a Glance: Combining Textures and Colors in Scientific Visualization. IEEE Transactions on Visualization and Computer Graphics 5(2), 145–167 (1999)

345. Herman, I., Delest, M., Melançon, G.: Tree Visualisation and Navigation Clues for Information Visualisation. Computer Graphics Forum 17(2), 153–165 (1998)

346. Herman, I., Melancon, G., Marshall, M.S.: Graph Visualization and Navigation in Information Visualization: A Survey. IEEE Transactions on Visualization and Computer Graphics 6(1), 24–43 (2000)

347. Hetzler, E., Turner, A.: Analysis experiences using information visualization. IEEE Computer Graphics and Applications 24(5), 22–26 (2005)

348. Hewagamage, K.P., Hirakawa, M., Ichikawa, T.: Interactive Visualization of Spatiotemporal Patterns Using Spirals on a Geographical Map. In: Proceedings IEEE Symposium on Visual Languages, pp. 296–303. IEEE Computer Society Press, Los Alamitos, CA (1999)

349. Hibbard, W.: Top Ten Visualization Problems. Computer Graphics, 33(2), available online (May 1999)

350. Himsolt, M.: GraphEd: a Graphical Platform for the Implementation of Graph Algorithms. In: DIMACS International Workshop on Graph Drawing, pp. 182–193 (1994)

351. Hinckley, K., Pausch, R., Goble, J.C., Kassell, N.F.: A Survey of Design Issues in Spatial Input. In: UIST '94: Proceedings of the ACM Symposium on User Interface Software & Technology, pp. 213–222. ACM Press, New York, NY (1994)

352. Hinckley, K., Pausch, R., Proffitt, D., Kassell, N.F.: Two-handed virtual manipulation. ACM Trans. Comput.-Hum. Interact. 5(3), 260–302 (1998)

353. Hinckley, K., Pierce, J., Sinclair, M., Horvitz, E.: Sensing techniques for mobile interaction. In: UIST '00: Proceedings of the 13th annual ACM symposium on User interface software and technology, pp. 91–100. ACM Press, New York, NY (2000)

354. Hinckley, K., Ramos, G., Guimbretiere, F., Baudisch, P., Smith, M.: Stitching: pen gestures that span multiple displays. In: AVI '04: Proceedings of the working conference on Advanced visual interfaces, pp. 23–31. ACM Press, New York, NY (2004)

355. Hinckley, K., Sinclair, M., Hanson, E., Szeliski, R., Conway, M.: The Video-Mouse: a camera-based multi-degree-of-freedom input device. In: UIST '99: Proceedings of the 12th annual ACM symposium on User interface software and technology, pp. 103–112. ACM Press, New York, NY (1999)

356. Ho, J., Hong, S.-H.: Drawing Clustered Graphs in Three Dimensions. In: Healy, P., Nikolov, N.S. (eds.) GD 2005. LNCS, vol. 3843, pp. 492–502. Springer, Berlin Heidelberg (2006)

357. Ho, J., Manwaring, T., Hong, S.-H., Roehm, U., Fung, D.C.Y., Xu, K., Kraska, T., Hart, D.: PathBank: Web-based Querying and Visualization of an Integrated Biological Pathway Database. In: 3rd International conference on Computer Graphics, Imaging and Visualization (CGIV06), page submitted (2006)

358. Hochheiser, H., Baehrecke, E., Mount, S., Shneiderman, B.: Dynamic Querying for Pattern Identification in Microarray and Genomic Data. In: Proc. IEEE Int'l Conf. Multimedia and Expo, IEEE Computer Society Press, Los Alamitos, CA (2003)

359. Hoffman, P.E.: Table Visualizations: A Formal Model and Its Applications (PhD Dissertation). Technical report, Department of Computer Science, University of Massachusets Lowell (1999)

360. Holman, D., Vertegaal, R., Altosaar, M., Troje, N., Johns, D.: Paper windows: interaction techniques for digital paper. In: CHI '05: Proceedings of the SIGCHI conference on Human factors in computing systems, pp. 591–599. ACM Press, New York, NY (2005)

361. Holtzblatt, K., Beyer, H.: Contextual design: using customer work models to drive systems design. In: CHI 98 conference summary on Human factors in computing systems, pp. 149–150. ACM Press, New York, NY (1998)

362. Hong, S.-H., Merrick, D., do Nascimento, H.A.D.: The Metro Map Layout Problem. In: Pach, J. (ed.) GD 2004. LNCS, vol. 3383, pp. 482–491. Springer, Berlin Heidelberg (2005)

363. Hong, S.-H., Murtagh, T.: Visualisation of Large and Complex Networks Using PolyPlane. In: Pach, J. (ed.) GD 2004. LNCS, vol. 3383, pp. 471–481. Springer, Berlin Heidelberg (2005)

364. Hong, S.-H., Nikolov, N.S.: Layered Drawings of Directed Graphs in Three Dimensions. In: Asia Pacific Symposium on Information Visualisation (APVIS2005), vol. 45 of CRPIT, pp. 69–74. ACS (2005)

365. Hopgood, F.: Computer Animation Used as a Tool in Teaching Computer Science. In: Proceedings IFIP Congress (1974)

366. Hornbaek, K.: Usability of Information Visualization: Reading and Interaction Processes. PhD thesis, Department of Computing. Faculty of Science. University of Copenhagen (2001)

367. Hornbaek, K., Bederson, B., Plaisant, C.: Navigation patterns and usability of zoomable user interfaces with and without an overview. ACM Trans. Comput.-Hum. Interact. 9(4), 362–389 (2002)
368. Hornof, A.J., Halverson, T.: Cognitive strategies and eye movements for searching hierarchical computer displays. In: CHI '03: Proceedings of the SIGCHI conference on Human factors in computing systems, pp. 249–256. ACM Press, New York, NY (2003)
369. House, D., Bair, A., Ware, C.: On the Optimization of Visualizations of Complex Phenomena. In: Proceedings Visualization, pp. 87–94. IEEE Computer Society Press, Los Alamitos, CA (2005)
370. House, D., Interrante, V., Laidlaw, D., Taylor, R., Ware, C.: Panel: Design and Evaluation in Visualization Research. In: Proceedings IEEE Visualization, pp. 705–708. IEEE Computer Society Press, Los Alamitos, CA (2005)
371. Hu, Z., Mellor, J., Wu, J., Yamada, T., Holloway, D., Delisi, C.: VisANT: data-integrating visual framework for biological networks and modules. Nucleic Acids Research 33, W352 (2005)
372. Huang, M.L., Eades, P.: A Fully Animated Interactive System for Clustering and Navigating Huge Graphs. In: Whitesides, S.H. (ed.) GD 1998. LNCS, vol. 1547, pp. 374–383. Springer, Berlin Heidelberg (1999)
373. Huang, W., Eades, P.: How People Read Graphs. In: Asia-Pacific Symposium on Information Visualisation, pp. 51–58 (2005)
374. Huang, W., Hong, S.-H., Eades, P.: Layout Effects on Sociogram Perception. In: Healy, P., Nikolov, N.S. (eds.) GD 2005. LNCS, vol. 3843, pp. 262–273. Springer, Berlin Heidelberg (2006)
375. Huang, W., Hong, S.-H., Eades, P.: Predicting Graph Reading Performance: A Cognitive Approach. In: Asia Pacific Symposium on Information Visualisation (APVIS2006), CRPIT, vol. 60, pp. 207–216. ACS (2006)
376. Hughes, T., Hyun, Y., Liberles, D.A.: Visualising very large phylogenetic trees in three dimensional hyperbolic space. BMC Bioinformatics 5 (April 2004)
377. Hundhausen, C.D., Brown, J.L.: What You See Is What You Code: A Radically Dynamic Algorithm Visualization Development Model for Novice Learners. In: VL/HCC, pp. 163–170 (2005)
378. Hundhausen, C.D., Douglas, S.: SALSA and ALVIS: A Language and System for Constructing and Presenting Low Fidelity Algorithm Visualizations. In: IEEE International Symposium on Visual Languages (VL'00), p. 67. IEEE Computer Society Press, Los Alamitos, CA (2000)
379. Hundhausen, C.D., Douglas, S.A., Stasko, J.T.: A Meta-Study of Algorithm Visualization Effectiveness. Journal of Visual Languages and Computing 13(3), 259–290 (2002)
380. Hundhausen, C.D., Wingstrom, J., Vatrapu, R.: The Evolving User-Centered Design of the Algorithm Visualization Storyboarder. In: VL/HCC, pp. 62–64 (2004)
381. IBM Lakes Team: IBM Lakes: An Architecture for Collaborative Networking. R. Morgan Publishing, Chislehurst (1994)
382. IEEE: 11th International Symposium on Haptic Interfaces for Virtual Environment and Teleoperator Systems (HAPTICS 2003), 22-23 March 2003, Los Angeles, CA, USA, Proceedings. IEEE Computer Society Press (2003)
383. Igarishi, T., Hinckley, K.: Speed-dependent automatic zooming for browsing large documents. In: Proceedings of the 13th Annual ACM Symposium on User Interface Software and Technology (UIST'00), pp. 139–148. ACM Press, New York, NY (2000)

384. Ihantola, P., Karavirta, V., Korhonen, A., Nikander, J.: Taxonomy of effort-less creation of algorithm visualizations. In: ICER '05: Proceedings of the 2005 international workshop on Computing education research, pp. 123–133. ACM Press, New York, NY (2005)

385. Immersion Corporation: Various Interaction Devices, http://www.immersion.com (2006)

386. International Nucleotide Sequence Database Collaboration. http://www.insdc.org/

387. Ino, S., Shimizu, S., Sato, T.O.M., Takahashi, M., Izumi, T., Ifukube, T.: A tactile display for presenting quality of materials by changing the temperature of skin surface. In: Proceedings, 2nd IEEE International Workshop on Robot and Human Communication, Nov. 2003, pp. 220–224. IEEE Computer Society Press, Los Alamitos, CA (1993)

388. Inselberg, A.: The plane with parallel coordinates. The. Visual Computer 1(2), 69–91 (1985)

389. Inselberg, A., Dimsdale, B.: Parallel Coordinates: A Tool for Visualizing Multi-Dimensional Geometry. In: Proceedings of the 1st Conference on Visualization '90, pp. 361–378. IEEE Computer Society Press, Los Alamitos, CA (1990)

390. Iqbal, R., Sturm, J., Kulyk, O., Wang, J., Terken, J.: User-Centred Design and Evaluation of Ubiquitous Services. In: International Conference on Design of Communication: Documenting and Designing for Pervasive Information, pp. 138–145. ACM Press, New York, NY (2005)

391. Irani, P., Ware, C.: Diagrams based on structural object perception. In: Proceedings of the working conference on Advanced visual interfaces, pp. 61–67. ACM Press, New York, NY (2000)

392. Irani, P., Ware, C.: Diagramming information structures using 3D perceptual primitives. ACM Transactions on Computer-Human Interaction 10(1), 1–19 (2003)

393. Isenhour, P., Begole, J.B., Heagy, W.S., Shaffer, C.A.: Sieve: A Java-Based Collaborative Visualization Environment. In: IEEE Visualization '97 Late Breaking Hot Topics Proceeding, pp. 13–16. IEEE Computer Society Press, Los Alamitos, CA (1997)

394. ISO: ISO 13407: Human-Centered Design Processes for Interactive Systems (1998)

395. ISO: ISO 9241: Ergonomic requirements for office work with visual display terminals (VDTs) - Part 11: Guidance on usability (1998)

396. Itti, L., Koch, C., Niebur, E.: A Model of Saliency-Based Visual Attention for Rapid Scene Analysis. IEEE Transactions on Pattern Analysis and Machine Intelligence 20(11), 1254–1259 (1998)

397. Iwata, H., Yano, H., Uemura, T., Moriya, T.: Food Simulator: A Haptic Interface for Biting. In: VR '04: Proceedings of the IEEE Virtual Reality 2004 (VR'04), IEEE Computer Society Press, Los Alamitos, CA (2004)

398. Jacob, R.J.: Commentary on Section 4. Eye tracking in human-computer interaction and usability research: Ready to deliver the promises

399. Jaimes, A., Sebe, N.: Multimodal Human Computer Interaction: A Survey. In: Computer Vision in Human-Computer Interaction: Workshop on HCI, pp. 1–15 (2005)

400. Jain, A.K., Mao, J., Mohiuddin, K.M.: Artificial Neural Networks: A Tutorial. Computer 29(3), 31–44 (1996)

401. Jalview Alignment Editor: http://www.jalview.org/

402. Jankun-Kelly, T.J., Ma, K.-L.: Visualization Exploration and Encapsulation via a Spreadsheet-like Interface. IEEE Transactions on Visualization and Computer Graphics 7(3), 275–287 (2001)

403. Jankun-Kelly, T.J., Ma, K.-L.: MoireGraphs: Radial Focus+Context Visualization and Interaction for Graphs with Visual Nodes. In: In Proceedings of the 9th IEEE Symposium on Information Visualization (InfoVis'03), pp. 59–66. IEEE Computer Society Press, Los Alamitos, CA (2003)
404. Jennings, C.: Robust Finger Tracking with Multiple Cameras. In: International Workshop on Recognition, Analysis, and Tracking of Faces and Gestures in Real-Time Systems, pp. 152–160 (1999)
405. Jepsen, M.L.: Smoke, Mirrors, and Manufacturable Displays. IEEE Computer Society Press 38(8), 63–67 (2005)
406. Jerding, D.F., Stasko, J.T.: The Information Mural: A Technique for Displaying and Navigating Large Information Spaces. IEEE Transactions on Visualization and Computer Graphics 4(3), 257–271 (1998)
407. Johanson, B., Hutchins, G., Winograd, T., Stone, M.: PointRight: experience with flexible input redirection in interactive workspaces. In: UIST '02: Proceedings of the 15th annual ACM symposium on User interface software and technology, pp. 227–234. ACM Press, New York, NY (2002)
408. Johnson, B., Shneiderman, B.: Treemaps: A Space-Filling Approach to the Visualization of Hierirchical Information Structures. In: Card, S., Mackinlay, J., Shneiderman, B. (eds.) Information Visualization: Using Vision to Think, pp. 152–159. Morgan Kaufmann, San Francisco, CA (1999)
409. Johnson, C.: Top Scientific Visualization Research Problems. IEEE Computer Graphics and Applications 24(4), 13–17 (2004)
410. Johnson, C., Moorehead, R., Munzner, T., Pfister, H., Rheingans, P., Yoo, T.S. (eds)· NIH-NSF Visualization Research Challenges Report, 1st edn. IEEE Computer Society Press, Los Alamitos, CA, http://tab.computer.org/vgtc/vrc/index.html (2006)
411. Johnson, C., Moorhead, R., Munzner, T., Pfister, H., Rheingans, P., Yoo, T.S.: Visualization Research Challenges. Technical report, NIH/NSF (January 2006)
412. Johnson, C., Sanderson, A.: A Next Step: Visualizing Errors and Uncertainty. IEEE Computer Graphics and Applications 23(5), 6–10 (2003)
413. Johnson, D.S., McGeoch, L.A.: The Traveling Salesman Problem: A Case Study. In: Aarts, E.H.L, Lenstra, J.K. (eds.) Local Search in Combinatorial Optimization, pp. 215–310. Wiley, Chichester (1997)
414. Johnson, G., Ebert, D., Hansen, C., Kirk, D., Mark, B., Pfister, H.: Panel: The Future Visualization Platform. In: Proceedings IEEE Visualization, pp. 569–571. IEEE Computer Society Press, Los Alamitos, CA (2004)
415. Johnson, G., Elvins, T.T.: Introduction to collaborative visualization. SIGGRAPH Comput. Graph. 32(2), 8–11 (1998)
416. Johnson, J.: GUI Bloopers. Morgan Kaufmann, San Francisco, CA (2000)
417. Jolliffe, I.: Principal Component Analysis. Springer, Berlin Heidelberg New York (2002)
418. Jones, S., Scaife, M.: Animated Diagrams: An investigation into the cognitive effects of using animation to illustrate dynamic processes. In: Anderson, M., Cheng, P., Haarslev, V. (eds.) Diagrams 2000. LNCS (LNAI), vol. 1889, pp. 1–3. Springer, Berlin Heidelberg (2000)
419. Joseph, J., LaViola, J., Feliz, D.A., Keefe, D.F., Zeleznik, R.C.: Hands-free multi-scale navigation in virtual environments. In: SI3D '01: Proceedings of the 2001 symposium on Interactive 3D graphics, pp. 9–15. ACM Press, New York, NY (2001)
420. Jünger, M., Mutzel, P. (eds.): Graph Drawing Software. Springer, Berlin Heidelberg New York (2003)
421. Kadmon, N., Shlomi, E.: A polyfocal projection for statistical surfaces. Cartograph 15(1), 36–40 (1978)

422. Kaiser, E., Olwal, A., McGee, D., Benko, H., Corradini, A., Li, X., Cohen, P.R., Feiner, S.: Mutual disambiguation of 3D multimodal interaction in augmented and virtual reality. In: ICMI '03: Proceedings of the 5th international conference on Multimodal interfaces, pp. 12–19. ACM Press, New York, NY (2003)

423. Kakoulis, K.G., Tollis, I.G.: An Algorithm for Labeling Edges of Hierarchical Drawings. In: DiBattista, G. (ed.) GD 1997. LNCS, vol. 1353, pp. 169–180. Springer, Berlin Heidelberg (1997)

424. Kakoulis, K.G., Tollis, I.G.: A Unified Approach to Labeling Graphical Features. In: Proceedings of the 14th ACM Symposium an Computational Geometry, pp. 347–356. ACM Press, New York, NY (1998)

425. Kalman, R.E.: A New Approach to Linear Filtering and Prediction Problems. Transactions of the ASME - Journal of Basic Engineering 82, 35–45 (1960)

426. Kamada, T., Kawai, S.: An algorithm for drawing general undirected graphs. Information Processing Letters 31(1), 7–15 (1989)

427. Kamba, T., Elson, S.A., Harpold, T., Stamper, T., Sukaviriya, P.: Using small screen space more efficiently. In: CHI '96: Proceedings of the SIGCHI conference on Human factors in computing systems, pp. 383–390. ACM Press, New York, NY (1996)

428. Kannusmäki, O., Moreno, A., Myller, N., Sutinen, E.: What a Novice Wants: Students Using Program Visualization in Distance Programming Course. In: Proceedings of the Third Program Visualization Workshop, pp. 126–133 (July 2004)

429. Karavirta, V., Korhonen, A., Malmi, L., Stalnacke, K.: MatrixPro - A Tool for On-The-Fly Demonstration of Data Structures and Algorithms. In: Proceedings of the Third Program Visualization Workshop, pp. 26–33 (July 2004)

430. Kato, H., Billinghurst, M., Poupyrev, I., Imamoto, K., Tachibana, K.: Virtual Object Manipulation on a Table-Top AR Environment. In: ISAR '00: Proceedings of the International Symposium on Augmented Reality, pp. 111–119 (2000)

431. Katzenmaier, M., Stiefelhagen, R., Schultz, T.: Identifying the addressee in human-human-robot interactions based on head pose and speech. In: ICMI '04: Proceedings of the 6th international conference on Multimodal interfaces, pp. 144–151. ACM Press, New York, NY (2004)

432. Kaufmann, M., Wagner, D. (eds.): Drawing Graphs. LNCS, vol. 2025. Springer, Berlin Heidelberg (2001)

433. Kawachiya, K., Ishikawa, H.: NaviPoint: An input device for mobile information browsing. In: CHI '98: Proceedings of the SIGCHI conference on Human factors in computing systems, pp. 1–8. ACM Press/Addison-Wesley (1998)

434. Kaye, J.J.: Making Scents: aromatic output for HCI. interactions 11(1), 48–61 (2004)

435. KDE - The K-Desktop Environment, http://www.kde.org

436. Keim, D.A.: Information Visualization and Visual Data Mining. IEEE Transactions on Visualization and Computer Graphics 7(1), 1–8 (2002)

437. Keim, D.A., Kriegel, H.-P.: Visualization Techniques for Mining Large Databases: A Comparison. IEEE Transactions on Knowledge and Data Engineering 8(6), 923–938 (1996)

438. Keim, D.A., Panse, C., Sips, M.: Information Visualization: Scope, Techniques and Opportunities for Geovisualization. In: Dykes, J. et al. (ed.) Exploring Geovisualization, pp. 23–52. Elsevier, Amsterdam (2005)

439. W. Keith Edwards, V. Bellotti, A. Dey, and M. Newman. Stuck in the Middle: The Challenges of User-Centered Design and Evaluation of Infrastructure. In: ACM Conference on Human Factors in Computing Systems (CHI'03) (2003)

440. Kerren, A., Stasko, J.: Algorithm Animation - Introduction. In: Diehl, S. (ed.) Software Visualization. LNCS, vol. 2269, pp. 1–15. Springer, Berlin Heidelberg (2002)

441. Keyson, D.V.: Dynamic Cursor Gain and Tactual Feedback in the Capture of Cursor Movements. Ergonomics 12, 1287–1298 (1997)
442. Khan, A., Fitzmaurice, G., Almeida, D., Burtnyk, N., Kurtenbach, G.: A remote control interface for large displays. In: UIST '04: Proceedings of the 17th annual ACM symposium on User interface software and technology, pp. 127–136. ACM Press, New York, NY (2004)
443. Khan, A., Komalo, B., Stam, J., Fitzmaurice, G., Kurtenbach, G.: HoverCam: interactive 3D navigation for proximal object inspection. In: SI3D '05: Proceedings of the 2005 symposium on Interactive 3D graphics and games, pp. 73–80. ACM Press, New York, NY (2005)
444. Khan, A., Matejka, J., Fitzmaurice, G., Kurtenbach, G.: Spotlight: Directing users' attention on large displays. In: CHI '05: Proceedings of the SIGCHI conference on Human factors in computing systems, pp. 791–798. ACM Press, New York, NY (2005)
445. Khoudja, B.M., Hafez, M., Alexandre, J., Kheddar, A.: Tactile Interfaces. A State of the Art Survey. In: International Symposium on Robotics, March 23-26 2004 (2004)
446. Khoudja, M.B., Hafez, M., Alexandre, J.M., Kheddar, A.: Thermal feedback interface requirements for virtual reality. In: Proceedings of the EuroHaptics 2003 (July 2003)
447. Kijimam, R., Hirose, M.: Representative Spherical Plane Method and Comsposition of Object Manipulation Methods. In: VRAIS '96: Proceedings of the 1996 Virtual Reality Annual International Symposium (VRAIS 96), IEEE Computer Society Press, Los Alamitos, CA (1996)
448. Kindlmann, G., Reinhard, E., Creem, S.: "Face-based Luminance Matching for Perceptual Colormap Generation". In: Proceedings of the 13th IEEE Visualization 2002 Conference (VIS-02), pp. 299–306. IEEE Computer Society Press, Los Alamitos, CA (2002)
449. Kirstein, C., Müller, H.: Intearction with a Projection Screen Using a Camera-Tracked Laser Pointer. In: MMM '98: Proceedings of the International Conference on Multimedia Modeling, p. 191 (1998)
450. Klau, G.W., Mutzel, P.: Combining Graph Labeling and Compaction. In: Kratochvíl, J. (ed.) GD 1999. LNCS, vol. 1731, pp. 27–37. Springer, Berlin Heidelberg (1999)
451. Kleiner, B., Hartigan, J.: Representing Points in Many Dimensions by Trees and Castles. Journal of the American Statistical Association 76, 260–272 (1981)
452. Knoche, H., McCarthy, J.D., Sasse, M.A.: Can small be beautiful?: Assessing image resolution requirements for mobile TV. In: MULTIMEDIA '05: Proceedings of the 13th annual ACM international conference on Multimedia, pp. 829–838. ACM Press, New York, NY (2005)
453. Knowlton, K.: L6: Bell Telephone Laboratories Low-Level Linked List Language. 16-minute black-and-white film (1966)
454. Kobsa, A.: An empirical comparison of three commercial information visualization systems. In: Symposium on Information Visualization, InfoVis 2001, pp. 123–130. IEEE Computer Society Press, Los Alamitos, CA (2001)
455. Kobsa, A.: User Experiments with Tree Visualization Systems. In: Proceedings of the IEEE Symposium on Information Visualization (InfoVis'04), pp. 9–16. IEEE Computer Society Press, Los Alamitos, CA (2004)
456. Koch, T.: The Map as Intent: Variations on the Theme of John Snow. Cartographica 39(4), 1–14 (2004)
457. Kölling, M., Barnes, D.J.: Enhancing apprentice-based learning of Java. In: Proceedings of the thirty-fifth SIGCSE technical symposium on computer science education, pp. 286–290. ACM Press, New York, NY (2004)

458. Koren, Y., Carmel, L., Harel, D.: ACE: A Fast Multiscale Eigenvectors Computation for Drawing Huge Graphs. In: INFOVIS '02: Proceedings of the IEEE Symposium on Information Visualization (InfoVis'02), p. 137. IEEE Computer Society Press, Los Alamitos, CA (2002)

459. Korhonen, A., Malmi, L., Nikander, J., Silvasti, P.: Algorithm Simulation– A Novel Way to Specify Algorithm Animations. In: Proceedings of the Second Program Visualization Workshop, pp. 28–36 (June 2002)

460. Körner, O., Männer, R.: Implementation of a Haptic Interface for a Virtual Reality Simulator for Flexible Endoscopy. In: HAPTICS '03: Proceedings of the 11th Symposium on Haptic Interfaces for Virtual Environment and Teleoperator Systems (HAPTICS'03), IEEE Computer Society Press, Los Alamitos, CA (2003)

461. Kosara, R., Bendix, F., Hauser, H.: TimeHistograms for Large, Time-Dependent Data. In: Proceedings of the Joint EG-IEEE TCVG Symposium on Visualization (VisSym) '04), pp. 45–54, 340. IEEE Computer Society Press, Los Alamitos, CA (2004)

462. Kosara, R., Hauser, H., Gresh, D.: An Interaction View on Information Visualization. In: Proceedings of Eurographics 2003, State of the Art Reports, pp. 123–137 (Sept 2003)

463. Kosara, R., Healey, C., Interrante, V., Laidlaw, D., Ware, C.: User Studies: Why, how, and when? IEEE Computer Graphics and Applications 23(4), 20–25 (2003)

464. Kosara, R., Healey, C.G., Interrante, V., Laidlaw, D.H., Ware, C.: User Studies: Why, How, and When? Computer Graphics and Applications 23(4), 20–25 (2003)

465. Kosara, R., Miksch, S.: Visualization Methods for Data Analysis and Planning in Medical Applications. International Journal of Medical Informatics 68, 141–153 (2002)

466. Kosara, R., Miksch, S., Hauser, H.: Semantic Depth of Field. In: IEEE Symposium on Information Visualization 2001 (InfoVis 2001), pp. 97–104. IEEE Computer Society Press, Los Alamitos, CA (2001)

467. Kosara, R., Miksch, S., Hauser, H., Schrammel, J., Giller, V., Tscheligi, M.: Useful Properties of Semantic Depth of Field for Better F+C Visualization. In: Proceedings of the Joint Eurographics - IEEE TCVG Symposium on Visualization 2002 (VisSym'02), pp. 205–210. IEEE Computer Society Press, Los Alamitos, CA (2002)

468. Kosara, R., Miksch, S., Shahar, Y., Johnson, P.: AsbruView: Capturing Complex, Time-oriented Plans - Beyond Flow-Charts (1998)

469. Kosslyn, S.M.: Elements of Graph Design. W. H. Freeman and Company, New York (1994)

470. Koua, E.L., Kraak, M.-J.: A Usability Framework for the Design and Evaluation of an Exploratory Geovisualization Environment. In: Proceedings of the Eighth International Conference on Information Visualisation (IV '04), pp. 153–158 (2004)

471. Koua, E.L., Kraak, M.-J.: Geovisualization to Support the Exploration of Large Health and Demographic Survey Data. International Journal of Health Geographics 3 (2004)

472. Koussoulakou, A., Kraak, M.-J.: Spatio-Temporal Maps and Cartographic Communication. The. Cartographic Journal 29, 101–108 (1992)

473. Kraak, M.-J.: Geovisualization Illustrated. ISPRS Journal of Photogrammetry and Remote Sensing 57, 390–399 (2003)

474. Krackhardt, D.: Social networks and the liability of newness for managers. Trends in Organizational Behavior 3, 159–173 (1996)

475. Kron, A., Schmidt, G.: Multi-Fingered Tactile Feedback from Virtual and Remote Environments. In: HAPTICS, pp. 16–23 (2003)
476. Kron, A., Schmidt, G.: Haptisches Telepräsenzsystem zur Unterstützung bei Entschärfungstätigkeiten: Systemgestaltung, Regelung und Evaluation (Haptic Telepresence System for Support of Disposal of Explosive Ordnances: Design Issues, Control, and Evaluation). at - Automatisierungstechnik 53(3), 101–113 (2005)
477. Krum, D.M., Omoteso, O., Ribarsky, W., Starner, T., Hodges, L.F.: Speech and gesture multimodal control of a whole Earth 3D visualization environment. In: VISSYM '02: Proceedings of the symposium on Data Visualisation 2002, pp. 195–200. Eurographics Association (2002)
478. Krum, D.M., Ribarsky, W., Shaw, C.D., Hodges, L.F., Faust, N.: Situational visualization. In: VRST '01: Proceedings of the ACM symposium on Virtual reality software and technology, pp. 143–150. ACM Press, New York, NY (2001)
479. Krygier, J.B.: Sound and Geographic Visualization. In: MacEachren, A.M., Taylor, D.F. (eds.) Visualization in Modern Cartography, pp. 149–166. Pergamon Press, Oxford (1994)
480. Kujala, S., Kauppinen, M.: Identifying and Selecting Users for User-Centered Design. In: Nordic Conference on Computer-Human Interaction, pp. 297–303. ACM Press, New York, NY (2004)
481. Kulyk, O., Wang, J., Terken, J.: Realtime Feeback on Nonverbal Behaviour to Enhance Social Dynamics in Small Group Meetings. In: Renals, S., Bengio, S. (eds.) MLMI 2005. LNCS, vol. 3869, Springer, Berlin Heidelberg (2006)
482. Kulyk, O., Wassink, I.: Getting to know bioinformaticians: Results of an exploratory user study. In: British HCI'06 Workshop on Combining Visualisation and Interaction to Facilitate Scientific Exploration and Discovery (2006)
483. Kumar, S., Cohen, P.R.: Towards a fault-tolerant multi-agent system architecture. In: AGENTS '00: Proceedings of the fourth international conference on Autonomous agents, pp. 459–466. ACM Press, New York, NY (2000)
484. Künzler, U., Runde, C.: Kinesthetic Haptics Integration into Large-Scale Virtual Environments. In: WHC, pp. 551–556. IEEE Computer Society Press, Los Alamitos, CA (2005)
485. Kurtenbach, G., Buxton, W.: User Learning and Performance with Marking Menus. In: Proceedings of ACM CHI'94 Conference on Human Factors in Computing Systems. Pen Input, vol. 1, pp. 258–264. ACM Press, New York, NY (1994)
486. Laakso, M.-J., Salakoski, T., Gradell, L., Qiu, X., Korhonen, A., Malmi, L.: Multi-Perspective Study of Novice Learners Adopting the Visual Algorithm Simulation Exercise System TRAKLA2. Informatics in Education 4(1), 49–68 (2005)
487. Lamping, J., Rao, R.: Laying Out and Visualizing Large Trees Using a Hyperbolic Space. In: Proceedings of the ACM Symposium on User Interface Software and Technology (UIST '94), pp. 13–14. ACM Press, New York, NY (1994)
488. Lamping, J., Rao, R., Pirolli, P.: A Focus+Context Technique Based on Hyperbolic Geometry for Visualizing Large Hierarchies. In: Proceedings of the Conference on Human Factors in Computing Systems (CHI '95), pp. 401–408 (1995)
489. Lang, U., Peltier, J.P., Christ, P., Rill, S., Rantzau, D., Nebel, H., Wierse, A., Lang, R., Causse, S., Juaneda, F., Grave, M., Haas, P.: Perspectives of collaborative supercomputing and networking in European aerospace research and industry. Future Generation Computuer Systems 11(4-5), 419–430 (1995)
490. Laramee, R.S.: FIRST: A Flexible and Interactive Resampling Tool for CFD Simulation Data. Computers & Graphics 27(6), 905–916 (2003)

491. Laramee, R.S., Bergeron, R.D.: An Isosurface Continuity Algorithm for Super Adaptive Resolution Data. In: Advances in Modelling, Animation, and Rendering: Computer Graphics International (CGI 2002), pp. 215–237. Computer Graphics Society/Springer, Berlin Heidelberg (2002)

492. Laramee, R.S., Garth, C., Doleisch, H., Schneider, J., Hauser, H., Hagen, H.: Visual Analysis and Exploration of Fluid Flow in a Cooling Jacket. In: Proceedings IEEE Visualization 2005, pp. 623–630. IEEE Computer Society Press, Los Alamitos, CA (2005)

493. Laramee, R.S., Hauser, H.: Interactive 3D Flow Visualization Using Textures and Geometric Primitives. In: NAFEMS World Congress Conference Proceedings, p. 75. NAFEMS–The International Association for the Engineering Analysis Community, May 17–20 2005, full proceedings on CDROM

494. Laramee, R.S., Hauser, H., Doleisch, H., Post, F.H., Vrolijk, B., Weiskopf, D.: The State of the Art in Flow Visualization: Dense and Texture-Based Techniques. Computer Graphics Forum 23(2), 203–221 (2004)

495. Laramee, R.S., Ware, C.: Rivalry and Interference with a Head Mounted Display. ACM Transactions on Computer-Human Interaction (TOCHI) 9(3), 238–251 (2002)

496. Laramee, R.S., Weiskopf, D., Schneider, J., Hauser, H.: Investigating Swirl and Tumble Flow with a Comparison of Visualization Techniques. In: Proceedings IEEE Visualization, pp. 51–58. IEEE Computer Society Press, Los Alamitos, CA (2004)

497. Larkin, J., Simon, H.: Why a Diagram is (Sometimes) Worth Ten Thousand Words. Cognitive Science 11, 65–99 (1987)

498. Latour, B., Woolgar, S.: Laboratory Life, vol. 60 Sage, Beverly Hills, CA (1979)

499. Lauesen, S.: User interface design. Addison-Wesley, Reading, MA (2005)

500. LeBlanc, J., Ward, M.O., Wittels, N.: Exploring N-dimensional databases. In: VIS '90: Proceedings of the 1st conference on Visualization '90, pp. 230–237. IEEE Computer Society Press, Los Alamitos, CA (1990)

501. Lee, M.D., Reilly, R.E., Butavicius, M.E.: An empirical evaluation of Chernoff faces, star glyphs, and spatial visualizations for binary data. In: APVis '03: Proceedings of the Asia-Pacific symposium on Information visualisation, pp. 1–10. Australian Computer Society, Inc (2003)

502. Leganchuk, A., Zhai, S., Buxton, W.: Manual and cognitive benefits of two-handed input: an experimental study. ACM Transactions on Computer-Human Interaction 5(4), 326–359 (1998)

503. Lester, J., Converse, S., Kahler, S., Barlow, T., Stone, B., Bhoga, R.: The Persona Effect: Affective Impact of Animated Pedagogical Agents. In: CHI '97: CHI '97 extended abstracts on Human factors in computing systems, pp. 359–366. ACM Press, New York, NY (1997)

504. Levoy, M.: Spreadsheets for images. In: Proceedings of ACM SIGGRAPH 1994, Computer Graphics Procceedings, Annual Conference Series, pp. 139–146. ACM Press, New York, NY (1994)

505. v. Liere, R., de Leeuw, J., Mulder, J., Verschure, P., Visser, A., Manders, E., v. Driel, R.: Virtual Reality in Biological Microscopic Imaging. In: International, I.E.E.E. (ed.) Symposium on Biomedical Imaging, pp. 879–882. IEEE Computer Society Press, Los Alamitos, CA (2002)

506. Likert, R.A.: A Technique for the Measurement of Attitudes. Archives of Psychology 140, 1–55 (1932)

507. Lind, M., Bingham, G.P., Forsell, C.: The Illusion of Perceived Metric 3D Structure. In: IEEE Symposium on Information Visualization (InfoVis), pp. 51–56. IEEE Computer Society Press, Los Alamitos, CA (2002)

508. Lipton, R.J., North, S.C., Sandberg, J.S.: A method for drawing graphs. In: Proceedings of the first annual symposium on Computational geometry, pp. 153–160. ACM Press, New York, NY (1985)

509. Liu, A., Tendick, F., Cleary, K., Kaufmann, C.: A survey of surgical simulation: applications, technology, and education. Presence: Teleoper. Virtual Environ. 12(6), 599–614 (2003)

510. Lodha, S.K., Pang, A., Sheehan, R.E., Wittenbrink, C.M.: UFLOW: Visualizing Uncertainty in Fluid Flow. In: Proceedings IEEE Visualization '96, pp. 249–254. IEEE Computer Society Press, Los Alamitos, CA (1996)

511. Logitech: Logitech®Cordless Rumblepad^{TM}2 Vibration Feedback Gamepad, http://www.logitech.com (2006)

512. Longabaugh, W.J., Davidson, E.H., Bolouri, H.: Computational representation of developmental genetic regulatory networks. Developmental Biology 283, 1–16 (2005)

513. Longley, P.A., Goodchild, M.F., Maguire, D.J., Rhind, D.W.: Geographical Information Systems and Science. Wiley, Chichester (2005)

514. Lord, H.: Improving the Application Development Process with Modular Visualization Environments. Computer Graphics 29(2), 10–12 (1995)

515. Lorensen, B.: Panel Statement: On the Death of Visualization: Can It Survive Without Customers. In: NIH/NSF Fall 2004 Workshop on Visualization Research Challenges, http://visual.nlm.nih.gov (Sept 2004)

516. Lovegrove, S., Brodlie, K.W.: Collaborative Research Within a Sustainable Community: Interactive Multi User VRML and Visualization. In: Eurographics UK Conference, pp. 53–68. Eurographics (March 1998)

517. Lowenthal, M.: Intelligence: From Secrets to Policy. CQ Press, Washington, DC (2000)

518. Ma, K.-L.: Visualizing Visualizations: User Interfaces for Managing and Exploring Scientific Visualization Data. IEEE Computer Graphics and Applications 20(5), 16–19 (2000)

519. MacEachren, A.M.: How Maps Work: Representation, Visualization, and Design. Guilford, New York, NY (1995)

520. MacEachren, A.M.: An Evolving Cognitive-Semiotic Approach to Geographic Visualization and Knowledge Construction. Information Design Journal 10, 26–36 (2001)

521. MacEachren, A.M.: Moving Geovisualization Toward Support for Group Work. In: Dykes, J. et al. (ed.) Exploring Geovisualization, pp. 445–462. Elsevier, Amsterdam (2005)

522. MacEachren, A.M., Boscoe, F.P., Haug, D., Pickle, L.W.: Geographic Visualization: Designing Manipulable Maps for Exploring Temporally Varying Georeferenced Statistics. In: Proceedings Information Visualization '98, pp. 87–94. IEEE Computer Society Press, Los Alamitos, CA (1998)

523. MacEachren, A.M., Brewer, I.: Developing a Conceptual Framework for Visually-Enabled Geocollaboration. International Journal of Geographical Information Science 18(1), 1–34 (2004)

524. MacEachren, A.M., Cai, G., Sharma, R., Rauschert, I., Brewer, I., Bolelli, L., Shaparenko, B., Fuhrmann, S., Wang, H.: Enabling Collaborative Geoinformation Access and Decision-Making Through a Natural, Multimodal Interface. International Journal of Geographical Information Science 19(3), 293–317 (2005)

525. MacEachren, A.M., Edsall, R., Huag, D., Baxter, R., Otto, G., Masters, R., Fuhrmann, S., Qian, L.: Virtual Environments for Geographic Visualization: Potential and Challenges. In: Proceedings of the ACM Workshop on New Paradigms in Information Visualization and Manipulation (1999)

526. MacEachren, A.M., Gahegan, M., Pike, W., Brewer, I., Cai, G., Lengerich, E., Hardisty, F.: Geovisualization for knowledge construction and decision support. Computer Graphics and Applications, IEEE 24(1), 13–17 (2004)
527. MacEachren, A.M., Ganter, J.H.: A Pattern Identification Approach to Cartographic Visualization. Cartographica 27(2), 64–81 (1990)
528. MacEachren, A.M., Kraak, M.-J.: Research Challenges in Geovisualization. Cartography and Geographic Information Science 28(1), 3–12 (2001)
529. Machiraju, R., Johnson, C., Yoo, T., Crawfis, R., Ebert, D., Stredney, D.: Do I Really See A Bone? In: Visualization Panels, pp. 615–617. IEEE Computer Society Press, Los Alamitos, CA (2003)
530. Mackay, E., Wendy,: Ethics, lies and videotape. In: SIGCHI conference on Human factors in computing systems, pp. 138–145. Addison-Wesley/ACM Press, New York, NY (1995)
531. MacKenzie, I.S.: Movement time prediction in human-computer interfaces. In: Proceedings of Graphics Interface '92, pp. 140–150 (May 1992)
532. MacKenzie, I.S., Jusoh, S.: An Evaluation of Two Input Devices for Remote Pointing. In: EHCI '2001: Proceedings of the Eighth IFIP Working Conference on Engineering for Human-Computer Interaction, pp. 235–249 (2001)
533. MacKenzie, I.S., Ware, C.: Lag as a Determinant of Human Performance in Interactive Systems. In: INTERCHI'93 Conference on Human Factors in Computing Systems, pp. 488–493 (1993)
534. Mackinlay, J.D., Card, S.K., Robertson, G.G.: Rapid controlled movement through a virtual 3D workspace. In: SIGGRAPH '90: Proceedings of the 17th annual conference on Computer graphics and interactive techniques, pp. 171–176. ACM Press, New York, NY (1990)
535. Mackinlay, J.D., Robertson, G.G., Card, S.K.: The Perspective Wall: Detail and Context Smoothly Integrated. In: Proceedings of the Conference on Human Factors in Computing Systems (CHI '91), pp. 173–179 (Apr 1991)
536. Madhavapeddy, A., Ludlam, N.: Ubiquitous Computing needs to catch up with Ubiquitous Media. In: Pervasive 2005 UbiApps Workshop (May 2005)
537. Madhavapeddy, A., Scott, D., Sharp, R., Upton, E.: Using Camera-Phones to Enhance Human-Computer Interaction. In: Sixth International Conference on Ubiquitous Computing (Adjunct Proceedings: Demos) (2004)
538. Maizel, J., Lenk, R.: Enhanced Graphic Matrix Analysis of Nucleic Acid and Protein Sequences. In: Proceedings of the National Academy of Science, pp. 7665–7669 (1981)
539. Malik, S., Laszlo, J.: Visual Touchpad: A Two-Handed Gestural Input Device. In: ICMI '04: Proceedings of the 6th international conference on Multimodal interfaces, pp. 289–296. ACM Press, New York, NY (2004)
540. Malik, S., Ranjan, A., Balakrishnan, R.: Interacting with large displays from a distance with vision-tracked multi-finger gestural input. In: UIST '05: Proceedings of the 18th annual ACM symposium on User interface software and technology, pp. 43–52. ACM Press, New York, NY (2005)
541. Malmi, L., Karavirta, V., Korhonen, A., Nikander, J., Seppälä, O., Silvasti, P.: Visual Algorithm Simulation Exercise System with Automatic Assessment: TRAKLA2. Informatics in Education 3(2), 267–288 (2004)
542. Manning, J., Atallah, M.J., Cudjoe, K., Lozito, J., Pacheco, R.: A System for Drawing Graphs with Geometric Symmetry. In: Tamassia, R., Tollis, I.(Y.) G. (eds.) GD 1994. LNCS, vol. 894, pp. 262–265. Springer, Berlin Heidelberg (1995)
543. Marchette, D.J., Solka, J.L.: Using Data Images for Outlier Detection. Computational Statistics & Data Analysis 43, 541–552 (2003)
544. Mardia, K.V.: Multivariate Analysis. Academic Press, London (1979)
545. Marketmap: Marketmap, www.smartmoney.com/marketmap (2006)

546. Massie, T., Salisbury, J.: The PHANToM Haptic Interface: A Device for Probing Virtual Objects. In: Proceedings of the ASME Winter Annual Meeting, Symposium on Haptic Interfaces for Virtual Environments and Teleoperator Systems, Chicago, USA, pp. 295–302 (Nov 1994)

547. Maybury, M., Lee, J.: The Structure of Multimodal Dialogue - Multimedia and Multimodal Interaction Structure, vol. 2, pp. 295–308. John Benjamins, Amsterdam/Philadelphia (2000)

548. Mayhew, D.: The usability engineering cycle. Morgan Kaufmann Publishers, San Francicso, CA (1999)

549. Mayor, C., Brudno, M., Schwartz, J.R., Poliakov, A., Rubin, E.M., Frazer, K.A., Pachter, L.S., Dubchak, I.: VISTA: Visualizing global DNA sequence alignments of arbitrary length. Bioinformatics 16(11), 1046–1047 (2000)

550. McCormick, B., DeFanti, T., Brown, M.: Visualization in Scientific Computing. Technical report, The National Science Foundation (NSF) (1987)

551. McDonnell, K.T., Qin, H., Wlodarczyk, R.A.: Virtual clay: a real-time sculpting system with haptic toolkits. In: SI3D '01: Proceedings of the 2001 symposium on Interactive 3D graphics, pp. 179–190. ACM Press, New York, NY (2001)

552. McGrath, C., Blythe, J., Krackhardt, D.: Seeing Groups in Graph Layouts. Connections 19, 22–29 (1996)

553. McGrath, C., Blythe, J., Krackhardt, D.: The effect of spatial arrangement on judgments and errors in interpreting graphs. Social Networks 19, 223–242 (1997)

554. McMillan, W.W.: The robot's sense of touch: Some lessons from human taction. In: CSC '84: Proceedings of the ACM 12th annual computer science conference on SIGCSE symposium, pp. 95–97. ACM Press, New York, NY (1984)

555. Medina-Sánchez, M., Lázaro-Carrascosa, C., Pareja-Flores, C., Urquiza-Fuentes, J., Velázquez-Iturbide, J.: Empirical Evaluation of Usability of Animations in a Functional Programming Environment. In: Technical report, Departamento de Sistemas Informáticos y Programación, Universidad Complutense de Madrid. Technical report 141/04 (2004)

556. Mehrabian, A.: Communication Without Words. Psychology today : a general magazine about the disciplines of psychology 2(4) (1968)

557. Meissner, M., Zuiderveld, K., Harris, G., Lesser, J.R., Persson, A., Vannier, M.: Panel: End Users' Perspectives on Volume Rendering in Medical Imaging: A job well done or not over yet?. In: Proceedings IEEE Visualization, pp. 711–714. IEEE Computer Society Press, Los Alamitos, CA (2005)

558. Mine, M.R.: Virtual Environment Interaction Techniques. Technical report, University of North Carolina at Chapel Hill (1995)

559. Mine, M.R., Frederick, J., Brooks, P., Sequin, C.H.: Moving objects in space: exploiting proprioception in virtual-environment interaction. In: SIGGRAPH '97: Proceedings of the 24th annual conference on Computer graphics and interactive techniques, pp. 19–26. Addison-Wesley/ACM Press, New York, NY (1997)

560. Minnotte, M.C., Webster, R.: The Data Image: A Tool for Exploring High Dimensional Data Sets. In: 1998 Proceedings of the ASA Section on Statistical Graphics, pp. 25–33 (1998)

561. Mitchell, K., Race, N.J.P., Clarke, M.: CANVIS: Context-aware network visualization using smartphones. In: MobileHCI '05: Proceedings of the 7th international conference on Human computer interaction with mobile devices & services, pp. 175–182. ACM Press, New York, NY (2005)

562. Miyaoku, K., Higashino, S., Tonomura, Y.: C-blink: A hue-difference-based light signal marker for large screen interaction via any mobile terminal. In: UIST '04: Proceedings of the 17th annual ACM symposium on User interface software and technology, pp. 147–156. ACM Press, New York, NY (2004)

563. Moeslund, T.B., Granum, E.: A Survey of Computer Vision-Based Human Motion Capture. Comput. Vis. Image Underst. 81(3), 231–268 (2001)
564. Moeslund, T.B., Storring, M., Granum, E.: A Natural Interface to a Virtual Environment through Computer Vision-Estimated Pointing Gestures. In: Gesture Workshop, pp. 59–63 (2001)
565. Monkman, G., Taylor, P.: Thermal Tactile Sensing. IEEE Trans. Rob. Automat 9(3), 313–318 (1993)
566. Monmonier, M.: Geographic Brushing: Enhancing Exploratory Analysis of the Scatterplot Matrix. Geographical Analysis 21(1), 81–84 (1989)
567. Moody, J.: Peer Influence Groups - Identifying Dense Clusters in Large Networks. Social Networks 23, 261–283 (2001)
568. Moreno, A., Myller, N.: Producing an Educationally Effective and Usable Tool for Learning, The Case of the Jeliot Family. In: Proceedings of International Conference on Networked e-learning for European Universities (CD–ROM publication) (2003)
569. Moreno, A., Myller, N., Sutinen, E., Ben-Ari, M.: Visualizing programs with Jeliot 3. In: AVI, pp. 373–376 (2004)
570. Morgan, D.: Focus groups as qualitative research, 2nd edn. Sage, Thousand Oaks, CA (1997)
571. Morris, C.J., Ebert, D.S., Rheingans, P.L.: Experimental analysis of the effectiveness of features in Chernoff faces. 28th AIPR Workshop: 3D Visualization for Data Exploration and Decision Making 3905(1), 12–17 (2000)
572. Morris, C.J., Ebert, D.S., Rheingans, P.L.: Experimental Analysis of the Effectiveness of Features in Chernoff Faces. In: 28th AIPR Workshop: 3D Visualization for Data Exploration and Decision Making, Proc. of SPIE, vol. 3905, pp. 12–17 (2000)
573. Morris, M.R., Paepcke, A., Winograd, T., Stamberger, J.: TeamTag: Exploring Centralized Versus Replicated Controls for Co-Located Tabletop Groupware. In: CHI '06: Proceedings of the SIGCHI Conference on Human Factors in Computing Systems, pp. 1273–1282. ACM Press, New York, NY (2006)
574. Morris, S.A., Asnake, B., Yen, G.G.: Dendrogram seriation using simulated annealing. Information Visualization 2(2), 95–104 (2003)
575. Morrison, A., Chalmers, M.: A pivot-based routine for improved parent-finding in hybrid MDS. Information Visualization 3(2), 109–122 (2004)
576. Morrison, A., Ross, G., Chalmers, M.: Fast multidimensional scaling through sampling, springs and interpolation. Information Visualization 2(1), 68–77 (2003)
577. Morrison, G.D.: A Camera-Based Input Device for Large Interactive Displays. IEEE Computer Graphics and Applications 25(4), 52–57 (2005)
578. Morrison, G.D., Holmgren, D.: Toward a Touch-Sensitive Display Wall. SID Symposium Digest of Technical Papers 34(1), 1458–1461 (2003)
579. Morrison, J.B., Bétrancourt, M., Tversky, B.: Animation: Does it Facilitate Learning. In: Proceedings of the AAAI 2000 Spring Symposium Smart Graphics, pp. 53–60 (2000)
580. Moskal, B., Lurie, D., Cooper, S.: Evaluating the effectiveness of a new instructional approach. SIGCSE Bull. 36(1), 75–79 (2004)
581. Moustakides, G., Botto, J.-L.: Stabilizing the fast Kalman algorithms (see also IEEE Transactions on Signal Processing). IEEE Transactions on Acoustics, Speech, and Signal Processing 37, 1342–1348 (1989)
582. Müldner, T., Shakshuki, E., Kerren, A., Shen, Z., Bai, X.: Using Structured Hypermedia to Explain Algorithms. In: Proceedings of the 3rd IADIS International Conference e-Society '05, pp. 499–503. IADIS (2005)

583. Munzner, T., Guimbretière, F., Tasiran, S., Zhang, L., Zhou, Y.: TreeJexta-poser: Scalable Tree Comparison Using Focus+Contex with Guaranteed Visi-bility. ACM Transactions on Graphics (SIGGRAPH'03) 22(3), 453–462 (2003)
584. Munzner, T.: Exploring Large Graphs in 3D Hyperbolic Space. IEEE Comput. Graph. Appl. 18(4), 18–23 (1998)
585. Munzner, T.: Interactive visualization of large graphs and networks. PhD thesis, Stanford University (2000)
586. Myers, B.A.: Visual programming, programming by example, and program vi-sualization: a taxonomy. In: Proceedings of the SIGCHI conference on Human factors in computing systems, pp. 59–66. ACM Press, New York, NY (1986)
587. Myers, B.A.: Taxonomies of Visual Programming and Program Visualization. Journal of Visual Languages and Computing 1(1), 97–1232 (1990)
588. Myers, B.A., Bhatnagar, R., Nichols, J., Peck, C.H., Kong, D., Miller, R., Long, A.C.: Interacting at a distance: measuring the performance of laser pointers and other devices. In: CHI '02: Proceedings of the SIGCHI conference on Human factors in computing systems, pp. 33–40. ACM Press, New York, NY (2002)
589. Myers, B.A., Peck, C.H., Nichols, J., Kong, D., Miller, R.: Interacting at a Distance Using Semantic Snarfing. In: Abowd, G.D., Brumitt, B., Shafer, S. (eds.) Ubicomp 2001: Ubiquitous Computing. LNCS, vol. 2201, pp. 305–314. Springer, Berlin Heidelberg (2001)
590. Nakatani, M., Kajimoto, H., Kawakami, N., Tachi, S.: Tactile sensation with high-density pin-matrix. In: APGV '05: Proceedings of the 2nd symposium on Appied perception in graphics and visualization, pp. 169–169. ACM Press, New York, NY (2005)
591. Naps, T.L.: JHAVé – Addressing the Need to Support Algorithm Visualization with Tools for Active Engagement. In: IEEE Computer Graphics and Applica-tions, IEEE Computer Society Press, Los Alamitos, CA (2005)
592. Naps, T.L., Bressler, E.: A multi-windowed environment for simultaneous vi-sualization of related algorithms on the World Wide Web. In: SIGCSE '98: Proceedings of the twenty-ninth SIGCSE technical symposium on Computer science education, pp. 277–281. ACM Press, New York, NY (1998)
593. Naps, T.L., Cooper, S., Koldehofe, B., Leska, C., Rößling, G., Dann, W., Ko-rhonen, A., Malmi, L., Rantakokko, J., Ross, R.J., Anderson, J., Fleischer, R., Kuittinen, M., McNally, M.: Evaluating the educational impact of visualization. SIGCSE Bull. 35(4), 124–136 (2003)
594. T. L. Naps and S. Grissom. The effective use of quicksort visualizations in the classroom. *J. Comput. Small Coll.*, 18(1):88–96, 2002.
595. Naps, T.L., Rößling, G., Almstrum, V., Dann, W., Fleischer, R., Hundhausen, C., Korhonen, A., Malmi, L., McNally, M., Rodger, S., Velázquez-Iturbide, J.A.: Exploring the role of visualization and engagement in computer science educa-tion. In: ITiCSE-WGR '02: Working group reports from ITiCSE on Innovation and technology in computer science education, pp. 131–152. ACM Press, New York, NY (2002)
596. NASA Advanced Supercomputing Division (NAS). Flow Analysis Soft-ware Toolkit (FAST), http://www.nas.nasa.gov/Resources/Software/swdescriptions.html 2006
597. Nass, C., Steuer, J., Tauber, E.R.: Computers are social actors. In: CHI '94: Proceedings of the SIGCHI conference on Human factors in computing systems, pp. 72–78. ACM Press, New York, NY (1994)
598. National Research Council, Committee on Intersections Between Geospatial In-formation and Information Technology: IT Roadmap to a Geospatial Future. National Academies Press (2003)
599. NaturalPoint® Inc.: OptiTrack^{TM}, http://www.naturalpoint.com (2006)
600. NCSA. Habanero, http://www.isrl.uiuc.edu/isaac/Habanero/ (2006)

601. Neale, D.C., Carroll, J.M., Rosson, M.B.: Evaluating Computer-Supported Co-operative Work: Models and Frameworks. In: ACM Conference on Computer Supported Cooperative Work (CSCW '04), pp. 112–121. ACM Press, New York, NY (2004)
602. Nesbitt, K., Barrass, S.: Finding trading patterns in stock market data. IEEE Computer Graphics and Applications 24(5), 45–55 (2004)
603. Newsmap: Newsmap, http://www.marumushi.com/apps/newsmap/newsmap.cfm (2006)
604. Ni, T., Schmidt, G.S., Staadt, O.G., Livingston, M.A., Ball, R., May, R.: A Survey of Large High-Resolution Display Technologies, Techniques, and Appli-cations. In: VR 2006: Proceedings of the IEEE International Virtual Reality Conference, IEEE Computer Society Press, Los Alamitos, CA (2006)
605. Nickel, K., Stiefelhagen, R.: Pointing gesture recognition based on 3D-tracking of face, hands, and head-orientation. In: Proceedings of the International Con-ference on Multimodal Interfaces, pp. 140–146 (2002)
606. Nielsen, J.: Usability Engineering. Morgan Kaufmann, San Francisco (1994)
607. Nielsen, J., Levy, J.: Measuring usability: Preference vs. performance. Commu-nications of the ACM 37(4), 66–75 (1994)
608. Nielson, G.M., Hagen, H., Müller, H. (eds.): Scientific Visualization: Overviews, Methodologies, and Techniques. IEEE Computer Society Press, Los Alamitos, CA (1997)
609. Nijholt, A.: Algorithms in Ambient Intelligence. In: Multimodality and Ambient Intelligence. Philips Research Book Series, vol. 2, pp. 21–53. Kluwer Academic Publishers, Dordrecht (2003)
610. Nijholt, A., Hondorp, H.: Towards communicating agents and avatars in virtual worlds. In: Proceedings EUROGRAPHICS 2000, pp. 91–95 (August 2000)
611. Nijholt, A., Rist, T., Tuijnenbreijer, K.: Lost in ambient intelligence?. In: CHI '04: CHI '04 extended abstracts on Human factors in computing systems, pp. 1725–1726. ACM Press, New York, NY (2004)
612. Nixon, M.A., McCalum, B.C., Fright, W.R., Price, N.B.: The Effects of Met-als and Interfering Fields on Electromagnetic Trackers. Presence 7(2), 204–218 (1998)
613. National Library of Medicine, http://www.nlm.nih.gov
614. noDNA GmbH Realtime Interactive Solutions. X-IST DataGlove, http://www.nodna.com (2006)
615. Nöllenburg, M., Wolff, A.: A Mixed-Integer Program for Drawing High-Quality Metro Maps. In: Healy, P., Nikolov, N.S. (eds.) GD 2005. LNCS, vol. 3843, pp. 321–333. Springer, Berlin Heidelberg (2006)
616. Norman, D.: The Design of Everyday Things. MIT Press, Cambridge, MA (1988)
617. North, C., Rhyne, T.-M., Duca, K.: Bioinformatics Visualization: Introduction to the Special Issue. Information Visualization 4(3), 147–148 (2005)
618. North, C., Shneiderman, B.: Snap-together visualization: can users construct and operate coordinated visualizations?. International Journal of Human-Computer Studies 53(5), 715–741 (2000)
619. North, C., Shneiderman, B., Plaisant, C.: User controlled overviews of an image library: A case study of the Visible Human. In: Proceedings of the 1st ACM International Conference on Digital Libraries (DL'96), pp. 74–82. ACM Press, New York, NY (1995)
620. Northern Digital Inc. (NDI): Polaris®, http://www.ndigital.com/ (2006)
621. Nowell, L., Hetzler, E., Tanasse, T.: Change blindness in information visualiza-tion: a case study. In: IEEE Symposium on Information Visualization (InfoVis 2001), pp. 15–22. IEEE Computer Society Press, Los Alamitos, CA (2001)

622. Odell, D.L., Davis, R.C., Smith, A., Wright, P.K.: Toolglasses, marking menus, and hotkeys: a comparison of one and two-handed command selection techniques. In: GI '04: Proceedings of the 2004 conference on Graphics interface, pp. 17–24. Canadian Human-Computer Communications Society (2004)
623. Oh, J.-Y., Stuerzlinger, W.: Laser Pointers as Collaborative Pointing Devices. In: GI '02: Proceedings of the 2002 Conference on Graphics Interface (2002)
624. Olsen Jr., D.R., Nielsen, T.: Laser Pointer Interaction. In: CHI '01: Proceedings of the SIGCHI conference on Human factors in computing systems, pp. 17–22. ACM Press, New York, NY (2001)
625. Olwal, A., Feiner, S.: Interaction techniques using prosodic features of speech and audio localization. In: IUI '05: Proceedings of the 10th international conference on Intelligent user interfaces, pp. 284–286. ACM Press, New York, NY (2005)
626. ONERA/DRIS: CEC Projects, http://visu-www.onera.fr/ (2006)
627. Ostry, D.I.: Some Three-Dimensional Graph Drawing Algorithms. Master's thesis, Department of Computer Science and Software Engineering, The University of Newcastle, Australia (1996)
628. Otten, R.H.J.M., van Wijk, J.J.: Graph representations in interactive layout design. In: Proceedings IEEE International Symposium on Circuits and Systems, pp. 914–918. IEEE Computer Society Press, Los Alamitos, CA (1978)
629. Oviatt, S.L.: Mutual disambiguation of recognition errors in a multimodel architecture. In: CHI '99: Proceedings of the SIGCHI conference on Human factors in computing systems, pp. 576–583. ACM Press, New York, NY (1999)
630. Oviatt, S.L.: Ten myths of multimodal interaction. Commun. ACM 42(11), 74–81 (1999)
631. Oviatt, S.L.: Multimodal Interfaces. In: Oviatt, S.L. (ed.) The Human-Computer Interaction Handbook: Fundamentals, Evolving Technologies and Emerging Applications, pp. 286–304. Lawrence Erlbaum Associates, Mahwah, NJ (2003)
632. Oviatt, S.L., Cohen, P.R.: Multimodal Interfaces That Process What Comes Naturally. Communications of the ACM 43(3), 45–53 (2000)
633. Oviatt, S.L., Coulston, R., Tomko, S., Xiao, B., Lunsford, R., Wesson, M., Carmichael, L.: Toward a theory of organized multimodal integration patterns during human-computer interaction. In: ICMI '03: Proceedings of the 5th international conference on Multimodal interfaces, pp. 44–51. ACM Press, New York, NY (2003)
634. Owen, C.B., Xiao, F., Middlin, P.: What is the best fiducial?. In: Proceedings of the First IEEE International Augmented Reality Toolkit Workshop, pp. 98–105. IEEE Computer Society Press, Los Alamitos, CA (2002)
635. Pagendarm, H.-G.: HIGHEND, A Visualization System for 3d Data with Special Support for Postprocessing of Fluid Dynamics Data. In: Eurographics Workshop on Visualization in Scientific Computing (1990)
636. Pagendarm, H.-G., Walter, B.: A Prototype of a Cooperative Workplace for Aerodynamicists. Comput. Graph. Forum 12(3), 485–496 (1993)
637. Pang, A.: Spray Rendering. IEEE Comput. Graph. Appl. 14(5), 57–63 (1994)
638. Pang, A., Wittenbrink, C.: Collaborative 3D Visualization with CSpray. IEEE Comput. Graph. Appl. 17(2), 32–41 (1997)
639. Pang, A., Wittenbrink, C.M., Goodman, T.: CSpray: A Collaborative Scientific Visualization Application. In: Proceedings of the 1995 SPIE Conference on Multimedia Computing and Networking (MMCN 1995), pp. 317–326. ACM SIGMM/SPIE, Society of Photo-Optical Instrumentation Engineers (March 1995)

640. Park, J.-M., Choi, J.-H., Jung, J.-Y., Park, S.-H.: Design and Implementation of Navigation System for Protein Interaction Networks. In: 15th International Conference on Genome Informatics (2004)

641. Parker, J.K., Mandryk, R.L., Inkpen, K.M.: TractorBeam: Seamless integration of local and remote pointing for tabletop displays. In: GI '05: Proceedings of the 2005 conference on Graphics interface, pp. 33–40. Canadian Human-Computer Communications Society (2005)

642. Patterson, E., Woods, D., Tinapple, D., Roth, E., Finley, J., Kuperman, G.: Aiding the Intelligence Analist in Situations of Data Overload: From Problem Definition to Design Concept Exploration, ERGO-CSEL 01-TR-01. Technical report, Institute for Ergonomics/Cognitive Systems Engineering Lab., The Ohio State University, Columbus OH (2001)

643. Pausch, R., Burnette, T., Brockway, D., Weiblen, M.E.: Navigation and locomotion in virtual worlds via flight into hand-held miniatures. In: SIGGRAPH '95: Proceedings of the 22nd annual conference on Computer graphics and interactive techniques, pp. 399–400. ACM Press, New York, NY (1995)

644. Peng, W., Ward, M.O., Rundensteiner, E.A.: Clutter Reduction in Multi-Dimensional Data Visualization Using Dimension Reordering. In: Proceedings of the IEEE Symposium on Information Visualization, pp. 89–96. IEEE Computer Society Press, Los Alamitos, CA (2004)

645. Pennisi, E.: Modernizing the Tree of Life. Science 300, 1692–1697 (2003)

646. Perlin, K., Fox, D.: Pad: An Alternative Approach to the Computer Interface. In: Proceedings of the 20th Annual ACM Conference on Computer Graphics (SIGGRAPH '93), pp. 57–64. ACM Press, New York, NY (1993)

647. Pickering, J.A.: Touch-Sensitive Screens: The Technologies and Their Application. International Journal of Man.-Machine Studies 25(3), 249–269 (1986)

648. Pierce, J.S., Forsberg, A.S., Conway, M.J., Hong, S., Zeleznik, R.C., Mine, M.R.: Image plane interaction techniques in 3D immersive environments. In: SI3D '97: Proceedings of the 1997 symposium on Interactive 3D graphics, p. 39. ACM Press, New York, NY (1997)

649. Pierce, J.S., Stearns, B.C., Pausch, R.: Voodoo dolls: seamless interaction at multiple scales in virtual environments. In: SI3D '99: Proceedings of the 1999 symposium on Interactive 3D graphics, pp. 141–145. ACM Press, New York, NY (1999)

650. Plaisant, C.: The Challenge of Information Visualization Evaluation. In: Working conference on Advanced Visual Interfaces, pp. 109–116. ACM Press, New York, NY (2004)

651. Plaisant, C.: Information Visualization and the Challenge of Universal Usability. In: Dykes, J. et al. (ed.) Exploring Geovisualization, pp. 53–82. Elsevier, Amsterdam (2005)

652. Plaisant, C., Carr, D., Shneiderman, B.: Image-browser taxonomy and guidelines for designers. IEEE Software 12(2), 21–32 (1995)

653. Plaisant, C., Grosjean, J., Bederson, B.B.: SpaceTree: Supporting Exploration in Large Node Link Tree, Design Evolution and Empirical Evaluation. In: IEEE Symposium on Information Visualization (InfoVis 2002), pp. 57–64. IEEE Computer Society Press, Los Alamitos, CA (2002)

654. Plaisant, C., Milash, B., Rose, A., Widoff, S., Shneiderman, B.: LifeLines: visualizing personal histories. In: CHI '96: Proceedings of the SIGCHI conference on Human factors in computing systems, p. 221. ACM Press, New York, NY (1996)

655. Plaue, C., Miller, T., Stasko, J.: Is a picture worth a thousand words? An Evaluation of Information Awareness Displays. In: Conference on Graphics Interface, pp. 117-126. Canadian Human-Computer Communications Society (2004)

656. Polhemus: Fastrack, http://www.polhemus.com (2006)

657. Pollack, S., Ben-Ari, M.: Selecting a Visualization System. In: Proceedings of the Third Program Visualization Workshop, pp. 134–140 (July 2004)
658. Pook, S., Lecolinet, E., Vaysseix, G., Barillot, E.: Context and Interaction in Zoomable User Interfaces. In: Proocedings of the 5th International Working Conference on Advanced Visual Interfaces (AVI'00), pp. 227–231. ACM Press, New York, NY (2000)
659. Poppe, R.: Vision-Based Human Motion Analysis: An Overview. Computer Vision and Image Understanding (CVIU), 2007. To appear
660. Post, F.H., Vrolijk, B., Hauser, H., Laramee, R.S., Doleisch, H.: The State of the Art in Flow Visualization: Feature Extraction and Tracking. Computer Graphics Forum 22(4), 775–792 (2003)
661. Poupyrev, I., Ichikawa, T.: Manipulating Objects in Virtual Worlds: Categorization Empirical Evaluation of Interaction Techniques. Journal of Visual Languages and Computing 10(1), 19–35 (1999)
662. Poupyrev, I., Weghorst, S., Fels, S.: Non-isomorphic 3D rotational techniques. In: CHI '00: Proceedings of the SIGCHI conference on Human factors in computing systems, pp. 540–547. ACM Press, New York, NY (2000)
663. Pouteau, X.: Interpretation of Gestures and Speech: A Practical Approach to Multimodal Communication. In: Bunt, H., Beun, R.-J. (eds.) CMC 1998. LNCS (LNAI), vol. 2155, pp. 28–30. Springer, Berlin Heidelberg (2001)
664. Preece, J., Rogers, Y., Sharp, H.: Interaction Design: Beyond Human-Computer Interaction. John Wiley and Sons, New York (2002)
665. Pressman, R., Ince, D.: Software Engineering, 5th edn. McGraw-Hill, New York, NY (2000)
666. Price, B.A., Baecker, R.M., Small, I.S.: A principled Taxonomy of Software Visualization. Journal of Visual Languages and Computing 4(1), 211–266 (1993)
667. Pruitt, J., Grudin, J.: Personas: practice and theory. In: Conference on Designing for User Experiences, pp. 1–15. ACM Press, New York, NY (2003)
668. Purchase, H.C.: Which Aesthetic has the Greatest Effect on Human Understanding?. In: DiBattista, G. (ed.) GD 1997. LNCS, vol. 1353, pp. 248–261. Springer, Berlin Heidelberg (1997)
669. Purchase, H.C.: Which Aesthetic has the Greatest Effect on Human Understanding. In: DiBattista, G. (ed.) GD 1997. LNCS, vol. 1353, pp. 284–290. Springer, Berlin Heidelberg (1997)
670. Purchase, H.C.: Performance of Layout Algorithms: Comprehension, not Computation. Journal of Visual Languages and Computing 9(6), 647–657 (1998)
671. Purchase, H.C.: Effective information visualisation: a study of graph drawing aesthetics and algorithms. Interacting with Computers 13(2), 147–162 (2000)
672. Purchase, H.C., Allder, J.-A., Carrington, D.A.: User Preference of Graph Layout Aesthetics: A UML Study. In: Marks, J. (ed.) GD 2000. LNCS, vol. 1984, pp. 5–18. Springer, Berlin Heidelberg (2001)
673. Purchase, H.C., Allder, J.-A., Carrington, D.A.: Graph Layout Aesthetics in UML Diagrams: User Preferences. Journal of Graph Algorithms and Applications 6(3), 255–279 (2002)
674. Purchase, H.C., Carrington, D.A., Allder, J.-A.: Experimenting with Aesthetics-Based Graph Layout. In: Anderson, M., Cheng, P., Haarslev, V. (eds.) Diagrams 2000. LNCS (LNAI), vol. 1889, pp. 1–3. Springer, Berlin Heidelberg (2000)
675. Purchase, H.C., Carrington, D.A., Allder, J.-A.: Empirical Evaluation of Aesthetics-based Graph Layout. Empirical Software Engineering 7(3), 233–255 (2002)
676. Purchase, H.C., Cohen, R.F., James, M.: Validating Graph Drawing Aesthetics. In: Brandenburg, F.J. (ed.) GD 1995. LNCS, vol. 1027, pp. 435–446. Springer, Berlin Heidelberg (1996)

677. Purchase, H.C., Cohen, R.F., James, M.I.: An Experimental Study of the Basis for Graph Drawing Algorithms. ACM Journal of Experimental Algorithms 2, 4 (1997)

678. Qeli, E., Wiechert, W., Freisleben, B.: Visualizing Time-Varying Matrices Using Multidimensional Scaling and Reorderable Matrices. In: Proceedings of the 2004 International Conference on Information Visualization (IV2004), London, UK, pp. 561–567. IEEE Computer Society Press, Los Alamitos, CA (2004)

679. Qeli, E., Wiechert, W., Freisleben, B.: The Time-Dependent Reorderable Matrix Method for Visualizing Evolving Tabular Data. In: Proceedings of the 2005 IST/SPIE Conference on Visualization and Data Analysis, San Jose, USA, pp. 199–207. SPIE (2005)

680. Qeli, E., Wiechert, W., Freisleben, B.: Visual Exploration of Time-Varying Matrices. In: Proceedings of the 2005 International Conference on Information Visualization (IV2005), London, UK, pp. 889–895. IEEE Computer Society Press, Los Alamitos, CA (2005)

681. Qualisys Motion Capture Systems: ProReflex MCU Digital Cameras, http://www.qualisys.com/proreflex.html (2006)

682. Quek, F., Mysliwiec, T., Zhao, M.: FingerMouse: A Freehand Computer Pointing Interface. In: Proceedings of International Conference on Automatic Face and Gesture Recognition, pp. 372–377 (1995)

683. Quesenbery, W.: The Five dimensions of Usability. In: Content and Complexity: Information Design in Technical Communication, Lawrence Erlbaum Associates, Mahwah, NJ (2003)

684. Quigley, A., Eades, P.: FADE: Graph Drawing, Clustering, and Visual Abstraction. In: Marks, J. (ed.) GD 2000. LNCS, vol. 1984, pp. 197–210. Springer, Berlin Heidelberg (2001)

685. Qvarfordt, P., Jönsson, A., Dahlbäck, N.: The role of spoken feedback in experiencing multimodal interfaces as human-like. In: ICMI '03: Proceedings of the 5th international conference on Multimodal interfaces, pp. 250–257. ACM Press, New York, NY (2003)

686. Qvarfordt, P., Zhai, S.: Conversing with the user based on eye-gaze patterns. In: CHI '05: Proceedings of the SIGCHI conference on Human factors in computing systems, pp. 221–230. ACM Press, New York, NY (2005)

687. Raje, R.R., Boyles, M., Fang, S.: CEV: Collaborative Environment for Visualization Using Java-RMI. Concurrency - Practice and Experience 10(11-13), 1079–1085 (1998)

688. Ramage, M.: The Learning Way: Evaluation of Cooperative Systems. PhD thesis, Lancaster University (1999)

689. Randhawa, B., Coffman, W. (eds.): Visual Learning, Thinking and Communication. San Francisco, New York, San Francisco, London (1978)

690. Rao, R., Card, S.K.: The Table Lens: Merging Graphical and Symbolic Representations in an Interactive Focus+Context Visualization for Tabular Information. In: Proceedings of ACM CHI '94 Conference on Human Factors in Computing Systems, pp. 318–322. ACM Press, New York, NY (1994)

691. Rao, R., Card, S.K.: The Table Lens: Merging Graphical and Symbolic Representations in an Interactive Focus+Context Visualization for Tabular Information. In: Proceedings of the ACM Conference on Human Factors in Computing Systems (CHI '94), pp. 318–322. ACM Press, New York, NY (1994)

692. Rauwerda, H., Roos, M., Hertzberger, B., Breit, T.: The promise of a virtual lab in drug discovery. Drug Discovery Today 11, 228–236 (2006)

693. Reeves, B., Nash, C.: The media equation: How people treat computers, television, and new media like real people and places. CSLI Publications, Cambridge University Press (1996)

694. Reeves, L.M., Lai, J., Larson, J.A., Oviatt, S.L., Balaji, T.S., Buisine, S., Collings, P., Cohen, P.R., Kraal, B., Martin, J.-C., McTear, M., Raman, T., Stanney, K.M., Su, H., Wang, Q.Y.: Guidelines for multimodal user interface design. Commun. ACM 47(1), 57–59 (2004)
695. Reidsma, D., Jovanovic, N., Hofs, D.: Designing Annotation Tools based on Properties of Annotation Problems. Technical Report 04-45, CTIT (2004)
696. Reidsma, D., op den Akker, H., Rienks, R., Poppe, R., Nijholt, A., Heylen, D., Zwiers, J.: Virtual Meeting Rooms: From Observation to Simulation. In: Proceedings Social Intelligence Design 2005, p. 15 (March 2005)
697. Reingold, E.M., Tilford, J.S.: Tidier Drawing of Trees. IEEE Transactions on Software Engineering SE-7(2), 223–228 (1981)
698. Rekimoto, J.: Tilting operations for small screen interfaces. In: UIST '96: Proceedings of the 9th annual ACM symposium on User interface software and technology, pp. 167–168. ACM Press, New York, NY (1996)
699. Rekimoto, J.: Pick-and-drop: a direct manipulation technique for multiple computer environments. In: UIST '97: Proceedings of the 10th annual ACM symposium on User interface software and technology, pp. 31–39. ACM Press, New York, NY (1997)
700. Rekimoto, J., Ayatsuka, Y.: CyberCode: Designing augmented reality environments with visual tags. In: Designing Augmented Reality Environments, pp. 1–10 (2000)
701. Rekimoto, J., Matsushita, N.: Perceptual Surfaces: Towards a Human and Object Sensitive Interactive Display. In: Proceedings of the ACM Workshop on Perceptive User Interfaces, ACM Press, New York, NY (1997)
702. Rensink, R.A., O'Regan, J.K., Clark, J.J.: To See or Not to See: The Need for Attention to Perceive Changes in Scenes. Psychological Science 8, 368–373 (1997)
703. Repenning, A., Sumner, T.: Agentsheets: A Medium for Creating Domain-Oriented Visual Languages. Computer 28(3), 17–25 (1995)
704. Repokari, L., Saarela, T., Kurki, I.: Visual search on a mobile phone display. In: SAICSIT '02: Proceedings of the 2002 annual research conference of the South African institute of computer scientists and information technologists on Enablement through technology, pp. 253–253. South African Institute for Computer Scientists and Information Technologists (2002)
705. Rhodes, P.J., Laramee, R.S., Bergeron, R.D., Sparr, T.M.: Uncertainty Visualization Methods in Isosurface Rendering. In: Eurographics 2003, Short Papers, pp. 83–88. The Eurographics Association, September 1-5 (2003)
706. Rhyne, T.-M., Hibbard, B., Johnson, C., Chen, C., Eick, S.: Panel: Can We Determine the Top Unresolved Problems of Visualization?. In: Proceedings IEEE Visualization, pp. 563–565. IEEE Computer Society Press, Los Alamitos, CA (2004)
707. Rienks, R., Reidsma, D.: Meeting Annotation: a Framework for Corpus Based Research on Human-Human Interaction (June 2004)
708. Risden, K., Czerwinski, M.P., Munzner, T., Cook, D.B.: An initial examination of ease of use for 2D and 3D information visualizations of web content. International Journal of Human-Computer Studies 53(5), 695–715 (2000)
709. Robertson, G.G., Czerwinski, M., Baudisch, P., Meyers, B., Robbins, D., Smith, G., Tan, D.: The Large-Display User Experience. IEEE Computer Graphics and Applications 25(4), 44–51 (2005)
710. Robertson, G.G., Czerwinski, M., Larson, K., Robbins, D.C., Thiel, D., van Dantzich, M.: Data mountain: using spatial memory for document management. In: Proceedings of the 11th annual ACM symposium on User interface software and technology, pp. 153–162. ACM Press, New York, NY (1998)

711. Robertson, G.G., Horvitz, E., Czerwinski, M., Baudisch, P., Hutchings, D.R., Meyers, B., Robbins, D., Smith, G.: Scalable Fabric: Flexible task management. In: AVI '04: Proceedings of the working conference on Advanced visual interfaces, pp. 85–89. ACM Press, New York, NY (2004)

712. Robertson, G.G., Mackinlay, J.D., Card, S.K.: Cone Trees: Animated 3D Visualizations of Hierarchical Information. In: Proceedings of the ACM Conference on Human Factors in Computing Systems (CHI '91), pp. 189–194. ACM Press, New York, NY (1991)

713. Robinson, A.C., Chen, J., Lengerich, E.J., Meyer, H.G., MacEachren, A.M.: Combining Usability Techniques to Design Geovisualization Tools for Epidemiology. In: Proceedings of Auto-Carto (2005)

714. Rodgers, P.: Graph Drawing Techniques for Geographic Visualization. In: Dykes, J. et al. (ed.) Exploring Geovisualization, pp. 143–158. Elsevier, Amsterdam (2005)

715. Rogowitz, B.E., Kalvin, A.D.: The "Which Blair Project": A Quick Visual Method for Evaluating Perceptual Color Maps. In: Proceedings Visualization, pp. 183–190. IEEE Computer Society Press, Los Alamitos, CA (2001)

716. Rohs, M.: Real-World Interaction with Camera Phones. In: Murakami, H., Nakashima, H., Tokuda, H., Yasumura, M. (eds.) UCS 2004. LNCS, vol. 3598, pp. 74–89. Springer, Berlin Heidelberg (2005)

717. Rolland, J.P., Davis, L.D., Baillot, Y.: A Survey of Tracking Technologies for Virtual Environments. In: Fundamentals of Wearable Computers and Augmented Reality, pp. 67–112. Lawrence Erlbaum Associates, Mahwah, NJ (2001)

718. Rößling, G., Schüler, M., Freisleben, B.: The ANIMAL algorithm animation tool. In: ITiCSE '00: Proceedings of the 5th annual SIGCSE/SIGCUE Conference on Innovation and technology in computer science education (ITiCSE'00), pp. 37–40. ACM Press, New York, NY (2000)

719. Rost, U., Bornberg-Bauer, E.: TreeWiz: interactive exploration of huge trees. Bioinformatics 18(1), 109–114 (2002)

720. Roth, S., Mattis, J.: Data Characterization for Intelligent Graphics Presentation. In: CHI '90: Proceedings of the SIGCHI conference on Human factors in computing systems, pp. 193–200. ACM Press, New York, NY (1990)

721. Roweis, S.T., Saul, L.K.: Nonlinear Dimensionality Reduction by Locally Linear Embedding. Science 290, 2323–2326 (2000)

722. Rubin, J.: Handbook of Usability Testing, How to Plan, Design, and Conduct Effective Tests. John Wiley and Sons, New York (1994)

723. Rusdorf, S., Brunnett, G.: Real time tracking of high speed movements in the context of a table tennis application. In: VRST '05: Proceedings of the ACM symposium on Virtual reality software and technology, pp. 192–200. ACM Press, New York, NY (2005)

724. Russel, S., Norvig, P.: Artificial Intelligence: A Modern Approach, 2nd edn. Prentice-Hall, Englewood Cliffs (2002)

725. Saitek Elektronik Vertriebs GmbH: Cyborg evo Force, http://www.saitek.com (2006)

726. Saitek Elektronik Vertriebs GmbH: R440 Force Feedback Wheel, http://www.saitek.com (2006)

727. Sammon, J.W.: A Nonlinear Mapping for Data Structure Analysis. IEEE Transactions on Computers 18(5), 401–409 (1969)

728. Sandstrom, T.A., Henze, C., Levit, C.: The hyperwall. In: Proceedings of the Conference on Coordinated and Multiple Views In Exploratory Visualization, pp. 124–133. IEEE Computer Society Press, Los Alamitos, CA (2003)

729. Saraiya, P., Lee, P., North, C.: Visualization of Graphs with Associated Time-series Data. In: INFOVIS '05: Proceedings of the 2005 IEEE Symposium on

Information Visualization, IEEE Computer Society Press, Los Alamitos, CA
(2005)

730. Saraiya, P., North, C., Duca, K.: An Evaluation of Microarray Visualization
Tools for Biological Insight. In: 10th IEEE Symposium on Information Visualization, pp. 1–8. IEEE Computer Society Press, Los Alamitos, CA (2004)

731. Saraiya, P., North, C., Duca, K.: An Insight-Based Methodology for Evaluating
Bioinformatics Visualizations. IEEE Transactions on Visualization and Computer Graphics 11(4), 443–456 (2005)

732. Saraiya, P., North, C., Duca, K.: Visualizing biological pathways: requirements analysis, systems evaluation and research agenda. Information Visualization 4(3), 191–205 (2005)

733. Sawhney, N., Schmandt, C.: Nomadic radio: speech and audio interaction for
contextual messaging in nomadic environments. ACM Trans. Comput.-Hum.
Interact. 7(3), 353–383 (2000)

734. Schaffer, D., Zuo, Z., Greenberg, S., Bartram, L., Dill, J., Dubs, S., Roseman,
M.: Navigating Hierarchically Clustered Networks through Fisheye and Full-
Zoom Methods. ACM Transactions on Computer-Human Interaction 3(2), 162–
188 (1996)

735. Schena, M., Shalon, D., Davis, R.W., Brown, P.O.: Quantitative Monitoring of
Gene Expression Patterns with a Complementary DNA Microarray. Science 270,
467–470 (1995)

736. Scheuermann, G., Garth, C., Peikert, R.: Panel: Even more theory, or more prac-
tical applications to particular problems. In which direction will Topology-Based
Flow Visualization go? In: Topology-Based Methods in Visualization Workshop,
September 2005. Held in Budmerice, Slovakia (2005)

737. Schlag, M., Luccio, F., Maestrini, P., Lee, D.T., Wong, C.K.: Advances in Computing Research, Vol. II, VLSI Theory, chapter A Visibility Problem in VLSI
Layout Compaction. JAI Press Inc (1984)

738. Schneider, T.D., Stephens, R.M.: Sequence logos: a new way to display consensus
sequences. Nucleic Acids Research 18(20), 6097–6100 (1990)

739. Schnyder, W.: Embedding planar graphs on the grid. In: Proceedings of the first
annual ACM-SIAM symposium on Discrete algorithms, pp. 138–148. Society for
Industrial and Applied Mathematics (1990)

740. Schoenberg, I.J.: Remarks to M. Fréchet's article Sur la d'efinition axioma-
tique d'une classe d'espaces vectoriels distanci'es applicables vectoriellement
sur l'espace de Hilbert. Annals of Mathematics 36, 724–732 (1935)

741. Schreiber, F.: High Quality Visualization of Biochemical Pathways in BioPath.
In. Silico Biology 2(2), 59–73 (2002)

742. Schroeder, M.: Intelligent Information Integration: From Infrastructure
Through Consistency Management to Information Visualization. In: Dykes, J. et
al. (ed.) Exploring Geovisualization, pp. 477–494. Elsevier, Amsterdam (2005)

743. Schroeder, W.J., Martin, K.M., Lorensen, W.E.: The Visualization Toolkit, An
Object-Oriented Approach to 3D Graphics, 2nd edn. Prentice-Hall, Englewood
Cliffs (1998)

744. Scott, S.D., Carpendale, M.S.T., Habelski, S.: Storage Bins: Mobile Storage
for Collaborative Tabletop Displays. IEEE Computer Graphics and Applications 25(4), 58–65 (2005)

745. Sears, A., Plaisant, C., Shneiderman, B.: A New Era for High Precision Touchscreens. In: Advances in Human-Computer Interaction, vol. 3, pp. 1–33. Ablex
Publishing, Greenwich CT (1992)

746. Segen, J., Kumar, S.: Look ma, no mouse! Communications of the ACM 43(7),
102–109 (2000)

747. Seisenberger, K.: Termgraph: Ein system zur zeichnerischen darstellung von strukturierten agenten und petrinetzen. Technical report, University of Passau (1991)

748. SensAble Technologies: Haptics - Touch it!, http://www.sensable.com (2006)

749. Seo, J., Shneiderman, B.: Interactively Exploring Hierarchical Clustering Results. Computer 35(7), 80–86 (2002)

750. Seo, J., Shneiderman, B.: A Rank-by-Feature Framework for Unsupervised Multidimensional Data Exploration Using Low Dimensional Projections. In: 10th IEEE Symposium on Information Visualization, pp. 65–72. IEEE Computer Society Press, Los Alamitos, CA (2004)

751. Shafer, S., Shan, Y., Wu, Y., Zhang, Z.: Visual Panel: Virtual Mouse, Keyboard and 3D Controller with an Ordinary Piece of Paper. In: Proceedings of the ACM Workshop on Perceptive User Interfaces, ACM Press, New York, NY (2001)

752. Shah, N., Dillard, S., Weber, G., Hamann, B.: Volume visualization of multiple alignment of large genomic DNA. In: Moeller, T., Hamann, B., Russell, R. (eds.) Mathematical Foundations of Scientific Visualization, Computer Graphics, and Massive Data Exploration, Springer, Berlin Heidelberg New York (2006)

753. Shanbhag, P., Rheingans, P., desJardins, M.: Temporal Visualization of Planning Polygons for Efficient Partitioning of Geo-Spatial Data. In: Proc. IEEE Symposium on Information Visualization (InfoVis),, pp. 211–218. IEEE Computer Society Press, Los Alamitos, CA (2005)

754. Shaner, M.C., Blair, I.M., Schneider, T.D.: Sequence Logos: A Powerful, Yet Simple, Tool. In: Proceedings of the Twenty-Sixth Annual Hawaii International Conference on System Sciences, Volume 1: Architecture and Biotechnology Computing, pp. 813–821. IEEE Computer Society Press, Los Alamitos, CA (1993)

755. Shannon, P., Markiel, A., Ozier, O., Baliga, N.S., Wang, J.T., Ramage, D., Amin, N., Schwikowski, B., Ideker, T.: Cytoscape: A Software Environment for Integrated Models of Biomolecular Interaction Networks. Genome Research 13, 2498–2504 (2003)

756. Shi, K., Irani, P., Li, B.: An Evaluation of Content Browsing Techniques for Hierarchical Space-Filling Visualizations. In: Proceedings of the 2005 IEEE Symposium on Information Visualization (INFOVIS'05), p. 11. IEEE Computer Society Press, Los Alamitos, CA (2005)

757. Shiloach, Y.: Arrangements of Planar Graphs on the Planar Lattices. PhD thesis, Weizmann Institute of Science, Rehovot, Israel (1976)

758. Shneiderman, B.: Tree Visualization with Tree-Maps: A 2-D Space-Filling Approach. ACM Transactions on Graphics 11(1), 92–99 (1992)

759. Shneiderman, B.: The Eyes Have It: A Task by Data Type Taxonomy for Information Visualization. In: Proceedings of the IEEE Symposium on Visual Languages (VL'96), pp. 336–343. IEEE Computer Society Press, Los Alamitos, CA (1996)

760. Shneiderman, B.: Universal Usability. Communications of the ACM 43(5), 84–91 (2000)

761. Shneiderman, B., Maes, P.: Direct manipulation vs. interface agents. ACM Interactions 4(6), 42–61 (1997)

762. Shneiderman, B., Plaisant, C.: Designing the User Interface: Strategies for Effective Human-Computer Interaction, 4th edn. Addison-Wesley, Reading, MA (2005)

763. Shneiderman, B., Rao, R., Andrews, K., Ahlberg, C., Brodbeck, D., Jewitt, T., Mackinlay, J.: Panel: Turning Information Visualization Innovations into Commercial Products: Lessons to Guide the Next Success. In: Proceedings of IEEE Symposium on Information Visualization 2005 (InfoVis 2005), pp. 241–244. IEEE Computer Society Press, Los Alamitos, CA (2005)

764. Siirtola, H.: Interaction with the Reorderable Matrix. In: International Conference on Information Visualization (IV '99), pp. 272–279. IEEE Computer Society Press, July (1999)
765. Siirtola, H.: Combining Parallel Coordinates with the Reorderable Matrix. In: Coordinated and Multiple Views In Exploratory Visualization (CMV'03), pp. 63–74. IEEE Computer Society Press, Los Alamitos, CA (2003)
766. Siirtola, H., Mäkinen, E.: Constructing and reconstructing the reorderable matrix. Information Visualization 4(1), 32–48 (2005)
767. Silfverberg, M., MacKenzie, I.S., Kauppinen, T.: An Isometric Joystick as a Pointing Device for Handheld Information Terminals. In: GI '01: Proceedings of Graphics Interface 2001, pp. 119–126 (2001)
768. Simon, A.: First-person experience and usability of co-located interaction in a projection-based virtual environment. In: VRST '05: Proceedings of the ACM symposium on Virtual reality software and technology, pp. 23–30. ACM Press, New York, NY (2005)
769. Simon, A., Scholz, S.: Multi-Viewpoint Images for Multi-User Interaction. In: VR '05: Proceedings of the IEEE Virtual Reality Conference, pp. 107–113. IEEE Computer Society Press, Los Alamitos, CA (2005)
770. Slack, J., Hildebrand, K., Munzner, T., John, K.S.: SequenceJuxtaposer: Fluid Navigation For Large-Scale Sequence Comparison in Context. In: German Conference on Bioinformatics, pp. 37–42 (2004)
771. Slater, M., Usoh, M.: Presence in Immersive Virtual Environments. In: VR '93: Proceedings of the IEEE Virtual Reality International Symposium, pp. 90–96. IEEE Computer Society Press, Los Alamitos, CA (1993)
772. Slocum, T.A., Blok, C., Jiang, B., Koussoulakou, A., Montello, D.R., Fuhrmann, S., Hedley, N.R.: Cognitive and Usability Issues in Geovisualization. Cartography and Geographic Information Science 28(1), 61–75 (2001)
773. Slocum, T.A., Cliburn, D.C., Feddema, J.J., Miller, J.R.: Evaluating the Usability of a Tool for Visualizing the Uncertainty of the Future Global Water Balance. Cartography and Geographic Information Science 30(4), 299–317 (2003)
774. SmartMoney: Smartmoney.com - Investing, Saving and Personal Finance, 2003, http://www.smartmoney.com (2006)
775. Smith, D.C., Ludolph, F.E., Irby, C.H.: The desktop metaphor as an approach to user interface design (panel discussion). In: ACM '85: Proceedings of the 1985 ACM annual conference on The range of computing: mid-8's perspective, pp. 548–549. ACM Press, New York, NY (1985)
776. Smith, G.M., Schraefel, M.C.: The radial scroll tool: scrolling support for stylus- or touch-based document navigation. In: UIST '04: Proceedings of the 17th annual ACM symposium on User interface software and technology, pp. 53–56. ACM Press, New York, NY (2004)
777. Smith, M.A., Davenport, D., Hwa, H., Turner, T.: Object auras: a mobile retail and product annotation system. In: EC '04: Proceedings of the 5th ACM conference on Electronic commerce, pp. 240–241. ACM Press, New York, NY (2004)
778. Sohn, M., Lee, G.: ISeeU: Camera-based user interface for a handheld computer. In: MobileHCI '05: Proceedings of the 7th international conference on Human computer interaction with mobile devices & services, pp. 299–302. ACM Press, New York, NY (2005)
779. Somervell, J., McCrickard, D.S., North, C., Shukla, M.: An Evaluation of Information Visualization in Attention-Limited Environments. In: Proceedings of the Joint Eurographics - IEEE TCVG Symposium on Visualization 2002 (VisSym'02), pp. 211–216. IEEE Computer Society Press, Los Alamitos, CA (2002)
780. Sommer, R.: Personal Space. Prentice-Hall, Englewood Cliffs (1969)

781. Spakov, O., Miniotas, D.: Gaze-based selection of standard-size menu items. In: ICMI '05: Proceedings of the 7th international conference on Multimodal interfaces, pp. 124–128. ACM Press, New York, NY (2005)

782. Spell, R., Brady, R., Dietrich, F.: BARD: A visualization tool for biological sequence analysis. In: INFOVIS'03: Proceedings of the IEEE Symposium on Information Visualization, IEEE Computer Society Press, Los Alamitos, CA (2003)

783. Spence, B., Witkowski, M., Fawcett, C., Craft, B., de Bruijn, O.: Image presentation in space and time: errors, preferences and eye-gaze activity. In: Working Conference on Advanced Visual Interfaces, pp. 141–149. ACM Press, New York, NY (2004)

784. Spence, R.: Information Visualization, vol. 1. Addison-Wesley, Edinburgh Gate (2001)

785. Spotfire. Will better Usability Studies Help Swell Market for Bioinformatics Software? GenomeWeb, January 2005. BioInform, vol. 9 (2) (2005)

786. Srámek, M., Dimitrov, L.I.: f3d - A File Format and Tools for Storage and Manipulation of Volumetric Data Sets. In: Proceedings of the 1st International Symposium on 3D Data Processing Visualization and Transmission (3DPVT '02), pp. 368–371 (2002)

787. Stammers, R., Shepherd, A.: Task analysis. In: Corbette, N., Wilson, J. (eds.) The evaluation of human work, pp. 144–168. Taylor & Francis, Abington (1995)

788. Starner, T.E., Leibe, B., Minnen, D., Westyn, T., Hurst, A., Weeks, J.: The perceptive workbench: Computer-vision-based gesture tracking, object tracking, and 3D reconstruction for augmented desks. Machine Vision and Applications 14(1), 59–71 (2003)

789. Stasko, J.T., Domingue, J., Brown, M.H., Price, B.A.: Software Visualization. MIT Press, Cambridge, MA (1998)

790. Stasko, J.T., Patterson, C.: Understanding and Characterizing Software Visualization Systems. In: Proceedings of the 1992 IEEE Workshop on Visual Languages, pp. 3–10. IEEE Computer Society Press, Los Alamitos, CA (1992)

791. Stefani, O., Hoffmann, H., Rauschenbach, J.: Design of Interaction Devices for Optical Tracking in Immersive Environments. In: Human-Centred Computing: Cognitive, Social and Ergonomic Aspects Volume 3 of the Proceedings of HCI International 2003, Lawrence Erlbaum Associates, Mahwah, NJ (2003)

792. Steiner, E.B., MacEachren, A.M., Guo, D.: Developing and Assessing Light-Weight Data-Driven Exploratory Geovisualization Tools for the Web. In: Proceedings of the Workshop on Geovisualization for the Web. ICA Commission on Visualization & Virtual Environments (2001)

793. Stephen, D.K.M., Brewster, A., Miller, C.A.: Olfoto: Designing a Smell-Based Interaction. In: CHI '06: Proceedings of the IEEE Computer Human Interaction 2006, IEEE Computer Society Press, Los Alamitos, CA (2006)

794. Stern, R., Liu, F., Ohshima, Y., Sullivan, T., Acero, A.: Multiple Approaches to Robust Speech Recognition (1992)

795. Stevens, S.: On the theory of scales of measurement. Science 103, 677–680 (1946)

796. Stoakley, R., Conway, M.J., Pausch, R.: Virtual reality on a WIM: interactive worlds in miniature. In: CHI '95: Proceedings of the SIGCHI conference on Human factors in computing systems, pp. 265–272. Addison-Wesley/ACM Press, New York, NY (1995)

797. Stolk, B., Abdoelrahman, F., Koning, A., Wielinga, P., Neefs, J., Stubbs, A., de Bondt, A., Leemans, P., van der Spek, P.: Mining the Human Genome Using Virtual Reality. In: Eurographics Workshop on Parallel Graphics and Visualization, pp. 17–21. Germany Eurographics Digital Library (2002)

798. Stone, D., Jarrett, C., Woodroffe, M., Minocha, S.: User Interface Design and Evaluation. Morgan Kaufmann/Elsevier, Amsterdam (2005)

799. Stott, J.M., Rodgers, P.: Metro Map Layout Using Multicriteria Optimization. In: Proc. 8th International Conference on Information Visualisation (IV'04), pp. 355–362. IEEE Computer Society Press, Los Alamitos, CA (2004)

800. Streit, M.: Why Are Multimodal Systems so Difficult to Build? - About the Difference between Deictic Gestures and Direct Manipulation. In: Bunt, H., Beun, R.-J. (eds.) CMC 1998. LNCS (LNAI), vol. 2155, pp. 28–30. Springer, Berlin Heidelberg (2001)

801. Sturm, J.: On the Usability of Multimodal Interaction for Mobile Access to Information Services. PhD thesis, Raboud University (June 2005)

802. Succliffe, A.G., Ennis, M., Hu, J.: Evaluating the effectiveness of visual user interfaces for information retrieval. International Journal of Human-Computer Studies 53(5), 741–765 (2000)

803. Sugiyama, K.: Graph Drawing and Applications: for Software and Knowledge Engineers. World Scientific (2002)

804. Sugiyama, K., Tagawa, S., Toda, M.: Methods for Visual Understanding of Hierarchical System Structures. IEEE Transactions on Systems, Man, and Cybernetics 11(2), 109–125 (1981)

805. SUN: JavaBeans, http://java.sun.com/products/javabeans/ (2006)

806. Surakka, V., Illi, M., Isokoski, P.: Gazing and frowning as a new human-computer interaction technique. ACM Transactions on Applied Perception 1(1), 40–56 (2004)

807. Sutherland, I.: The ultimate display. Proceedings of the International Federation of Information Processing Congress 2, 506–508 (1965)

808. Sutherland, I.: Ten Unsovled Problems in Computer Graphics. Datamation 12(5), 22–27 (1966)

809. Swaminathan, K., Sato, S.: Interaction design for large displays. Interactions 4(1), 15–24 (1997)

810. Swayne, D.F., Cook, D., Buja, A.: XGobi: Interactive Dynamic Data Visualization in the X Window System. Journal of Computational and Graphical Statistics 7(1), 113–130 (1998)

811. Szalay, A., Gray, J., Kunszt, P., Thakar, A.: Designing and Mining Multi-Terabyt Astronomy Archives: The Sloan Digital Sky Survey. In: Proceedings of ACM SIGMOD, pp. 451–462. ACM Press, New York, NY (2000)

812. Takatsuka, M., Gahegan, M.: GeoVISTA Studio: A Codeless Visual Programming Environment for Geoscientific Data Analysis and Visualization. The. Journal of Computers and Geosciences 28(10), 1131–1144 (2002)

813. Talbert, N.: Toward human-centered systems. IEEE Computer Graphics and Applications 17, 21–28 (1997)

814. Tamassia, R.: On embedding a graph in the grid with the minimum number of bends. SIAM Journal on Computing 16(3), 421–444 (1987)

815. Tamassia, R., Battista, G.D., Batini, C.: Automatic graph drawing and readability of diagrams. IEEE Transactions on Systems, Man. and Cybernetics 18(1), 61–79 (1988)

816. Tamassia, R., Tollis, I.: Tessellation representation of planar graphs. In: Proceedings of Twenty-Seventh Annual Allerton Conference on Communication, Control and Computing, pp. 48–57 (1989)

817. Tan, D.S., Meyers, B., Czerwinski, M.: WinCuts: manipulating arbitrary window regions for more effective use of screen space. In: Proceedings of ACM CHI 2004 Conference on Human Factors in Computing Systems. Late breaking result papers, vol. 2, pp. 1525–1528. ACM Press, New York, NY (2004)

818. Tan, D.S., Robertson, G.G., Czerwinski, M.: Exploring 3D navigation: combining speed-coupled flying with orbiting. In: CHI '01: Proceedings of the SIGCHI conference on Human factors in computing systems, pp. 418–425. ACM Press, New York, NY (2001)

819. Tan, D.S., Stefanucci, J.K., Proffitt, D., Pausch, R.: The Infocockpit: Providing Location and Place to Aid Human Memory. In: Workshop on Perceptive User Interfaces 2001 (2001)

820. Tavanti, M., Lind, M.: 2D vs 3D, implications on spatial memory. In: IEEE Symposium on Information Visualization (InfoVis 2001), pp. 139–148. IEEE Computer Society Press, Los Alamitos, CA (2001)

821. Taylor, M.M.: Response Timing in Layered Protocols: A Cybernetic View of Natural Dialogue. In: The Structure of Multimodal Dialogue, pp. 159–172. North-Holland, Amsterdam (1989)

822. ten Bosch, L., Boves, L.: Survey of spontaneous speech phenomena in a multimodal dialogue system and some implications for ASR. In: International Conference on Spoken Language Processing ICSLP (2004)

823. Tenenbaum, J.B., de Silva, V., Langford, J.C.: A Global Geometric Framework for Nonlinear Dimensionality Reduction. Science 290, 2319–2323 (2000)

824. The Mathworks: Statistics Toolbox, http://www.mathworks.com/products/statistics (2006)

825. Theisel, H., Ertl, T., Hagen, H.-C., Noack, B., Scheuermann, G.: Panel: Why are topological methods not included in commercial visualization systems. In: Topology-Based Methods in Visualization Workshop, September 2005. Held in Budmerice, Slovakia (2005)

826. Thomas, J.J., Cook, K.A.: Illuminating the Path: The Research and Development Agenda for Visual Analytics. IEEE Computer Society Press, Los Alamitos, CA (2005)

827. Tobler, W.: Thirty Five Years of Computer Cartograms. Annals of the Association of American Geographers 94(1), 58–73 (2004)

828. Toffler, A.: Future Shock. Bantam Press, London (1970)

829. Tory, M., Moeller, T.: Evaluating Visualizations: Do Expert Reviews Work?. Computer Graphics and Applications, IEEE 25(5), 8–11 (2005)

830. Tory, M., Möller, T.: Human Factors in Visualization Research. IEEE Transactions on Visualization and Computer Graphics 10(1), 72–84 (2004)

831. Tory, M., Möller, T.: Rethinking Visualization: A High-Level Taxonomy. In: IEEE Symposium on Information Visualization (INFOVIS'04), vol. 00, pp. 151–158. IEEE Computer Society Press, Los Alamitos, CA (2004)

832. Trafton, G.J., Kirschenbaum, S.S., Tsui, T.L., Miyamoto, R.T., Ballas, J.A., Raymond, P.D.: Turning pictures into numbers: extracting and generating information from complex visualizations. International Journal of Human-Computer Studies 53(5), 827–850 (2000)

833. Tricoche, X., Garth, C., Kindlmann, G., Deines, E., Scheuermann, G., Hagen, H.: Visualization of Intricate Flow Structures for Vortex Breakdown Analysis. In: Proceedings IEEE Visualization 2004, pp. 187–194. IEEE Computer Society Press, Los Alamitos, CA (2004)

834. TriSenx Holding Inc.: The Scent Dome^{TM}, http://www.trisenx.com (2004)

835. Tufte, E.R.: Envisioning Information. Graphics Press, Cheshire, CT, USA (1990)

836. Tufte, E.R.: Visual Explanations: Images and Quantities, Evidence and Narrative. Graphic Press, Cheshire, CT, USA (1997)

837. Tufte, E.R.: The Visual Display of Quantitative Information, 2nd edn. Graphics Press, Cheshire, CT, USA (2001)

838. Tukey, J.W.: Exploratory Data Analysis. Addison-Wesley, Reading, MA (1977)

839. Tunkelang, D.: A Practical Approach to Drawing Undirected Graphs. Technical report, Carnegie Mellon University, Pittsburgh, PA, USA (1994)

840. Urquiza-Fuentes, J., Velázquez-Iturbide, J.: A Survey of Program Visualizations for the Functional Paradigm. In: Proceedings of the Third Program Visualization Workshop, pp. 2–9 (July 2004)

841. Urquiza-Fuentes, J., Velázquez-Iturbide, J.: R-Zoom: a Visualization Technique for Algorithm Animation Construction. In: Proceedings of the IADIS International Conference on Applied Computing 2005, pp. 145–152 (2005)

842. van Dam, A., Forsberg, A.S., Laidlaw, D.H., L. Jr., J.J., Simpson, R.M.: Immersive VR for Scientific Visualization: A Progress Report. IEEE Computer Graphics and Applications 20(6), 26–52 (2000)

843. van Dam, A., Laidlaw, D.H., Simpson, R.M.: Experiments in Immersive Virtual Reality for Scientific Visualization. Computers & Graphics 26(4), 535–555 (2002)

844. van der Sluis, I.F.: Multimodal Reference. PhD thesis, University of Tilburg, december (2005)

845. van der Veer, G., del Carmen Puerta Melguizo, M.: Mental Models. In: Human Factors And Ergonomics (2002)

846. van Es, I., Heylen, D., van Dijk, B., Nijholt, A.: Gaze behavior of talking faces makes a difference. In: CHI '02: CHI '02 extended abstracts on Human factors in computing systems, pp. 734–735. ACM Press, New York, NY (2002)

847. van Ham, F., van Wijk, J.J.: Beamtrees: Compact Visualization of Large Hierarchies. Information Visualization 2(1), 31–39 (2003)

848. van Kreveld, M., Speckmann, B.: On Rectangular Cartograms. In: Albers, S., Radzik, T. (eds.) ESA 2004. LNCS, vol. 3221, pp. 724–735. Springer, Berlin Heidelberg (2004)

849. van Welbergen, H.: A virtual human presenter in a 3D meeting environment. Master's thesis, Human Media Interaction Group, University of Twente (2005)

850. van Welie, M., van der Veer, G., Koster, A.: Integrated Representations for Task Modeling. In: Tenth European Conference on Cognitive Ergonomics, pp. 129–138 (2000)

851. van Wijk, J.J.: Image Based Flow Visualization. ACM Transactions on Graphics 21(3), 745–754 (2002)

852. van Wijk, J.J.: The Value of Visualization. In: Proceedings IEEE Visualization '05, pp. 79–86. IEEE Computer Society Press, Los Alamitos, CA (2005)

853. van Wijk, J.J., Nuij, W.A.A.: Smooth and efficient zooming and panning. In: IEEE Symposium on Information Visualization (InfoVis 2003), pp. 15–23. IEEE Computer Society Press, Los Alamitos, CA (2003)

854. van Wijk, J.J., Nuij, W.A.A.: A Model for Smooth Viewing and Navigation of Large 2D Information Spaces. IEEE Transactions on Visualization and Computer Graphics 10(4), 447–458 (2004)

855. van Wijk, J.J., van de Wetering, H.: Cushion Treemaps: Visualization of Hierarchical Information. In: INFOVIS '99: Proceedings of the 1999 IEEE Symposium on Information Visualization, p. 73. IEEE Computer Society Press, Los Alamitos, CA (1999)

856. van Wijk, J.J., van Ham, F., van de Wetering, H.: Rendering hierarchical data. Commun. ACM 46(9), 257–263 (2003)

857. Varci, A.C., Vieu, L.: Frontiers in Artificial Intelligence and Applications Systems. In: Formal Ontology in Information Systems, 3rd edn. IOS Press (2006)

858. Velázquez-Iturbide, J., Pareja-Flores, C., Urquiza-Fuentes, J.: An evaluation of the effortless approach to build algorithm animations with WinHIPE. Computers & Education. In press

859. Vernier, F., Nigay, L.: A Framework for the Combination and Characterization of Output Modalities. In: Palanque, P., Paternó, F. (eds.) DSV-IS 2000. LNCS, vol. 1946, Springer, Berlin Heidelberg (2001)

860. Vincente, K.: Cognitive Work Analysis: Toward Safe, Productive, and Healthey Computer-Based Work. Lawrence Erlbaum & Associates, Mahwah (1999)

861. Visenso GmbH: Visual Engineering Solutions, http://www.visenso.de (2006)

862. VisionCue: LLC. In: ALVA Braille Displays, http://www.visioncue.com (2006)

863. Vogel, D., Balakrishnan, R.: Interactive public ambient displays: transitioning from implicit to explicit, public to personal, interaction with multiple users. In: UIST '04: Proceedings of the 17th annual ACM symposium on User interface software and technology, pp. 137–146. ACM Press, New York, NY (2004)

864. Vogel, D., Balakrishnan, R.: Distant freehand pointing and clicking on very large, high resolution displays. In: UIST '05: Proceedings of the 18th annual ACM symposium on User interface software and technology, pp. 33–42. ACM Press, New York, NY (2005)

865. Wagner, C.R., Lederman, S.J., Howe, R.D.: A Tactile Shape Display Using RC Servomotors. In: Symposium on Haptic Interfaces for Virtual Environment and Teleoperator Systems 2002, pp. 354 – 356 (2002)

866. Wahlster, W. (ed.): SmartKom: Foundations of Multimodal Dialogue Systems. Cognitive Technologies, vol. XVIII. Springer, Berlin Heidelberg New York (2006)

867. Waldeck, C., Balfanz, D.: Mobile Liquid 2D Scatter Space (ML2DSS). In: Proceedings of the 8th International Conference on Information Visualisation, pp. 494–498 (2004)

868. Wang, N., Johnson, W.L., Rizzo, P., Shaw, E., Mayer, R.E.: Experimental evaluation of polite interaction tactics for pedagogical agents. In: IUI '05: Proceedings of the 10th international conference on Intelligent user interfaces, pp. 12–19. ACM Press, New York, NY (2005)

869. Wang, X., Miyamoto, I.: Generating Customized Layouts. In: Brandenburg, F.J. (ed.) GD 1995. LNCS, vol. 1027, pp. 504–515. Springer, Berlin Heidelberg (1996)

870. Ward, K., Heeman, P.A.: Acknowledgments in human-computer interaction. In: Proceedings of the first conference on North American chapter of the Association for Computational Linguistics, pp. 280–287. Morgan Kaufmann, San Francisco, CA (2000)

871. Ward, M.O., Theroux, K.J.: Perceptual Benchmarking for Multivariate Data Visualization. In: DAGSTUHL '97: Proceedings of the Conference on Scientific Visualization, pp. 314–321. IEEE Computer Society Press, Los Alamitos, CA (1997)

872. Ware, C.: Information Visualization: Perception for Design. Morgan Kaufmann, San Francisco, CA (2000)

873. Ware, C.: Information Visualization: Perception for Design, 2nd edn. Morgan Kaufmann, San Francisco, CA (2004)

874. Ware, C., Bobrow, R.: Motion to support rapid interactive queries on node–link diagrams. ACM Transactions on Applied Perception 1(1), 3–18 (2004)

875. Ware, C., Bobrow, R.: Supporting visual queries on medium-sized node-link diagrams. Information Visualization 4(1), 49–58 (2005)

876. Ware, C., Fleet, D.: Context sensitive flying interface. In: SI3D '97: Proceedings of the 1997 symposium on Interactive 3D graphics, p. 127. ACM Press, New York, NY (1997)

877. Ware, C., Franck, G.: Evaluating stereo and motion cues for visualizing information nets in three dimensions. ACM Transactions on Graphics 15(2), 121–140 (1996)

878. Ware, C., Jessome, D.R.: Using the bat: a six dimensional mouse for object placement. In: Proceedings on Graphics interface '88, pp. 119–124. Canadian Information Processing Society (1988)

879. Ware, C., Mikaelian, H.H.: An evaluation of an eye tracker as a device for computer input. In: Graphics Interface '87 (CHI+GI '87), pp. 183–188 (Apr 1987)

880. Ware, C., Osborne, S.: Exploration and virtual camera control in virtual three dimensional environments. In: SI3D '90: Proceedings of the 1990 symposium on Interactive 3D graphics, pp. 175–183. ACM Press, New York, NY (1990)

881. Ware, C., Plumlee, M.: 3D Geovisualization and the Structure of Visual Space. In: Dykes, J. et al. (ed.) Exploring Geovisualization, pp. 567–576. Elsevier, Amsterdam (2005)

882. Ware, C., Purchase, H., Colpoys, L., McGill, M.: Cognitive measurements of graph aesthetics. Information Visualization 1(2), 103–110 (2002)

883. Wasserman, S., Faust, K.: Social network analysis: methods and applications Cambridge University Press, Cambridge (1994)

884. Watson, B., Luebke, D.P.: The Ultimate Display: Where Will All the Pixels Come From?. IEEE Computer Society Press 38(8), 54–61 (2005)

885. Wattenberg, M.: Arc Diagrams: Visualizing Structure in Strings. In: INFOVIS '02: Proceedings of the IEEE Symposium on Information Visualization 2002 (InfoVis'02), p. 110. IEEE Computer Society Press, Los Alamitos, CA (2002)

886. Wehrend, S., Lewis, C.: A problem-oriented classification of visualization techniques. In: Proceedings of the 1st conference on Visualization '90, pp. 139–143. IEEE Computer Society Press, Los Alamitos, CA (1990)

887. Welch, G., Bishop, G.: An Introduction to the Kalman Filter. Technical report, University of North Carolina at Chapel Hill (1995)

888. Welch, G., Bishop, G.: An introduction to the kalman filter. In: SIGGRAPH 2001, course 8, Computer Graphics, Annual Conference on Computer Graphics and Interactive Techniques, Addison-Wesley, Reading, MA (2001)

889. G. Welch and E. Foxlin. Motion Tracking: No Silver Bullet, but a Respectable Arsenal. *IEEE Computer Graphics and Applications*, 22(6):24–38, 2002.

890. Westerman, S.J., Cribbin, T.: Mapping semantic information in virtual space: dimensions, variance and individual differences. International Journal of Human-Computer Studies 53(5), 765–787 (2000)

891. Wickens, C.D., Hollands, J.D.: Engineering Psychology and Human Performance Prentice-Hall, Englewood Cliffs (1999)

892. Wiener, N.: Extrapolation, Interpolation, and Smoothing of Stationary Time Series MIT Press, Cambridge, MA (1964)

893. Wierse, A.: Performance of the Covise Visualization System under Different Conditions. In: Visual Data Exploration and Analysis. SPIE, vol. 2410, pp. 218–229 (1995)

894. Wierse, A., Lang, U., Ruhle, R.: A System Architecture for Data-Oriented Visualization. In: Lee, J.P., Grinstein, G.G. (eds.) Database Issues for Data Visualization. LNCS, vol. 871, pp. 148–159. Springer, Berlin Heidelberg (1994)

895. Wikipedia: Human-Computer Interaction, http://en.wikipedia.org/wiki/Human-computer_interaction (2006)

896. Wilkinson, L.: Presentation Graphics, http://www.spss.com/research/wilkinson/Publications/iesbs.pdf (2006)

897. Williams, M., Munzner, T.: Steerable, Progressive Multidimensional Scaling. In: Proceedings of the IEEE Symposium on Information Visualization, pp. 57–64. IEEE Computer Society Press, Los Alamitos, CA (2004)

898. Wills, G.J.: NicheWorks - Interactive Visualization of Very Large Graphs. In: DiBattista, G. (ed.) GD 1997. LNCS, vol. 1353, pp. 403–414. Springer, Berlin Heidelberg (1997)

899. Wilson, A.D.: TouchLight: An imaging touch screen and display for gesture-based interaction. In: ICMI '04: Proceedings of the 6th international conference on Multimodal interfaces, pp. 69–76. ACM Press, New York, NY (2004)

900. Wilson, A.D.: PlayAnywhere: A compact interactive tabletop projection-vision system. In: UIST '05: Proceedings of the 18th annual ACM symposium on User interface software and technology, pp. 83–92. ACM Press, New York, NY (2005)

901. Wilson, T.: Models in information behavior research. Journal of Documentation 55(3), 249–270 (1999)
902. Winckler, A., Marco, P., Palanque, M.D.S., Freitas, C.: Tasks and scenario-based evaluation of information visualization techniques. In: 3rd annual conference on Task models and diagrams, pp. 165–172. ACM Press, New York, NY (2004)
903. Wise, J., Thomas, J., Pennock, K., Lantrip, D., Pottier, M., Schur, A., Crow, V.: Visualizing the non-visual: spatial analysis and interaction with information from text documents. In: INFOVIS '95: Proceedings of the 1995 IEEE Symposium on Information Visualization, IEEE Computer Society Press, Los Alamitos, CA (1995)
904. Wong, P.C., Bergeron, R.D.: 30 Years of Multidimensional Multivariate Visualization. In: Scientific Visualization, Overviews, Methodologies, and Techniques, pp. 3–33. IEEE Computer Society Press, Los Alamitos, CA (1997)
905. Wong, P.C., Mackey, P., Perrine, K., Eagan, J., Foote, H., Thomas, J.: Dynamic Visualization of Graphs with Extended Labels. In: Proceedings of IEEE Symposium on Information Visualization, pp. 73–80. IEEE Computer Society Press, Los Alamitos, CA (2005)
906. Wong, P.C., Thomas, J.: Visual Analytics. IEEE Computer Graphics and Applications 24, 20–21 (2004)
907. Wood, J.: Collaborative Visualization. PhD thesis, University of Leeds (1997)
908. Wood, J., Kirschenbauer, S., Döllner, J., Lopes, A., Bodum, L.: Using 3D in Visualization. In: Dykes, J. et al. (ed.) Exploring Geovisualization, pp. 295–312. Elsevier, Amsterdam (2005)
909. Wood, J., Wright, H., Brodlie, K.W.: CSCV - Computer Supported Collaborative Visualization (1995)
910. Wood, J., Wright, H., Brodlie, K.W.: Collaborative Visualization. In: Visualization '97, Proceedings, pp. 253–259 (1997)
911. Woodruff, A., Landay, J., Stonebreaker, M.: Constant Information Density in Zoomable Interfaces. In: Proocedings of the 4th International Working Conference on Advanced Visual Interfaces (AVI'98), pp. 110–119. ACM Press, New York, NY (1998)
912. Woods, D.: Drawing planar graphs. PhD thesis, Department of Computer Science, Stanford University (1982)
913. Xiong, R., Donath, J.: PeopleGarden: creating data portraits for users. In: UIST '99: Proceedings of the 12th annual ACM symposium on User interface software and technology, pp. 37–44. ACM Press, New York, NY (1999)
914. Yanagida, Y., Kawato, S., Noma, H., Tetsutani, N., Tomono, A.: A nose-tracked, personal olfactory display. In: GRAPH '03: Proceedings of the SIGGRAPH 2003 conference on Sketches & applications, p. 1. ACM Press, New York, NY (2003)
915. Yanagida, Y., Noma, H., Tetsutani, N., Tomono, A.: An unencumbering, localized olfactory display. In: CHI '03: CHI '03 extended abstracts on Human factors in computing systems, pp. 988–989. ACM Press, New York, NY (2003)
916. Yang, C.C., Wang, F.L.: Fractal summarization for mobile devices to access large documents on the web. In: WWW '03: Proceedings of the 12th international conference on World Wide Web, pp. 215–224. ACM Press, New York, NY (2003)
917. Yang, J., Stiefelhagen, R., Meier, U., Waibel, A.: Visual tracking for multimodal human computer interaction. In: CHI '98: Proceedings of the SIGCHI conference on Human factors in computing systems, pp. 140–147. Addison-Wesley/ACM Press, New York, NY (1998)
918. Yee, K.-P.: Peephole displays: Pen interaction on spatially aware handheld computers. In: CHI '03: Proceedings of the SIGCHI conference on Human factors in computing systems, pp. 1–8. ACM Press, New York, NY (2003)

919. Yost, B., North, C.: Single Complex Glyphs versus Multiple Simple Glyphs. In: Extended Abstracts Proceedings of the Conference on Human Factors in Computing Systems, CHI, pp. 1889–1892 (2005)

920. Young, G., Householder, A.S.: Discussion of a Set of Points in Terms of Their Mutual Distances. Psychometrica 3, 19–22 (1938)

921. Young, M., Argiro, D., Worley, J.: An Object Oriented Visual Programming Language Toolkit. Computer Graphics 29(2), 25–28 (1995)

922. Yu, E.S.-K.: Modelling strategic relationships for process reengineering. PhD thesis, University of Toronto (1995)

923. Zhai, S.: User performance in relation to 3D input device design. Computer Graphics 32(4), 50–54 (1998)

924. Zhai, S.: What's in the eyes for attentive input. Communications of the ACM 46(3), 34–39 (2003)

925. Zhai, S., Morimoto, C., Ihde, S., Center, R.: Manual and Gaze Input Cascaded (MAGIC) Pointing. In: Proceedings of ACM CHI 99 Conference on Human Factors in Computing Systems. Gaze and Purpose, vol. 1, pp. 246–253. ACM Press, New York, NY (1999)

926. Zhang, J.: A representational analysis of relational information displays. International Journal of Human-Computer Studies 45, 159–174 (1996)

927. Zhang, J., Johnson, K., Malin, J., Smith, J.: Human-Centered Information Visualization. In: International Workshop on dynamic Visualizations and Learning. Digital Enterprise Research Institute, University of Innsbruck (2002)

928. Zhao, W., Chellappa, R., Phillips, P.J., Rosenfeld, A.: Face recognition: A literature survey. ACM Comput. Surv. 35(4), 399–458 (2003)

929. Zhu, Z., Fujimura, K., Ji, Q.: Real-time eye detection and tracking under various light conditions. In: ETRA '02: Proceedings of the 2002 symposium on Eye tracking research & applications, pp. 139–144. ACM Press, New York, NY (2002)

Author Index

Index

Lecture Notes in Computer Science

For information about Vols. 1–4525

please contact your bookseller or Springer

Vol. 4573: M. Kauers, M. Kerber, R. Miner, W. Windsteiger (Eds.), Towards Mechanized Mathematical Assistants. XIII, 407 pages. 2007. (Sublibrary LNAI).

Vol. 4572: F. Stajano, C. Meadows, S. Capkun, T. Moore (Eds.), Security and Privacy in Ad-hoc and Sensor Networks. X, 247 pages. 2007.

Vol. 4571: P. Perner (Ed.), Machine Learning and Data Mining in Pattern Recognition. XIV, 913 pages. 2007. (Sublibrary LNAI).

Vol. 4570: H.G. Okuno, M. Ali (Eds.), New Trends in Applied Artificial Intelligence. XXI, 1194 pages. 2007. (Sublibrary LNAI).

Vol. 4569: A. Butz, B. Fisher, A. Krüger, P. Olivier, S. Owada (Eds.), Smart Graphics. IX, 237 pages. 2007.

Vol. 4566: M.J. Dainoff (Ed.), Ergonomics and Health Aspects of Work with Computers. XVIII, 390 pages. 2007.

Vol. 4565: D.D. Schmorrow, L.M. Reeves (Eds.), Foundations of Augmented Cognition. XIX, 450 pages. 2007. (Sublibrary LNAI).

Vol. 4564: D. Schuler (Ed.), Online Communities and Social Computing. XVII, 520 pages. 2007.

Vol. 4563: R. Shumaker (Ed.), Virtual Reality. XXII, 762 pages. 2007.

Vol. 4562: D. Harris (Ed.), Engineering Psychology and Cognitive Ergonomics. XXIII, 879 pages. 2007. (Sublibrary LNAI).

Vol. 4561: V.G. Duffy (Ed.), Digital Human Modeling. XXIII, 1068 pages. 2007.

Vol. 4560: N. Aykin (Ed.), Usability and Internationalization, Part II. XVIII, 576 pages. 2007.

Vol. 4559: N. Aykin (Ed.), Usability and Internationalization, Part I. XVIII, 661 pages. 2007.

Vol. 4558: M.J. Smith, G. Salvendy (Eds.), Human Interface and the Management of Information, Part II. XXIII, 1162 pages. 2007.

Vol. 4557: M.J. Smith, G. Salvendy (Eds.), Human Interface and the Management of Information, Part I. XXII, 1030 pages. 2007.

Vol. 4556: C. Stephanidis (Ed.), Universal Access in Human-Computer Interaction, Part III. XXII, 1020 pages. 2007.

Vol. 4555: C. Stephanidis (Ed.), Universal Access in Human-Computer Interaction, Part II. XXII, 1066 pages. 2007.

Vol. 4554: C. Stephanidis (Ed.), Universal Acess in Human Computer Interaction, Part I. XXII, 1054 pages. 2007.

Vol. 4553: J.A. Jacko (Ed.), Human-Computer Interaction, Part IV. XXIV, 1225 pages. 2007.

Vol. 4552: J.A. Jacko (Ed.), Human-Computer Interaction, Part III. XXI, 1038 pages. 2007.

Vol. 4551: J.A. Jacko (Ed.), Human-Computer Interaction, Part II. XXIII, 1253 pages. 2007.

Vol. 4550: J.A. Jacko (Ed.), Human-Computer Interaction, Part I. XXIII, 1240 pages. 2007.

Vol. 4549: J. Aspnes, C. Scheideler, A. Arora, S. Madden (Eds.), Distributed Computing in Sensor Systems. XIII, 417 pages. 2007.

Vol. 4548: N. Olivetti (Ed.), Automated Reasoning with Analytic Tableaux and Related Methods. X, 245 pages. 2007. (Sublibrary LNAI).

Vol. 4547: C. Carlet, B. Sunar (Eds.), Arithmetic of Finite Fields. XI, 355 pages. 2007.

Vol. 4546: J. Kleijn, A. Yakovlev (Eds.), Petri Nets and Other Models of Concurrency – ICATPN 2007. XI, 515 pages. 2007.

Vol. 4545: H. Anai, K. Horimoto, T. Kutsia (Eds.), Algebraic Biology. XIII, 379 pages. 2007.

Vol. 4544: S. Cohen-Boulakia, V. Tannen (Eds.), Data Integration in the Life Sciences. XI, 282 pages. 2007. (Sublibrary LNBI).

Vol. 4543: A.K. Bandara, M. Burgess (Eds.), Inter-Domain Management. XII, 237 pages. 2007.

Vol. 4542: P. Sawyer, B. Paech, P. Heymans (Eds.), Requirements Engineering: Foundation for Software Quality. IX, 384 pages. 2007.

Vol. 4541: T. Okadome, T. Yamazaki, M. Makhtari (Eds.), Pervasive Computing for Quality of Life Enhancement. IX, 248 pages. 2007.

Vol. 4539: N.H. Bshouty, C. Gentile (Eds.), Learning Theory. XII, 634 pages. 2007. (Sublibrary LNAI).

Vol. 4538: F. Escolano, M. Vento (Eds.), Graph-Based Representations in Pattern Recognition. XII, 416 pages. 2007.

Vol. 4537: K.C.-C. Chang, W. Wang, L. Chen, C.A. Ellis, C.-H. Hsu, A.C. Tsoi, H. Wang (Eds.), Advances in Web and Network Technologies, and Information Management. XXIII, 707 pages. 2007.

Vol. 4536: G. Concas, E. Damiani, M. Scotto, G. Succi (Eds.), Agile Processes in Software Engineering and Extreme Programming. XV, 276 pages. 2007.

Vol. 4534: I. Tomkos, F. Neri, J. Solé Pareta, X. Masip Bruin, S. Sánchez Lopez (Eds.), Optical Network Design and Modeling. XI, 460 pages. 2007.

Vol. 4533: F. Baader (Ed.), Term Rewriting and Applications. XII, 419 pages. 2007.

Vol. 4531: J. Indulska, K. Raymond (Eds.), Distributed Applications and Interoperable Systems. XI, 337 pages. 2007.

Vol. 4530: D.H. Akehurst, R. Vogel, R.F. Paige (Eds.), Model Driven Architecture- Foundations and Applications. X, 219 pages. 2007.

Vol. 4529: P. Melin, O. Castillo, L.T. Aguilar, J. Kacprzyk, W. Pedrycz (Eds.), Foundations of Fuzzy Logic and Soft Computing. XIX, 830 pages. 2007. (Sublibrary LNAI).

Vol. 4528: J. Mira, J.R. Álvarez (Eds.), Nature Inspired Problem-Solving Methods in Knowledge Engineering, Part II. XXII, 650 pages. 2007.

Vol. 4527: J. Mira, J.R. Álvarez (Eds.), Bio-inspired Modeling of Cognitive Tasks, Part I. XXII, 630 pages. 2007.

Vol. 4526: M. Malek, M. Reitenspieß, A. van Moorsel (Eds.), Service Availability. X, 155 pages. 2007.